Selling Black History for Carter G. Woodson

Selling Black History for Carter G. Woodson

A Diary, 1930–1933

LORENZO J. GREENE

Edited with an Introduction by

ARVARH E. STRICKLAND

UNIVERSITY OF MISSOURI PRESS
COLUMBIA AND LONDON

University of Missouri Press, Columbia, Missouri 65201
Printed and bound in the United States of America

5 4 3 2 1 00 99 98 97 96

Library of Congress Cataloging-In-Publication Data

Greene, Lorenzo Johnston, 1899–
Selling Black history for Carter G. Woodson : a diary, 1930–1933 / Lorenzo J. Greene ; edited, with an introduction, by Arvarh E. Strickland.
p. cm.
Includes bibliographical references (p.) and index.
ISBN 0-8262-1068-6 (alk. paper). —ISBN 0-8262-1069-4 (pbk. : alk. paper)
1. Woodson, Carter Godwin, 1875–1950. 2. Greene, Lorenzo Johnston, 1899– —Diaries. 3. Afro-American—historians—Biography. 4. Historians—United States —Biography. 5. Afro-Americans—Historiography. 6. Booksellers and bookselling—United States. I. Strickland, Arvarh E. II. Title.
E185.97.W77G735 1996
973'.0496073—dc20 96-8542
CIP

∞™ This paper meets the requirements of the American National Standard for Permanence of Paper for Printed Library Materials, Z39.48, 1984.

Designer: Kristie Lee
Typesetter: BOOKCOMP
Printer and binder: Thomson-Shore, Inc.
Typefaces: Bembo, Nuptial Script

For Thomasina Talley Greene
and Willie Pearl Elmore Strickland

Contents

Editor's Acknowledgments

Editing this book, as was the case with editing *Working with Carter G. Woodson, the Father of Black History,* was a labor of love. This time, however, there was a great difference. My dear friend Lorenzo Johnston Greene died on January 24, 1988. Consequently, he was not with me to wrack his brain to try to recall dimly remembered names and events. Also, he had not worked on the entries in these notebooks to the same extent that he had those that comprised the earlier volume. This time, I was on my own in reading his handwriting. Nevertheless, he was there in spirit.

I owe a special debt of gratitude to Thomasina Talley Greene, Lorenzo Thomas Greene, and Deborah Foster Greene. Without their cooperation, this project could not have been completed. They made the notebooks constituting the diary available to me, gave me access to all pertinent manuscript materials, and shared their recollections with me.

My search for often obscure facts about people, events, and places sometimes caused me to stretch the bonds of friendship far beyond normal limits. My already immense indebtedness to John Hope Franklin became greater. While he was a guest in my home and was in Columbia to deliver the 1993 Paul Anthony Brick Lectures, I pressed him into service to read sections of the diary dealing with Oklahoma. At that time and later, he provided names and explanations that greatly facilitated my work. That gracious lady of Houston, Texas, Pearl Suel, permitted herself to be imposed upon to render a similar service on sections related to her city. Soon after we met, Richard Allen Morton was called on to search for information at Clark Atlanta University. He, too, became an obliging friend.

Over the six years that this project lasted, many others helped in various ways. I am deeply grateful to Antonio F. Holland for all he did on my behalf. Regina Drake helped me to contact those who could provide assistance at Howard University and was of immeasurable aid herself. My friend Thomas B. Alexander not only gave assistance, but also placed me in touch with others, such as Frances Cabiniss Roberts of Huntsville, Alabama, who responded to my request for help.

No historian can be productive without the help of archivists and librarians. I am especially appreciative to Elizabeth Wilson, director of Page Library at Lincoln University, and her staff, and I particularly want to thank Howard University's archivist and the librarians at the Moorland-Springarn Collection. Anne Edwards, June DeWeese, and Paula Roper of the University of Missouri–Columbia's Ellis Library are outstanding reference librarians and great friends. The staffs at the Library of Congress, the Western Historical Manuscripts Collection, the State Historical Society of Missouri Library, and the University of Illinois at Urbana-Champaign Library assisted me in many ways.

Janet Thornton, typist, word processor, and assistant without equal, played a crucial role in this project. She contributed greatly to the transcribing of the material from longhand to a typescript and to the establishment of the first version of the text. This greatly facilitated the work of the editor. What turned out to be a six-year project would have taken much longer without her efficient work.

I would also like to thank August Meier for recognizing the historical value of the diaries and for bringing them to the attention of Beverly Jarrett. Working with her and her staff has been a delightful experience. I particularly appreciate the work of my editor, Julie Schroeder.

It is not possible to name all of the people who deserve recognition for their contributions to this project, but I owe special thanks to Marie Sloan, Mary Oates, Nancy Taube, Carolyn Dorsey, Maria DeLongoria, Jimmie L. Franklin, Robert Weems, Jr., Tritobia Hayes Benjamin, Carl Patterson, Nesta Bernard, and Gregory Wilson.

Several University of Missouri administrators contributed, in various ways, to the completion of this work. These included Richard Wallace, Larry Clark, John Bullion, and K. C. Morrison.

The inclusion of my wife, Willie Pearl Elmore Strickland, in the dedication is a token of my appreciation for the support she has provided throughout my career. Also, the love and support of Duane, Hope, Bruce, Pamela, and my grandchildren make it all worthwhile.

Selling Black History for Carter G. Woodson

Editor's Introduction

Serving the "Cause"

At the close of the 1930 Negro History Week celebration in Washington, D.C., Lorenzo Johnston Greene confessed to his diary that he had experienced a conversion. He said that the events of the final evening made him "a confirmed and dedicated associate" of Dr. Carter G. Woodson. He pledged an even higher commitment to the Association for the Study of Negro Life and History, the organization founded by Woodson on September 9, 1915. "The Association," Greene said, "is indelibly stamped upon me. It is my cause and shall transcend everything else, even my allegiance to Woodson."[1]

Greene was the last of a succession of bright young scholars whom Woodson nurtured and converted to the field of African American history. He was born in Ansonia, Connecticut, on November 16, 1899, and received his elementary and secondary education in the schools of that town. After graduating from high school, he entered Howard University in Washington, D.C., with the intention of earning a degree in medicine. There, however, he came under the influence of three able African American historians—Professors Walter Dyson, Leo Hansberry, and Charles H. Wesley—and decided to make history his life's work. Consequently, he entered Columbia University to pursue graduate work in history.

In the meantime, Greene became associated with Woodson and was inspired by him to devote himself to African American history. Woodson holds the undisputed title of father of African American history. His life story is one of hardship, struggle, and dedication. Woodson was born in rural Virginia on December 19, 1875, to parents who had been slaves and who struggled to support their nine children by farming. The elementary school in Buckingham County, where Woodson grew up, was in session

1. Lorenzo J. Greene, *Working with Carter G. Woodson, the Father of Black History: A Diary, 1928–1930,* 464.

only five months a year, but he was unable to attend regularly even during these months. So, in large measure, he was self-educated in the rudiments of an elementary education.

At twenty years of age, he began high school and completed the work in one and a half years. After finishing high school, he entered Berea College in Kentucky, which at that time was still integrated, where all students paid their way by working on campus. He left college in 1900, after two years, and became principal of the high school he had attended in Huntington, West Virginia. He continued to attend Berea in the summers and completed a bachelor's degree in 1903. In 1908 he earned another bachelor's degree, as well as his master of arts degree, from the University of Chicago. In 1912, Woodson became only the second African American to earn a Ph.D. in history from Harvard University. The first was W. E. B. Du Bois, who received his degree from Harvard in 1895.

Woodson devoted his life to correcting misconceptions about the history of black people. On September 9, 1915, he and five other persons founded the Association for the Study of Negro Life and History (now the Association for the Study of Afro-American Life and History). In 1916, he began publishing the *Journal of Negro History;* in 1926, he began the celebration of Negro History Week, which has now become African American history month; and in 1937, he began publishing the *Negro History Bulletin.* In addition to editing the *Journal* and the *Bulletin,* Woodson produced an impressive number of scholarly works. Before the publication of John Hope Franklin's *From Slavery to Freedom* in 1947, Woodson's *The Negro in Our History* was the standard general treatment of African American history.

Through the years, at times Greene's dedication to Woodson the man was severely tested; however, he never wavered in his dedication to Woodson the scholar. Moreover, his devotion to the Association remained unshaken over the next almost six decades of his life.

The immediate manifestation of this dedication and devotion was the bookselling odyssey Greene undertook to provide needed funds for the Association and to promote the study of African American history. On June 21, 1930, Greene and four young men who were students at Howard University left Washington in a Model A Ford to sell books published by the Associated Publishers. Their tour took them through Virginia, North Carolina, a little of South Carolina, Tennessee, Georgia, Alabama, across the northeastern tip of Mississippi, and into Arkansas, Louisiana, Texas, Oklahoma, Missouri, Illinois, and Pennsylvania. Greene left an account of this journey in a diary he kept in a series of notebooks.

This was not a journey for the timid or the fainthearted. The South of the 1930s and, for that matter, over the next four decades, was not a place where five young African American men were expected to travel without encountering serious racial problems. The black press in 1930 and 1931 headlined the lynchings and other acts of violence suffered by African Americans in both the South and the North. The National Association for the Advancement of Colored People (NAACP) recorded twenty-five lynchings in 1930, and twenty-four of the victims were African Americans. Georgia led the nation with seven, followed by Alabama and Texas with four each.[2]

Greene only expressed misgivings about encountering racial violence when he left Tennessee and crossed into Georgia. Here and there, he mentions hostile stares and a few catcalls from white youth, but the team experienced surprisingly little direct hostility. Greene did inquire of informants at the places they visited about the climate of race relations. This information he recorded in his diary. He also left vivid descriptions of the people, geography, and other attributes of the routes they traveled.

Greene's diary, however, was much more than a travelogue. Before leaving Washington, he completed proofreading *The Negro Wage Earner.* His work on this study made him sensitive to and an acute observer of economic conditions in the South. His observations gave him firsthand knowledge of what was taking place in the black communities of the cities he visited. This made him one of the most knowledgeable scholars about economic conditions among African Americans at the advent of the Great Depression in 1930–1931.

When the agents arrived in a town or city, their first contact was with black business and professional people. In many places, they could seek potential buyers through names furnished by Woodson. School ties provided Greene access to professionals in a number of places. He knew doctors, dentists, lawyers, and teachers who were in school at Howard University with him during his undergraduate years. Several of the men were fellow members of Kappa Alpha Psi Fraternity. Invariably, these men and women were suffering from the effects of the depression, but most of them were cooperative.

Greene and his fellow agents found black college campuses hospitable places to market their books. These campuses hosted meetings of teachers, musicians, ministers, agricultural agents, and other likely customers. Because of the sales team's connection to Woodson, college presidents often provided them with free lodging and meals. The diary contains, therefore, Greene's impressions of the physical plants, the administrative leadership, the faculty members, and the academic quality of these institutions.

2. National Association for the Advancement of Colored People, *One Year's Work in Race Relations: 1930, 21st Annual Report,* 35–39.

At the end of the tour, Greene stayed in Philadelphia for about two months selling books in that city and in neighboring towns and cities in New Jersey, Maryland, and Delaware. He returned to some of these places several times and wrote detailed accounts of school, church, business, and social conditions in these northern and border areas.

Greene's life as a protégé of Woodson was not always easy. Woodson served as a role model because of his struggle for an education and his singular dedication to his cause. Still, Woodson was a person of human dimensions. Various individuals described him as "arrogant," "cantankerous," and "domineering." While agreeing with this characterization, Greene found Woodson to be an extremely complex man. Throughout his life, Greene remained ambivalent in his attitude toward his mentor. He respected and admired Woodson as a scholar and for the sacrifices he made in his struggle to preserve the African American past and to correct the myths and errors commonly found in American histories. This is what Greene and others labeled the "cause." On the other hand, Greene resented Woodson's patronizing attitude toward him and his failure to ever recognize him as a colleague.

Throughout Woodson's life, Greene endured his bluntness and directness. Greene often responded respectfully, but directly, to jabs taken by Woodson. Overall, the relationship was beneficial to both men. Greene contributed greatly to the support of the Association for the Study of Negro Life and History by selling books, spreading the gospel of "Negro History," and helping to organize branches and Negro History Study Clubs.

On the other hand, Woodson helped to train Greene as a researcher, afforded him the prestige of having his name associated with that of his own and the Association for the Study of Negro Life and History, provided him with work, awarded him fellowships, and recommended him highly for academic and other positions. Woodson obviously was quite fond of Greene and respected him. He discussed matters related to the Association with him, sought his advice, and followed courses of action he recommended. An example of this was Greene's role in devising the plan that led to the bookselling campaign recorded in the diary.

As the tour progressed, Greene became more and more aware of the importance of his relationship with Woodson and the importance of Woodson's name to the success of the bookselling campaign. When Greene identified himself as an investigator for the Association and as an associate of Dr. Woodson, doors opened to him that may otherwise have been closed. This was true in Durham, North Carolina, where C. C. Spaulding, president of the North Carolina Mutual Insurance Company, showed him every courtesy. Greene said that Spaulding "grasped my hand very warmly and seemed delighted to know that I was an assistant to Dr. Woodson and was engaged in carrying on his work."

In Atlanta, his connection with Woodson served to gain him the assistance of Dr. John Hope, president of Atlanta University, and also, through Dr. Hope, gained him the hospitality of the Atlanta University and Morehouse College staffs. At Bishop College in Texas, President Joseph J. Rhodes invited him to return to speak at the campus as Woodson's surrogate, and also provided the team with names and addresses of potential customers in Dallas.

In October 1930, Greene found himself stranded in Chicago. He was down on his luck and without enough money to return to Washington. Woodson's name again served him well. Mentioning Woodson's name to a total stranger led to the sale of several sets of books and provided him the money to leave Chicago.

His experiences during the campaign both in the South and in the Philadelphia area, along with the activities he had engaged in as Woodson's employee over the past two years, gave Greene more confidence in himself as a historian. He began to feel that he deserved to be recognized as a scholar. He especially wanted Woodson to treat him as a colleague.

Nevertheless, Woodson refused to give Greene the type of recognition he desired and for the rest of his life kept a certain distance between them. It was always "*Dr.* Woodson and *Mr.* Greene"; Woodson never let Greene forget that it was a relationship between protégé and mentor. By 1931, Greene was becoming restless in this relationship and resentful that Woodson would not acknowledge him as a colleague and peer.

This resentment came to a head over the authorship of *The Negro Wage Earner.* When Greene left Washington in July 1930, the book was ready to go to press, and the manuscript listed Greene as sole author. The published book, however, listed Greene and Woodson as coauthors. Greene wrote to Woodson in September expressing his resentment, and he poured out his bitterness to his friends.

Entries in Greene's diary during the researching and writing of the book evidenced Woodson's deep involvement in the project. Woodson was paying Greene to do the research; he arranged for Greene to use the Library of Congress; and he made other connections for him in governmental agencies. Woodson also went over the data, corrected errors, and made decisions about the organization and interpretation of material. Moreover, Woodson's name on the book probably gave the work greater acceptability.

On the other hand, the reason for Greene's anger is apparent. Greene did all of the research and drafted the narrative. This is not evident from the book's introduction, where Woodson stated: "Most of the data in this treatise were collected by Mr. Lorenzo J. Greene. These findings were then checked, corrected, and supplemented by the undersigned, who reduced the work to literary form."[3] Greene called this statement "an *infamous* lie." He continued: "I myself not only collected the data, but also put it in virtually the exact form, with the exception of a few expurgations, in which the book now stands."

This incident continued to poison the relationship between the men. Woodson, however, continued his usual paternal and patronizing behavior, seemingly oblivious of Greene's feelings, and Greene, like an unappreciated son, continued to seek the approval and recognition of the father. He also remained dependent upon Woodson for financial assistance. He confided to his diary, however, his antagonism toward his mentor and idol.

Greene went to Washington from Philadelphia to visit with Woodson on March 2, 1931. He said that Woodson seemed happy to see him and to know that he "had been able to interest people in the Negro's past." The visit began to go downhill from there. Greene was not happy when Woodson informed him that he had not submitted his name for a position at Morgan College because he "knew" that Greene "did not care for teaching."

Greene also felt Woodson to be ungrateful for the work he had done selling books. Woodson said that no money was being made and that too many books were being returned. "Yet," Greene noted, "had it not been for such he would have been virtually bankrupt this winter. . . . He sees only the black, unpleasant side of the other fellow's labors." Two months later, in an article in the *Afro-American,* Woodson boasted about the role that agents had played in 1930 in increasing the sale of books. Woodson reported that ten thousand volumes were sold, with his work, *The Negro in Our History,* leading other books in sales.[4]

On February 7, 1931, Greene received an invitation to speak to a class from the head of the economics department at Dartmouth College. He felt that this was the first step in his being "vindicated as the author of *The Negro Wage Earner.*" Woodson had received the letter, read it, and sent it on to him without comment. There is no indication in the diary or in available correspondence as to the role Woodson may have played in getting this invitation for Greene. The diary does contain Greene's reaction to the unwelcomed advice he received from Woodson on how to deport himself at Dartmouth. Although it was unwelcomed, Greene followed the advice.

Woodson showed his pride in Greene's being invited to speak at Dartmouth in a laudatory note in the *Journal of Negro History.* "As a result

3. Lorenzo J. Greene and Carter G. Woodson, *The Negro Wage Earner,* vi.

4. "House to House Agents Help to Popularize Books," *Baltimore Afro-American,* May 2, 1931, 4.

of Mr. Lorenzo J. Greene's work in the production of *The Negro Wage Earner,*" the note read, "he has been invited to speak to several scholarly bodies on this topic. Probably the most appreciative of such circles was the student body of Dartmouth College which he addressed on the 19th of March."[5] After the Dartmouth trip, Greene, at Woodson's invitation, returned to Washington to help conduct a survey of Negro employment. During the time he worked on the survey, he exhibited his usual concern about not making a bad impression on Woodson. Several months later, Woodson informed Greene that his fellowship to support study at Columbia University had been renewed for the fall of 1931. His bluntness and sarcasm notwithstanding, Woodson obviously thought very highly of Greene.

Of course, the diary contains much that is autobiographical, and these sections provide a case study of one of the few African Americans who were maturing as scholars in the 1930s. In 1930, Greene was thirty-one years of age, unmarried, and well on his way to completing work on his doctorate. His ideas about what was expected of a scholar and academician reflected the views of the period, and these ideas helped to govern both his personal and professional behavior.

The teachers in African American schools—whether elementary, secondary, or college—were expected to live in strict conformity to the moral values and mores of the communities in which they worked. Those caught deviating from accepted conduct were subjected to loss of employment and often to public disgrace. Standards differed somewhat from community to community, but sexual misconduct was universally frowned upon. The editors of black newspapers reserved prominent places in their papers for stories of such misconduct. In most communities, African American women teachers were severely restricted in their social relations. They outnumbered men teachers, and few other men in the community were on their educational and social levels.

This situation was both a boon and a danger to Greene. He was educated, attractive, and adept at gaining the favor of young women. They welcomed him and his fellow agents as escorts to parties, as card players, as dance partners, and in other social roles. Greene exploited these situations to sell these women books and to obtain their help in selling to others.

Still, Greene was ever aware of the danger to both his and the women's reputations should they violate community mores and this become public knowledge. Moreover, he saw himself as the older, mature scholar who was the leader of and role model for the young men on his team. Although the younger men might take certain liberties in violation of community standards, he had to set a good example for them. He also had to maintain

5. "Notes," *Journal of Negro History* 16 (April 1931): 250.

a good reputation in order to gain acceptance by the ministers and church members, another large group of potential book buyers. Nevertheless, he developed relationships that went beyond the platonic with several young women who hoped to stand before an altar with him.

His greatest embarrassment probably came from Woodson's knowledge of his involvement with women while he was on the bookselling tour. Of course, this became the subject of some sarcastic barbs from Woodson. After Greene returned to Columbia University, for example, Woodson wrote: "We are getting various letters here from women who express their love in poetry and in fervent song. . . . We are holding these things here because we understand very clearly that you cannot give your attention to women and to song [and] at the same time study diligently."[6]

In his diary, Greene rationalized that given his financial situation it would be unwise and irresponsible for him to marry. Implicit in much that he wrote, however, was the belief that marriage would jeopardize the achieving of his career objectives. Consequently, it is not surprising that he delayed getting married until he had a relatively secure position at Lincoln University and until he had completed his doctorate. This was a delay of almost a decade after his impulsive, but futile, proposal of marriage to Lenora Pritchett in 1932.

Greene met Thomasina Talley, his future wife, soon after he arrived in Missouri, but they did not become romantically involved at that time. Talley was born in Nashville, Tennessee, to Ellen Roberts and Thomas Washington Talley. Her father was head of the chemistry department at Fisk University. She began piano lessons at age five, graduated from Fisk University at fifteen, and entered the Juilliard School of Music. Juilliard awarded her a certificate in piano in 1932, and she began her teaching career in the segregated high school in Columbia, Missouri.

Talley left Missouri soon after Greene arrived, however, to accept a teaching position in Texas. Later, she moved to North Carolina. In 1939, she received a Rockefeller Fund Fellowship and returned to New York City to study at Columbia University. Greene received a Rosenwald Fund Fellowship in 1940 and returned to Columbia University to complete his

6. Carter G. Woodson to Lorenzo J. Greene, October 14, 1931, papers in the possession of the Greene family, Jefferson City, Missouri. Unless otherwise indicated, all letters and manuscript materials cited hereafter are from these papers. Soon after Lorenzo Greene's death, the family deposited a major portion of his papers in the Library of Congress. Later, they began sending pictures and other materials on both Lorenzo J. Greene and Thomasina Talley Greene to the Western Historical Manuscripts Collection at the University of Missouri–Columbia. In order to facilitate the work of the editor, the family temporarily retained possession of the letters and other materials germane to the editing of this part of the diary.

dissertation. They renewed their friendship, fell in love, and were married on December 19, 1941. They were both awarded degrees by Columbia University in 1942 and came to Jefferson City, Missouri. Thomasina Greene opened a music studio, received national recognition as a concert pianist, and, from time to time, taught at Lincoln University. Their son, Lorenzo Thomas Greene, was born in 1952.

Much about the South fascinated Greene, but he remained the consummate New Englander. He generally measured things southern against things New England, and this outlook shaped his view of the South and those who lived there. This tendency revealed a regional pride that sometimes led to intolerance of differences and to failure to understand or appreciate the reason for some conditions. At times, as when he criticized the quality of free meals and lodging provided by institutions or individuals, this pride bordered on arrogance and led to an appearance of ingratitude. Increasing maturity and residence in Missouri moderated this tendency.

His earlier work on the church survey made him a critical, albeit biased, observer of the black church.[7] Churches were important sources of clients. The second, if not the first, contact the team made in a community was a minister. If the agents were invited to address a congregation or church organization, such as youth groups and women's and men's clubs, this usually led to sales and a widening circle of contacts. These contacts with ministers resulted both from referrals by Woodson and from invitations received by Greene from ministers he met at the Hampton Institute ministerial conferences. By and large, southern ministers were helpful even though, in many cases, they were struggling to survive as leaders of impoverished congregations.

Even while profiting from their assistance, however, Greene was strongly critical of black ministers. He reserved his strongest invectives for Bishop Charles Emmanuel "Daddy" Grace, founder of the United House of Prayer for All People. Several of Greene's relatives attended Grace's church in Washington, D.C. Greene characterized Grace and other leaders of his cult as the "vilest type of miscreant—seducers of the weak and illiterate, parasites who suck the life's blood out of a people, already bled white, so to speak, by 300 years of servitude."[8]

7. In 1928, Woodson received a grant to study the black church. He commissioned Charles H. Wesley, assisted by Greene, to undertake a pilot study of the black church in an urban and in a rural setting. Greene worked on the survey in Baltimore, Maryland, and in Suffolk, Virginia. His anticlericalism stemmed in large measure from his encounters, while making the survey, with ministers he characterized as ignorant, morally corrupt exploiters of their followers. See Greene, *Working with Carter G. Woodson,* 18–146.

8. Ibid., 161.

Ministers in Baptist, Methodist, and other mainline churches were not spared Greene's condemnation. He was especially critical of those who "gave the people what they wanted" and appealed to their emotions. His ideal minister was Vernon Johns, who was Martin Luther King, Jr.'s predecessor at Dexter Avenue Baptist Church in Montgomery, Alabama. Johns ranked with Mordecai Johnson and Howard Thurman as among the most distinguished African American preachers of the period.

Johns was learned but unconventional. He abhorred emotionalism, favored the establishment of black businesses, and was an active opponent of discrimination. Had Greene been a member of Dexter Avenue church during Johns's tenure, however, he probably would have been as uncomfortable as were some Alabama State University faculty members. Greene's anticlericalism was, in part, based on social class behavior. The diary revealed that he was uncomfortable with those who were not middle class in dress and demeanor. Johns, on the other hand, was militantly anti-elitist and often unconventional in both dress and behavior.[9]

Greene's views on the black church and its leaders received public attention in November 1930 when he went to Lynchburg, Virginia, to speak at Virginia Seminary, where Johns was president. While there, he delivered his speech on "unemployment among Negroes, its causes and its remedies" to an audience at the Court Street Baptist Church. This speech was based on observations made during his journey through the South. He described the displacement of black workers on farms, in hotels, in homes, as garbage collectors, and in other occupations traditionally reserved for them.

The audience expected this kind of analysis, but, according to a newspaper account, it was not ready for what followed. Greene "astounded his listeners by asserting that the Negroes' own unreliability, lack of responsibility, want of training, and their general failure to take care of their jobs have all collaborated to drive [them] out of [their] customary employment."

His remedies were less disturbing. He advocated returning to the land to truck farm, patronizing black-owned businesses, and the creation of more black businesses. He voiced limited support for boycotting white businesses to gain more jobs for African Americans. He also called for restricting immigration.

Then, he again shocked his audience with a discussion of the black church. First, he called for a moratorium on the building of new churches and for diverting the money that would be used for this purpose into "productive channels by erecting factories and stores." Next, he recommended consolidating churches and selling some of the buildings to obtain capital to support

9. Taylor Branch, *Parting the Waters: America in the King Years, 1954–1963,* 1–26.

businesses. The proliferation of churches, he said, constituted a "financial millstone about the neck of the race." Moreover, this situation impeded the "economic rise of the entire group for certain so-called leaders primarily interested in their own self-aggrandizement."[10]

Greene was identified in the *Norfolk Journal and Guide* as research investigator of the Association for the Study of Negro Life and History. Ironically, given his own views, Woodson rebuked Greene for critizing the church. He wrote:

> You will find it difficult to get into the churches, since you have begun to attack the institution. I was asked by a newspaper man yesterday for a rejoinder to Rev. R. R. Wright's reply to your attack on the church. Those who have heard of it are hot in the collar. Go on with your reform, if you like; but do it as a "freelance." Do not send out any more releases as an investigator of the Association. Do not tell any one that you are connected with the Association. We believe that the church should be reformed, but this is not our task.[11]

This admonishment may have been more a reminder to Greene of his place than a criticism of his action. Only Woodson could launch attacks in the name of the Association. "All releases," he said, "sent out in the name of the Association must proceed from this office." The irony was that a number of releases criticizing the black church had proceeded from that office, and more would follow. Greene's views were, in large part, those of Woodson. R. R. Wright, Jr., who responded to Greene's remarks, accused Woodson of being biased against the church and its leaders and refused to appear on the Association's annual meeting program in 1931.[12]

Although he was loath to admit it, Greene learned much from the African American ministers he criticized so vehemently. He saw that the most effective among them had mastered the art of holding the attention of audiences and of bending audiences to their wills. As the tour progressed, Greene became more and more adept at "preaching the gospel of Negro History." If he were permitted to address an audience, he was almost certain

10. *Norfolk Journal and Guide,* November 22, 1930, 4.

11. Woodson to Greene, December 3, 1930.

12. In an article in the *Norfolk Journal and Guide,* October 10, 1931, 5, Woodson expressed opinions almost identical to those attributed to Greene. The story on Wright's refusal to appear on the Association program appeared in the *Pittsburgh Courier,* November 14, 1931, 10. Woodson responded in the *Pittsburgh Courier,* December 5, 1931, 10. For other newspaper articles by Woodson on the black church, see those listed in Sister Anthony Scally, comp., *Carter G. Woodson: A Bio-Bibliography,* 177–87.

to sell some books. After an especially exhilarating experience before an audience preaching on the contributions of Africans to world civilization or the causes and remedies of unemployment among African Americans, he would confide to his diary, "I gripped them."

In September 1931, Greene returned to Columbia University to continue work on his doctorate. Evidently, he found little time for writing in his diary during the two academic years he spent in New York City. No entries were found for the period from September 5, 1931, to September 30, 1932, and the only entries for the remainder of 1932 related to his unrequited love for Lenora Pritchard. The next entries told of his arrival and first days in Jefferson City, Missouri, in September 1933, to begin his teaching career at Lincoln University.

Nevertheless, the missing months and years were an eventful, but not always happy, period in Greene's life. He completed the course work for his doctorate and passed the oral examination. In addition, he continued to sell books, to fill speaking engagements, and to serve Woodson and the "cause."

The annual meeting of the Association was scheduled to be in New York City in November 1931, and Greene returned just in time to get involved in the preparations. During a visit to the city in December 1930, he participated in setting up a branch of the Association, and he helped to draw up a petition to the Board of Education calling for the adoption of books on African Americans as supplemental textbooks. Members of the new branch circulated the petition to "obtain the endorsement of churches, social, fraternal, educational institutions, business and professional organizations in the effort."[13]

Greene was able to resume work on his degree and to remain in school for two academic years, thanks to his bookselling abilities, his oratorical skills, and his relationship with Woodson. During the academic year 1931–1932, he was relatively free from financial worries. Woodson gave him a twelve-hundred-dollar fellowship, and he continued to sell books. As in the past, however, Greene did not always find working with Woodson enjoyable. Words of appreciation and praise did not flow as easily from Woodson's pen as did sarcasm and criticism. Greene learned to respond in kind, but in a more refined and gentle manner. Their harsh words, however, did not keep Greene from continuing to call upon Woodson for help and did not keep Woodson from giving advice and help whenever possible.

Planning for the 1931 annual meeting began in September. Woodson went to New York City and met with Greene and his friends Harcourt Tynes and Emile Holley. Tynes, who lived in New York City, was active in

13. Greene to Woodson, December 29, 1930.

the new branch. Holley had left his teaching position at Howard University and returned to Columbia University to continue work on his doctorate in English. By October a planning committee was at work, and the local people were already at odds with at least one of the area's leaders and with Woodson. The committee failed to involve Dr. L. H. King, pastor of St. James Presbyterian Church, in early planning sessions, and he notified the committee that he would not take part in the program. By the time the meeting opened, however, King had been placated, and the opening session convened at his church.[14]

Problems connected with the Musicale, scheduled as a major attraction on the second day of the meeting, were more difficult to resolve. On October 24, Greene warned Woodson that the music situation was in disarray. There was no chairman for the music committee. Woodson had alienated Melville Charlton, the choir director at St. James Presbyterian Church, who then resigned from the committee. Woodson explained, probably to Greene's amusement, that he was accused of writing Charlton an "insolent letter." He said that he "did not mean to do such a thing. I may have done so accidentally." Charlton's alienation placed in doubt the participation of his friend Harry Burleigh. Another well-known musician, Carl Diton, tried to chair the music committee, but he gave up in frustration. Finally, Greene gently chided Woodson for his interference and informed him that the members of the general committee "now feel that it is best to leave all arrangements for the Musicale to you."[15]

The committee only suggested what was already the case. Woodson was making all decisions from Washington, but he depended upon Greene to help with his plans. Still, he was highly critical of Greene's suggestions and actions. When, for example, Greene suggested that they try to get the Hall Johnson Choir for the Musicale, Woodson dismissed the suggestion immediately. Actually, Woodson had not heard of Hall Johnson or his choir, and he probably thought of the group as just another church choir. Earlier he had confided to Greene that he was "anxious to avoid church choirs and church aggregations for strictly artistic work." He explained that "We do not want persons who are singing merely to edify people's souls on Sunday."[16] He was willing to have the Hall Johnson Choir sing at the opening

14. Woodson to Greene, September 24, 1931; Greene to Woodson, October 25, 1931; and Carter G. Woodson, "Proceedings of the Annual Meeting of the Association for the Study of Negro Life and History, Held in New York City, November 8–12, 1931," *Journal of Negro History*.

15. Greene to Woodson, October 24, 1931; Woodson to Greene, October 24, 1931; Woodson to Greene, October 25, 1931; and Woodson to Greene, October 30, 1931.

16. Woodson to Greene, October 20, 1931.

session, since Charlton's choir would not sing, but he did not want it for the Musicale.[17]

Greene responded by providing Woodson a brief introduction to the Hall Johnson Choir and letting him know that this was not just another church choir. He told Woodson that the choir "is quite famous throughout the country. They have appeared at Town Hall and Carnegie Hall here, as well as in Boston, Philadelphia, and other cities."[18] Woodson relented and informed Greene that he was willing to have the Hall Johnson Choir perform at the Musicale. But, when he learned that the choir would not perform free, he vetoed the choir's participation.[19]

A few days later, Woodson was ready to change his mind again. He said that there had been requests for the Hall Johnson Choir. He was now willing to use "four or six or eight persons who can give a better interpretation of music than the entire choir." Still, however, he would only use them if they would perform free.[20]

Greene learned that there was, indeed, a small group from the choir that was used for radio performances.[21] Woodson already knew about this group, for, on October 27, several days before Greene wrote to him, Woodson expressed misgivings about this group to Harcourt Tynes. Woodson understood that the Hall Johnson Choir was supposed to be in Chicago with the stage production of *Green Pastures.* He wondered if he was being offered a "sort of truncated inefficient group left in New York City." He confided to Tynes that he was beginning to feel the frustration that others obviously had been feeling for some time. "This Musicale is giving me so much trouble that I feel like giving it up. I do not think it is worth all the pain it is giving me."[22] This group, whatever its quality, could not be secured without charge, and this ended the matter.

On Monday, November 9, the Musicale was held at the Riverside Church, without the Hall Johnson Choir. The participating artists were Charlotte Wallace Murray, contralto; Louia Vaughn Jones, violinist; R. Nathaniel Dett, pianist-composer; and Mercer F. Bratcher, tenor soloist of the Hampton Institute Choir. Woodson gave Emile Holley the honor of having

17. Woodson to Greene, October 24, 1931; and Woodson to Greene, October 25, 1931.

18. Greene to Woodson, October 24, 1931.

19. Woodson to William Lloyd Imes, October 28, 1931; Greene to Woodson, October 29, 1931; and Woodson to Greene, October 30, 1931.

20. Woodson to Harcourt A. Tynes, November 2, 1931.

21. Greene to Woodson, November 5, 1931.

22. Woodson to Tynes, October 27, 1931.

his name listed on the program, "only to fill the space," as chairman of the music committee.[23]

In addition to serving as a middle man in planning the Musicale, Greene accepted other responsibilities. When writing to make a demand on Greene's time, Woodson always prefaced his request with the statement that he did not want Greene to do anything that would interfere with his studies. Woodson would then proceed to explain that what he was about to ask would not take much time. In mid-October, he asked Greene to help publicize the meeting by distributing "throwaways"; later in the month, he sent ten thousand leaflets to be distributed. Additionally, Greene and Holley worked together on a "big publicity drive." Woodson also put Greene in charge of the exhibit of the Association's publications.[24]

As soon as the annual meeting ended, Greene turned his attention back to the campaign to get books handled by the Association adopted by the New York City Board of Education as supplemental textbooks. The books presented were Woodson's *The Negro in Our History, Negro Makers of History,* and *African Myths* and Maurice Delafosse's *Negroes of Africa.*[25]

Although Greene had been instrumental in having the New York City branch begin this project, Woodson's published account of it made it appear as something he started following the annual meeting. He wrote: "It was most encouraging . . . that principals of schools teaching numbers of Negro children sought the assistance of the Director in bringing before the educational authorities the importance of adopting as texts certain books which give the background of the Negro. This matter is now being taken to the New York Board of Education."[26]

On November 13, 1932, Woodson instructed Greene on how to go about getting the books adopted. A principal, Anne E. Lawson, suggested to Woodson that the way to proceed was to get letters from principals stating that if the books were listed, they would buy them. The next place to go was to the appropriate associate superintendent. Greene contacted principals, but he also continued to solicit signers for the petition. This brought a sharp

23. Woodson, "Proceedings of the Annual Meeting," 2; and Woodson to Emile T. Holley, October 31, 1931.

24. Woodson to Greene, October 14, 1931; Woodson to Greene, October 28, 1931; Woodson to Greene, October 30, 1931; Greene to Woodson, November 5, 1931; and program of the Annual Meeting of the Association for the Study of Negro Life and History, November 8–12, 1931.

25. Greene to Woodson, February 19, 1932.

26. Woodson, "Proceedings of the Annual Meeting," 7.

rebuke from Woodson for Greene's failure to follow his instructions.[27] "It was not refusal to follow your plan that impelled me to pursue the course I did in reference to the books," Greene responded. He continued: "This procedure had the endorsement of interested individuals and school teachers on the scene here. Yet I shall gladly drop my method and adopt yours, if that will insure success. Like you, I am interested in results; not methods."[28]

Getting the books before the Board of Education for adoption was a long and tedious process. Greene continued to gather names on the petition, contact school officials, and follow the procedures they prescribed.[29] In the meantime, Woodson waxed hot and cold on what Greene was doing. On February 3, he sent him a gracious letter thanking him for his efforts. A week later, he wrote criticizing him for not working through the principals. "Sending a petition to the Board of Education," Woodson admonished, "does not amount to much. They get thousands every day and readily send them to the waste basket." Again, Greene patiently explained to Woodson that he had contacted the principals as instructed.[30]

Both Woodson and Evarts B. Greene, Greene's advisor at Columbia University, reminded Greene from time to time that work toward his degree should have first priority. His preliminary report in Professor Greene's seminar was due in late November, and the final oral report followed in January. Also, examinations in all other courses came at the end of January.[31] Greene prepared for and took these course examinations in spite of advice to the contrary from his adviser and other members of the history faculty. These faculty members felt that he could spend his time to better advantage

27. Woodson to Greene, November 13, 1931; and Woodson to Greene, December 30, 1931.

28. Greene to Woodson, January 1, 1932.

29. An indication of the time and effort Greene invested in this project can be gleaned from the correspondence related to it. For example, the following correspondence shows Greene's dedication to the project: Greene to Woodson, December 15, 1931; Greene to Woodson, February 2, 1932; Greene to Board of Education of New York City, February 5, 1932; Joseph Miller, Jr., to Greene, February 8, 1932; Greene to Board of Education of New York City, February 8, 1932; William J. O'Shea to Greene, February 9, 1932; Eugene A. Colligan to Greene, February 10, 1932; Greene to O'Shea, February 11, 1932; Greene to Colligan, February 12, 1932; Colligan to Greene, February 16, 1932; Miller to Greene, February 17, 1932; Woodson to Greene, February 20, 1932; Greene to Colligan, February 18, 1932; and Greene to Woodson, February 19, 1932.

30. Woodson to Greene, February 3, 1932; Woodson to Greene, February 9, 1932; and Greene to Woodson, February 19, 1932.

31. Woodson to Greene, November 23, 1931; Evarts B. Greene to Greene, November 20, 1931; Memorandum from Evarts B. Greene, December 10, 1931; Greene to Woodson, January 20, 1932.

preparing for the broader doctoral examinations. Columbia, unlike Harvard, followed the German practice and did not require students beyond the master's degree to take course examinations. Greene told Woodson that he took the course examinations because "I believe you would desire it and because I wished to check up on myself."[32]

Woodson's admonitions to place schoolwork before all else did not keep him from making demands on Greene's time. During the examination period in January 1932, he sent the galley proof for the study of unemployment in the District of Columbia and urged Greene to read it immediately. In response to Greene's excuses for delay, Woodson said that he only wanted Greene to check figures and for gross inaccuracies. He believed that this could be done in two or three hours.[33]

Then, in early February, Woodson found another assignment for Greene. The Associated Publishers had recently released *George Washington and the Negro* by Walter H. Mazyck, and Woodson was seeking agents to sell this book. Percy E. Newbie, a friend of the author, expressed an interest in acting as agent in New York City. Woodson asked Greene to screen agents there. Greene then contacted Newbie and began negotiating with him, presumably with authority from Woodson to act.[34]

Newbie, who had just finished law school and was without resources, agreed to follow the procedures that the agents used during the summer of 1930. He would take orders, collect his commission, and have the books sent C.O.D. from Washington. Greene agreed for Newbie to work on these terms, but Woodson, to Greene's embarrassment, rejected Newbie. "I wrote you," Woodson said, "that inasmuch as Mr. Newbie had nothing, that is could not pay five or ten dollars in advance, we do not care to have any dealing with him. It is not safe to transact business with paupers."[35]

Obviously disgusted, Greene wrote reproving Woodson for his action. "It seems that you have the wrong idea about bookselling," he said. "Millionaires do not sell books. Furthermore, the Associated Publishers, Inc. cannot lose one penny through the selling plan followed by us for the last two summers."[36]

In the midst of the Newbie episode, Woodson asked Greene to help collect data for the study then underway of African Americans in the

32. Greene to Woodson, January 28, 1932.

33. Woodson to Greene, January 19, 1932; Greene to Woodson, January 20, 1932; and Woodson to Greene, January 22, 1932.

34. Woodson to Greene, February 5, 1932; and Greene to [Percy E.] Newbie, February 8, 1932.

35. Greene to Woodson, February 27, 1932; and Woodson to Greene, March 15, 1932.

36. Greene to Woodson, March 18, 1932.

professions. He suggested that Greene could spend his Easter vacation doing this interviewing. When Greene informed him that he would not have an Easter vacation and that he had to write his seminar paper, Woodson would not excuse him from participation. "It is not expected," he said, "that you will take off time from your studies to fill out the questionnaires. You need a change from day to day, however, and this will suffice." He also sent Greene a check for one hundred dollars to cover expenses incurred in conducting the interviews.[37]

The check was probably to help salve hurt feelings over a financial dispute the men were having. This began when, on March 9, Greene asked Woodson to send the next installment of his fellowship. The response was an acrimonious letter upbraiding Greene for his spending habits. Woodson said that the next installment of three hundred dollars was not due until May, "if you are still in school and doing satisfactory work." He pointed out that Greene had received nine hundred dollars during the past six months, and this was more than Woodson was living on. "During the last fiscal year," he concluded, "the Association was able to pay me only $750 on my salary."[38]

In a less biting but equally direct reply, Greene assured Woodson that he was not spending money recklessly. In fact, he said that he was "exercising the greatest frugality in" his "expenditures." After explaining his expenditures, he expressed to Woodson understanding of and appreciation for the "sacrifices which you have made, and are making in promoting the work of the Association." "I hope," he said in closing, "the explanation contained herein will convince you that . . . I have carefully planned my expenditures, so that the $1,200.00 fellowship will not only carry me through the school year, but also will defray expense incurred for the benefit of the Association."[39]

Greene was careful not to go too far or to use injudicious language in writing Woodson. Largely thanks to Woodson, he enjoyed a rather good year financially. The fellowship, the income from lectures and selling books, and money earned from *Social Science Abstracts* made it a fairly lucrative year. The future, however, was uncertain.

With the nation in the throes of the Great Depression, employment prospects were bleak. The heads of colleges Greene had visited in 1930 and who had expressed an interest in employing him were not hiring in 1932. The only encouraging word about a job came from Harry J. Carman, a member of the Columbia history faculty. Carman recommended Greene

37. Woodson to Greene, March 14, 1932; Woodson to Greene, March 24, 1932; Greene to Woodson, March 26, 1932; and Woodson to Greene, March 28, 1932.

38. Greene to Woodson, March 9, 1932; and Woodson to Greene, March 12, 1932.

39. Greene to Woodson, March 14, 1932.

to Will Alexander, president of the new Dillard University in New Orleans. Alexander promised to keep Greene in mind, but, as it turned out, Alexander did not need a historian until the fall of 1934.[40]

With no prospects for employment, Greene decided to remain in school another year. He planned to complete all requirements for the degree by October 1933 at the latest. He also hoped against hope that Woodson would come through again and provide him with some support. Woodson let him know emphatically that this would not be the case. In fact, he had gotten rid of the car that Greene had used. Agents would have to provide their own transportation and work strictly on commission. Greene refused to work the Virginia Tidewater, the area Woodson offered him, on these terms.[41] Even so, Woodson invited Greene to come to Washington to see him. "I have nothing definite to offer," he warned him, "but I may give you some good advice."[42]

At this point, Greene became almost totally dependent upon income from selling books. Often this meant that he had to accept speaking engagements, with only his expenses covered, in order to have an opportunity to sell books after his speech. Usually, evidenced by the orders he sent off to Washington, these events resulted in at least a few sales.

As the depression deepened in 1933, Greene's financial situation became desperate. Woodson reminded him periodically how tight things were economically and informed him that things were also desperate with the Association. "If it were not for the fact that I am sacrificing every thing for the work," Woodson wrote in January, "we would have to close up." In February 1933, Greene resumed his search for employment with the same negative results he experienced the previous year.[43] He even applied for a job with the New York City Home Relief Bureau as an emergency investigator. He found that corruption and discrimination against black men stood in the way of his chances of employment with this agency.[44]

40. Harry J. Carman to Greene, April 5, 1932; Greene to W. R. Banks, April 15, 1932; W. R. Banks to Greene, April 11, 1932; F. D. Bluford to Greene, April 19, 1932; W. J. Hale to Greene, April 21, 1932; Charles W. Florence to Greene, April 30, 1932; Evarts B. Greene to Greene, October 24, 1933; and Evarts B. Greene to Greene, October 26, 1933.

41. Woodson to Greene, May 23, 1932; Greene to Woodson, May 24, 1932; Woodson to Greene, June 2, 1932; Greene to Woodson, June 17, 1932; Woodson to Greene, June 20, 1932; and Greene to Woodson, June 22, 1932.

42. Woodson to Greene, June 23, 1932.

43. Woodson to Greene, January 21, 1933. Among the institutions to which Greene applied for employment in 1933 were Miners Teachers' College, Johnson C. Smith University, Samuel Huston College, and the Tuskegee Institute. He inquired of Charles H. Wesley about the prospects of an opening at Howard University.

44. Greene to S. A. Allen, March 8, 1933; and Greene to Woodson, April 4, 1933.

The sale of books remained his only source of income. Many of those who subscribed for books were not able to pay the balance due and accept them when they arrived C.O.D. To add to his woes, Columbia University began dunning him for past due payments on a long-term loan the university had made to him earlier. Then, in April, Harriet Coleman Greene, his mother, was hospitalized, and the family expected him to contribute toward the hospital expenses.[45] His mother died in June. By this time, thanks to Woodson, Greene had the promise of a job for the fall of 1933.

President Charles W. Florence of Lincoln University in Missouri informed Woodson that he had a vacancy for a teacher of political science and history for the fall of 1933. Woodson recommended Greene, and President Florence wrote to Greene, through Woodson, inviting him to apply for the position.[46]

Characteristically, Woodson gave Greene detailed instructions on how to act in this situation. Above all, he was not to reveal that Woodson had anything to do with sponsoring him for the job. He went on to say: "You will see that the way is very clear and that you will succeed in getting this job unless you write a rather long letter, say things which you ought not to say, and make demands which you do not need to make. You will have a fine opportunity. I shall expect you, then, to proceed wisely."[47]

Woodson then proceeded to instruct Greene on how many paragraphs to include in the letter, what to say in each paragraph, and how long the letter should be. As to salary, Woodson advised, "I would suggest $3,000 a year, if he asked me to suggest the amount; but do not suggest it yourself. Let him bring the salary up himself. Say nothing about it at first."[48]

Greene followed Woodson's advice, in every detail, in writing the letter, and he probably did the same in regard to the salary question. President Florence, however, outlined for him the salary schedule at Lincoln. He wrote, "We have a regular salary schedule in which a full professor and head of a department receives $3,000 per year and an assistant professor receives $2,400. The only position open at present is an assistant professorship, which we are offering to you. This means $200 per month for twelve months."[49]

Greene accepted the appointment and worked at Lincoln University for his entire teaching career. He remained Woodson's loyal supporter and was always ready to serve the "cause."

45. Woodson to Greene, January 21, 1933; Charles S. Danielson to Greene, April 6, 1933; and Thomas Coleman to Greene, April 24, 1933.

46. Charles W. Florence to Greene, April 26, 1933.

47. Woodson to Greene, April 28, 1933.

48. Ibid.

49. Greene to Florence, May 2, 1933; and Florence to Greene, June 14, 1933.

1

Planning the Bookselling Campaign

A Reminiscence

[For the diary covering his bookselling odyssey, Greene left several drafts of introductions explaining how the sales campaign came about. He wrote these at least thirty years after his travels. This reminiscence is from one of these drafts.]

At the end of May [1930] Woodson suggested that I take a two-week vacation, then come in and talk with him upon my return. Having completed the study of Negro Employment in the District of Columbia,[1] I was happy to leave for New York.

On Monday, June 16 [the date recorded in the diary, Sunday, June 1, 1930, was probably the correct date], after two delightful weeks spent in New York and Newark and a few days with my family in Connecticut (where I was happy to find Mother and Dad well), I returned to Washington. I was also glad to see former high school classmates and friends in Ansonia.

Arriving in Washington at 2:30 p.m., I went directly to the office. Woodson was glad to see me and expressed the hope that I had got some much-needed rest, to which I nodded assent.

He then said he wanted to talk to me concerning the books of the Association, which were mildewing in the basement. I knew that [they were]. Then he asked whether I had any suggestions for disposing of them. I responded in the affirmative. "But how?" he asked, "I am sending out 2,000 letters a month advertising the books, but few orders come to [the]

1. Actually, Greene had just completed *The Negro Wage Earner* with Carter G. Woodson. The study of employment in the District of Columbia, which is covered in this volume, was not conducted until 1931.

office as a result. Last fall, I paid Paul Miller $14.00 to train salesmen, but few or no books were sold." I remembered that all too well also.

"Mr. Greene," he went on, "how can we get the public to purchase these books?" I briefly recounted my experience with the Union Circulation Company of New York City three summers ago, when at the head of a team of four students, I sold magazines over approximately one-fourth of the country.

"Well?" he inquired.

In reply, I stated, "Do what the magazine companies do."

"What is that?" he snapped.

"Well, take some of your best books, figure the total price, then cut that price to the bone. Send out salesmen; they will sell books."

"What are you proposing?"

"Choose some of these books," I responded, "which would sell for about $18.50. My proposal is to strike a line through that figure and peg the new price at $9.98."

Woodson nearly collapsed. "Why, that's a giveaway," he exploded, "are you trying to ruin the Association?"

"Well, Dr. Woodson, the books are mildewing in the basement. You are not selling them, although you are sending out two thousand letters a month. Paul Miller's plan failed and so did [Thomas] Georges's."

"How will the salesmen be paid?" he asked. "We don't have any money."

"You don't need money. The agents will collect their salary by receiving 40 percent of the sales price. If they sell books, they eat; if they don't, they starve. But it will cost the Association nothing."

"Mr. Greene, you mean to tell me that we shall sell books worth $18.50 for $9.98; the salesmen will receive $4.00 and the Association will net only $5.98? And what assurance do I have that the Association will receive even that much?"

He bristled up so, I feared he would have a stroke.

"Well, Dr. Woodson," I countered, "it's a question of getting something out of the books or letting them continue to rot in the basement. The $5.98 balance due will be collected C.O.D. by the postman when the books are received. In this way neither the subscriber nor the Association can lose. Especially will the Association be assured of its $5.98. It cannot lose."

Whether he was silenced or convinced, I did not know. Whatever the case, Woodson gave me a quizzical stare, then asked, "When can you start?"

"As soon as I can recruit a couple of salesmen and secure transportation," I replied.

Again that stare. "Transportation? What do you mean by transportation?"

"A car, an automobile, Dr. Woodson."

He just glared at me. "Well, I'll see what can be done," he said.

I left him and went to the Kappa [Alpha Psi] Fraternity House. There I was able to interest three students in selling books. [John Wesley] Poe and Noble Payton were glad to find some work for the summer after listening to my tale of the fun we had while selling magazines in 1927. Further, since they had no jobs, they had nothing to lose. The third chap, named [James Cecil] Wilkey, said he had a job on Lake Champlain that would earn him $200 a month. However, I was able to persuade him to forgo that employment for the opportunity of seeing the country, the possibility of making more than his job would pay him, and especially because of the people he would meet and the diversion that would be ours as we met students in the various towns and cities we would visit. Wilkey decided to go with us. All three promised to have surety for $100, which Woodson demanded.

When I returned to the office, lo, Woodson had bought a used Model A Ford. When I thanked [him], he advised me to take good care of it and by all means be careful on the road. He also advised that I make certain the students posted the $100 surety bond. I assured him I would see that the fellows complied.

The balance of the afternoon [was] spent reading the page proof [of *The Negro Wage Earner*]. Woodson finally advised that I go home and get a good night's rest so that I could pass the test for my driver's license if I intended to leave tomorrow. Taking his advice, I went home to prepare for what I hoped would be a successful bookselling campaign.

[The only diary entry found that covers this event was made on June 1, 1930.]

Returned from Newark after three weeks' absence from D.C. Met Dr. Woodson at 2:45 p.m. Showed me list of four books: *Negro in Our History, Plays and Pageants, Negro Orators and Orations,* and *African Myths.* Proposed selling them for $8.50. Regular price $12.00. Thought well of it. But persuaded him to add two more—*Veiled Aristocrats* and *Everlasting Stain*—neither of which is selling. That boosted the total regular price to $16.50. I suggested they be sold for $10.00, giving agent 40 percent. Woodson agreeable. Deputed me to draw up some sort of subscription blank.

Met [Thomas] Georges. He was overjoyed at seeing me. Yet, chided me for not writing him. Very despondent over failure to graduate from Howard. Threatened suicide. He even attempted it. Told him he was foolish, that he ought to leave school and finish without being forced to worry over the bare necessities of life.

Called I____. Overjoyed to hear my voice. Called upon her later. What a welcome. And I felt all my resolutions vanishing into nothingness before the passion of her greeting and the warmth and sweetness of her presence.

Called upon Bertha. Was out.

Went into the House of Prayer. Here the most pathetic yet the most grotesque and at once the cruelest travesty upon the name of Christianity met my eyes. It was about 10:20 p.m. The meeting had been presided over by the so-called Bishop [Charles Emmanuel] Grace, who had stirred his hearers to an incredible degree of religious frenzy, climaxing it by having them line up to receive his blessing as they filed by, while others yelled, shouted, and danc[ed] in demoniacal fury. Some screeched, others gibbered inarticulately. One woman evidently simulating repeated "oh su-su-su-su-su." Others fell down on the sawdust-covered floor, jerking, rolling, moaning, weeping, and crying, "O Jesus, O Jesus!" Women, girls, boys, and men, all in one indiscriminate heap in all manner of positions fell down smitten with the power. Those still retaining their senses sang, moaned, and chanted a ragtime tune. Others beat cymbals. Still others blew brass instruments.

Then at the height of this emotional orgy, the Bishop [was] suddenly escorted out by a double line of brawny, sweating, white-gloved, sword-wearing ushers. I wondered what the children of God needed with swords. With the departure of the Bishop, the hubbub tended to die down. I then ventured nearer the front to ascertain the extent of the casualties.

2

We Go to Hampton and Suffolk

SATURDAY AND SUNDAY   JUNE 21 AND 22, 1930

On my way to the office this morning [I] tried unsuccessfully to secure a Model T Ford in which to take my road test. Did not feel capable of passing it in a gearshift Model A. Failing in this, however—Bright could not help me—I decided to stake all in passing the exam successfully in the Model A Ford [Carter G.] Woodson had purchased the day previous. [James Cecil] Wilkey accompanied me. Passed the test without any trouble and received a 10-day temporary permit—regular permit will be issued at the end of that period.

Returned to the office to complete the reading of the proof of the "Negro Wage Earner."[1] Woodson seemed pleased to know that I had secured a permit. Is anxious for us to start.

By the way, I reminded him that one of the tires was flat this morning. He gave me a letter to take to the salesman demanding it be replaced by a serviceable one. This was done. Upon the return to the office I gave the boys the fright of their lives although it left me unperturbed. I narrowly missed striking a parked auto while rounding a curve at 14th and Penn. Ave. In doing so, I did not notice until almost too late that I was almost upon a boy riding a bicycle. By maneuvering the car carefully, however, I avoided colliding with him. I laughed at the fellows' discomfiture and apprehension. Yet had I struck that boy, my temporary permit would have been revoked on the very day of its issuance. That would have been an extremely unfortunate affair for it would have detained us indefinitely.

1. Greene and Woodson, *The Negro Wage Earner.*

It was finally decided by me that we would leave at 6:00 p.m. for Newport News, Virginia. [John Wesley] Poe, [Noble F.] Payton, and Wilkey, all Howard students, are to accompany me as canvassers. [Oliver] LaGrone, a fellow recommended by Wilkey, I heard had called to see me and left a letter of credit at the office, filled out with a surety of only $10. Woodson and I both agreed that it was too small. I called him, had him come to see me, and advised that he get surety for $100 (one hundred dollars). He promised to do so but said he could not leave before Sunday.

I also told Woodson of the need for a luggage carrier. He expressed himself against it, stating that our luggage could go inside. Also did not see why I desired to carry four men. What would I do with them? I explained my plan to distribute them in the various cities. He finally, as I knew he would, brought back a luggage carrier and a lantern.

Poe and Payton were ready at 6:00 p.m. I was reading page proof of "The Negro Wage Earner." Woodson finally decided I had better finish it at the expiration of 10 days.

We met at the office at 8:30. Gave the boys final instructions, told them what was expected of them, that this 10-day period was largely probationary, and that their results therefrom would decide who would go south with me.

Left the office at 9:30. Had Wilkey to drive me to the barber shop. Before going there, however, went to say goodbye to the Mickeys [Lillian and Bushrod]. Not at home. Met them on the outside as I was leaving. Chatted with them for [a] half hour. Mrs. Mickey asked that I stop to see her in Asheville, N.C. She appears in better health than when last I saw her.

After a long wait in the barber shop and a longer wait for Wilkey to return with the car, I went home to pack my things. Did not feel safe leaving tonight for some reason. I had fears that Wilkey, who seems somewhat drowsy even by day, might fall asleep while driving, with disastrous results to us all. Told the boys that upon my return to the car. Wilkey assured me he could remain awake indefinitely. I overruled him, however, and with the weight of the other fellows (except Poe, who stated he was willing to take any sort of chance), we decided to leave at 3:00 a.m. LaGrone invited the fellows to his former lodging. I say "former" because he had just given it up. Then he had the temerity to invite us—five in all—to rest for the time in "his" room. He must have felt that the landlady was tender-hearted to an extreme. I could not invite them to share my room because of its condition.

Up to LaGrone's, therefore, we went. I had no intentions of going in but, having seen the boys cared for, would have returned to my aunt's. Just what I expected. All the boys went along with LaGrone only to have two [of them] return with the announcement that only two could sleep in the bed. Three would break it down. Payton and Poe, then, were couchless. Therefore, I could do nothing less than sleep with them in the car.

Telling Wilkey we would return for them at 3:00 a.m.—it was 12:30 now—I drove the car over to an inconspicuous place on Girard Street where we settled down to our repose. I dozed fitfully. Payton did likewise. Poe, however, was more adaptable and actually slept.

Returned for Wilkey and LaGrone at 3:45. Could not wake them, although I sounded the horn several times. Had to desist for fear of arrest for disturbing the peace at that ungodly hour. Therefore, settled down to watchful waiting. Just to illustrate the Negro's conception of time; although I had informed the fellows that we would leave at 3:00 a.m., they actually set the alarm on their clock for 4:05. It went off with considerable racket at that time.

Within five minutes we were off. Filled the car with gas. The trip to Richmond gave us our first thrill. We also had an opportunity to behold the stately Potomac in its most beautiful dress. Dawn was just breaking as we left Washington. And as we crossed the Long Bridge a most gorgeous panorama engaged the eye on every side. Above, the mist was rising, disclosing an azure sky from which the stars vanished one by one. Clouds, varying in color from dark blue to white, scudded heavenly eastward. On both sides spread the green-clad banks of the river, rising in verdant grandeur until they lowered their heads under the weight of the horizon. And between this, the river. Never have I seen it more beautiful. It glistened even though there was neither moon nor sunlight to illumine it. It was placid, calm, silvery. It almost appeared wintry. Whatever it was, it evoked exclamations of rhapsody from us all.

Leaving this behind we attended to the serious business of getting to Richmond. Wilkey, who was driving, not only failed to impress me as a driver, but even frightened me at times. He seemed unable to make turns, especially on the right, without great effort, almost turning the car over in several attempts and causing all of us to become extremely anxious. Moreover, he evinced a marked tendency to run off the road. And in places where a drop of several inches exists between the pavement and the dirt lining, to do so might spell disaster for us at any time, especially while traveling at a forty-mile[-an-hour] gait. We had already passed an overturned automobile. Once Wilkey dozed, ran off the road, brought the car back, and zigzagged to such an extent that I bade him give over the wheel to me. He assured me, of course, that he was awake, that the fault lay in the unevenness of the road. It reminded me of [Sidney] Wells in 1927.[2]

I took the driving job for a while. Showed Wilkey how to take right-hand curves without causing the fellows to hold the sides of the car in consternation lest they be overturned. Also demonstrated how to make a curve seem no curve. He did not manifest any umbrage at my giving him advice. I must confess that I gave the boys considerable apprehension on two occasions by the swaying of the car while traveling at 45 miles an hour.

It was Wilkey, however, who made the crowning stroke. Trying to pass between a parked car and a bus traveling downhill on his left, he ran into the former. Why he did not stop in order to avoid it is a mystery. The owner of the car, however, a Maryland poor white, was in good humor, evidently, for he assured us that outside of a dent in his fender, his car was unhurt. Did not even ask to see our license. Our fender was bent a trifle. Wilkey blamed the man. True, he was technically at fault because he had parked on a state highway. But I blamed Wilkey, for although he had the right of way, he certainly was not justified in jeopardizing our lives by running into an obstacle in his path.

Reached Richmond without further ado about 7:30. Stopped at Glenn Carrington's at 305 Leigh St.[3] Unable to awaken anyone. Called on Joscelyn at 1212 N. 31 St. He is one of our agents. Came to Richmond without books or subscription blanks. Has spent a week without doing anything. Wrote a distressful letter to our office last week for money. Still has plenty of energy, dash, and guts. Believe he will make good. Gave him additional subscription blanks. He did not relish the fact that we were to work his territory. I told him, however, that I would be responsible for his getting to South Carolina.

After leaving him, for the first time, I became conscious of our wretched financial condition. Went to Slaughter's Cafe for breakfast. I ordered cereal, fruit, bacon and eggs, and milk. The other fellows followed suit, Wilkey, however, getting ham instead of bacon. The proprietor had no fruit. Could scarcely believe this was the Slaughter's Cafe of 1927, when we could order almost anything within reason and get it. After the meal three of the fellows,

2. Sidney Wells and Greene traveled together during the summer of 1927 selling magazines for the Union Circulation Company. See Greene, *Working with Carter G. Woodson,* 12–13, n. 1.

3. Greene met Glenn Carrington while they were students at Howard University. After graduating from Howard, Carrington attended the New York University School of Social Work. Later, he attended Harvard University on a fellowship secured for him by Carter G. Woodson to study anthropology. See Greene, *Working with Carter G. Woodson,* 258–61, 280–81, and 283.

I find, are absolutely penniless. One, Payton, had $2.00. The total bill was $3.15. I had to pay for Wilkey and LaGrone; Payton for Poe. I was astounded, as well as provoked, for had I known that the boys were in such pressing straits, I should never have left Washington until Monday. I was left with $2.50. By the time I bought gas and oil, only 80 cents remained.

It seemed that the financial condition of the men had been somewhat misrepresented. Wilkey did not tell me he was penniless. Neither did Poe. Wilkey had also assured me that LaGrone had money, for he had been working. Payton had said nothing. I was in a quandary, for we would be unable to sell anything until Monday.

Where would we stop overnight? Insofar as I was concerned, I could easily find accommodations at Hampton Institute. But I could not do so and permit the fellows to sleep in the car. Yet in my capacity as a man in the public, I could not go to Hampton or any other place and ask that the boys be put up gratis. I could accept but not solicit a favor. I realized that the fellows, Poe excepted, probably did not understand my point of view.

Not only did lack of money plague us but tire trouble was soon added. The rear right tire, we discovered, had a break on the side, evidence of rottenness. Not far from Richmond, it went flat. We had to put on the spare tire, which, if it lasts for 100 miles, will certainly surprise me. In addition, we had no pump in the car. The Ford agent certainly made a fool of us. We ought to have been outfitted with new tires all around.

We reached Hampton without further trouble, tired, sleepy, and hungry, at 2:00 p.m.

It had been an otherwise enjoyable ride through historic Fredricksburg, where remains the only slave auction block in the United States, past the home of ~~Martha~~ [Mary] Washington,[4] mother of George; the spot also where he supposedly threw a silver dollar across the river; the law office of James Monroe; and the beautifully terraced battleground of Fredricksburg.[5] It is a typically Southern town—lazy and quiet. It is as near Colonial in architecture as Alexandria, perhaps even more so.

4. Here Greene confused the names of George Washington's mother and wife. The house in Fredericksburg belonged to Washington's mother, Mary Ball Washington. Washington's sister, Elisabeth (Betty) Washington Lewis, also had a house in Fredericksburg. For a description of Fredericksburg landmarks and historic sites as they probably were at the time of Greene's visit, see, Paul Wilstach, *Tidewater Virginia,* 259–79.

5. The Union Army of the Potomac commanded by General Ambrose E. Burnside was defeated by Confederate forces under General Robert E. Lee at Fredericksburg on December 13, 1862. This was one of the bloodiest battles of the Civil War, with Union casualties numbering over twelve thousand and Confederate losses at about five thousand. Bruce Catton, *Never Call Retreat,* 12–24.

Richmond on her seven hills reminds me of the Eternal City. Two rivers, the Rappahannock and the James, flow through it. The city is beautiful. Many of the Negroes have beautiful homes, especially on East Leigh and East Clay streets. There is considerable Negro business here—insurance companies, [a] building and loan, grocery stores, drug stores, and the like. Many Negroes also work in the industries here, especially the tobacco factories. Others find employment in flour mills, iron factories, and in common labor. Most of the women, except those in tobacco factories, are domestics.

One cannot but be shocked at seeing the wretched hovels tenanted by many Negroes in the heart or outskirts of this great city. On side streets, near the river and railroad station, and in alleys, they live in wretched shacks unpainted, unsanitary, and in all stages of dilapidation. Their inmates seem coarse, vulgar, and ignorant. Most of those seen by us were black Negroes. They were untidy, unclean, and careless even to exposing their persons. Of course this applies only to the rougher, more illiterate element of the Richmond Negro population. Most of the streets upon which they live are unpaved. In many of them the toilet accommodations and water are on the outside.

Leaving Richmond we passed through Williamsburg, the seat of the second oldest university in the country—[the College of] William and Mary. It was founded in 16[93]. Some of the old buildings are still standing. The entire architectural scheme is colonial and of recent years, through the munificence of John D. Rockefeller, Jr., the entire university is being restored and enlarged in all its quaint colonial glory.[6] Several new buildings have already been constructed. Williamsburg has the atmosphere of Alexandria or Fredricksburg—quiet, dignified, and strongly reminiscent of the historic past.

Another wonder en route was the James River Bridge, one of the longest in the world stretching 4½ miles stately across the James River from Hilton

6. At the time of Greene's visit, the restoration of Colonial Williamsburg was still in process. John D. Rockefeller, Jr., became interested in restoring the city through the efforts and influence of Dr. W. A. R. Goodwin, rector of the Bruton Parish Church. Rockefeller visited Williamsburg in 1926, and the following year, the purchase of property and the restoration began. The restoration "as to form" was completed by 1935, but some details were still left to be done. The three College of William and Mary buildings constructed in the eighteenth century—the Wren Building, the President's House, and the Brafferton—underwent restoration between 1928 and 1932. See "The Restoration of Colonial Williamsburg in Virginia," 357–62; Colonial Williamsburg, Inc., *Official Guidebook*, 55–59; and Writers' Program of the Work Projects Administration in the State of Virginia, 313–20.

to within a few miles of Jamestown. It was opened in 1928. The state could not build it on account of insufficient funds; therefore, it was constructed by a private corporation.

Then into beautiful Hampton. Hampton with its lovely campus stretching like an enormous green carpet, its stately buildings, alluring charm, never to be forgotten. Hampton!

I called upon Capt. [Walter R.] Brown, my friend of 1927. He is assistant to the commandant, Major [Allen W.] Washington, and is one of these princes whom every now and then it becomes one's good fortune to meet.[7] He was not at his office but was resting. I learned Major Washington also was out. Called upon Dr. Nathaniel Dett, world-famous musician, but could not find him at home.[8]

Finally called upon Capt. Brown at his home. Greeted me affably. We talked over the campaign of 1927, mentioned [Hosea] Campbell.[9] He was pleased to learn that I had accomplished a little during the interim. Gradually I led him to ask our mission this time. Told him of the book campaign. Asked whether he could lodge my four men. Replied he would be glad to do so, but the incoming of 300 ministers to their Annual Conference would make it a little difficult. But Capt. Brown is such an excellent man that he made room for the boys by putting extra cots in the summer students' rooms in order to accommodate them. He asked whether I desired a room. Told him at first that I was going to Suffolk. Finally, decided to remain here. Each of us bunked with three fellows.

Frankly, I am disappointed in today's outcome. I had hoped to arouse interest in the work in all the larger tidewater cities such as Norfolk, Portsmouth, Suffolk, and Newport News, by sending a man to each of

7. Allen Wadsworth Washington graduated from Hampton in 1891 and was employed as assistant to Major Robert Russa Moton, the commandant of Hampton Institute. Washington became commandant in 1916, when Moton left to become Booker T. Washington's successor as the principal of Tuskegee Institute. Walter R. Brown graduated from Hampton in 1913, and after teaching in the preparatory department of Morehouse College for two years, he returned to Hampton as an assistant in the commandant's office. Brown became commandant when Washington died in 1930. See John A. Kenny, "Allen Wadsworth Washington," *Southern Workman* 59 (October 1930): 444–45; "New Commandant," *Southern Workman* 59 (November 1930): 525.

8. Robert Nathaniel Dett (1882–1943) taught at Hampton from 1913 to 1932. Although he was an accomplished pianist, he is best known as a composer and as the organizer and director of the Hampton Institute Choir.

9. Hosea Campbell convinced the Union Circulation Company of New York City to use teams of African American students to sell magazines. In 1927, Campbell led a team and was in charge of all teams of African American students. Greene was a team leader, and both his team and the team led by Campbell were at Hampton in August 1927.

them. Because of lack of funds, however, I was unable to do this and thus open the way for a good start on Monday.

Went to dinner at the cafeteria. The boys, three of whom were penniless, took a waffle and coffee. I gave half of my 56 cents to Wilkey and LaGrone. I took peas, beets, and milk. Cost 27 cents. This was worse than 1927.

Incidentally, I went to chapel along with Poe, LaGrone, and Payton. LaGrone went to sleep. How he could possibly do so is more than I could fathom for surely the remarks of the speaker left me spellbound. He was Bishop Samuels of South Africa, a big princely looking dark man. He told of the oppression of natives under English rule. Negroes, he said, are not allowed abroad after nine at night, except they have passes. They are brought from the interior into the cities to work for little or nothing and they pay a pound a year as a head tax. Last year they paid to the government £750,000 in taxes. He told of the various restrictions under which the Bantu natives lived, their meager pittance for laborious work, segregated quarters, which finally if carried to completion would result in the virtual extermination of seven millions of people. In biting sarcasm, he spoke of the Negro's *understanding* the white man. Such a fine speech was absolutely wasted on LaGrone, for while Poe, Payton, and I sat there spellbound, LaGrone went fast asleep. I had to tell Poe to nudge him. Poor fellow, I presume he was both hungry and tired, hence welcomed a chance to close his eyes.

This is a good time to take stock of my companions. Poe is a gentleman, tall, spare, and exceedingly lean of face. He is of a reddish hue. A most agreeable companion, well read, soft spoken, a good conversationalist, and possessing an engaging personality. He is a lady's man; more truthfully, the ladies admire him easily. He has just received his B.A. degree and will study law at Winchester. Is self made. Both mother and father died when he was a child.[10] Is of the irrepressible type.

In contrast to Poe, there is Payton. Noble Payton! What an uncommon name for a Negro. He wears the cognomen well, is tall, reserved, almost to an extreme. Where Poe is buoyant, he is coldly calculating. He is refined, soft spoken, an excellent talker, so I hear, a logical reasoner, and very careful about his sartorial appearance. His reserve is accentuated by the fact that he wears glasses and rectangular ones at that. He comes of a good New Jersey

10. This statement is contradicted by information contained in entries made in August 1930. John Wesley Poe was from Huntsville, Alabama, and Chapter 6 has an account of Greene's visit to the home of Poe's mother and stepfather there. Poe completed a bachelor of science degree in Howard University's College of Liberal Arts in 1930. Although he left the bookselling campaign before the end of the tour, later in 1930 he rejoined Greene in Philadelphia. He remained in Philadelphia after Greene left in early 1931.

family. Expects to specialize in law at Harvard. He lacks stick-to-itiveness, according to Poe, and is easily dismayed. He and the latter are good friends.[11]

Still another picture is presented by LaGrone. A fine physical type of fellow such as football coaches would like to grace their teams. Heavily built, strong muscled, and heavy jawed, he could also perhaps be mistaken for a prize fighter. He is loquacious, almost to a fault, sometimes propounding the most asinine queries. But there are two qualities that stand out prominently in him. He has initiative, plenty of it, he is irrepressible; and he has guts. He ought to make a good salesman under a little coaching. He is an Oklahoman and expects to become a lawyer. Is a junior at Howard U. Complexion brown.[12]

Last but not least comes Wilkey, the fellow whom I persuaded to relinquish a $200-a-month job on Lake Champlain to come with me. Wilkey is the youngest of all. Just 21. Very dark, not good looking, with reddish eyes. He has great initiative and is a hard worker. He is also very thoughtful. Although an unobtrusive type of fellow, he has a way of his own. Lacks polish, but underneath this rough exterior, I believe that there lies true mettle.[13]

11. Noble Frank Payton received the bachelor of science degree from Howard University in 1931 and the master of arts in chemistry from Howard in 1934. He taught chemistry at Howard and several other institutions, including Mississippi Industrial College, North Carolina College (now North Carolina Central University), Livingstone College, and Hampton Institute (now Hampton University). He also served as president and plant manager of the Suburban Chemical Company (Julian Laboratories) in Franklin Park, Illinois, and president of PharmChem Corporation in Chicago. From 1953 to 1964, he was director of development at Meharry Medical College, and in 1964, he became director of alumni affairs at Howard. Howard University Official News Release, July 1, 1964; *Howard University Magazine,* October 1964, 26, Data File, Howard University Office of Alumni Affairs.

12. This and subsequent comments about Clarence Oliver LaGrone show that Greene failed to recognize a kindred creative spirit in this young man. LaGrone was born in McAlester, Oklahoma, on December 9, 1906. He did not return to Howard after participating in the bookselling campaign. He earned a bachelor of arts degree from the University of New Mexico in 1938. In addition, he studied at Wayne State University and the Cranbrook Art Academy. He became a teacher, sculptor, and poet. He taught in the Detroit Public Schools and at Pennsylvania State University. His sculptures include pieces on George Washington Carver, Langston Hughes, and Nelson Mandela. His published works include *Dawnfire and Other Poems* (1989) and his poetry has appeared in several anthologies. In 1992, when the editor interviewed LaGrone by telephone at his home in Hamlet, North Carolina, the octogenarian was still actively exhibiting his works and lecturing.

13. James Cecil Wilkey was born on September 16, 1908, in Morristown, Tennessee. His father, Thomas W. Wilkey, was a barber there. In 1930, he transferred to Howard University from Morristown College. He remained with Greene to the end of the tour in 1930. In 1933, he returned to Howard University for two semesters and took courses in commerce, but he did not complete a degree at Howard. Howard University Office of the Registrar, Application Blank and Scholastic Record of Wilkey, James Cecil.

I was so tired that I returned at 9:50 and despite the efforts of the fellows in the room to talk with me, I fell off to sleep leaving them to follow soon after.

The first day of the trip had ended. We were in a precarious predicament. I had a $10 check and three or four cents. The only way to get breakfast would be to cash the check. God grant that might be done early in the morning, for the boys are hungry and broke.

Monday June 23, 1930

Ways and Means

Something in the air here must be conducive to sleep, else I was fatigued to an extreme. Whatever the case, I enjoyed the best night's rest that I have experienced in years.

At 6:40 I awoke fully refreshed. The sun shone brilliantly and the campus seemed even more inviting than yesterday. The fellows with whom I stay, Parham and Gates, are splendid chaps. Make me feel right at home. Both are cooking here during the summer in order to earn money for school in the fall.

We were still in a serious predicament as far as money was concerned. No one had any. The boys went to bed hungry last night. Early this morning Wilkey and LaGrone came to my room. I admonished them that the sooner they sold subscriptions, the sooner they could eat. They started out with a will.

Halfway across the campus, I met Poe [and Payton?] and LaGrone. They introduced me to a bald headed, pleasant looking man of possibly 38 or 40. He was Mr. [Ernest] Hays, the organist here. Through him, I was able to cash the $10 check. He also gave the fellows some leads for Hampton City. Took them over there. Introduced us to Negro druggists, a banker—there is a building and loan association there operated by Negroes. I attempted to sell the druggists, but both of them pleaded lack of funds. They were moving their drug store from downtown and one of them remarked that he could not even buy castor oil. Met Mr. Ashwan, head of the school of electricity at Hampton Institute. Promised to see me later.

Left Poe and Payton in Hampton with my blessings and returned to the campus. Called upon Capt. Brown relative to an introduction to the director of the summer school. I desired to have his permission to speak in chapel before the summer school students. There are more than 750 here, the largest summer school Hampton has ever experienced. That augurs well for educational progress.

Capt. Brown was not in. Fortunately, however, I looked in the adjoining office and espied Major Washington, the commandant. A large, kindly, elderly man who had been so kind to us in 1927. He was glad to see me and seemed happy to know that I had accomplished a little since he last saw me. I replied that one of my greatest pleasures lay in showing him that his aid in 1927 had not been wasted upon us, but that with the exception of [Sidney] Wells, who is ill, we have been striving to vindicate the faith which he inspired in us. I told him of Martin's success in the New York University School of Law.

Relative to speaking in chapel, he advised me to see Dr. [George Perley] Phenix, the President.

Called upon the latter. He had just stepped out but his secretary assured me that he would return within a few minutes. We chatted about the beauty of Hampton while I awaited his return.

I had not long to do so, for in less than five minutes he entered. He is white, small of stature, almost my height with a tendency to stoutness. He is almost deaf and uses an ear-hone. He listened with much interest to my participation in the work of Dr. Woodson, praised the latter, but told me he would be unable to grant me a chance to speak at chapel because every hour was filled until next Monday. The Ministers' Conference opening today was responsible. He told me, however, that he would be glad to read a notice in chapel for me and that I might have one of my men sit at a table with the books on exhibition in the lobby of the chapel—Ogden Hall.

We discussed for some little time the occupational trend of the Negro, touched upon the loss of the Negro in the trades since the Civil War and the change in sentiment of intellectual Negroes to trade schools and manual training. I asked him about what percentage of his trade graduates actually followed their trades. He could not tell me exactly, but called the proper sources and gave the proportion at 60 percent. That also included teaching trades. He admitted, however, that the school was becoming increasingly academic. That is the trend among Negro schools today.

Leaving Dr. Phenix, I interviewed Mr. [Isaac] Fisher at Clark Hall. Mr. Fisher is the executive secretary of the Ministers' Conference and the head of the Y.M.C.A. here. He is a small, dark man, slight of stature, with a large head and possessing a nervous and dynamic temperament. Very kind. I asked him whether he could present me to the president of the Ministers' Conference in order that I might speak to them for a moment or two. He assured me that as soon as Dr. [Erasmus Lafayette] Baskerville, the president, arrived, he would do so. He, himself, however, could not give me permission to do so.

As I left Mr. Fisher, Mr. Hays called me. He introduced me to a Mrs. [Mary Rose] Reeves Allen, regular Howard University instructor, now teacher of physical education for the women here. She promised to introduce me to Dr. [Charles W.] Coulter, the teacher of Negro History here, that

I might speak to his classes and thus be able to induce his students to take some of the books.[14] She advised me to meet her at the girls' dormitory at 6:30 for that purpose.

My next move was to find Wilkey and LaGrone and take them to dinner. (By the way, the biggest meal of the day is served at noon here, which is very sensible.) They have not enjoyed a good meal since yesterday morning. However, they did help to consume a pound of prunes, which I bought in Hampton, after which I advised them to drink plenty of water. Both of them were ravenously hungry and it was only with great difficulty that I could persuade them to wait until noon for dinner. They, like [Ernest] B[acote] and [Harry] H[ipp],[15] lose their sense of proportion entirely when hungry. Such a phenomenon is exceedingly strange to me for it seems that education should permit one to suppress the appetites to such a degree that only under the most extreme conditions should they become patent to the observer. I have frequently done so during my school days.

TUESDAY JUNE 24, 1930

Rose 6:45. Wrote in diary until 8:00. Missed breakfast trying to locate Dr. Baskerville, the president of the Ministers' Conference meeting here. Finally found him. Is a tall, dark, jovial man. An Episcopalian from Charleston, South Carolina. A firm and loyal supporter of our work. Contributes five dollars each year. Told me he would have to allot me only five minutes to speak for their program was full. Would let me speak this afternoon. Dr. [Chantise T.] Murray of the Vermont Avenue Baptist Church was right there to help me out.

Had to go to Hampton City, thereafter, for breakfast. Best available place was wretched. Full of flies and, as usual in Negro places, no fruit nor cereal. Just bacon and eggs. Did not even give me butter. When it was finally brought, it cost me a dime extra. May Allah shrive me! Could not enjoy my meal. The flies ate as much as I. Finally, had to go across the street and get a

14. Both Mary Reeves Allen and Charles W. Coulter were at Hampton Institute in 1930 to teach in the summer school. Allen was director of physical education for women at Howard University, and Coulter taught sociology at Ohio Wesleyan University. "The Summer School," *Southern Workman* 59 (August 1930): 378.

15. Ernest Bacote and Harry Hipp were close friends of Greene's at Howard University. Bacote was from Greene's hometown of Ansonia, Connecticut, and they had been schoolmates there. He earned an M.D. degree from Howard in 1926 and practiced medicine in Lawnside, New Jersey; Syracuse, New York; and Newark, New Jersey. Hipp and Greene met at Howard. After earning an A.B. from Howard, Hipp went to work for Standard Oil of New York. Greene, *Working with Carter G. Woodson,* 12–13, nn. 1, 2.

pint of milk and some raw prunes. If my stomach can stand up under this, I'll live to a ripe old age.

While Poe and Payton canvassed in the city of Hampton, I returned to the Institute to work.

Met the physical education teacher, Mrs. Allen, who introduced me to Dr. Coulter, [a] white sociologist teaching Negro History. Using [Jerome] Dowd's book, *The Negro in American Life.* The book is written with a bias. Dowd is a Southerner. Coulter defends his use of the book on the grounds that he desires his students to get both points of view. Therefore, he did not use Woodson's [*Negro in Our History*]. Latter is too plain spoken, I feel. Coulter told me that Wilkey had come to him yesterday and interrupted his class to ask him for names of his students. Told him he could not do so and to go to the registrar. I had to apologize for this. Coulter said he felt a little reticent, on that account, to talk with me. Finding out my connections, however, he quickly offered me an opportunity to speak to his classes at 8:00 a.m. and 9:00 a.m. respectively tomorrow.

The Ministers' Conference is really a nuisance. Some few take it seriously. Most, however, regard it as a pleasure or sight-seeing trip. When Dr. [James H.] Dillard was speaking this morning, fully one-half the ministers were absent.[16] Many were playing croquet, others were visiting or sight-seeing in Norfolk or Portsmouth, while a goodly number of others sat on the lawn either flirting with the summer school teachers or arguing trivial biblical points.

Spoke to the ministers at 2:30. Supposed to have five minutes. Took nine. The topic of the conference, "How to Keep Youth in the Church" ["The Church and Its Young People"], afforded me an opportunity to tell them the truth about youth's growing failure to attend or support the church. I gave the findings of our ([Charles H.] Wesley and my) survey of 1928. Told them youth itself was dissuaded from going to church for three reasons. First, that the Negro Church had failed to keep pace with worldly progress; second, that the church still frowned upon such innocent diversions as dancing, card-playing, and theater-going; and third, that the church was giving youth an impractical doctrine—one that's like a brand new suit, [which] could only be used on Sunday. I explained that youth was tired of being taught to die or of being preached into heaven or hell. He wanted to be taught how to live. Told them also that youth should be given a place in the church to demonstrate its talents. This could be consummated by organizing church

16. James H. Dillard was president of the Anna T. Jeanes Fund and the John F. Slater Fund. His topic for the conference was "The Kingdom of Heaven." Isaac Fisher, "Hampton Ministers' Conference," *Southern Workman* 59 (August 1930): 351.

clubs like Negro History clubs, dramatic clubs, poetry clubs, musical clubs, etc. In this way, youth would be kept in the Church, also, [that] the cause of Negro History would be served. I also explained that the books we were selling were admirably adapted to such uses and exhorted the ministers to see me and purchase them.

Whatever my talk did, it aroused such a storm of debate among the ministers that I feared I had wrecked the meeting. Led by Dr. [A. G.] Galvin of Newport News [pastor of First Baptist Church], a fiery dispenser of the gospel of the Old School, many of the ministers swore that they would not let down the bars in order to keep their young people in the church. One suggested that they be allowed to go their errant way. Another vowed that he would stop preaching before he would submit to such a thing. Then, others sought to minimize the problem by stating that they had difficulty in getting the old people into the church. I could readily discern, however, that such a stand was merely a self-defensive mechanism in which little or no truth was inherent. Old Galvin, a crusader, if ever there was one, took the floor again and waxed so eloquent against what I had said that I felt like congratulating him (only for his oratorical ability, however).

Against this determined stand of the conservative older preachers stood the younger, more intelligent, and the more liberal older preachers. Fewer in number; yet because of superior intelligence they waged a mighty struggle on the floor to dispense with some of the old social prohibitions. Among this group was Dr. [Richard H.] Bowling [pastor of First Baptist Church] of Norfolk, Virginia, and Dr. Murray of Vermont Ave. Baptist Church, Washington, D.C. For half an hour the struggle waxed in intensity. I finally had to leave in order to get a little milk. I had not eaten since early morning and had a splitting headache. I smiled as I reached the outside, knowing full well that I had precipitated the storm.

To my surprise, however, the argument soon turned out to my advantage. When I returned to the campus, the ministers were just leaving the meeting. Some of them spied me and after congratulating me, asked to see the books. One said, "If these books will keep my people in the church, let me have them." A Reverend [J. S.] Shaw from Greenville, North Carolina [pastor of York Temple African Methodist Episcopal Zion Church], told me he wanted the books and also desired me to come down to address his people on Negro History. Another from Raleigh, Dr. Dawson, told me to write when I could come [to Raleigh] and [then] come on [and speak at his church]. Ministers crowded about to such an extent on the campus, that in a half hour, with the aid of Wilkey and LaGrone, we had sold 12 sets of books. For such a result, I would gladly start another argument. Poe and Payton sold two sets each in Hampton. It was a fine day for the exchequer.

Tonight was beautiful. Never have I seen the stars so near the earth. They seemed to be just above the tree tops. There was no moon and the stars were so thick and so clear that they appeared like gold dust scattered over the blue-domed heaven. And the campus, now hidden save for the tower of the chapel, seemed so restful, so quiet. There is almost something inviting in the very atmosphere, something that seems to call to one's soul. It gripped me so until all unawares I found myself stretching forth my arms to the star-bedecked heavens, as if to pluck down a handful of its precious jewels.

[No entries were found for June 25 and 26.]

Friday June 27, 1930

Awoke at 6:30 this morning. Beautiful, brilliant morning. Took the car to the Hampton garage. Had it greased, the horn fixed, and [the] flat tire repaired. Went through Hampton tailor shop. Surprised at the fine work done by the students. A German teacher is in charge.

On the way to Suffolk, I picked up two white men who hailed me for a ride as I was going across the James River Bridge. Unthinking of the hazard, I picked them up. One sat beside and the other behind me. It was only after I had admitted them that I felt the imbecility of giving them a ride. So many tales of violence done to sympathetic motorists had reached my ears. And I was alone with them on a bridge 4½ miles long stretching over a vast expanse of water. It was a high bridge and as far as I could see I was the only motorist on it. How easy it would have been for them to have slugged me and thrown my body into the river. Cognizant of such, I stepped on the gas and traveled at 60 miles an hour until I reached the crossroads going to Norfolk and Suffolk. Arrived there; I presume my guests were as glad to be rid of me as I of them. They thanked me and turned off the road to Norfolk. Both parties no doubt breathed a sigh of relief.

Arrived at Suffolk an hour and a half later with no further incidents. Went first to Nansemond High School where Mr. [William] Huskerson is principal. Is doing a fine work here, but is still being opposed by ignorant Negroes. He has, notwithstanding, been able to get the school accredited. [He had to fight] President [John] Gandy of Virginia State, but [he] also succeeded in having the school classified as an accredited summer school.

Promised him a set of books for the school in case I could sell 20 sets of books. Asked me to come to speak to class tomorrow.

Called upon Mrs. [Bessie?] Skeeter. Was well. Remembered me. Asked about daughters. Saw youngest daughter, Ovieda.

Went to Mrs. [Odella] Peele's. Engaged room there. Had stayed there in 1928. Sold Dr. [Richard Henry] Bland, classmate of mine, a set of books. Made appointment with lawyer [J. H.] Fulcher for Monday. Could not see Dr. [Herbert] Warren. Dr. [name not in diary] said he was not in position to buy. Had lost quite a deal of money. Suffolk seemed quite dead to me. Ira [Skeeter] was not there. Most of the other girls had left town. Called on the Bryants [George C. and Fannie?]. They were not at home, however.

Saturday June 28, 1930

Got up late, and went to Nansemond High School at 12:00. Spoke to the students. About 35. Very poor. All teachers, except a few, poorly paid. Could not take books. Saw Miss Lillian Bryant, but she hurried home before I could speak to her.

Was terribly hot. Called upon Dr. Warren. He could do nothing for me, however. Some professional men are in a bad way, due to the depressed conditions. Some of the peanut factories are closed, others are on a reduced working schedule. Several of the lumber plants have moved south—one was burned but was not rebuilt. It was estimated that 2,000 Negroes were out of employment here.

During my travels over the city later in the day, I noted that several peanut factories were working on short time. One or two were closed.

About 2:00 p.m. Mr. Huskerson came over to Mrs. Peele's to take me to a Sunday School Convention. It took place at a church, Lakeview, in what is known as Saratoga. [Huskerson] arranged to have me speak there at 11:00 a.m. [the] next day. Most of these people are country folk. Huskerson also tried to arrange for me to speak at the Church of God and Saints of Christ Colony at Belleville, Virginia, tomorrow. I am to go down anytime in the day.

Returned to Mrs. Peele's about 4:00. Took Mrs. Peele and Vivian to Smithfield. Met the Misses [Salome and Mary] Shivers. One teaches there; the other is a student at Virginia State. Mr. [W. F.] Shivers, who is rapidly turning white, conducts one of the best Negro markets I have ever seen. Ships hams, fish, and oysters as far north as Boston. Owns his own boats, too. His children seem to have no interest in the business.

Miss Shivers seemed interested in the books. Waited a long while trying to interest Mr. Shivers. Too busy. She took me to see Mr. Crawley, the furniture man. He temporized; told me to see his son, that he could not read, and the like. Then, in a serious vein, told me to see him Monday. Mr. Crawley told me he has the oldest furniture business in Smithfield. He started Shivers's business, but sold out to him. Told me [that the Shivers] children don't help the father in his business.

The daughters are interesting. They took me to meet several prospective customers. Told me they would be down to Suffolk to hear me speak in the morning and would subscribe then. Oh, yes, I had secured permission from Rev. [J. B.] Williams, the roly-poly young minister of the First Baptist Church to speak for a few minutes at his church tomorrow. He succeeded Rev. [James A.] Harrell. I am to go to Smithfield Monday.

Sunday June 29, 1930

This was one of the busiest days I have yet experienced. At 9:30 I spoke before the Sunday School at the African Methodist Episcopal Church on Pine Street; from there, I visited the Lakeview Baptist Church in Saratoga. The audience ranged from the most illiterate to school teachers. Here I made my best effort so far. Brought forth a series of amens and applause from the audience by recounting the achievements of the race. Spoke about 35 minutes. The people were thrilled. One man asked me whether I had any pamphlets that I could leave with him. Told me that the books were too long for him to read. Old Mr. [A. J.?] Holland, who resembles Robert E. Lee, waxed eloquent. Told me he would take books before I left, for his niece.

From the Lakeview Baptist Church, I rushed to the First Baptist. Spoke 15 minutes, although Rev. Williams told me I could have only 7½ minutes. The sermon was delivered by a Reverend [P. D.] Price of Danville, Virginia. He is a powerful speaker, philosophical, yet practical. His sermon was so gripping that it fascinated me. Then he spoiled it by an impassioned appeal to the emotions that started the church shouting.

He was impressed by what I had to say on Negro History. Told me to come to Danville at any time. Just write and let him know when I was coming.

Went to Bryant's. [He] took nothing. Then over to Lakeview Baptist Church again. Insufferably hot there. The program was pitiful to hear. Yet these country people were doing the best they could. Singing consisted of hymns and recitations of poetry delivered in a sing-song manner.

Left soon afterwards for Belleville. Arrived at 6:00 p.m. This is the home of the Church of God and the Saints of Christ. They have a remarkable place, as I have already mentioned elsewhere, when Drs. Woodson and Wesley and I visited here in 1928.[17] The Bishop, Father Abraham ([William Henry] Plummer), was playing tennis. Told me his son would attend to the

17. See Greene, *Working with Carter G. Woodson*, 133–37.

business. The latter, Howard, a law graduate, took an entire set and then two extra books, giving me a $6.00 deposit.[18]

Although this colony has its own oyster beds and farms, they will plant no crops this year. It is their custom to let the ground lie fallow for an entire season every seven years. They put aside enough of the crops from the preceding harvest to last over that period. Potatoes are dried, fruits likewise; vegetables are canned; and every means known concerning the preservation of food is taken to enable the colony to experience this seven[th] year non-planting custom without hardship.

Not only is this a remarkable plant, city lighting, engineering, and boat system, it has the best buses in Virginia. Here also are located the finest tennis courts owned by Negroes in the state and among the best in the country. So much so that the Negro state tennis tournament will take place here in a few weeks. They have a permanent judges' stand erected, something that the others lack.[19]

Met also a Mr. Mackey and another young fellow who are very much interested in Negro History. They wanted to learn how I held the people's attention while speaking to them. Knowing that I was to speak at the Pine Street Baptist Church, they came along. When I arrived, hot as it was, a "Sister" Wallace was screaming and perspiring in the midst of a revival sermon. Strange that they have such in summer. At home (Connecticut), February is the month. Sister Wallace spoke until 10:50. I spoke five minutes. I was utterly fatigued. Another such day would kill me. When I arrived home, Mrs. Peele gave me $3.50, which the people from the Lakeview Sunday School Convention had left for me. Retired about eleven thirty.

Monday June 30, 1930

Rose later than usual. Terrific strain of the last week has been telling on me. A beautiful day. There has been no rain here for over a month and the fields and roads are parched by a broiling sun.

18. Howard Zebulun Plummer (1899–1975) was born the same year as Greene. He succeeded his father as head of the church in 1932 and was succeeded by his son, Levi Solomon Plummer, in 1975. Elly M. Wynia, *The Church of God and Saints of Christ: The Rise of Black Jews,* 32–39.

19. Bishop William H. Plummer received some unwelcome attention in the press in 1930, shortly before Greene's visit. A disgruntled former minister, E. T. Yancy, charged that Plummer was living extravagantly, while others at the Belleville colony received only the bare necessities of life. P. Bernard Young, Jr., son of P. B. Young, publisher of the *Norfolk Journal and Guide,* went to Belleville to interview Plummer. His description of the operation agrees with Greene's, and Young was equally impressed with Plummer as head of the church. See *Norfolk Journal and Guide,* May 3, 1930.

I took Vivian Peele and her girlfriend to Smithfield. Stopped by Mr. Shivers's. Expected him to take books, but he told me that he had educated his children; now they must buy their own books. It was said with such finality that I took him at his word. I knew him well enough to feel that he meant what he said.

The librarian, a Mr. [name not in diary] at the beautiful Rosenwald School here, promised to send in an order for a set of books. The school is ideally located with bookcases made in the wall in every room. There are large basketball courts outside, and provision is now being made for tennis courts. There are several acres to be developed.

Did fairly good business today. I sold the Misses Williams, school teachers, and several others.

The largest order of the day, however, was sold to Mr. Davis, the head of the Davis Bus Line. Mr. Peele took me over to see him at 12:00. We had to wait until he played several violin selections, which he does excellently. Then, he talked on endlessly, until finally when I had almost despaired of bringing his attention to books again, he decided to take not only the set, but two more. I left Mr. Davis, having over $30 worth of checks and $34 in cash.

3

Canvassing in North Carolina

SUNDAY JULY 6, 1930

The Greenville Fiasco

At 5:15 a.m. I was making preparations for leaving Emporia, Virginia, and the fine hospitality of Dr. Cartwright. [I] was just half dressed when [James Cecil] Wilkey and the other fellows drove up. [I was] so fearful lest they should blow the horn and awaken the doctor that I rushed to the window and signaled to them to be quiet. I was none too soon.

A half hour later, we were thundering over the roads to North Carolina with Rocky Mount our first objective. It lay about 60 miles away.

The morning was cool; the sky overcast by clouds. But the scenery was beautiful and the roads excellent. Extensive farms or plantations stretched along both sides of the road. The fields were green with growing cotton, sweet potatoes, corn, and tobacco. This is especially a tobacco section. The cotton in some places ranged from a foot down to about eight inches in height, but the tobacco, in most cases, had already matured. In some cases, it was turning a brownish color.

In the midst of these plantations stood the large, well painted home of the planter. Dotted hither and thither, like soiled spots on a white tablecloth, appeared the huts of the Negro tenants—unpainted, windowless in many instances, and most of them containing one room. Where the windows had been, they were effectively replaced by boards, which not only shut out the air but the light as well. It's no wonder these people die of consumption and other diseases. In other cases, the windows are stuffed with burlap, calico dress remnants, paper, or any other material that happened to be at hand.

These cabins are of the "shotgun" type. There are two doors—one front and one rear—and when both are open one can stand in front of the hut and look into the backyard. In front of these hovels grew the gardens of the tenants, for the planter usually allows them a half acre or sometimes an acre to grow vegetables or whatnot for their families.

Living conditions naturally are terrible. These people with no other diversion except sex naturally have large families. In one instance, I saw eight children ranging in ages, it appeared to me, from 3 to 17, emerging from one of these one-room affairs. In another instance, we could see the inmates still asleep in their shack—men, women, and children, lying about indiscriminately, and with only the privacy that one room could give them. Such conditions as these naturally keep the moral tone at low ebb. A situation more forced upon these unfortunate people than deliberately entered into. Most of the women and girls whom we saw were scantily clad; the greater part wearing neither shoes nor stockings.

A considerable number of Negroes, however, own fairly large farms. Some are well kept; others show lack of attention. Some of these farmers with their families were working their crops on Sunday. They undoubtedly were small farmers, who work on the white plantations during the week and tend their own plots of ground at their only possible opportunities—Sundays and holidays. Their crops are chiefly cotton, tobacco, sweet potatoes, and corn. I saw one or two cows on such farms, but they were thin and obviously underfed. Nine prosperous farmers had well painted houses and some of them sat smoking on their verandas or reading their Bibles.

All along here, the signs point to Rocky Mount and Wilson as marketing points for tobacco. I was exceedingly anxious to reach Rocky Mount for the place held much sentimental interest for me. It is the home of Miss Nannie Hagans, another of my "lost" loves.

Reached Rocky Mount at 8:00 p.m. Went directly to Rev. Battle's, at whose church I was to have spoken on July 4th. Wonder of wonders, when I saw his home, I nearly lost my speech. It was a little cabin containing not more than two tiny rooms at best, unpainted and wholly uninviting. I was astounded.

I woke the good Reverend. He came to the door in his bathrobe. Told me he was expecting me Tuesday. A young fellow, not 28, I daresay. [I] apologized for my failure to see him on July 4th. [He] told me the town was full of people who had no place to go. One excursion had even come down from Petersburg. [I] tried to make an engagement for the week, but the Reverend gentleman explained that prayer meeting [was] on Tuesday, the missionary convention on Thursday, and a number of other things would prevent it. [I] asked where his church was located, and was agreeably surprised to learn that it was a large brick structure. Told him I would return to speak at night. His rejoinder was that it would be impossible to get the people out at night.

The Reverend asked me to leave a man in Rocky Mount since I could not stay to speak at the eleven o'clock services. Promised to turn it over to me if I would do so. Told him my engagement in Greenville took precedence, however.

Left [John Wesley] Poe in Rocky Mount. Consigned him to the tender mercies of the people, for Poe was penniless. And I had naught to give him for I had spent my money buying gas, etc. Then, too, my illness of Thursday had nearly depleted my exchequer. Sent [Noble] Payton to Wilson, a larger town than Rocky Mount, and one of the leading tobacco markets of the country. Both these towns offer fine possibilities. They have a considerable number of Negro professional and business men and also of intelligent and cultured Negroes. Payton took a bus. Told them to speak in as many churches as possible.

Took [Oliver] LaGrone to Tarboro, about 18 miles east of Rocky Mount. Admit the town did not look any too inviting. Put LaGrone in the charge of a deacon of the St. Paul Baptist Church and left him with instructions to meet me in Rocky Mount Tuesday at 6:00 p.m.

Wilkey and I then continued the 27 miles to Greenville, another important tobacco mart, to the south. East of Greenville, nearly ran out of gas and was forced to put in two gallons, leaving me with $1.35. A fine capital with which to be entering a strange town. Felt, however, that after my speech in the morning at Rev. [J. S.] Shaw's church, my financial fortune would rise.

Arrived in Greenville. We were shown to the reverend gentleman's home by the chief of police. On the way, we had an opportunity of seeing much of the town. It is beautiful, with many fine homes, well kept lawns, flowers, and shrubbery. The name Greenville is very appropriate.

Disappointed in the worthy reverend's dwelling from outside appearances. On a dirt street (Clarke)—a straggling house, one story that smacked more of a store than a dwelling. Down in a hollow, too. Instinctively, I rebelled against such quarters. The worthy divine came to the door. He was fat, black, and sweating profusely. "Sorry, I cannot invite you in. Place not suitable, for my wife is away. Have you eaten? No, then you can find a good place over near my church," pointing across the way. Again, I was annoyed. Here I had been invited as his guest, yet he had no place to receive me, nor even whereabouts for me to wash my face. Told him I was tired, hungry, and dirty, after a four hour drive, and desired to wash up. Referred me to a Mrs. Wilkinson, who took in boarders. I was disgusted. Felt like going back to Rocky Mount. Nevertheless, went over to find Mrs. Wilkinson.

When I saw her, I immediately knew that I could not stay at her home. She was ugly, black, untidy, ignorant, and her house lacked the atmosphere that I desired. She relieved me by stating that all her rooms were occupied, leaving nothing but the parlor divan, which I could use. I hastily refused. Coming out of there, we were hailed by a boy from a second story window who asked whether we desired to have breakfast. Responded affirmatively, whereupon he directed us into a side door of a store. We found a small kitchen, absolutely barren of furniture with the exception of a long table covered with a soiled white tablecloth. One part of the room had been walled off and this served as a place where the food was cooked. A tall, scanty-haired woman, exceedingly garrulous and ignorant, presided with a young girl as her assistant. I wanted to go immediately, but Wilkey had to leave for Washington (North Carolina), and I too was in a hurry; therefore, I ordered some soft-boiled eggs and toast. Wilkey told me that he did not have the wherewithal, whereupon, I made him eat, but [also] keep within my own [financial] bounds. He ordered fried eggs.

Horrors! The woman did not even know how to prepare toast. She began by buttering the bread first, then putting it in the oven. With a wood fire, God only knows when it would have been ready. For putting butter on two pieces of toast, she wanted 15 cents. I took it as an excuse to leave. She immediately made it 10 cents. But when I beheld them toasting my bread atop of the stove and saw it handled first by the mother, then the daughter, and last, by the son, who had just come in (and God only knows whether any of them had washed their hands), I made excuses, gave Wilkey my eggs, paid his bill and left. Such a place! God help me! The flies would have eaten more of the food than I.

While waiting for Wilkey, I met a man and asked him whether there were any professional men in the town, for it was clearly evident to me that I had gotten in with the wrong class of people—and this despite the fact that I am very democratic. He told me there were two physicians and a dentist here, that they lived (or one of them did rather) near Rev. [J. A.] Nimmo's Church. This was the First Baptist Church [Sycamore Hill Baptist Church], a nice looking brick structure standing near the new bridge just as one enters the town. Forthwith, I went to seek him as soon as Wilkey emerged from his "breakfast." The Lord only knows how he ate there. Still, the fact that he is from the South may have accustomed him to such places.

In our attempt to find Rev. Nimmo, I happened upon a man who was to mean more to me than anyone else in the town. I noticed a short, stocky, dark, kindly faced gentleman about forty-two years of age going toward the church. I inquired where I might find Rev. Nimmo. He was so courteous, so soft-spoken, that I immediately recognized in him a man of intelligence and culture. He turned out to be Professor [G. R.] Whitfield, the supervisor of the rural schools of the county in which Greenville is located.

Mr. Whitfield took me to Rev. Nimmo, a tall, brown, bald headed gentleman who was engaged in teaching a class in Sunday School. He seemed pleased to meet me and invited me to speak at the Young People's Meeting at 5:30. He also remembered me from Hampton. Mr. Whitfield then took me to his home, I having promised Rev. Nimmo to speak at the designated hour.

How hospitable Mr. Whitfield was. Took me to his home and after learning that my stomach did not permit me to eat the sort of fare common here, sent out his son to get me what I desired. He himself boiled the eggs. The first were too hard, but on the next attempt they proved to be just right. He then made me some toast, and with [this and] a glass and a half of milk, my appetite was immediately satisfied. He just killed me with kindness. His wife had gone to her church in the country, and he begged me to make myself at home, which I proceeded to do. Invited me also to stop with him. He has a large home not sumptuously furnished, but clean. There are eight of the largest rooms I have ever seen and all on one floor.

When I finally cleaned up, shaved, and was ready to go, it was ten minutes to twelve. Mr. Whitfield was kind enough to get one of the deacons to take me to the church [York Temple African Methodist Episcopal Zion Church]. It turned out to be a brick affair, about half completed. Church services were held in the basement. The church itself, when completed, will be a good sized edifice capable of seating about 500. When I arrived, the pastor, Rev. Shaw, was in the midst of his sermon. He had taken a text from some chapter of Matthew and was raising the roof in an effort to arouse his listeners. He certainly disappointed me as he bawled, whined, shouted, and sweated in an effort to lift his congregation into the delectable realms of a spiritual heaven. [He] even reminded them of the loved ones who had gone to the Great Beyond—a favorite but much worn method of emotional excitation. It had the desired effect, however.

Most of the people are illiterate. The majority were "grownups," proving the old theory that it is difficult to entice the young folks to church nowadays. The congregation numbered about 100. After puffing, blowing, and finally leading up to a crescendo of apostrophes on heaven, Shaw fumbled about in a hymnal until he secured a song to his liking. Having done so, he first recited—as in the old Greek chorus—the words while his rapt listeners chanted the tune after him.

I was disgusted. Wondered when he would cease his harangue in order to give me a chance to speak.

Finally, when I had almost succumbed to the unbearable heat, he did so. He then attempted to introduce me, but could not remember my name, my connection, nor the place from which I had come. It was embarrassing to me to stand before the people while he asked my name. He had told them I was from Hampton and Howard.

I corrected that, however. [He] told me the young people wanted me to speak at night. Therefore, I merely acquainted the people with the origin, purpose, and achievements of the Association and bade them come out tonight with pencil and paper and I would try to give them something to think about.

After I had spoken, a Professor [C. M.] Epps, the Negro school principal, rose to say a word. He recounted the strenuous times in Greenville and urged the Negroes to begin organizing to help themselves, for the whites would shortly tire of doing so. He spoke of the deplorable situation existing since last Xmas when the factory owners and the city had to feed the people. He reminded them of the great scarcity of jobs, and touched upon the fact that the whites are pushing the Negroes not only out of the desirable jobs, but also taking such jobs as street sweepers, drivers of wagons of all sorts, and even doing domestic service. He also made the statement that the factory owners, during the incoming winter, would only take care of their own employees.

I met the good professor, who is well acquainted with Woodson. Yet he seemed a little cold to me. Perhaps thought he was being eclipsed, at least for the time being.

Now the collection. With much oratory, persuasion, and continued dogging, along with the terrific heat, the deacons finally succeeded in extracting $19.46 from these poor people. Of this, ten dollars went to the minister as part of his salary; the remainder was to be applied upon the building and loan fund.

After the services, I met some of the people; many of them promised to come out tonight.

Rev. Shaw took me to his house. He drives a dilapidated Ford which I almost blushed to enter. Then too, the Reverend frightened me sorely, for he has a cork leg, I believe, and is unable to bend it, but keeps it thrust forward when driving and, consequently, he is unable to use but one of the foot pedals. Whenever he stops, therefore, it must be the result of using the hand and the foot brake instead of the foot brake and clutch. Time is thereupon lost, which once nearly proved fatal when he narrowly avoided crashing into a car.

The good Reverend finally invited me into his home. It was a rambling house containing several very large old-fashioned rooms. They were dirty, and like the typical Negro [home], there was a place to eat and a place to sleep. The rooms were barren, seemingly devoid of a woman's touch. There was running water—and that out in the backyard. The toilet was a septic tank outside. There was no bath. The only redeeming feature about the house was the library. He was a fine collector of more than a thousand volumes. A library fit to grace any man's home. History, philosophy, classics, and all sorts of commentaries, economics, psychology, books on anything or any topic. I congratulated him upon it. Told me he had secured many from secondhand stores.

He invited me to dinner. I was so anxious to leave that I took up my briefcase. He assured me, however, that we were only going next door. Thither we went and way back into a little dining room where dinner was served. The place was tolerably clean. But it was insufferably hot and the flies were everywhere. I swear that Greenville must contain the largest fly population in the world. For dinner there were: cabbage (fried and boiled), sliced tomatoes, onions, cucumbers, (swimming in vinegar). I could not eat anything but managed to take a small piece of tomato and cucumber. [I] asked for a piece of toast, but what little I took was almost eaten by flies before it was brought. I felt wretched. Just wanted to leave this place.

Dr. Shaw finally took me back to Mr. Whitfield's. It was certainly a relief to get back to this kindly and understanding man. He derived immediately that I desired to eat. Of course, I told him "no," that "perhaps later." Recounted my attempts to eat where Shaw had taken me. He regarded me with sympathy.

[Mr. Whitfield] introduced me to Mrs. Little, an elderly school teacher who lives next door. She looked at the books and seemed much impressed, but told me she would see me tomorrow.

Left to speak at Rev. Nimmo's Church. Only a handful at the B.Y.P.U. [Baptist Young People's Union] meeting. Rev. Nimmo introduced me after a solo by a pretty young girl and a recitation by another. I spoke on some of the achievements of the Negroes in Africa. My time was about 15 minutes for it was frightfully hot.

After speaking I demonstrated to the young people the various points of interest in the books. Persuaded a young fellow named [Arthur L.?] Norcott to take a set. He plays the organ here. [He] took them for his sister. It was a godsend to sell him, for otherwise, I would have been virtually destitute in this town, with only 50 cents. Rev. Nimmo promised to see me tomorrow.

Upon my return to Mr. Whitfield's he advised me to take something to eat. Took me to a restaurant, the "Busy Bee." Oddly enough, this is the town's best eating place. It fronts two streets. On the Main St. entrance whites are accommodated; on the rear street, Negroes. The place is owned by Greeks. It is clean, however; no flies. Yet I could not overcome my disinclination to eat in a Greek place, remembering their uncleanliness from my hometown. Therefore, I took milk and graham crackers. Then, too, my stomach was in none too robust shape. Very fine of Mr. Whitfield to take such an interest in me. I made an effort to pay for the food out of my last half dollar. Mr. Whitfield, however, refused to countenance my effort to do so. I was his guest. He will never know the embarrassment he saved me.

Returned to Mr. Whitfield's and changed my clothes preparatory to speaking at Rev. Shaw's church. Somehow, I was filled with misgivings. Mr. Whitfield's son, a fine young fellow, accompanied me there. Had to walk since Wilkey had the car. About a mile and a half.

Arrived at the church, found it dark. [It] had not even been opened. A few people sat outside who assured me that, although most people did not come to church at night, they were sure to get here about 8 o'clock.

Finally went in about 8 o'clock. Rev. Shaw, limping and sweating, came puffing in about 8:30, giving me profuse excuses for his delay. There were about seventy-five people in the church when I started to speak. These had increased to 100 before I finished.

Spoke about 50 minutes. What I said about the Negro (I spoke generally on his contributions in Africa and America) either must have interested them or they were mighty fine actors. They interrupted me several times with applause. Dr. Shaw then made a stirring appeal to the people to show their appreciation for the information that I had brought to them. I sold several sets of books. Received $12.00 for myself. Shaw embarrassed me. Asked for contributions for me as I sat on the platform. Collected $14.00 for me. [He] later gave it to me wrapped in [a] paper napkin. I put it in my pocket. When I got home, I found I had but 85 cents, mostly in pennies.

Monday July 7, 1930

It was terrifically hot today. The temperature must have been well over 100 degrees. It was 110 degrees in Rocky Mount.

Mr. Whitfield took me to the store with him and bought just what I desired to eat. He is so fatherly.

After breakfast, I met Mrs. [M. P.?] Evans, wife of a former bricklayer, who told me of the extreme poverty of the people here. Many are starving and have been doing so since last Xmas. Many destitute children are forced to resort to eating out of garbage pails. She also told me of a very brutal attack on a colored youth. It seems that two years ago he had struck or talked impudently to two white boys. They resented it, but waited two years before securing an opportunity to take revenge. Sunday, she said, they enticed the Negro youth out of town, beat him terribly, kicked him, and threw him into the Tar River. They shot at him, but the bullets went wild. He saved himself from drowning by clinging to a sand bar. He was finally rescued. I was horrified and asked what steps had been made to prosecute his assailants. She replied that warrants had been issued for them, but to date no further action had been taken. The town, she said, is totally dependent upon work in the tobacco factories, but since last Christmas there has been almost no work.

Some of the owners have taken care of their help since that time, but in what way? By raising the funds from the meager salaries of those poor Negroes who are working and donating it as their own gift. In this manner, Person and Garrett, one of the largest tobacco factories, raised $300 last winter and distributed it among the starving Negroes. The richest man in the town, Mr. Flanagan, who works 500 Negroes, also secured $500 in this manner, yet donated it as his personal gift. Such a thing would be unheard of in the North, where men of wealth know how to give money. They have not only a civic, but a humane spirit.

The city, too, has had to bear a large part of the burden in caring for destitute Negroes. It has been feeding many of them since last winter.

Mrs. Evans, who keeps a boarding and lodging house, told me that employment here is seasonal. It lasts but 4 months, from September to Xmas. Then everyone has money and everyone spends it. After that there is little or nothing to do. The work during that time consists chiefly of sorting, packing, and shipping tobacco. There are several huge warehouses here and farmers from the surrounding country come here to sell their tobacco.

With Mrs. Evans there came a cute little lady, Mrs. [Oneda] Faison. She was soft-spoken, charming, and for the first time, I met a woman in the town who could be really attractive as well as entertaining. She also had a fine sense of humor. Told me she knew a fine young teacher, a Miss [Lillie Mae?] Edmonds, whom she wished me to meet. Suggested I bring my books and come down either this afternoon or in the evening. Told her I would come in the latter. She stressed the fact that Miss Edmonds would be there in order that Mr. Whitfield might not give it the wrong interpretation.

Now for business. I succeeded in persuading Rev. Nimmo of the First Baptist Church [Sycamore Hill Baptist Church] to subscribe but could get only his postdated check. Two other worthy gentlemen of the cloth, Rev. [J. J.] Lang and Rev. [J. L.] King pleaded lack of funds, took my address, and promised to send for the books later. Of course, any salesman knows enough to discount such promises.

What a terrible predicament in which the professional class of Negroes now find themselves! With the Negro masses unable to find employment, consequently they lack means of paying the doctor, dentist, and preacher. This was reflected in my attempts to sell these people. Dr. [W. M.] Capehart was not at home. He was playing checkers somewhere. Better this than worrying, or to sit idly in his office, or to attend persons without prospects of remuneration.

Called upon Drs. [J. A.] Battle and [Archibald L.] Banks. The former is a doctor, the latter a dentist. Both were out. They have a fine office; each using one side of a specially constructed one-story building with an office for a nurse and a waiting room in between. Fine offices, well equipped and clean. So different from most Negro physicians' offices in small towns.

Mrs. Flanagan, the nurse, who is also the wife of an undertaker, readily subscribed. Later she brought in the doctors. Both of them were interested, although I had to create the interest in Dr. Battle. So typical of Negro physicians. He pleaded lack of money; his car was being repaired, and he was rushing to a case. Yet, he spent a half hour talking with me. In the case of the dentist, he was too busy to talk, had no interest in books (which doubtless was true) and no money. Yet he consumed an hour and a half of my time and became even more interested than Battle. I had to take his word, however, as being "broke."

Called upon Mr. [T. J.?] Allen who keeps a fairly well stocked grocery store on Fifth St. Not so intelligent, but likes books. He readily subscribed. Told me he had formerly been a member of a corporation that owned the store. It was then in another location. It burned down, however. He bought out the others and started the present store with $50 a few years ago. Now he owns a fairly fine grocery store. He told me that there were three others in town, also a cleaning and pressing club, two filling stations, and an ice-cream parlor.

Met Mr. [John H.] Dupree, the county farm demonstration agent, while talking to Mr. Allen. [He was] still enthusiastic over my speech of last night. Told me, in answer to my query, that Negro farmers are getting scant benefit from the Federal Farm Board, first because they are unorganized, (it is one of the express conditions that farmers must organize in order to secure loans), and second, [because] their farms are already so heavily mortgaged that there is no security for the bank even if they were organized to apply for loans. He also told me that many of the farmers were turning to diversified agriculture, such as the raising of corn, wheat, and other foodstuffs. That is certainly a hopeful sign. Told me to be sure to see him in Raleigh, where he wants me to speak to the agents. Promised him I would do so.

Went home to a dinner of string beans, milk, and graham crackers. After dinner Mr. Whitfield's sons came in. One had worked all day stripping tobacco leaves from the stalk; the other handing tools to a mechanic. The former received $2 a day for backbreaking work, the latter 50 cents a day. Meager wages, but better than nothing.

Went down to Mrs. Faison's about 7:00. A walk of about 20 minutes. She has a beautiful home. Entertained her with poetry, etc. Miss Edmonds, she said, waited all afternoon for me. Was convinced I was not coming. She sent a note for her, but the lady evidently was not at home.

Met a Mrs. Hagans. Had a nice looking daughter. She is much too tall for me, but we had lots of fun. Both of them knew Nannie's people, but not her. Spoke of the Stanback case where Nannie's brother-in-law had misappropriated funds from a Negro bank in Wilson, North Carolina, causing it to fail. He is now serving a 5-year sentence at hard labor.[1]

Left Mrs. Faison's at 10:15. Promised to return at 2:00 p.m. tomorrow. She also promised me that Miss Edmonds would be there.

Stopped at the drug store and bought a bottle of citrate of magnesia. Could not find anything with or upon which to open it after reaching Mr. Whitfield's, and the household was asleep. Happily, however, one of the boys came in just as I despaired of opening it and performed that service for me. It was terribly hot when I retired about 11:30.

I forgot to state that I sold a set of books to a young lady by the name of [Ruby] Vines. She was so anxious to have them, but her mother was unable to take them because she could not collect rent money from her tenants. So, I gave her a dollar off my commission. I did it because here was a fine opportunity to have the gospel of Negro History spread through the young people.

[No entry was found for July 8.]

Wednesday July 9, 1930

Made preparations for trip to Raleigh. Went to Rev. Battle's [in Rocky Mount] to pay the fellows' bill. Felt he should have had nothing for tricking

1. On September 24, 1929, the state of North Carolina closed the Commercial Bank of Wilson. The closing resulted from an investigation following a fire in the bank's vault. The fire destroyed several books and records. A grand jury indicted J. D. Reid, the bank's vice president, and Harry S. Stanback, cashier, charging them with two counts of embezzlement, two counts of forgery, receiving deposits knowing the bank to be insolvent, and making false entries in the bank records. In February 1930, they were convicted on the charges of unlawfully receiving deposits. The other charges were held over for trial later. The men dropped their appeals in March 1930, forestalling prosecution on the remaining charges, and they began serving their five-year sentences. Also, efforts to remove Mrs. Eleanor Reid, wife of the convicted vice president, from her job as principal of a school in Wilson ended. *Norfolk Journal and Guide,* January 11, February 22, and March 1, 1930.

me in the first instance. Had to borrow money from Wilkey to pay him. Charged them $5. Took boys to hotel to breakfast. En route, Poe showed me fried potato cakes he had taken from the table in order to give the impression that he had eaten them. They were sour, the potatoes having been cooked Sunday. En route to hotel to buy milk, found it impossible to do so. Could only buy it at the drug store, 25 cents a quart. A & P clerk told me this was the first time that a grocery store could not sell milk. Forbidden on account of typhus fever raging. Had to buy shredded wheat, milk, and bananas to help out breakfast. Negro restaurants don't have such things.

Arrived [in] Raleigh at 12:30. Passed capitol, etc. Saw Mr. [Lawrence] Oxley.[2] [He] secured us a nice place to stay on North Tarboro St. at Mrs. Higgs's. Took dinner with him. Saw Mr. [H. L.] Trigg, assistant director of Education for the state (Negro). Fine fellow. Oxley told me of Glenn [Carrington]'s impracticability. Wrote thesis while he went to Europe instead of doing work. Had to fire him with 2 months advance salary. Told me to see Mr. [Nathan Carter] Newbold and Mrs. Hillard[?]. Latter will be in town Saturday. Went to tennis court. Fun with Miss Reid and little girl from Halifax. Met Prof. [Reginald] Lynch and [J. H.] Holmes [of St. Augustine's College]. Old fellows who can't afford to take books, however, at least so they say. St. Augustine school has potentialities. Built three new buildings last year. Campus fair. County Demonstration Agents meeting here. Went over to see them. Met Mr. [J. W.] Mitchell, General Agent. Told me he would be glad to help me. Would tell me whether I should speak in the morning or evening. Invited me to supper, but I declined. Two hundred boys and girls here for short course—boys in farm work and girls in domestic science.

Return to house. Went downtown. Relations between races good here.

Thursday July 10, 1930

Enjoyed a good breakfast at the Arcade. Fine hotel here owned by Mr. Rightner and brother. They have a large office building too, across the street. Good breakfast. Best, yet. Hotel excellently appointed.

Went to St. Augustine. Agents out on sightseeing tour. Waited until noon meeting, going to see nurses in interim. Too busy to be approached just then.

Mr. Mitchell advised me I had best speak at night. Attended meeting. Heard Mrs. [Jane S.] McKimmon make fine address.

2. In 1930, Lawrence Augustus Oxley, a social worker, was director of the Division of Negro Work, North Carolina State Board of Charities and Public Welfare. Under the New Deal, he served as chief of the Division of Negro Labor in the Department of Labor and was a member of Franklin D. Roosevelt's "Black Cabinet."

Went to dinner. Ate ham and cabbage. From there went to see Trigg and Oxley. Talked with Trigg about possibilities of getting books on school list. Told me it might be done. Referred me to Newbold.

Went to meeting of Interracial Commission. Dr. Petite elected Pres., Mr. Oxley Vice Pres. Recognized Mr. Reynolds's good works. I talked. Told them of origin, purposes, and some of the achievements of our organization. People enthusiastic, congratulated me . . . [phrase not decipherable]. I tell them of Sebastian Gomez.[3] Leave with Lightner. Dinner. Try to sell Dr. [Rufus Samuel] Vass. To St. Augustine.[4] Speak before agents. Sold 2 sets. To party. Home to bed.

Friday July 11, 1930

After breakfast this morning, I immediately wrote out a report to Woodson. No doubt he feels that I have stopped selling books, for no report has been received from me in a week. Sent him 9 orders, eight of them mine. Not very encouraging in view of the fact that we sent in 84 orders from the Tidewater District of Virginia in ten days.

While writing in the car, Dr. [L. E.] McCauley came up to congratulate me upon my little talk before the Raleigh Interracial Commission yesterday. He told me that the members were very favorably impressed with me. I felt happy because of Woodson. Dr. McCauley then went on to tell me that each year his fraternity, Phi Beta Sigma, holds a large celebration during which they usually bring before them some prominent speaker, such as Mordecai Johnson, Charles Johnson, or [W. E. B.] Du Bois. He added that yesterday convinced him that I ought to know a lot of history and, consequently, they would be pleased to secure me for this year as their speaker. He asked me to communicate with him. Promised to buy books later. Again I felt gratified, especially since I had impressed the whites who were present.

Leaving Dr. McCauley, I called upon Mr. Trigg. Failed to find him in, however. Wanted to secure his frank opinion upon my talk of last night. Mr. Dickinson, his secretary, took me over to the office of Mr. Newbold, the Secretary of the Board of Education [State Agent for Negro Education]. A very splendid man. His greeting was just as cordial as a Negro could expect

3. Sebastian Gomez (1646–1682) was a Spanish painter of African descent. The painter Murillo freed him from slavery, adopted him as a son, and instructed him in painting. Gomez rose to a prominent place in Spanish society. See Wilhelmena S. Robinson, *International Library of Negro Life and History: Historical Negro Biographies,* 20; and Leslie B. Rout, Jr., *The African Experience in Spanish America: 1502 to the Present Day,* 18.

4. St. Augustine's Normal and Collegiate Institute, now St. Augustine's College, was founded in 1867 under the auspices of the Protestant Episcopal Church.

to receive from any Northern white man and, if anything, perhaps more genuine.

I congratulated him upon the fine work his state was doing in behalf of Negro education. Told him truthfully that throughout the length and breadth of the country people looked at North Carolina as the foremost commonwealth in its attempt to enlighten its Negro citizens. To this Mr. Newbold responded that the work had not yet reached the goal for which they had set out, but he felt some little progress had been made. Even now he was busy preparing a report for Hoover's Child Commission Study, which is to take place later in the month. He showed me a large collection of data from South Carolina, Mississippi, and North Carolina—all of which he must read and incorporate in his report.[5]

I finally brought the conversation to the subject in which I was most interested, namely the possibility of getting some of our publications upon the North Carolina supplementary reading list. In this connection I suggested *African Myths.* Here, I told Mr. Newbold, was a fine collection of 36 folk tales, handed down by word of mouth for generations by these people. Not only are they charmingly told and carefully selected for children from the third to the fourth grades, but they contain no reference whatsoever as to race and, therefore, could be read and enjoyed by whites and blacks as well.

I asked Mr. Newbold had Dr. Woodson sent him a copy. He did not know, saying that he receives so many publications that he has little chance to do more than acknowledge their receipt. However, upon glancing at his book cases—one of which contained only books dealing with the Negro—I saw that he did have a copy. I took it down and asked him to look through it. He seemed to be agreeably impressed, so much so that he told me if Dr. Woodson could reduce the price from $1.00 to 60 or 75 cents he would urge upon the school board its acceptance.

After such an encouraging beginning I then turned to the only other of our publications that could be used in the grades. This was the *Negro Makers of History,* an elementary version of *The Negro in Our History,* suitable for children from the 6th to the 9th grades. Mr. Newbold agreed that the books ought to be in the system for Negroes, and added that, as in the case of *African Myths,* it would be necessary to reduce the price somewhat in order to bring it within the buying power of the Negro family. He remarked, and truthfully, that so low stood the spending ability of the Negro population, on account of their correspondingly meager earning power, that it would be necessary to reduce the cost of the books in order to insure their fairly

5. Newbold chaired the section on Negro Schools of the Committee on the School Child. See White House Conference on Child Health and Protection, 584.

large sale. I promised to write Dr. Woodson asking his best terms, then to communicate with him. He advised me to do so, stating that he would urge their adoption upon the school board in case the reductions were made.

He also introduced me to Mr. [G. H.] Ferguson, [Assistant State Agent] who has charge of making up the Extension Courses for Negro schools among his other duties. Mr. Ferguson, like Mr. Newbold, seemed to be a fine type, gripped my hand cordially, and even seemed reluctant to release it. He told me that Brawley's *History*,[6] and Woodson's also, were used in the Extension Courses and that more than 5,000 persons had taken the course last year. He promised to see me tomorrow morning at 10:30 in order that we might talk over the matter at greater length.

Went to see Mr. Trigg in order to acquaint him with the progress I had made. Failed to find him in. Therefore, I went to the bank to secure what information I could relating to the Negro business and professional men.

It was now time for us to start for Durham. LaGrone, however, found that he had to see someone. During the interim, the rest of us started packing. Mrs. Higgs offered us some homemade cake, which none of us—even I who am not supposed to eat it—proved slow in accepting. I had a few more things to add to my wardrobe, for this morning I invested in a shirt (90 cents), bought a comb and brush, and some hair tonic. All, except the shirt, I bought from Woolworth's.

6. Probably Benjamin Brawley's *A Short History of the American Negro.*

4

More Canvassing in North Carolina

FRIDAY JULY 11, 1930 (CONTINUED)

Durham

Finally left Raleigh at 3:05 p.m. Durham was 37 miles distant. It proved an uneventful ride save for the beauty of the farms, the unique architecture of the North Carolina State Fair Building, and North Carolina State College. The latter is just on the outskirts of Raleigh. It is a very large institution, contains large and stately buildings, and reminds me somewhat of Ohio State University. Its campus, from my superficial observance, might have more or less beauty, yet it could not cope with Hampton.

All of us felt our spirits rise as we came nearer [to] Durham. Arriving in the city we passed tobacco, cotton, and flour mills and also saw hundreds of colored women and girls just emerging from their day's work in the tobacco factories. It is the industrial character of Durham that differentiates it from the cities of eastern North Carolina and Raleigh. This is apparent too in the ability even of the Negro workers to purchase books. I should add that this is one of the greatest tobacco marts in the world and that Negro women and girls are the chief workers in the unskilled processes.

We went directly to the North Carolina College for Negroes[1] of which Dr. [James Edward] Shepard is President. I met him some time ago in Washington. Is a friend of Woodson's. Glad to see me. Dr. Shepard is about 50, tall, spare, brown of color, and with a pleasing and kindly personality. Inquired of my book [*The Negro Wage Earner*]. I told him that it was virtually ready for publication. Thanked him for the help he gave me during its composition. He was sorry he could not have given me greater aid.

1. Now North Carolina Central University.

I congratulated him upon the magnificent buildings lining the campus. The administration building alone is one of the most beautiful I have seen on any campus. Reminds me of the one at West Virginia Collegiate. Dr. Shepard told me that the institution had been recently engaged in a building campaign during the course of which three new buildings had been erected. The main building, which contains the administrative offices and classrooms, consists of three stories. The classrooms are large and airy and the registrar's, treasurer's, and president's offices are equipped with the most modern furnishings.

The hospitality of the Southerner surpasses the understanding of the person from above the "line." And one of the finest demonstrations of such was given by Mr. Shepard. He, after inquiring how long we were to stay in town, called a hotel [and] told the manager to accommodate us and send the bill to him. It was a magnificent expression of his appreciation of the work we are trying to do. And I know that Dr. Woodson will certainly feel gratified. He (Dr. Shepard) is a Kappa man; perhaps that influenced him somewhat. We were delighted, for the funds of the exchequer had sunk to a few dollars.

The hotel proved to be the Biltmore, located on Pettigrew Street within two blocks from the railroad station. It is a new building, well furnished with hot and cold water in every room. With its awnings and green slated roof it makes a very imposing appearance. Too bad its location opposite the railroad tracks and in an undesirable location detracts somewhat from its beauty. Its manager is a very alert and well informed woman—a Mrs. Johnson. She is short, plump, and about 38 years of age. She wore no stockings.

The fellows were delighted with their new quarters. In our room there were three windows looking out upon the railroad tracks, however. Nevertheless, we all decided that with such fine quarters we would quickly start making money.

There is a restaurant connected with the hotel. Thither we went to dinner. The food was excellently cooked but, horrors, there were four vegetables and all were starches. I asked for some tomatoes and lettuce which added somewhat in balancing the dinner. Mrs. Johnson and I had a little friendly argument over the serving of poached eggs with a vegetable dinner. I had frequently received them with such. She ridiculed the idea. It ended by a little humorous sally on her part that caused us all to laugh. She is sophisticated to an extreme, friendly with everyone, especially the men, whom she joshes, pets, but in such a way that all respect her. And strange to add, she told us that even the ladies like her.

One of the objects of her witticism, as well as meaningless affection, was a handsome and intelligent looking fellow who sat at a table in front of us. I asked his name. She told me he was a contractor and was building the theater next door. Told her I'd like to meet him. She introduced us. He came and sat down at our table. He turned out to be Mr. Boykins, a graduate of Massachusetts Institute of Technology, one of the leading schools of its kind in the country. He knew [Percy] Julian (chemist), Johnny Burr (physical education instructor at Howard University), Dr. [J. B.] Watson (president of Arkansas A.M.&N. in Pine Bluff), Dr. [Bill] Knox (a Howard classmate from Massachusetts), and many other acquaintances of mine. Lives in Scanlin[?], N.C., where his father also is a contractor. Mr. Boykins has a fine personality, but stammers terribly. And how Mrs. Johnson kidded him about it. She mocked him at every turn. He took it good naturedly, however, but I believe that I might have been ruffled under similar conditions. Left him after a very pleasant chat of a half hour.

We then set out to get in contact with some of the Negro ministers. Went up Fayetteville Street, which is the leading Negro residential thoroughfare here. Never have I beheld more pretentious residences. No home owned by rich whites in my home town can measure up in pretentiousness. All about lay an atmosphere of wealth, culture, and refinement. Mr. C[harles] C[linton] Spaulding, Mr. [William Gaston] Pearson, and others have homes that anyone would be proud to own.

Called on the pastor of St. Joseph A.M.E. Church [Vincent Hodges], the largest of its kind here. Could not find him, however. Was out of town. The church itself is a large brick structure. Called upon a Rev. Williams, who pastors a small baptist Church on a street running parallel with Fayetteville, but a woman returned such uncivil answers that I left with my mission unfilled. I learned later that the Reverend was out. The third pastor, Rev. Grady, who has a small Baptist Church, we found in overalls, down on his hands and knees in a hole in the yard of his home. He irritated me first because he could return no direct answers; and second, because of his loquacity. Upon my asking what he was doing in the hole, he responded that he was reading an electrical meter. We returned home to consider ways and means of best canvassing Durham. I have no desire to duplicate calls upon persons that prove not only profitless, but also annoying to the persons thus interviewed. [James Cecil] Wilkey, of all the others, objected. Late as it was, he desired to begin canvassing tonight. I overruled him, however.

Back at the house we played whist and ate half a watermelon. Then [John Wesley] Poe and I played [Noble] Payton and [Oliver] LaGrone for a quart of ice cream and lost. This ended the day, and we retired about 12:00 p.m. [a.m.].

Saturday July 12, 1930

This day shall be long remembered by me. First I secured the first real bath in a week. Sought to get in touch with Mr. C. C. Spaulding, President of the North Carolina Mutual Insurance Company. [I] called the office, but he had not yet arrived. Expecting to find him, I drove there. Disappointed. Returned to hotel, took breakfast, then went back to the North Carolina Mutual Insurance Co. The building itself is located in Parrish Street, the second largest business street of Durham. It is a six-story structure, all of which is given over to the insurance company. Entering, an elevator operator took me to the third floor where Mr. Spaulding has his offices. I was astonished at the surroundings; elaborately furnished offices on every hand. A girl told me that Mr. Spaulding had just left his office for a few minutes but would be back shortly.

In a few moments he appeared. I recognized him immediately. He is just a trifle taller than I, about a shade or two lighter, with a thatch of white hair that lends him a conspicuous dignity. He grasped my hand very warmly and seemed delighted to know that I was an assistant to Dr. Woodson and was engaged in carrying on his work. He told me that he would be available in a few minutes but that someone was awaiting him in his office.

A girl came shortly to tell me that Mr. Spaulding would see me. I went in, congratulated him on the fine work he was doing, and told him of my efforts in behalf of the Associated Publishers. He told me in response to my compliments over his splendidly appointed offices and well managed business that the property was owned unencumbered. He then called a young lady to show me over the building.

The trip became a succession of marvels for me. First we went to the basement where the stockroom is located. There everything was immaculately clean and in place. A very complicated stamping, folding, and sealing machine and a paper cutter showed that no facility for the expedition of the company's business was lacking. On the ground floor is the Farmers and Mechanics Bank, largely controlled by the Spaulding interests, with assets of $800,000. The other floors are given over wholly to insurance. Offices of the treasurer, industrial department, claims department, policy writing department, photostat rooms, [and] cashiers office all evoked exclamations of wonderment and gratification from me. One of the most unique features, however, was the Medical Department, in [the] charge of Dr. [Clyde] Donnell, a Howard and a Harvard graduate. Almost an entire floor is given over to this work. There are X-ray rooms, special rooms for treating transient patients, nurses' rooms, [and] consultation and operating rooms. In short, every available means for preserving the health of their subscribers is employed by the company. I met all the heads of the departments, also. Outstanding was Mr. [Edward Richard] Merrick, the treasurer and son of the founder of the company.[2] He is a tall, spare man who resembles Mr. Simmons of the Y.M.C.A. of New York City. He is a young man, too.

There was also another interesting character, an old gentleman who writes the policies. His color defied description, but his penmanship was something at which to marvel. I gasped at his uncanny ability to illustrate many of the different styles of penmanship.

When the young lady brought me back after a tour through the building, I felt so inspired that I could scarcely wait to congratulate Mr. Spaulding. He was busy and sent word to his secretary to take me to the Forum. This is a truly remarkable institution for a Negro business, or indeed for any other business, and shows well the farsighted vision of the president. A cafeteria is usually operated here, but on every Saturday from 11:00–12:00 various problems, ways, and means are discussed, addresses given, or other meetings held. Everyone can take part in the discussions. In this way, each one is not only posted upon the state and progress of the business but, thereby, feels that he has a personal interest in the company.

The meeting today was under the auspices of the conservation department. The speaker was Asa Spaulding, the nephew of C. C. Spaulding. He told of his experiences at the School of Business at New York University. He had been graduated "magna cum laude," the first time such an honor had been granted or conferred upon a Negro. He was also inducted into an honorary fraternity. Told of his experiences in a cabaret, how he was humiliated the first year by one of his professors, and of the prejudice of an occasional Southern woman. On the other hand, he told of the fine friendship existing between him and a white professor from South Carolina. He made a splendid record, and told it very modestly. His speech charmed and frequently brought forth ripples of laughter. He himself is of small stature, slight of build, and almost bald. He wears glasses.

Mr. Spaulding had come up during the interim. Later he introduced me. I told of the achievements of the Association, after stressing its origin and purposes. I recounted Dr. Woodson's early struggles then climaxed it with relating the tribute paid to us by Dr. Carlton Hayes. I also informed them of Mr. Newbold's promise to recommend several books of the Association to the North Carolina State School Board as supplementary readers, in case *African Myths* could be reduced from $1.00 to 75 cents; and *Negro Makers of History* from $1.50 to $1.00. Also told them of the extraordinarily critical economic position of the American Negro. They seemed impressed,

2. Edward Richard Merrick was the oldest son of John Merrick.

if one could judge from their applause. I also told them that our work required funds, and that to refrain from seeking charity, we were offering this marvelous sale of books at little more than cost. I told them it was the duty of all Negroes—ministers, teachers, professional classes, and laborers—to assist in this work, which had for its aim the uplifting of all classes of the Negro race.

Mr. Spaulding commented favorably upon my remarks, told the group that he was a staunch supporter of our work, and advised them to buy the books. He asked me to place his order. He then proceeded to admonish his force against unnecessary expenditures. Told them they should buy nothing they did not need. Not only that but they should eschew living above their means, spending excessively for dress. Said he, the working Negro who buys a 50 cent shirt is infinitely wiser than the man who, in the midst of this financial and business chaos, insists upon wearing $5 silk shirts. He himself had never bought one although several had been given him. Even now he wore a plain white broadcloth shirt that could not have cost more than $1.95. This was common sense, but it certainly militated against my selling books.

After Mr. Spaulding, Mr. Merrick, the treasurer, rose to say that many of the employees receiving salaries from the North Carolina Mutual were carrying deposits with the white banks. Moreover, they carried Metropolitan instead of North Carolina Mutual insurance. Such a condition or actions, he added, may be styled racial treason, for none of the white companies, save only a few of the lesser ones, will employ Negroes in the capacity of agents. Mr. Merrick vowed, accordingly, that if he found any employee of the company guilty of such actions, he would use his powerful influence, regardless of who they were, to have them discharged. Such a statement smacks of economic paternalism, but Henry Ford is an outstanding example of such benevolent despotism. Mr. Spaulding rose and reiterated the same sentiments as Mr. Merrick, adding that if, in view of the struggle the company is making to give and to secure them in their jobs, they persist in aiding white institutions by banking their moneys with them and by supporting white insurance companies, then he would be the first one to weed them out.

In a measure such actions would be justified, for when a Negro company has proven its ability to serve its race even better than the white institutions of like character; when that establishment is creating jobs for members of the race; and when these individuals depend upon such work entirely for their livelihood, give their business to help further develop white institutions, they are pulling down the walls of the structure under which they have gathered for survival, and Samson-like shall perish by their own folly. In this case, I heartily agree with Mr. Spaulding. Economic advancement among

Negroes can only be gained by rallying all Negroes around the standards of legitimate, well managed, race businesses.

Another official, Mr. [William Jesse] Kennedy[, Jr.], likewise spoke against the Negro's penchant for show when he lacks the wherewithal to support it. Like the preceding speakers, he deplored the tendency of the average Negro to fritter away his earnings in boom times, only to find himself destitute when business depression and retrenchment set in. He called attention to merchants in the main business streets here, who were actually cutting their store space in half in an endeavor to adjust themselves to economic changes. Mr. Spaulding, in commenting, told them that the company might be compelled to do a similar thing here. I marvel. They have not yet felt the depression.

After the Forum, Mr. Spaulding took me to his office where he showed me the books of the company. They now have in force over $35,000,000 worth of insurance and own nearly all the real estate, land and buildings, in that block of Parrish Street. They also have other assets of more than $3,300,000. Everything is done upon a strictly business basis and the institution is ranked by state examiners as one of the safest and firmest institutions operating within North Carolina.

One of the secrets of the phenomenal success of the North Carolina Mutual Insurance Company I gleaned from Mr. Spaulding's speech. He likes young men: young men with the theory and advanced ideas of business gained in the best schools of commerce in the country, who can blend their theory and initiative with the experience and practice of the older men and therefore make for a pliable and progressive organization. In such cases the impetuosity of youth will be somewhat tempered by the practical wisdom and experience of age, while the graybeards, what few there are, will find their reactionary or overcautious tendencies mellowed by the new blood. In my humble opinion, that is the best way to build up a great and durable business structure. Asa Spaulding, a nephew of Mr. C. C. Spaulding, who has just been graduated from N.Y.U. School of Business, will now be able to step into a responsible position. Then C. C.'s own son was recently graduated from Clark University of Massachusetts and will enter the business school next year. Mr. Spaulding plans to train him as auditor of the company, which he said is the best paying position in an insurance firm.

Another feature about the company is Mr. Spaulding's habit of rewarding diligence, efficiency, and interest in the business as portrayed by his employees. The cashier is a woman, a Mrs. [Bessie Alberta Johnson Whitted].[3]

3. According to Walter B. Weare, Whitted became an officer of the company in 1906 and remained with the company until her retirement in 1957. She served as chief bookkeeper

According to Mr. Spaulding, she has never attended a business school, yet is one of the best cashiers in the South and is probably the highest paid Negro business woman in this section. He showed me several reports which she had made out. Spaulding told me she started in the business 25 years ago as a little girl. He considers her invaluable. He also gave me a list of the affiliated enterprises connected with the North Carolina Mutual in which he has a large interest. These include the Farmers and Mechanics Bank, the only Negro banking institution with a branch (it is located in Raleigh); a fire insurance company, loan companies, etc.

One of the most unique aspects of the North Carolina Mutual is the firm loyalty and ardent enthusiasm of the employees and officials. They think in terms of the company. Mr. Spaulding is the symbol, the hub about which things revolve. I left the office inspired as I have seldom been.

Went to the colored library located on Fayetteville Street. It is an unpretentious structure, the ground floor of cement and the second story of frame. It has, despite its small size, a fair collection of books. A Mrs. Booten is librarian.

[No entries were found for July 13–16.]

Thursday July 17, 1930

Returned to Greensboro. Terrible day. Rain. Stop in Burlington. Meet Dr. [Roscoe Albert] Wooten. Calls for physician. Wrote [Ernest] Bacote. Meet Odean Day. On to Greensboro. People disappointed at my failure to arrive. Go to dinner. See again Miss Ringles, Belson Lawson, and [Lois] Jones[4] and [Gertrude Parthenia] McBrown. Three former and I play blackjack. Later we go to a dance at the college [North Carolina A and T].

Friday July 18, 1930

Rise at 8:30. Do not feel well. Eat no breakfast save few peaches. Put in laundry. Fail to see Mr. Bullock. Go to dinner. See Miss McBrown, poet and dramatist. Show her some of my poetry. Is pleased. Like "Will

---

and cashier (*Black Business in the New South: A Social History of the North Carolina Mutual Life Insurance Company,* 90).

4. In 1930, Lois Mailou Jones, a native of Boston, was teaching at the Palmer Memorial Institute in Sedalia, North Carolina. She was a graduate of the art school of the Boston Museum of Fine Arts, and she attended the Massachusetts College of Arts, the Designers Art School of Boston, and Harvard University. She left North Carolina in 1930 to join the faculty of Howard University. See Darlene Clark Hine, ed., *Black Women in America: An Historical Encyclopedia,* 649–53.

You Sit and Weep," "June Night,"[5] and "When I Lost You." I spoke to students. Thought I did fairly well, but students were interested in their grades. Yet managed to interest two persons. A Mr. Connor stubbornly held out on me. Remained there until dinnertime. After dinner went to see Miss [Beatrice M.] Beaumont, supervisor of schools for county. Could not subscribe, but would do what she could. Returned. Met Laura Ringles. Went to see Mrs. [S. P.] Sebastian. Has beautiful home. Danced. Took them to movies. Returned to Wilkey's girl's home. He brought another girl. She was angry but concealed it. Wilkey and Miss [Iola] Jackson took me to meet Miss Sellers. Danced. Had nice time.

Saturday July 19, 1930

Went to Burlington at 8:00. Met a Mr. Scarborough over there who proceeded to direct me around. Dr. Siet took more than an hour. Bought nothing. Then Reverend Boykins bought nothing. From there to Prof. [J. F.] Gunn. Was won to him immediately. Has fine library, is humorous, liked me. Told Scarborough if he finds more like me to bring them there. Sold him easily. Went across the street. Sold Mrs. Jeffries [Mrs. W. J. Jeffreys?], much to Scarbrough's astonishment. Missed on Reverend Hawkins. His house had been sold. Finance company failed. Called on Mrs. Petterman [Pittman?], wife of leading doctor. Sold her easily. Heard me speak yesterday. Mrs. Albright. Missed her. Got Miss Cable, though she swore she could not buy. Just put my pen in her hand and laughingly pushed her from the car to write me a check. Failed with Mrs. Ivy, Mrs. Tyson. Left for Greensboro at 4:40. Due there 12:30; had phoned fellows, though. Arrived 5:30. Went to dinner. Boys exasperated. All right when learned I had done business. Went to laundry. Back to art exhibit, where I saw sketches of boys by Miss Jones. Very good. Lots of fun. I analyzed their portraits, also the girls. Likeable, all of them. Social and economic conditions discussed.

Away to Winston-Salem at 7:20. Beautiful road, beautiful country. Arrived at 9:00. Went to Teachers College.[6] Dr. [S. J.] Atkins referred us to Ideal Hotel. Hilly city like Lynchburg. Rooms: boys' $3.00, mine $1.50. Cheap. Girl next door.

5. See appendix.

6. Winston-Salem Teachers College was founded in 1892 as the Slater Industrial Academy. The state assumed control of the school in 1905, and it became a state normal school for the training of African American teachers. In 1925, the state legislature granted the institution a new charter under the name Winston-Salem Teachers College. For the school term 1926–1927, the enrollment was 179 and the faculty numbered sixteen. See U.S. Department of the Interior, Bureau of Education, *Survey of Negro Colleges and Universities,* 573–580.

Sunday July 20, 1930

Spoke at St. Paul M[ethodist] E[piscopal] Church. Fine sermon by Dr. Sweeny. Dinner. Meet Mrs. Scales. The spell of the summer upon me. Hate to retire.

Monday July 21, 1930

Very eventful day. By 8:00 we are breakfasting. Have to buy fruit and cereal and bring it to lunchroom. Service abominable. To post office. No mail. Can't find notebook. Take Poe and Payton to their districts. Call on Mrs. Hairston of Y.W.C.A. Is in West Virginia. Y.W.C.A. is large, barnlike structure. Raising money for new building. Mrs. Henry refers me to Miss Hall. She liked my speech of Sunday. Couldn't see me. Must return at 5:00 p.m. Referred to Mrs. Bruce. Call. Said Wilkey offended her; had been rude, they told me. Mollified and sold them. Then to Prof. [U. S.] Reynolds. Boys falling over one another. Must prevent this. While speaking to Reynolds, Payton came in. LaGrone had already interviewed Bishop [Lynwood Westinghouse] Kyles and Miss Cash.[7] Is omnipresent. Does no business. Dr. Eaton.

To Atkins's, fine conversation. Discusses the Negro Church, outlook and salvation of Negro race. Young Negroes must save church. Is going to ruin. Negro must develop economic stability. J. C. Price and [Charles N.] Grandison were the greatest Negro orators.[8] One's death, [and the] latter's waywardness, paved the way for Booker T. Washington's rise. Race has had no leader since. Fraternities should buy railroad stock instead of buying buildings.

Received letters and books from office. E. Franklin Frazier is here.[9] I may not speak tomorrow. May wait till Wednesday. Called on Miss Hall; charming, has beautiful smile. A trifle stout, however. Is former sweetheart of Reverend [Vernon] Johns.[10] Plays organ in the church. Could not buy

7. Lynwood Westinghouse Kyles, a native of Virginia and a graduate of Lincoln University in Pennsylvania, was elected a bishop in the African Methodist Episcopal Zion Church in 1916. In 1930, he was living in Winston-Salem, North Carolina.

8. These two contemporaries of Booker T. Washington were both presidents of colleges in North Carolina. J. C. Price was president of Livingstone College, and Charles N. Grandison was president of Bennett College.

9. In 1930, the distinguished sociologist Edward Franklin Frazier (1894–1962) was teaching at Fisk University and completing work on his doctorate at the University of Chicago. He left Fisk in 1934 to spend the remainder of his teaching career at Howard University.

10. Vernon Johns set the standards in belief and style that Greene used to evaluate other ministers. Greene met Johns while selling magazines in Charleston, West Virginia, where

books, however; lack of funds. Father, too, could not buy. To dinner. LaGrone embarrasses me at dinner by arguing about price. Terrible slam by Mrs. Blunt, waitress, brought on by own stupidity. Got haircut. Party. Miss Marie Strange. Take her from LaGrone. Letter from Harry [Hipp]. Can't go South. To relieve me of embarrassment he would withdraw from our friendship. I sat at table dumbfounded. My best friend. His friendship is worth 10,000,000 degrees, professorships, etc. Sought only to stir him to action.

Tuesday July 22, 1930

Spoke at Winston-Salem Teachers College. Met E. Franklin Frazier, Chandler, Dot Atkinson and husband, Miss Williams from Atlantic City, etc. Took Payton with me. Miss ____ will send order to Charlotte. Sold 3 sets. Went to High Point at night with girls after disappointing Mrs. Blount about playing cards. Girl cried. High Point fine town, furniture factories, cotton mills, etc. Negroes have fine homes. Whites doing much of work. Wilkey will work it.

[No entry was found for July 23.]

Thursday July 24, 1930

Charlotte

After breakfast, we began a systematic canvass of Charlotte. LaGrone, the ambler, was assigned to the district called Brooklyn, where live the largest number of Negroes. Most of them are poor people, yet since there is no exclusive residential section here for Negroes as in Winston-Salem or Durham, he ought to at least make two sales. Allotted the professional men to Poe. He will sell them if they possibly can be sold. Payton, I took with me. LaGrone could not conceal his chagrin at the territory given him, but it was far better than to have him roaming at large, spoiling sales. Instructed him to remain in his territory, yet I assured Poe and Payton that within twenty minutes he would be in the Negro business and professional building.

What a stupid fellow. And just will not accept information. Has an inflated ego that needs puncturing if he is ever to make any success in life. At the breakfast table he entered into an argument with Payton on what is

---

Johns was pastor of White Rock Baptist Church. They became friends when Johns moved to New York City to head the Baptist Educational Center. Johns also served as president of the Lynchburg Theological Seminary. Later, he became pastor of Dexter Avenue Baptist Church in Montgomery, Alabama, and was the predecessor of Martin Luther King, Jr., there. Branch, *Parting the Waters,* 1–26, discusses Johns as a "forerunner" of King.

knowledge. It was induced when he began bringing in the argument of the behavioristic school of psychology to settle an argument. Yet, he knew nothing concerning the tenets of this group, nor of any other school of thought, psychologically speaking. He has read a little psychoanalysis by that popular bamboozler, Andre Tridon, and being unable to discriminate the probable true from the false (the entire science is still in the realm of the hypothetical) has accepted verbatim what he has taken in. I tried, by analogy, to point out that no man was fit to discuss a subject or to form his point of view until he had familiarized himself with every possible angle from which the subject is, or might be, presented. He then changed the point at issue to lead us into extraneous channels, by saying that any science of knowledge was derived from actual physical experiences with concrete images. Although all of us tried to show him the error in his reasoning, he was finally more silenced than convinced. All of us, even Wilkey, considered his case as almost hopeless. He just will not listen, always thinks someone is trying to disparage him and attempts to settle every argument by some stock illustration from psychoanalysis of which he knows little or nothing. Sometimes, I believe he is nothing more than a first class moron.[11]

Went to the Carnegie Library. Met a charming lady, Miss Marshall. She has been here but two weeks, having come from Elizabeth City State Normal School. She is small, good looking, with plenty of personality and is a splendid conversationalist. Her home is in Little Rock, Arkansas. She knows Dorothy Gillam and other friends of mine from Howard University. Spent almost two hours with her. She told me that books are bought by the white library. Referred me to a Mrs. Pierce who was librarian. At first she advised me not to interview her because of her prejudice against Negroes. Told her I would go, notwithstanding. She can do no more than refuse to see me. Met a Miss Lanns, a social worker with whom Miss Marshall stays. Promised to see her tonight.

Called upon Robert D. Greene, classmate of mine at Howard. Is practicing medicine here. Asked me to come to see him at 8:00 p.m. Wanted to show me around. Promised I would.

Went to the white library. Mrs. Pierce, I learned, was out, but the white girls at the desk extended to me every civility. I could have asked for no more consideration in Massachusetts. I was informed that Mrs. Pierce would be in at 10:00 a.m. tomorrow, at which time I might see her. Payton, who sat in the car, had seen me enter with evident misgivings.

11. Many years later, when editing a transcription of this entry, Greene added to this entry: "God forgive me! Maybe *I* am the stupid one."

From the library we went down South Tryon Street, one of the main business thoroughfares, to the Ford agency and service station. This is a very large building of three stories, with an underground shop where cars are repaired. The trouble with the car was diagnosed as carbon and too much play in the steering wheel. I also told the mechanics to drain oil, change the oil, repair a tube, and to tighten all bolts and nuts. The total cost was placed at $10.25. That means we must sell books. Only a few Negroes are employed in this company and they are cleaners, washers, porters, and greasers. We were treated with every courtesy.

En route back up town, I noticed white men working on the streets. There was only one Negro among them. In the large hotels and restaurants on North Trade Street, the chief business highway here, white girls performed nearly all of the work as waitresses. In only one large restaurant did I see Negro waiters. Even in the Greek places, white girls are used. These people come in from the hills and work almost as cheaply as Negroes. Yet, they are displacing the latter because the white man cannot generally bear the sight of his own race idling while the Negro works. Then, too, in many instances, white girls give better service, are more reliable and even neater than the Negroes. Moreover, the whites like to be waited upon by them. This situation is truly remarkable and manifests clearly the abolition of racial lines in occupations caused by the necessity of earning bread and butter.

Later in the afternoon, I called upon Dr. C. E. Davis. He is the Rosenwald representative for North Carolina. An elderly man of about sixty-two—small, very fair and a fine conversationalist. He taught chemistry, physics, and biology at Johnson C. Smith here for 35 years and proudly exhibits a physics textbook that he used as a student and that he subsequently employed in his courses.[12] It is an old and rare edition printed in 1813 by an English publishing house. The author was a certain Hulton. The book was used at the Royal Academy in London. It contains no such literacy features as the physics books of today, but teaches entirely by propositions. In Mr. Davis's opinion, specialization is ruining the young people. They are one-sided, know something in only one branch of their field and none other. I ventured to suggest that they were victims of the present universal demand for men who can do one thing and do that well. In other words, training today is intensive rather than extensive. He agreed but felt that the old fellows could

12. Johnson C. Smith University was founded in 1867 by the board of missions of the Presbyterian Church in the United States as Biddle University. The name was changed to Johnson C. Smith University in 1923. In 1926–1927, the school had a college enrollment of 211 and a faculty of fourteen. U.S. Department of the Interior, Bureau of Education, *Survey of Negro Colleges and Universities,* 522–35.

put us to shame insofar as all-around information is concerned. I agreed with him.

We discussed the Negroes' economic plight. He felt that the Negro's salvation lay in developing experiences that would give employment to his own group. Deplored the trend of industrial schools away from the original purpose to become more and more academic institutions. Cited Hampton and Tuskegee as outstanding examples. Felt also, even as I, that manual training in this machine age as taught in Negro industrial schools is a waste of time and an injustice to the students who, upon graduating, find it impossible to measure up in efficiency with the whites, hence, unable to get a job. Felt that the Negroes should have two great technical schools comparable to Massachusetts Institute of Technology. I was forced to agree with him. Told me of the loss of several occupations—such as street cleaning, garbage, and scavenger collecting—throughout North Carolina by Negroes.

Mr. Davis then diverted to a discussion of Negro orators induced by his looking over Woodson's *Negro Orators and Their Orations.* He placed Frederick Douglass ahead of all others. Next he ranks Grandison, whom he claims was a greater orator than either Booker T. Washington or John C. Price. The latter was Dr. S. J. Atkins's choice. But according to Mr. Davis, Price had only one speech, which he wrote soon after his graduation from Lincoln. At his first public appearance in Laurenceburg, North Carolina, Mr. Davis introduced him. He (Mr. Davis) was a teacher there. According to him, Price read his speech but the effect was so great that white men and women [were] thrilled and moved by his eloquence, [and] showered bouquets of flowers upon him. Later he memorized the speech. Grandison, in his opinion, was a far greater orator, but drink and women ruined him. Mr. Davis ended by taking a set of books. Told me he would try to get the books into the school system during the winter. I left quite uplifted.

Failed to sell Reverend Wells, a Presbyterian minister, a set. Told me had I come yesterday I might have done so. Had to buy a tire and pay insurance. Assured me, however, that after he had preached a few revivals, he would be able to do so. Would send in for order. Has fine personality.

Called upon Mr. Harstin, a plasterer. Could not take any but gave me a bit of information. The Negro plasterers seem to be strong here. They have a local with 30 members besides 60 unaffiliated. Negro carpenters are almost nonexistent; the whites do most of the work. Bricklayers fare better. Neither Negro bricklayers nor carpenters are organized, which accounts, in large measure, for their ability to sell their labor. Whites, too, are unorganized. Both races work together, sometimes both on the same scaffold.

Both Mrs. Anderson and Mr. Stinson failed to take books. The former, who is librarian for one of the schools here, told me she would send for 20 copies of *African Myths* in the fall. The latter is confined with a broken leg. Could not see him.

Met Dr. [Robert T.] Greene. He took me to see some of his friends. Met a Miss H____, who is very charming. Also saw the Russell[?] girl. I hear she does not do credit to her parents. Her brother, too, was shot by a female friend of his.

I met a Miss Partee who lives on the campus. Daughter of a minister and school teacher.

Friday July 25, 1930

We planned to leave at noon today. My first office was to interview Mr. Gunn, a young fellow who has charge of the library at Johnson C. Smith University where we are stopping. Induced him to take two sets of books to take effect in October. Would have been consummated now, but Dr. [Henry Lawrence] McCrorey, the president, is now attending summer school at Chicago University, and his signature is necessary for all such transactions. Mr. Gunn also promised to persuade Dr. McCrorey to take a set for his personal library.

From Mr. Gunn's office, we proceeded to breakfast. While the other fellows were interviewing "prospects," I called at the colored library to see Miss Marshall. It is a small one-story building containing a couple of thousand volumes, most of which are juvenile literature. The city supports it. This is quite unique, for in most Southern towns, the Negroes must support their own library if they desire one. Miss Marshall had advised me to see Miss Pierce, the librarian of the white library, who does the buying of books for the colored branch. [Miss Marshall] did not feel as if it were of any use, for Miss Pierce was "Rebbish," so much so that even the girls of her own race who worked under her feared her. I told Miss Marshall I would go nevertheless and take my chances upon being refused admittance or being thrown out. She smiled and wished me "bon voyage."

Before seeing Miss Pierce, however, we attempted to cash some checks to pay for the repairs of the car. Verdi Robinson, the nephew of Marie Burbridge, now manager of the National Benefit Insurance branch office here, cashed a check apiece for Payton, Poe, and me. In the confusion of exchanging bills for checks, poor Verdi nearly became the loser by $1.98 and I the innocent offender.

The car cost $9.90. Had to have the carbon removed, the brakes tightened, steering wheel adjusted in order to remove the play that caused the car to wobble over the road, and the bolts and nuts tightened. That was just about $1.98 a man. It was worth it, for the car ran like new.

Returned to the library. While talking with Miss Marshall, I met Reverend Jones, a Methodist minister. Young, fairly intelligent. Prevailed upon him to buy a set of books. Will be sent C.O.D. on August 15. He took Poe to sell the Reverend Mr. Weatherspoon. I should mention that Poe had entered during the interim. A fine fellow, every inch a gentleman. He is really the only member whose company does not bore me.

At the white library I was treated with every courtesy by the white girls at the desk. They received my query as to where I might find Miss Pierce with the utmost civility.

5

The Journey to Atlanta

Western North Carolina, South Carolina, and Beautiful Tennessee

SATURDAY[?] JULY 26, 1930[?]

[Not many] miles from Asheville, [North Carolina]. Broad river flowing between peaks. Road beautiful, winding. Wild uninhabited parts of mountains. Poor whites, dirty, look as if they had been eating clay.

Entering Buncombe County, elevation 2,400 feet. View of mountains, plateaus, farms, series of peaks—one immense panorama of inspiring and majestic grandeur. Descending road has whole succession of tiers below us. Fine red-brick school. Astounding curve. Put car in second gear. Rifle-carrying mountaineers eye us suspiciously. When we stopped seven miles from Asheville, another beautiful view, white house standing out against sea of mountain peaks. Tunnel under mountain going into Asheville.

SUNDAY JULY 27, 1930

Went to West Asheville. Spoke at Reverend [E. W.] Dixon's church. Latter gave people what they wanted. Had them "falling out." After church I went home. Took pie and milk. Went to Tryon, North Carolina, with Dixon. View from mountain's top was one of the most beautiful I have ever seen. Dixon preaches. Sets church on fire. Negroes and whites in religious frenzy. White girl walks up and down pulling up dress, cries hallelujah, and falls out facing pulpit. Man palsied, so to speak, just cries out "My God! My God!" I spoke to people. Were enthusiastic. Dixon told me I ought to remain there. A Mrs. Patten told me to come down and sell to her daughter.

Back over mountains to Asheville. No Negro farmers here. Farmers are white, laborers also. Beautiful valley between mountains. Hendersonville[, North Carolina,] in it. In Hendersonville, Negroes are mostly servants. Summer recruits; a few mechanics.

Stopped by Rev. [E. B.] King's, arrange for speech at his church in Hendersonville tomorrow night at 8:00 p.m. Back to Asheville. [James Cecil] Wilkey has taken car. I was hot. Had to speak at 8:30 at Rev. [J. W.] Hairston's Church. Waited until 8:10. Wilkey did not return. I went to church. Was crowded. Hairston preached good sermon, an exposition on faith and baptism. He then ruined it by ardent appeal to emotions. Went back to Wilkey's house. So incensed I could not talk to [Noble] Payton. Wilkey came. I took the car keys from him. He argued with me. Left him. Went home.

Monday July 28, 1930

Arose early. Wrote letter to Helen [Notis?]. After breakfast drove up to Wilkey's. Boys out. Met [John Wesley] Poe in Dr. Middleton's office. Interesting man. Left him. Went to post office. No mail. Went to West Asheville. Met Helen Williams. Promised to send $4.00 to Knoxville for me. Interesting. Left. Kilgore, young preacher, took me to county courthouse to see Commissioner of Education for county. Beautiful building. Commissioner not in. Went to High School to see Superintendent of Education for city. Not in also. Persuaded Poe to go to Greenville[, South Carolina,] tomorrow. I would go to Spartanburg, South Carolina. Kilgore would go along and drive Poe to Greenville. Left at 7:00 p.m. Arrived in Hendersonville at 7:50. Excellent drive. Called upon the Methodist pastor, since the church at which I was to speak was dark. I tried to sell books. Wife blocks sale. On to King's at 9:00 p.m. Latter going to bed. Could see wife undressing from window. Argued with him over books. Suggests I stay in Hendersonville overnight and work the town tomorrow. Furthermore, he would help me. Called a member of his church, a Miss Young. Could take us at 50¢ per [night]. He has good ideas although a little egotistic. Went to Young's. Fine home. Rooming house. Had to pay 75¢ per in advance. Poe was broke. So was Kilgore. I had 43¢ left. Many of the roomers not as desirable. Keeps cafe also. Very attractive woman. Must confess that equanimity not only of myself but of Poe also was disturbed. Poe left ostensibly for cigarettes. I went down to the cafe. Both of us were activated by the same motive—the lure of a woman's body. Returned quite disturbed. I believe my good brother was [word not decipherable] agitated.

TUESDAY JULY 29, 1930

At 6:00 a.m. I called Poe. Kilgore was already up and dressed. They left about 6:45. Hated to see them go, for I had 43 cents and couldn't buy breakfast. At 8 o'clock I was knocking at King's door. By the Great Horn Spoon—he invited me to breakfast. I had already eaten my fruit. A very nice breakfast. My hostess was charming and refined; Reverend King, although loquacious, was very entertaining.

Immediately after breakfast King took me to see some of his members. His theory is [the] "big" Negro will argue with you and always cry broke; the "little" Negro will buy and think you are doing him a favor to take up time with him; the big Negro thinks he's doing you a favor. First one was a Mrs. Powell. She pleaded broke. The second was a Mrs. Bolding, a woman of fair intelligence but who has a son and daughter in school. Sold her on the strength of her buying inspiration for her children that they could not get in school.

Went to a Mr. Rackins, a common laborer. Owns his home. Sold them also, after telling them of the glory of Negro History. These were the "little Negroes." The "big Negroes," like Mrs. McBeth[?], Mrs. Williams, Mrs. Framsbly[?], Mrs. Tyson, Professor [O. T.] Robinson [science instructor at Henderson Institute], and others, gave me much talk. They had books or could not make out check without the consent of husband. Professor Robinson's. Here I met a Miss Davenport from Charleston, South Carolina, fine young woman. Mrs. Owens called Reverend King a big bluff. [King] felt [his] time [was] worth $10 a day. [He was] not [worth this] to me. I took $3.00 off his subscription. Sold it to him for $1.00. Fine dinner.

Poe and Kilgore returned at 5:10 p.m. Made nothing. Doctors' offices burned down last night in Spartanburg. Bad roads, bad "crackers." Negroes in condition of squalor. Fine farms worked by Negroes.

Lunchroom expensive. Had to send out for eggs, bacon, and bread as ordered.

I made $10 in Hendersonville. A life saver for me.

Got lonely. Dressed for speech at West Asheville. Went to party. Girls and fellows came by for me. Miss Michael, H_____, and Howell. Left. Went by Miss Michael's. Late for talk. People leaving. They returned. Made most effective speech yet. People applauded forever. After that another party. Met charming Miss Howell. Attracted me as no other girl has on trip. Almost persuaded her to leave Wilkey. Charmed by a Miss Hightower of Memphis, also.

Wednesday July 30, 1930

French Broad River runs through narrow gorge less than 1,400 feet wide. From Marshall, [North Carolina,] [we go through] mountains midst tobacco and corn growing area. Whites do own farming. Lean, gaunt mountaineers on horseback. Iron kettles. Entire mountainside is corn. Ring of mountains stretching before us, peak after peak. Haze appears like blue smoke. Gorges hundreds of feet below. Pisgah National Forest. Whites work on roads. Beautiful valley outside Hot Springs[, North Carolina]. . . . Mountains fall away. In highland meadow.[1]

Good road when we crossed Tennessee line.[2]

[No entries were found for July 31 and August 1.]

Saturday August 2, 1930

Nashville

Instead of awakening at 3:00 a.m. as I had planned, it was 6:00 when I rose. Woke Wilkey. Dressed hurriedly. Disappointed, for I had hoped to be in Chattanooga at 10:00. Went over to Poe's quarters (he stayed with his brother) in the men's dormitory. Went into the wing reserved for women by mistake. Poe was fast asleep. Told me that he had risen at 3:00 a.m. but upon my failure to come had gone back to sleep. My rejoinder was that I had been there twice since 2:00 a.m. but could get no response. Each one knew the other was lying.

Went over to the dormitory where I bade farewell to Mr. Carpenter, a county farm demonstration agent from Savannah, Georgia. He is one of the 150 meeting there for a course being sponsored by the Julius Rosenwald Fund. What a benefactor he [Rosenwald] is to the Negro race. Carpenter wants me to come to Prairie View, Texas, at the time of the session there. Told him I would think it over.

1. This entry was made in a temporary notebook in which Greene probably made notes while riding in the car. Some of these notes, including this one, were almost illegible. He included some information from these notes in summary entries that he made later in the more carefully kept diary he used during the trip. Not all entries from the temporary notebooks and scraps of paper were rewritten and entered in the main diary, however.

2. After crossing into Tennessee, Greene stopped making entries in the temporary notebook he used in the car. He turned to composing a poem, "To A Lady." After making several drafts of the verses, he arrived at his final version, which appears in the appendix of this volume.

Before leaving, I spied Dr. [William Jasper] Hale sitting on his porch reading the morning paper.[3] He was comfortably attired in BVDs and a robe. Went over and thanked him for his hospitality. Told me he was glad to help out in this little measure. Congratulated him upon the fine school of which he is president. Told him that, next to Hampton, it was the most beautiful Negro school I have yet seen. I have not seen Tuskegee. But North Carolina State College for Negroes; Teachers College, Winston-Salem; A & T at Greensboro; Johnson C. Smith; Knoxville College; and all others recede into the background when compared to Tennessee State. I pointed out the many fine buildings and the beauty of the grounds as concrete proof of his great work here. He told me that it had been a difficult struggle; whites and blacks had fought him, the whites because they felt that the school was superfluous since there already existed Fisk, Walden, Roger Williams, and Meharry;[4] the Negroes because they felt that Hale laid undue emphasis upon agricultural training. Oh, my people, how they endeavor in every way to forsake that which better than any other pursuit would return them a comfortable living if only they prepared themselves even as they train their minds for the ministry, medicine, law, or teaching.

3. William Jasper Hale (1876–1944) was the founding president of Tennessee State Agricultural and Industrial Normal school, now Tennessee State University.

4. In 1930, Nashville was an important center of African American higher education. Tennessee Agricultural and Industrial State Normal University (Tennessee State University) was formally opened on June 19, 1912, as an 1890 land-grant institution. By 1927, it had an enrollment of 422 students, a faculty of sixteen instructors, and a physical plant of twelve buildings, three of which were completed in 1927.

Fisk University was founded in 1865 by the American Missionary Association and several years later became independent. By 1927, Fisk had an enrollment of 563 students, taught by twenty-eight full-time and two part-time faculty members. There were nineteen buildings on a forty-acre campus.

Walden College, which was established in 1865 by the Methodist Episcopal Church, and Roger Williams University, founded in 1866 under the auspices of the American Baptist Home Missionary Society, were in decline at the time of Greene's visit and would close in a few years. In 1926, Roger Williams had only 67 students in the college and normal department. Walden, in 1927, was a two-year college with only 41 students enrolled.

Meharry Medical College, which began in 1876 as a part of Central Tennessee College (which became Walden University in 1900), was a growing institution. In 1926, Meharry had 700 students enrolled in its schools of medicine, dentistry, pharmacy, and nursing. The college had already turned out over 4,000 graduates in these fields.

U.S. Department of the Interior, Bureau of Education, *Survey of Negro Colleges and Universities,* 723–57; James P. Brawley, *Two Centuries of Methodist Concern: Bondage, Freedom and Education of Black People,* 383–90 and 501–8; Joel Schor, *Agriculture in the Black Land-Grant System to 1930,* 144–49.

Hale went on to say that the school was founded in 1912, that his troubles began when soldiers quartered there during the war were charged $7,000[?] a month. Forbes, who commanded them, refused to pay the money, and when Hale declined to nullify the expenses of maintaining them, threatened to close the school, have Hale thrown out, and started a general war against him. The struggle reached an acute stage a few years later when charges of misappropriation of funds and immorality [were made against Hale]—in fact Hale said every charge except murder was hurled against him. To such a point did the criminations and recriminations reach that Hale turned to the Governor of Tennessee, who had accused him wrongfully and called him a "liar" right to his face. And this was while the governor sat on the platform at his own (Hale's) school. One more attempt was made to dislodge this fearless and fighting president when the Board of Examiners came to chapel one day and decided that the school would have to be closed, because agriculture, which constituted the main reason for the founding of the school, was not being taught. Now came Hale's capital stroke. He rose, told the student body and friends what had been said, and called upon everyone who was taking agriculture to stand. Marvelous to relate and to his intense and happy surprise everyone stood, male and female, old and young, visitors and students. Even his gray-haired mother who was visiting him stood. The board was discomfited, withdrew in a huff, but [was] convinced that the school could not be closed on that ground.

After this, Hale's troubles largely ended. The school, he confided, receives $600,000 a year from the state, a larger appropriation than any other colored school. I admired Hale; we need other men who can be men when occasion demands and not [men who] eternally surrender all principles and virility when the whites suggest or demand something that the Negro knows to be contrary to the best interests of his group.

Dr. Hale then told me of his interest in me, how he had been impressed by my manner of approach, my appreciation for what little courtesy he had shown us. I thanked him. He asked what was my connection with Dr. Woodson. I told him. He was surprised yet happy to discern that I could still remain on the ground. The trouble with most young men, he said, is when they earn their master's or doctor's degree or accomplish a little something, they begin to suffer with self-inflation, set themselves upon a pedestal, and become well nigh unapproachable. Commended me and asked whether I intended to remain with Dr. Woodson. Offered me a position as teacher of history if I desired it. Otherwise, he told me he would be glad to have me on his lecture staff. I assured him that anything I could do to assist him in my line, I would be happy to do. This is my life work.

He had tried to persuade me to remain for breakfast. I had pleaded my desire to get an early start to Atlanta. The fellows, too, were already waiting in the car. For this reason I did not sit, and we had stood talking almost an hour. It was so near breakfast time that I yielded to his last invitation. He gave me a note to give to the lady in charge of the dining room ordering a special breakfast for five of us. He then expressed his keen interest in our program. Said Dr. Woodson was doing a fine piece of constructive work. Told me to be sure Mr. Payton, whom I am leaving here, takes stock of the books they have on hand and that he would buy whatever was needed. Thanked him, and finally pulled myself away, highly impressed with him.

How the boys welcomed the news of a free breakfast. They even forgot that they had waited for me almost an hour. The dining room, a cafeteria, is located in the western wing of the administration building. The very first sight was a revelation as well as a spur to whet the appetite. It was large, spacious, clean, airy. Every chair and table was immaculately white; the food counters of white tile and glistening nickel made the food even more attractive. I found the directress, Mrs. [Elliot], a rather stout lady, who welcomed us and waited upon us personally. I have never seen in any Negro cafeteria or dining room such a varied collection of food. For fruit—which very few Negro eating places serve—there were peaches, grapefruit, baked apples, orange juice, bananas, prunes, and cantaloupe; four kinds of meat including chicken and lamb chops (these were the first lamb chops I had seen in a colored lunch room since I left D.C.); cereal from Post-Toasties to oatmeal; rice and four kinds of bread, even brown bread. We all partook with relish. All echoed my sentiments that this was the best meal of the entire trip.

I interrupted my breakfast to awaken Payton and LaGrone. Both were overjoyed to know such arrangements had been made. Poe's brother also told us that the students are allowed 50 cents a day for board and that a breakfast of fruit, cereal, hot bread, chicken, rice, baked apples, and coffee or milk costs only 45 cents. How depressing on the contrary when one thinks of Howard where the students eat the unsavory food served to them by exploiting and, in many cases, unclean Jews.

Met Mrs. Brown from ____, Ky. Her husband is a good friend of Dr. Woodson's. Saw Miss Brown and other girls, who tried to persuade us to remain over. Bade farewell to Mr. Sanford and Mr. Carpenter. Promised to see the latter at Prairie View, Texas.

Off now at 7:50 for Chattanooga. Had to stop in Nashville to ascertain the cause of a squeak in the car. Mechanic told us it was the oil pan.

Nashville—what was its impression? Not so favorable as a city. Disappointing. Knoxville was far more impressive. As for the Negroes, their general housing conditions leave much to be desired. In many cases, in the typical Negro sections, their houses sit in the rear of houses on main streets, near creeks, down by the railroad tracks, and in other undesirable and disease breeding places. On [one] street were groups of unpainted small shacks where the water and privy are outside. In a section very near Fisk and Tennessee State, the same thing obtained. Roads are unpaved, except where the best class of Negroes live, and even some of these are not. I saw no playground for Negroes, although Fisk has a golf course. The usual amusements must therefore obtain: poolrooms; theaters owned by either whites, where they are segregated, or by Negroes, where the fixtures and environment are in many instances demoralizing; dance halls where fights and brawls usually occur; or just streetwalking or doing nothing.

The Negroes here engage chiefly in domestic service for a livelihood. Even here, however, as in all other Southern cities, this work is being done more and more by whites. Many engage in some form of common labor or as workers in some of the factories. There are some Negro carpenters, bricklayers, plasterers, and so forth, but they are barely holding their own insofar as living is concerned. As in all other cities, the Negroes are bewailing the fact that they can't find work. They will have to make jobs for their people.

Insofar as educational facilities are concerned, this town is unique. It is a city of schools. There are several white universities here including Vanderbilt. The outstanding Negro schools, of course, are Fisk and Tennessee State. The former was disappointing to me. Its campus showed no forethought in its development. Buildings were just put up here and there. In fact, there are only two buildings here worthy of mention, Jubilee Hall and the new library now in process of erection. This is a million-dollar structure of brick, rising to an impressive height. Its design is Gothic and reminds me of the buildings at Yale University. Still, the buildings do not make the school, and with its splendid faculty and energetic and farseeing president, Fisk stands second only to Howard, and even bids fair to pass it shortly, insofar as collegiate work alone is concerned.

Tennessee State, however, impresses with its buildings, arranged in the shape of a quadrangle, and its beautiful terraced campus between them. Every building here is modern, beautiful, and ample. The library is the best yet, with the possible exception of Howard's. Never have I seen dormitories so cleanly kept as here. The science building, on the extreme right as we enter the grounds, and the administration building, a large structure covering nearly the entire northern section of the campus, are quite outstanding. There is an atmosphere of culture and refinement here that Fisk lacks, but which makes Tennessee State compare favorably with Hampton. The guest rooms here, with their immaculate showers, baths, and other conveniences including plenty of cold water for drinking purposes, certainly endeared the school to me. Then, of course, the all-pervading spirit of hospitality. Some 150 teachers, women and men, (mostly the former) are attending summer school. In addition, 150 county farm demonstration agents who work among Negroes will be here for a short course. They will come from Florida, Alabama, Tennessee, and Georgia. 'Twill be an excellent place for Payton. I should also state that this school pays the largest salaries, I am told, of any Negro school in the East.

The ride to Chattanooga proved a succession of scenic wonders. It seemed that nature vied with herself to make and to create a number of vast and inimitable pictures of indescribable beauty. All the way there, these scenes brought forth exclamations of wonder and astonishment from us. Especially was this true of the mountains. On two occasions, once when about 40 miles from Nashville, nearing historic Murfreesboro, we looked down from a height of several thousand feet and beheld a gorgeous mountain-locked valley stretching before us on every hand. Far down below we could see the white farmhouses [and] the neatly laid-off fields: some of them [were] filled with corn or cotton, others held a few cows listlessly grazing hither and thither. Then the valley seemed to yield to the call of the mountains and gradually grew higher and higher until it merged into the green-clad slopes of the peaks swathed in a deep blue haze. I could have gazed interminably upon this sight, but we had to go on.

A little later on, about thirteen miles from Chattanooga, we passed through the gorgeous Sequatchie Valley. Beautiful as it was on the level, it was indescribably so from the top of Bowers Peak, a mountain that rises almost a mile above it. From its summit we looked through a natural window made, it seems, by the omniscient deity so that the toiler up the mountainside might be rewarded for his labors by a glimpse at one of the most magnificent of her creations. If the view of the valley just outside of Murfreesboro was magnificent, the Sequatchie Valley was heavenly. It seemed, as if in some ecstatic mood, nature had suddenly created this inimitable scene and dropped it down as a treasureland of beauty. And as if to safeguard it from wantonness, she had surrounded it with a stalwart ring of giants in the form of the blue, mist-covered Cumberland Mountains. Such beauty uplifted me, made me feel that after all, man with all his marvelous creations, in comparison to the vast workings of nature, was puny indeed. It also made me realize that there must be some divine, some supernatural force—mightier, nobler, and grander than man, free from his numerous prejudices and weaknesses—an all-pervading, all-powerful, omniscient spirit, which ruled over mortal destinies and which, in playfulness of spirit, wrought miracles of grandeur on an unbelievably large and gigantic canvas.

About one o'clock we drove into Chattanooga. Its appearance was far more pretentious than that of Nashville, which seemed dead and dingy in comparison. The streets here were wide and well paved and gave every indication of being a bustling town. Wilkey took us to Seventh Street, the Negro district, where he met his friend the son of an undertaker named Mr. ____. They have a large undertaking establishment with a fleet of cars. The son, I was gratified to observe, worked along with his father in order that he might learn the business from the ground up.

I was anxious to reach Atlanta before dark, therefore got Wilkey and Mr. ____ to show us the way to the route leading to that city. Filled up with high speed gasoline at a station nearby. When Poe inquired my reason, I responded that it was [an] added precaution so that, if any trouble occurred in Georgia, I could get away from Mr. Charlie (the whites). He laughed but took the trouble to see that the crank and an iron used as a jack handle were within easy distance so that they could be wielded, were we attacked. Of course, they were to be employed only after all conciliatory and diplomatic means had proved futile and violence was attempted to our persons.

Within two miles we were over the Georgia border and it seemed as if everything suddenly changed and not for the better. My attitude changed. Security gave place to uncertainty. Came to roads metamorphosed into bumpy asphalt. Tennessee license plates, with which we had been familiar for more than a week, were now replaced by that of Georgia. All the unpleasant things I had heard of Georgia now rose before me. Each car full of people; each white on the street, about the gasoline station, or stores, were potential enemies. I was filled with a desire to reach Atlanta as quickly as possible. Still, nothing happened.

On the road to Atlanta! Gone was the sublime grandeur of Tennessee's valleys and mountains. Gone the good roads. And in their places came first a detour of 12 miles over the worst road I have ever witnessed in the past two months. Dust nearly blinded and choked us. Sometimes, especially when a car passed us, it was impossible to see the road at all. And it was so rocky that I was afraid lest the car shake to pieces. Then to cap the climax, we even had to drive through a creek that crossed the road. I was disgusted, irritated, and disappointed, for I had been told that the road to Atlanta was paved all the way. And during this interminable stretch of bad thoroughfare we had been passing the Chickamauga National Park which, incidentally, comprises the battlefield of one of the most sanguinary encounters of the Civil War. This was the battle of Chattanooga, in which [General George H.] Thomas carved for himself the name of "the Rock of Chickamauga." We went on, making fairly good time, after meeting pavement again at Rossville, until we came to a second detour 42 miles from Atlanta. What a road. If anything, worse than the first detour. Then, to make matters worse, we missed the detour and found ourselves on the most terrible road imaginable. Along it we went for about 3 miles, past gaping holes and ruts which threatened to overturn us, and over a road just wide enough for one car to pass. Had one come suddenly from the opposite direction, I, being black, would have been compelled to back almost a mile in order to let the white man pass. If not, trouble, and on this lonely road in the midst of a cornfield, God only knows what might have happened.

On we went, bumping along until it suddenly dawned upon me that this could not be the road to Atlanta. Surely no detour could be this bad. My doubts were verified a little later by my hailing a car bearing a Michigan license, which, happily, we met at a place where only by my getting dangerously near the gutter on the side of the road was the car permitted to pass. As it did so, I hailed the driver—a white man, his wife and daughters—and asked whether this was the road to Atlanta. He told me what I had feared—that we had missed the detour. He offered to pilot me while I turned around. Through his kindness we were put on the right road again. The pointing of an arrow at the crossroads confused us. Such would never have happened in Tennessee and, especially, North Carolina.

Without further trouble, we reached Atlanta about 6:30. We had experienced no trouble. Only once did we hear the word "nigger" and that by a group of young white hoodlums whom we passed on the road and who perhaps hated to see Negroes riding while they walked. Our relationships with the whites, however, we found exceedingly cordial all the way from Nashville. Whenever we stopped, whether at a garage in Nashville or at a little refreshment stand in the mountains, we were overwhelmed with kindness. It was "Mr." and "No Sir" and "Yes Sir." Strange to relate, it was Poe and I with our Northern training who unconsciously would say "no" and "yes," and people down South look upon that as a sign of improper training.

What was the economic condition over this route of nearly 300 miles? Very bad in some instances. In the mountain regions of Tennessee the prolonged drought has played havoc with crops. Streams and creeks, upon which the farmers depend in large measures for irrigation for their fields or as water for their cattle, have dried up. In one instance a stream about 25 feet wide was absolutely arid. The French Broad River in some places was absolutely devoid of water, and even the lordly Tennessee showed the ravages of the prolonged dry spell. In some places no rain has fallen since the first week in June. Fields have burned up; the grass has been scorched until it is as brown and withered as one would expect to find it in October. Cattle graze patiently on the brown stubble, which cannot furnish them sufficient food, and farmers are compelled to buy feed for them. Tobacco has turned yellow from the effects of the glaring sun; cabbage has burned up; even corn, which thrives on hot, dry weather, has begun to dry up. Lima beans and potatoes showed the same tendency. The only crop that looked encouraging was the cotton of northern Georgia, and God only knows what will happen to that once the boll weevil begins its depredations. And the time is almost ripe for it, because the bolls are just opening.

Through most of this county the farming is done by whites. One sees very few Negroes. Especially is this applicable to Tennessee, where the Negroes are leaving the farms and congregating in cities. In Georgia, particularly as we neared Atlanta, we found Negroes keeping small farms of their own. This was true between Dalton and Marietta. We stopped at the home of one of them for a drink of water.

As we drove into Atlanta we at once realized that we were entering a metropolis. Diversified manufacturers met us on every hand. There were plow factories, medicine factories, paper factories, cotton mills, etc. We went directly to Atlanta University, thanks to the piloting of a Negro. Dr. John Hope, the president, was not in. But Mr. Hughes, [this was probably Alexander S. Huth][5] the superintendent to whom I had been sent, advised me to see Mr. Waldrom [probably Charles Hamilton Wardlaw][6] at Morehouse, just about a quarter mile away. We found the gentleman, who very graciously installed us in the guest chamber of the men's dormitory there. Not as elaborate as [at] Tennessee State, but then a nice room with two beds, private bath. We were utterly fatigued. Washed, took a little refreshment, and retired.

This city is still agog over the murder of young Hubert by white hoodlums. One has been sentenced to from 12 to 15 years in the penitentiary, something heretofore unheard of in Georgia.[7] The whites are aroused and

5. Huth is listed in the *Atlanta University Bulletin,* series 2, no. 74, April 1928, 4, as superintendent of Buildings and Grounds. He is listed in the *Atlanta University Bulletin, 1935–1936,* 6, as superintendent of Buildings.

6. Morehouse College, *Annual Catalogue, 1929–1930,* 7, and *1930–1931,* 8, both list Charles Hamilton Wardlaw as superintendent of Buildings and Grounds.

7. On June 15, 1930, Dennis Hubert, a sophomore at Morehouse College, was killed on the playground of Crogmann School. A grand jury indicted seven white men for the crime. The men claimed that they attacked Hubert because he had insulted two white women earlier that day. Evidence, however, placed Hubert in Sunday school and church and at the homes of his parents and grandparents at the time the alleged incident took place. Two days after a bail hearing for the accused men, the home of Hubert's father, Rev. G. J. Hubert, pastor of Glenn Street Baptist Church, was burned. A few days later, a tear-gas bomb was

Mr. Waldrom [Wardlaw] informed us that he feared reprisals. Negroes are forbidden to buy guns, or at least white storekeepers are not to supply them. The idea is clearly seen. If a riot comes, for God's sake have the Negro defenseless in order that the white casualties will be as small as possible. Nevertheless, many of the Negroes, especially the lower element, are well supplied and ready for any emergency. They buy from Jews and very fair Negroes buy from Gentiles, thus putting to good account their preponderance of white blood. I hope, however, that it will not be necessary to resort to the use of arms.

[No entry was found for Sunday, August 3, 1930.]

Monday August 4, 1930

Rose at 6:20 quite refreshed. Gathered together some laundry and sallied forth to the post office. Found letters from Woodson, Bertha [Baylor], and Prudential Bank. This is quite a city. It has a large variety of industries and its thoroughfares remind one of a small New York. As I drove through the crowded streets I bethought me of Wilkey who feared that I could not drive in Knoxville, Tennessee, which boasts one main street. Here are dozens of traffic-laden streets.

Inquired our way to the Negro business district on Auburn Avenue. Arriving there, [I] was astonished. Negro insurance companies, bank, hotels, undertaking parlors, two newspaper offices, drug stores, groceries, and other stores met our eyes. There was the *Atlanta Independent* Building in which Ben Davis, the Negro politician and editor, holds forth.[8] Our laundry we took to a colored concern.

[No entries were found for August 5–8.]

---

thrown into a mass meeting of African Americans. According to the police, a group of white men threw the bomb.

Young Hubert's reputation and the prominence of the Hubert family caused an unusual reaction to the murder and the incidents which followed. An editorial in the *Atlanta Constitution* called the murder a "test case of the right of all persons, white and black, in life, liberty and the pursuit of happiness in the sovereign State of Georgia." Ministerial groups protested and a movement was launched to raise funds to rebuild the Hubert home.

A jury found T. L. Martin, the first of the seven white men brought to trial, guilty of voluntary manslaughter and set his sentence at from twelve to fifteen years in the state penitentiary.

See *New York Times,* July 29, 1930, p. 5, and August 3, 1930, sec. 3, p. 6.

8. Benjamin Jefferson Davis, Sr. (1870–1945), was active in the Republican Party. He served as National Republican Committeeman for Georgia until 1928, and he served as an at-large delegate to the Republican National Convention for twenty-five years. In 1930, he was the editor of the *Atlanta Independent,* a weekly newspaper.

6

Alabama and Arkansas

SATURDAY AUGUST 9, 1930

Leaving Atlanta

Before we could get out Saturday, Miss Estes had come to the tennis tournament ostensibly to watch the matches, but in reality to see [John Wesley] Poe. The most likable girl we have met with on the trip. She is our girl. Her fingers still pained from my catching them in the door of the car last night.

Wrote Dr. Woodson. Could not finish letters to Mae and others.

No mail. Took breakfast at Mrs. Sutton's instead of [at] James [Cafe], fools that we were [for having eaten at James Cafe in the first place]. Here [at Mrs. Sutton's] we had enough food for five men—fruit, cereal, chicken (three poached eggs in my order), candied sweets, steak, hash, rice, marmalade, hot rolls, and all the milk we desired. And just sixty cents apiece. The food was excellently cooked and the service all that could be desired. And what was better, not a fly could be seen in the place. It was so well appointed that it was a pleasure to eat there. And I had to literally drag Poe in. Just to think Monday I had paid 85 cents for a breakfast of poached eggs, bacon, and fruit at James Cafe. Our people drive business away from them by overcharging.

Took car to filling station before going to breakfast. Had oil changed, tire fixed, springs, etc., lubricated, and tank filled with gas. Cost $5.41.

While it was being done I called upon Mrs. Gatewood to bid her farewell. Had previously called her sister, Emma. From there went to Mr. C. W. Washington's office (Urban League Secretary). Told me of case of peonage near Atlanta, where two Negro boys, 11 and 13, respectively, were held on the farm of a white named Peters. He refused to send them to the mother on the ground that they were indebted to him for board and other expenses to the amount of $16.50. Yet, they had worked sawing wood, plowing, picking cotton, and at sundry other chores for nine months. Peters had itemized both the boys' debts and credits, of course, in his favor. The mother, distracted, had appealed to the Urban League, and Mr. Washington, after quite a lengthy battle, succeeded in having the boys returned to her. Peters was illiterate and his letters show his average intelligence being scarcely that of the third grade and his penmanship about illegible.

Could not say farewell to Miss Hall the way I wanted to because of the presence of Mr. Washington. She looked at me so wistfully as if to say, "Is this goodbye?"

Out now to Poe who has had the car put in shape to travel. We experienced no trouble getting out of town. A beautiful concrete road took us past fields of cotton, which was just beginning to blossom. In many of the fields could be seen red and white blossoms against the green stalks, which presented a beautiful picture. For hundreds of acres these cotton fields stretched along the road. The fields were deserted, for the farmhands do not work on Saturday afternoon. Of course most of these were Negroes. Some of the cotton fields were broken here and there with a patch of corn. Little diversified farming, such as food crops, was seen. All the way to Tuskegee I saw no wheat, oats, vegetables—that is to any extent—and only one haystack.

These plantations, of course, had their small unpainted gunshot shacks sitting haphazardly amidst the cotton field. To see them one would not marvel at the high death rate among Negroes. Most of them had no windows. Some had two, some more. In other cases the windows were boarded up, and in Alabama, we saw huts that had no windows at all. Just a door, front and back. Most of them contain two rooms; many one. And in these ill-founded quarters whole families are housed. From the road we can see bed, stove, and everything else in the one room.

[No entry was found for August 10.]

MONDAY AND TUESDAY AUGUST 11 AND 12[?][1]

Montgomery, Alabama

Awoke Monday 8:30. Woke Poe. [There are] 1,100 summer school teachers at [the] Normal School [State Normal School, now Alabama

1. This entry was marked July, but Greene did not reach Alabama until August. The entries from August 11 to August 24 were entered in a small notebook. Some sections were out of chronological order, and several words and phrases were illegible.

State University]. Physical Equipment: Campus wretched. Buildings old and unattractive with exception of one dormitory, [the] girls'. School has a large appropriation, $300,000 to $400,000 a year. New buildings, girls' dormitory and administration building, are good. [We had] trouble finding person in authority.

Monday August [11], 1930

Go to Montgomery School, large . . . campus. Speak at classes, Miss Moore, Trenholm, M_____. Sell books in hall. Russell; Gilchrist. Met Beatrice Mcfadden. Take her for ride. M_____ takes us to party. Miss Banks from Sheffield. Before, met Whitley, frat brother. Wife introduces me to her sister. Charming. Bertha _____. Came back under pretext of looking for pen. Play cards, leave at 9:00.

Tuesday August [12], 1930

To school early. Speak at chapel. Sold books in hall. See many attractive girls. Saw Bea at noon. Make arrangements for ride at 8:00. Sold 12 sets of books. Russell takes me in hand. Promised to give him a set of books if I can sell 10. Takes me to Mrs. Weeks of Mobile; sell her 2 books. Reverend buys nothing, offers good time. But I'm due at Whitley's. Started to party, looking for Bea. Finally find her. Take her for *ride.* Back to St_____. Changed clothes. Go to dinner and party 1 and ½ hours late. Forgiven. Meet Mr. _____, a railway mail clerk. No discrimination he tells me. A never-to-be-forgotten evening with Bertha. Oh, yes, during the day, Mrs. Moore took me to see Dr. Carey. Sold him.

Wednesday August 13, 1930

Rush back to Tuskegee. Do it in 1 hour flat (40 miles). Speak at Bush's English class, then at chapel. Make impression there. I am thrilled. Sell books in hallway, four sets. Meet Mrs. [Portia Washington] Pittman, B. T. Washington's daughter, and Mrs. Peters from University of Maine, English teacher. Sell with Roberts's cooperation until 4:30. Dress, go to dinner with Bryant. Meet Miss Maggie Pierce. Most charming woman met with on trip. Remind me of Beth Sinkford. Invited us to her home. Irene _____ from Thomasville, Georgia, with us. I am enamored of her but see Miss Ingersoll of Columbus, Georgia, at the party at Veterans Hospital. Spend most of time with her. Take her and Irene for ride. God knows I did not have whom I desired. Finally retired at 1:15.

THURSDAY AUGUST 14, 1930

Went back to my accustomed place in Huntington Hall. This was my biggest day. Cut initial installment to $2.00, due to pleas of teachers that they could not pay four dollars, and also to my own need of funds. Spoke to Bryant's class at 10:00 a.m. Netted me finally about four sales. Several sales from teachers as widely scattered as Georgia, Texas, Louisiana, Florida, North Carolina, and Alabama. Miss Holliday[?], Mrs. Addison[?]. One woman paid for 2.

Miss Ingersoll came to see me. Too busy, however, to talk to her. Took dinner at cafe. Lucky because everyone [else] got sick from drinking ambrosia or eating bad food. Told Jesse Atkins mortals had no business quaffing of the nectar of the gods.

Left Huntington Hall about 4:00 p.m. Raining. Missed D_____ at Veterans Hospital. Returned by home; was sitting, waiting. Took me to see Mrs. Delaney[?], librarian at Veterans Hospital. Talkative, interesting, typical New Yorker as to dress. Appeared in almost nothing. Former librarian at 135th Street Branch in New York City. Trains librarians. Knows everyone. Exceedingly well read. Will take large order for library. Beautiful home. Husband ill. From there went to Veterans Hospital to call upon Dr. and Mrs. Callis [Henry Arthur and Myra Colson Callis]. Interesting, she is social science student. Knows Woodson. Discussed Negro from every angle. Made me forget [Henry Lee] Moon's engagement, or rather, I could not leave.[2] Tried to do so at 6:40. Let them see our list of books. Mrs. Callis took them immediately. Then the greatest surprise of all came—Mrs. Shepherd, a friend of Callis's, actually asked to buy a set.

FRIDAY AUGUST 15, 1930

Today left Tuskegee at 8:10 after bidding all goodbye. Left many unwritten orders there. Terrific rain en route to Montgomery. Saw Bertha. On [the] way, saw Negroes driving mules and working in field. Stopped one. Found Negroes were working for $15 a month on farms and boarding themselves. This is less than wages in northern Alabama, due perhaps to greater demand for labor in the mines and factories. Saw Negro women chopping cotton,

2. Henry Lee Moon (1901–1985) and Greene probably met at Howard University, where Moon earned an undergraduate degree in 1923. The following year, he received a degree in journalism from Ohio State University and went to work as a press agent for Tuskegee Institute. In later years, he served as public relations director for the NAACP, and from 1965 to 1974, he edited *Crisis* magazine. Joseph Berger, "Henry Lee Moon Dead at 84; Ex-N.A.A.C.P. Spokesman," *New York Times,* June 8, 1985, p. 45, C4.

etc. Huts of tenants with no windows. En route to Birmingham, saw whites working with Negroes on railroad. Doing same kind of work. Slowly eliminating Negroes out of these jobs.

Saturday August 16, 1930

Before breakfast I set out to find Mr. Parker, principal or director of the summer school here. I had expected Poe to work, but he failed to do so. Doesn't feel anything is to be made from teachers. I disagree. Found Mr. Parker at the school. Summer session had closed, however, therefore, my trip was in vain. Mr. Parker himself was not interested. There still remained a few teachers who were so absorbed in their work of getting out reports that I would not bother them.

The school itself is unique. A peach-colored cement affair of one story. It is rambling, covers a lot of ground and is composed of several units. Has a large auditorium. Mrs. [Eunice Vivian] Adamson, a teacher, tells me that its physical appearance is the result of the "hat in hand" attitude of the principal, Mr. Wood, a half-illiterate man who accepts anything the whites give him and who admonished his teachers and the parents of the students to do the same. There ought to be a place for such fellows.

Went downtown about eleven o'clock. Called upon Mr. R. F. Brown, proprietor of the Fraternal Hotel. Name given me by Woodson. Has been dead a year. Wife running business. Pretty fair hotel. Went into the Masonic Temple, a large, seven-story building on the corner of 4th Avenue and _____ streets. Bigger than the Independent building of Atlanta. Cleaner, has two elevators. About this section cluster Negro businesses such as drug stores, dry goods stores, real estate, hotels, lunch rooms, beauty parlors, etc. I noticed with regret, however, that two of the biggest and best places for Negroes to eat are owned by whites. I learned from Dr. [Garland Norman] Adamson that such a condition is not only an evidence of exploitation, but also gives a clear index of the power of choice and big business. Stopped in the library to see Mrs. Driver, the librarian.

Met Poe, who asked me to take him to a Dr. Bryant's on 12½ Terrace. [I] did not want to go, feeling that it would be only a wild goose chase, that Dr. Bryant was passing the buck. Went, notwithstanding. Had trouble finding the way. En route, passed a number of homes of similar design fenced off. Found from a Negro grocery man that it was Tuggles Institute. Took Poe to Bryant's. Told him to come by the Institute for me. Entering, I met the principal, a woman of average height and build, brown, unmistakably Negroid. Saw the value of books immediately. Don't believe she had any in their school. Took set, although she desired me to have them billed $9.98 collect. Told her it could not be done. Gave me her check.

I asked about the school. Told me it was founded by Mrs. Carrie Tuggles in 1902. Remained principal until 1924. It was founded for the benefit of the neglected colored children of Birmingham. It is now supported by such fraternal orders as the Court of Calanthe, the Rising Sons and Daughters of Protection, and the Knights of Pythias. Naturally, the endowment of the school is small and uncertain. Yet it has 200 students ranging from the grades to Normal school capacity. Seventeen men and women constitute the faculty. The present member has held her position only since May.

Back to Adamson's, ate and prepared to leave. Thanked Mrs. Adamson for her fine exhibition of hospitality.

Off now to Decatur. Stopped at Pythian Building to cash check. Poe cashed his. I was unsuccessful. What a long time it takes to get out of Birmingham. A large city in acreage.

Birmingham

HOUSING: Company owns [a] lot of houses for Negroes. Running water, lights. Rent low, $7 or $8 a month. Negroes abuse the privileges. Burn lights all day.

EDUCATION: About 15 colored schools. 400 teachers. Tennessee Coal and Iron Railroad Company furnishes schools for Negroes. Pays teachers higher salaries than city. Tennessee C.I.R. Co. has 11 schools for Negroes. 8 kindergartens for Negroes and three for whites. (Mrs. Adams, kindergarten teaching for years.) All principals are ladies, only 2 men employed and they are welfare directors. Nine months school. Teachers paid for ten. City starts one with $60 for grades, $70 for high school. In Tennessee C.I.R. [schools, the teachers receive] $70 a month start[ing pay] for grades. Tennessee C.I.R. schools [are] frame buildings, but schools well equipped. All do welfare work. Have kindergartens. City schools don't have them. Even milk they drink furnished by the company. Pay 25¢ a month for crackers. Negroes don't want to pay it. Schools kept immaculate. Have maids. Everything kept in good repair. Men have that job alone. Schools attractive. Company gives pageant every other year. Want to give them every year. About 2,000 children participate. All costumes furnished by company. Given free. Children brought in trains. Some get first ride. Have natural bowl with concrete seats. Music furnished by ____ victrola. In little house, can't be seen.

HEALTH: Have health campaign each year, clean up week. Impress them with necessity of such. Have clinics, dental and medical. Doctors take care of entire family. Negroes have own physicians, but are handicapped because their trade goes to company physicians who treat Negroes free. Many of latter too ignorant to effectively treat them. Refuse to send children to have teeth cared for, tonsils removed, etc.

HOSPITALIZATION: Company has million-dollar hospital. Take in Negroes. Negroes have wards in Charity Hospital in Birmingham. Children's Home hospital only one run by Negroes. Negroes have four-room hospital, only place where Negro physician can practice.

LABOR: Acute for Negroes. Tennessee C.I.R. Company, largest employer of labor here, on short working schedule. Men get 1 to 3 days a week. Wages 31 to 35 cents per hour. Most unskilled. Skilled workers get more.

MINERS: Many of them Negroes. Mine much of coal and most of iron. Italians and other whites also work there. Many out of work. Negro named Dumas told me he was let go yesterday. Ensley virtually run by company. Steel mills hire. Work in Birmingham, porters, janitors, etc.

Outside the city, we were soon in the coal mining districts. We passed mines. Evidently, they were just closing, for white and black miners were returning. First time I had ever seen them. Negroes outnumbered whites. Walk along streets side by side. Some have lamps burning on their caps.

Started to rain. Poured. Ran out of it after half hour. Passed through Cullman, Alabama, where it is said no Negro is allowed to stay overnight. Beautiful road. Sped. Raced Train. Latter too much for me.

Reached Decatur about seven o'clock after racing a train for about ten miles. Failed to find [Noble] Payton at the station. On the way to the other railroad station we met [James Cecil] Wilkey. He had not seen Payton. My telegram had been received by Wilkey. He had stayed at Undertaker Sykes's last night. Met him, took us to meet his wife. Has beautiful home. Wife refined and cultured.

About 1,200 Negroes in Decatur. Work at railroad shops. Conditions of labor are trying. Little work. Whites taking jobs in railroad shops and driving teams. Mr. Sykes tells me virtually no skilled Negro labor there. Have lost out to whites. Good colored drug store and several other small businesses such as lunch rooms, barber shops, etc.

Left Decatur about 8:00 for Huntsville, Poe's home. Good gravel road all the way. Wilkey drove. Frightened me once by nearly overturning the car. Ran out of water. Feared bearings would be ruined. Luckily, they were not. Secured water at gas station just as proprietor was closing. Reached Huntsville about 9:30. Enclosed by mountains. Everyone knows Poe. Call him John Wesley. Is certainly popular in his hometown.

Took us to his home. Beautiful. Stepfather is painter. Dining room and parlor done in metallic-colored paint. Wife [Poe's mother] almost white.

Extremely courteous, hospitable, and motherly. We just had to stay there overnight. Our bedroom reeked with fresh paint, but that, we reasoned, could be obviated by opening the windows. By the way, Mr. D_____ made the bricks for the porch.

Poe took us to meet some of his friends. Some were storekeepers, especially Mr. Williams, a druggist. Among the other interesting persons was a Mr. Hendley, a lawyer whose father was formerly federal land agent for Northern Alabama. His commission hanging on the wall shows that he was appointed by President [Benjamin Harrison] in 1889. His office was in the post office. He also published the *Huntsville Gazette.* He left a splendid library to his son. The latter appears to be his father's only son. Also met my former classmate, Clayton Binford. Is now a physician. Just as untidy and careless about his person as he was in college. To add to this, he has become so ungodly fat that he looks like an ogre. And he is just about my height. I would not have recognized him. Don't see how anyone could patronize him. Failed to find others home. Went home, retired about midnight.

Huntsville, Alabama

Fine little town. Hemmed in by mountains. Negro drug store, grocery and meat market, ice cream parlor, gas filling station, Negro gin mill (Jordan), poolroom, and theater. About 5,000 Negroes, 4 dentists, 6 doctors. Hendley, lawyer, interesting, as son of [Charles] Hendley one of two federal land custodians for northern Alabama appointed by General Harrison in 1889. Huntsville has the two greatest limestone springs in America. Capacity 5,000,000 gallons a day. Hemmed in by mountains.

Race Relations: Good. Never had lynching. *Schools:* One grade and high combined, good school. Normal school at Normal, Alabama. *Labor:* Work in quarries, cotton mills, farms, bottling works, porters, and janitors. Bricklayers, painters, etc. Negroes work at some mills.

SUNDAY AUGUST 17, 1930

Saw Huntsville after breakfast. Could not send telegram to Payton. Office closed. Left for Athens after fun with two girls. Had leak in pump fixed by friend of Poe's. Blowout between Huntsville and Athens. Mr. McWillliams tells me of labor conditions. Laborers $20 a month with board, $25–30 without. Day labor $1.00 to $1.50. Negro peasants in fairly good shape in country. Farm owners have holdings of 20–158 acres. Drought has ruined corn. Cotton better. Domestic service: only one white home hires white servants, Negroes do rest of it. Trades: Negro work at them. Number lessening due to Negroes' failure to make selves proficient, also attraction of trades to white men. Driving Negroes out. Latter had contractor who boasted of money made. Was given jobs at so much per 1,000 bricks laid. Did work on school. Good dinner. Buttermilk.

Left about 3:40. Good gravel road to Florence. Few Negroes. Poor mountain whites. Live in dilapidated, one-room shacks. Large number of children. Men in overalls sitting about. Wilkey frightens us to death at curves, nearly overturns car. Going too fast. Terrific storm comes up. Road like glass. I drive from Florence. . . . Stopped in Sheffield at Mrs. Mathews's for night. Wife of school principal. Took us to a Mrs. Taylor. People afraid of lightening. Terrified of putting on light. Stayed all night at Taylors'.

Monday August 18, 1930

Beautiful Mary Sieveg, attractive, from Sheffield. Saw Negroes going to work. White man had group. As we crossed Mississippi line, [we] see Negroes working in sand pit. Whites carrying gun. Wilkey bends, anticipating shot. Wretched hovels lived in by whites, bed, stove, table, all in one room. Children in excess. Saw about 15 in one house. Cotton in northeast Mississippi does not look so good. Lumber mill near Iuka, Mississippi. Saw 20 Negroes working. Passed Iuka mineral springs. Negro in Corinth, Mississippi, tells me that some Negro farmhands receive $25 and board, bacon and cornmeal. They work from sunup till sundown. Three or four fellow Negroes work in lumber mills. Whites work in service. Whites and Negroes work on streets and railroads. Saw groceries. Wide highway going into Memphis. One of the most beautiful highways from Tennessee-Mississippi border, nothing for miles. Killed dog! Stop in Corinth, Mississippi. Negro restaurant owner surprised me by [the] way he spoke to white insurance man. Is from Louisiana.

Tuesday August 19, 1930

Memphis to Little Rock

Had to fix flat tire this morning. Lodging and breakfast 50 cents. Lovely Mississippi. Large island in center, but water not as muddy as I anticipated. Crossing from Memphis older wooden bridge alongside. Into Arkansas. . . . Whites and blacks working in road. Negroes serving in bayous of the Mississippi bottoms. Wide new concrete bridge over parts of bottoms: whites working on road. One of largest cotton fields I've ever seen, stretching for miles. On both sides of road. . . .

Secured valuable information from Negro trucker Jones. Told me wages are meager and farming, for Negroes, is thing of the past. Negroes get 75 cents a day with board and $1.00–1.25 without board. The plight of Negro renters is pathetic. They cannot make money because of high rental plus the drought. Last year they made a little money but the landlords, in order to prevent their either buying land or leaving them, virtually doubled the rental. Last year no land cost more than $8–10 an acre. This year it has been increased from that price to $15–15.50 an acre. The Negro tenants are virtually the slaves of the planters.

These flat bottomlands, with their rich black loam, grow luxuriant crops, but [for] the drought. After last night's rain, the mud in some places has been washed on the pavement from the shoulders of the road, which makes it extremely dangerous to drive.

Saw cotton in all degrees of health and growth. Great planters have own gins. Overseers as managers have no diversification. Cotton only.

Fairly good gravel road. Segregation pervasive. Louise, Arkansas, has railroad station about 9 by 19 [feet,] and even this divided for whites and colored. Shows how ridiculous as well as costly segregation can be.

Wrote Woodson, sending him name of Miss Heard as agent. Told him of Payton. [Oliver] LaGrone, as we passed Claybrook, Arkansas, told me that a Negro farmer, Claybrook, owns 2,000 acres.

Saw small school on plantation, about 10 by 20 feet. Children and grownup barefooted, bowlegged. Male teacher. LaGrone gets boll of cotton. Explained how they develop. Plantation churches for Negroes. In midst of cotton fields. Small, unpainted. Corn burnt up.

White tenant homes on plantations are pathetic, 4 families each. Containing each about 2 rooms. None of Negro tenant homes have screens. Flies rampant.

Corn burnt up or stunted. Grass looks as if it had been burnt over. Saw rice grow for first time. Done by irrigation.

Whites kind. Exceedingly so in Little Rock. Terrible time getting to Little Rock. Had to come 18 miles on flat tire. Money gave out. Tires not worth spending money for new tubes.

Arrived in Little Rock about 9:30. Met Mr. Reynolds, Grand Scribe and treasurer of masonic[?] Templars. Hospitable, kind. Allowed us to wash up in his office, which was excellently furnished. Secured us quarters in Hotel Grayson. Called Seifert Jones. Going out of town. Referred me to Mr. A. E. Bush, real estate man, and Luther Moore, lawyer. Said they would do for me what they could. Mr. Reynolds there, but in work. Told me of John E.

Bush, late President of Templars. Son squandered money. Introduced me to Mr. Brown, fire insurance man. See him next morning.

Called Dot Gillan, engagement for 9:30 a.m. Met Hargrove[?], who keeps finest Negro lunchroom I've seen. Reservation to see him in the morning. Is frat brother. Went to Grayson's. Clean. Just large house. Board and live there. Retired so tired I could not even bathe. Little Rock looks promising.

Wednesday August 20, 1930

Saw Dot Gillan at 9:30. Left her and went to see Mr. Bush. Fine office. Slim, cultured mulatto. Looks like [Ernest E.] Just. Took first set of books. Referred me to Luther Moore. Went there. LaGrone interviewing him. (Lost sale.) Was able then to eat breakfast. Saw Mr. Henderson.

[No entries were found for August 21–23.]

Sunday, Monday, and Tuesday August 24–26, 1930

Hot Springs

Left Little Rock Saturday, about 1:30. Original intention to send Wilkey to Pine Bluff. Could not secure car for him, however. I had to take him with Poe and me. His main desire was to see the place. Good road (for Arkansas) all the way. I drove.

All along the road the ravages of the drought are in evidence. Brooks, rivulets, and creeks are dry. Some of them fifty feet wide, ordinarily, show not one drop of water. Trees stand denuded, desolated as if a fiery holocaust had swept over them. Grass is burnt up. Cotton will yield nothing. Farmers are hard put to it to find forage for their cattle, and the cattle wander aimlessly along the road nibbling a little burnt grass here and a little there. Lack of long feed has also reduced the milk supply.

The drive to Hot Springs was beautiful. The road wound about the Ozark hills continuously. The air was fresh, crisp, and flavored with the invigorating aroma of the pines.

Reached Hot Springs in one hour and twenty five minutes (60 miles). What a surprise. Magnificent hotels greeted us on every side of its one extremely long street. The Arlington Hotel is one of the most beautiful that I have ever beheld. There appear to be literally dozens of bathhouses, where persons from all over the world come to bathe in the healing waters of these celebrated hot and cold springs with their arsenates and calcium, lithium, magnesium, and iron salts. Then too, there is secured here the famous Mountain Valley water.

What was most outstanding as well as gratifying to me was the two fine buildings here owned by Negroes. The Woodmen of the Union building, which occupies a square and includes baths, hospital, office building, and the Home of the Woodmen, is the most beautiful building I have ever seen owned by Negroes. The Pythian Building in the block above it is not so pretentious from the exterior, but outdoes the Woodmen's from the interior. This building is also essentially a hotel with baths, offices, stores, etc. I should have remarked that John L. Webb, the guiding spirit of the Woodmen, is one of the most powerful Negroes in the Southwest. I was to have spoken at their convention here on the eighth of August, but was unable to do so.

We had been told in Little Rock that all the business in Hot Springs was on one street. So were the residences. What was my surprise to find here a large number of fine Negro homes. And in no case did I see the dilapidated structures such as Little Rock, Memphis, and other Southern towns presented. The reason, no doubt, is that the riffraff are discouraged from coming here because of the absence of any other work than hotel work for the unprepared Negro, and for the large opportunities for educated Negroes due to the fact that the home offices of two insurance companies are located here. Then too, the Negro resident here gets contact from all over the world.

I met several classmates of mine. One was Sam[uel] Lassiter, who was graduated a year ahead of me. He is married, a member of the executive committee of the Century Life Insurance Company, and one of their most energetic young men. He is married to a very charming woman. Met Sheppard Acme. He runs a drug store. Fairly well stocked. Claims business is bad, however. Recently lost his wife. Met Drs. Collier and Andrews, the former an intern, the latter practicing in Parsons, Kansas. Played tennis with him. Met Miss Bea Hollingsworth. Very interesting. Back to Hot Springs. Called upon two ladies. Introduced by Dr. Thane[?], effeminate and incapacitated brother of Mrs. Watkins. One Miss Diggs, bookkeeper, took a set. Called on Rev. Sims of Vesters Temple. Dark, slim, straight man. Intelligent. Had all our books. Knew [Roland] Hayes personally. Told of Hayes singing in kitchen of white home, bemoaning his expulsion from Fisk for singing spirituals.[3] Warranted interest of white woman guest at home,

3. Hayes entered Fisk University's preparatory department in 1905 as an eighteen-year-old sixth grader. He came to Fisk seeking formal training in classical music, and he received such training from the music faculty. Professor Jennie Robinson, head of the music department, recognized his talent. She fostered his training by secretly raising money to cover his tuition. She did not approve of his singing spirituals and popular music, however, with the famed Fisk Jubilee Singers. It was she who had him expelled from the university. See Edgar A. Toppin, *A Biographical History of Blacks in America since 1528,* 315–17.

who made musical education possible. Secured appointment for Wilkey to speak here tomorrow. Passed Roanoke Baptist, [the] most famous Negro Church in [the] South, and Haven Memorial. I shall speak at former, Poe at the latter. Played game of golf. Bought a shirt. Finances low, have but 4 dollars. Poe broke.

[No entry was found for Wednesday, August 27, 1930.]

7

Going to Texas

Hot Springs, Arkansas, to Marshall, Texas

Thursday August 27 [28], 1930

At 7:45 we began making preparations for leaving Hot Springs. Went to see Mr. Wyatt, who promised to take a set of books. No one came to the door although it was only 8:15. Tire was a quandary. Took it to garage to have it repaired. Tube rotten. Tire, fairly likewise. Just cheated in Little Rock out of $13.50. Decided to go back to secure redress or adjustment on them, but could not spare money for such. Concluded to go to Texas.

None of the fellows except [John Wesley] Poe had any money. I had only $1.65. And we needed a tube, the oil ought to have been changed long ago, gas was to be bought, and meals purchased; and everyone broke. [Oliver] LaGrone made me especially angry. During the last two days he made $8.50, yet spent it foolishly either on golf or girls and saved but 50 cents as his share for traveling expenses. Yet, I cautioned him several days ago we had to travel 204 miles. I was exasperated. I was tired [of] "carrying" him and [James Cecil] Wilkey. I can save nothing. They look to me for everything. Poe is not included. He is a gentleman. Whatever I lend him he will repay. Then, too, he is my friend.

En route to Texarkana we saw many interesting things. Not the least of them was the dirt road, one of the worst I have ever seen. Cotton was everywhere. On one side of the road a large acreage had been cleared; the trees cut down, leaving only the stumps. It evidently had been cleared for grazing purposes or for planting.

The effects of the drought were everywhere. The fields are baked, the very mountainsides are parched, the corn is destroyed, the cotton stunted and small. The yield of necessity will be small. The dry weather has caused forest fires, which were burning with great gusto between Hot Springs and Arkadelphia, doing great damage to timber lands. Along the same road, construction was going on and all the workers were white. Not a Negro could be seen, not even as waterboy. We passed several gangs of them.

Passed two enormous fields of cotton stretching for acres and acres along both sides of the road. It represented a large loss to the farmer, however, for the terrific heat had not only retarded its growth, but had forced the bolls to open prematurely. It was only 9 to 12 inches high, yet the bolls were already opening.

We passed another gang of road workers. All were white. They were driving teams, steam shovels, grading, building bridges, etc., yet not a Negro was in evidence. The dust was choking. It was as fine as powder. The roads were the worst over which I have ever traveled, worse than those of Tennessee. We finally had a respite from such, however, for five miles of concrete highway loomed ahead of us. It was certainly welcome.

Stopped in Arkadelphia, a little town about 30 miles from Hot Springs, to earn a little quick and much-needed money. Told the fellows to sell one book. Sent Wilkey to see Dr. Swayzi. Is a Meharry grad of 1899. I found this out when Wilkey returned to the car informing me that the doctor had summoned to his office two school principals and wanted me to talk with them. The doctor looked like a farmer, small and wizened, and his office had the appearance of a barn. It was untidy, dirty, and unsanitary. The principals presented a more imposing appearance, relatively speaking. One, Mr. Marchbank, seemed quite intelligent. There are two colored schools here, he told me, with about twelve colored teachers. Bought nothing.

There is a large milling plant here, but I saw no Negroes working there. Most of them work on farms. Here, too, jobs are scarce. Some of the cotton in the near vicinity looks very good, but we soon passed another enormous field that was burned brown.

On the way to Hope, Arkansas, we saw Negroes and whites working together at a lumber mill. Some of the Negroes were running machines. I was interested in seeing a number of small Negro farmers with plots, I judged, ranging from 10 to 20 acres. These tillers of the soil will not be able to break even on their crops because of the drought. No doubt the farmer himself performed other work, leaving most of the labor on his patch to his wife and children. There were plenty of the latter. No one seemed to be doing anything.

Forest fires as a result of the 91-day drought or the carelessness of motorists or campers were everywhere. The woods on both sides of the road were burning fiercely for miles and miles. The smoke rolled up and across in huge white billows almost obscuring the road. Thousands of dollars worth of valuable pine and spruce timber were being consumed. And no one was fighting it. What amazed me was that, although the flames were gradually licking their way toward the farmhouses, both whites and blacks sat on their porches watching the fires with the most complete indifference.

At Smithton, Arkansas, the station manager lay asleep on top of a large baggage truck, while a half mile away, forest fires were crackling and burning over a large acreage.

This entire region is sparsely settled, which accounts, to a large degree, for the lack of roads. For miles at times, we passed through nothing but woods. Before leaving the mountains again, there was nothing to be seen save mountains and the road. There is no crop diversification. One sees corn and cotton only, the great curse as well as the wealth of the South. There are plenty of watermelons, however, but the supply exceeds the demand; hence, one buys them at unbelievable prices. We got two at Hope, which is said by white farmers to be the best watermelon section in the country, for five cents apiece.

We saw other things of interest between Prescott and Texarkana. Near Wheeler Springs, the doors of the Negro farmers were open in some cases, and we could see women stretched out on the floor sound asleep. All the steam road machines we passed were driven by whites. All the creeks we passed were dry. Near Prescott we saw cotton in mule-drawn carts being brought to the gin. They were driven by whites in every instance. This was the first time I had ever witnessed such. I wanted to go into a cotton gin, but time did not permit. Saw the familiar sight of Negro men, women, and children picking cotton, dragging their huge sacks after them. They are earning from 45 to 50 cents an hour, a white man told me in Prescott. We passed another forest fire. A little farther on, I saw the first all-Negro railroad gang in hundreds of miles of traveling.

Arrived at Texarkana, Arkansas-Texas, at 5:00 p.m. Instructed fellows to canvass the physicians and dentists as quickly as possible in order that we might go on to Marshall. The town was larger than I had expected. It is a true border city. State Line Avenue cuts the town in two, and one can ride up that street with half of his car in Texas and the other half in Arkansas. We worked the Texas side. There was a beautiful new office building at the corner of 2nd and Oak streets, where most of the Negro professional men had their offices. Across from this stood a large home before which whites and blacks sat with watermelons for sale.

Met Dr. A[ustin] H[ervin] A[rchibald] Jones. Young dentist. Howard grad (1925). Persuades me to stay over, backed up by the same arguments from a Dr. McPeters[?]. Incidentally, he was the first man I sold. I brought to bear upon him my strongest sales arguments, showed him the great ignorance common to both races concerning the Negro. Informed him of the omission of worthwhile things concerning the Negro in schoolbooks and also recounted some of the deliberate and vicious propaganda circulated in books to demean, debase, and belittle the Negro in order to keep him feeling inferior and the whites superior. For these reasons, I added, these books should be in every home. He looked at me amazed, but I was talking for bread. He finally—after pleading broke—took *The Negro in Our History* and *African Myths,* giving me $1.60 deposit.

Jones, my former classmate, told me he would take care of all of us if we would remain. Decided to do so. Told me we could make money here. Met Mr. J. J. Jones. Could not sell him. Sold his wife who teaches at Arkansas A & M College at Pine Bluff.

Poe in the meantime had arranged dinner for all of us at Rev. Plant's. He is the father of M. L. Plant, a friend or rather acquaintance of mine in D.C., a senior law student. Had a fine dinner. Fine service.

Dr. Jones came later, bringing with him one Mr. Hawk. I recognized him as soon as I beheld him, but could not call his name. He had sold magazines with me in 1927. Is married here now. Selling real estate. Invited me to his home. Could take one more. I took Poe. Hawk has a charming wife and a nice home. We played whist until 11:00, at which time we retired.

Friday August 29, 1930

After a fine night's rest and a good breakfast, we set forth to interview a Mr. Pendleton, recommended to us by Mr. Hawk. I accompanied Poe in order to help reinforce his sales argument, for he needs to make some money badly. Is penniless and feels it keenly. Mr. Pendleton is a railway mail clerk. His best two things are a fine library and ten children. His home is ill-furnished, even untidy. Discouraged both of us at first by telling us he was not interested in any more books. Played upon his ego, however, for he is well read, although not having received very much school training. Then, too, he realizes it. The upshot of the matter was he took a set of books, although he was forced to give a postdated check.

Following the sale, Mr. and Mrs. Hawk and the latter's mother took us to their farm. The farm is owned by Mr. and Mrs. Williams, Mrs. Hawk's parents.

En route there, several things of interest attracted me. An oil boom had just been started in this part of Texas and companies and individuals are busy locating wells. I, accordingly, saw my first oil well near Texarkana. It was not gushing but I learned that oil had already been found on the spot and the lessee was procrastinating in order to secure the most favorable sale terms from the owner by pretending that the first strike had already petered out. The well itself stood in the center of a cotton field. This section of Texas is more than 60 percent Negro and we passed many small colored farms. Mrs. Williams told me that they did not, as a rule, exceed twenty acres, with most of them 10–15 acres. Very few were well kept. The dwelling homes of some, however, were in fair condition. Most of these farmers are pure Negroes. Very few mulattoes were in evidence.

Farmhands, I was told, received a higher wage here than in either the lower South or Arkansas, $1.50 a day. Of course this is without board. The pickers get from 60 to 75 cents a hundred. Mrs. Williams pays her pickers 75 cents a hundred. According to her, the best pickers can make 300 pounds a day. Most of them, however, fall considerably below that figure.

We passed a large truck farm. It was one of the few I have seen in the South. Whites go into this pursuit seldom. Negroes almost never. Latter don't understand such cultivation. This section too, according to my hostess, is one of the greatest watermelon growing sections of the South. Evidences abound on every hand. On the roads, at filling stations, at ice houses, one finds this fruit everywhere. And strange to see, Negroes do not consume the largest supply either, as one generally believes.

We also noted some immense plantations along the road. The big house, of course, was beautiful, neatly painted, with well kept lawns, while the shacks of the Negro tenants were mere lean-to's containing one and two rooms. The most conspicuous article of furniture in them all is the bed.

We finally arrived at Mrs. Williams's farm. They have about fifty acres but are nonresident. Her husband is a hostler in one of the railroad shops. An old lady was shelling beans on the front porch of the house, while three or four young girls were cutting corn off the cob. All looked as if a bath were quite unknown to them. But then it was not Saturday. The old lady, Aunt Fannie she is called, told us some interesting stories of different parts of Texas.

The farm was interesting to me. It is kept by a tenant who works on thirds. The crops were somewhat diversified. For instance, I saw corn, cotton, watermelons, sweet potatoes, blackeyed peas, and peanuts. Then, too, there was some fruit—peaches and pears. The latter trees were laden with large fruit that would ripen, I was told, some time in September. Of course, corn and cotton abounded. It was the best corn that I had seen in hundreds of miles, green, tall, and luxuriant. Here also was some of the best cotton, standing tall, firm, and green. The bolls were not yet open. Aunt Fannie was drying peaches on top of a shed. Strange to say, I found no cows.

I told Mrs. Williams of the advantages of truck farming. She seemed eager to try it for she confided that the farm paid her nothing on her investment. And how could it, when all the farmers are raising the same things for a highly limited market? I told her that if their 50 acres were planted in food crops, she could realize a goodly profit before the summer was half spent, without the necessity of basing everything upon a hazardous cotton crop. She replied that the latter was all the Negroes knew how to raise. I met Mr. Wallace, a small, halfway intelligent man who runs the farm. I congratulated him on his corn and cotton. Asked him about wages. Told me farmhands got $1.50 a day without board, $1.00 with meals. Cotton pickers, he confided, were receiving less this year than formerly because of the great abundance of labor due to unemployment. Most of them were glad, he said, to receive 50 cents a hundred. Many receive less. Around New Briton most of the pickers, according to my informant, receive from 35 cents to 50 cents a hundred. The average cotton picker could pick 150 pounds a day. Some can pick much more.

He also told me that many colored farmers are in dire straits. Many of them, indeed, are giving up farming, and are allowing their land to lie idle. Others remain but are not growing paying crops. Lack of organization and inability to avail themselves of the farm loan act account for this. The white man usually secures the loan, then charges an exorbitant rate of interest to the Negroes. Many of these farmers have quit in disgust, and work in the pipe and other plants about Texarkana. A case in point given was that of one Al Jacobs whose 80-acre farm lay just across the branch but who for several years has been working at the creosoting plant. There was also the case of Mr. Williams working at the roundhouse despite his 50-acre farm.

On the way back we passed Dunbar High School. It is an attractive brick building with several portable schools surrounding it. We also went back to the fine office building on 3rd and Oak Streets. Here I met one of the proprietors, Mr. W_____. Here are the offices of most of the physicians upstairs, while downstairs there are a drug store, a shoe repair shop, and a tailor shop. I also saw my first Mexicans, one of whom was hurrying with his dinner, which consisted of tomatoes and bread. They remind me of the Italians in my home. These people, Mexicans, have swarmed across the border since the war and seriously undermined labor for the Negroes. They live cheaper, hence, sell their labor cheaper and, as a result, they are driving the Negro workers from the farms in the Southwest, from the railroads, and, also, from other fields of common labor.

I saw a large lumber mill here where a goodly number of Negroes are employed. In the Texarkana Post Pipe Company, the largest in the Southwest, according to Mr. Hawk, nearly all the employees are Negroes.

Other Negroes find employment in the Cotton Belt roundhouse. Many of them hold responsible positions such as hostlers, boiler helpers, etc. There are no firemen. A colored man (Mr. Easly) is manager of the baggage department at the Union Station here. Still, other Negroes find employment in the sand and gravel works and in cement. Other Negroes are employed as truck drivers. Most of the Negro women are domestics. A few whites perform the same work. There is a dearth of eligible men here for educated Negro women.

After dinner we took our leave from the Williamses. I went to Rev. Plant's. There I found that I had suffered an irreparable loss in my address book. How I lost it I could not say. I believed at first that I left it at Mrs. Jones. Called. It was not there. Nor at Mrs. Hawk's. And all the leads for the entire trip—New Orleans, Texas, etc.—were contained therein. Mrs. Jones was visibly perturbed over it and assured me she would send it to me in Houston in case she found it. I made Rev. Plant an agent. We also ate our final meal there. Shall never forget the hospitality of these people, here. Rev. Plant has 10 children.

Left for Marshall. I drove all the way. Wilkey refused to drive because I refused to allow him to have the keys. I am responsible to Woodson for the car, therefore, think [it] best that I should know where the car is at all times. The ride was uneventful save for a sharp storm that came up.

Arrived in Marshall about 8:15. I should say that Texas does not show the effects of the drought such as characterized Arkansas. The grass and trees were green and the odor of the pines was certainly invigorating. Marshall surprised me. It has a very large hotel. It is also the county seat, and about the courthouse is the largest square that I have ever seen in any city.

Reached the college. Called on Dr. [Matthew Winifred] Dogan, the president. Was bathing preparatory to retiring. Sent his sons to care for our lodging. Is graduate of law school, Northwestern University. Fine fellow. I was given [Oliver] Crump's room, but LaGrone and Wilkey scattered their clothes all over it. Therefore, I let them have it and with Poe took a student's room adjoining. The Misses Dogan, whom we had met, sent for us to come over. They cooked for us at 11:30. We talked until 12:00. Told us to be sure and return. Promised. Retired about 12:30.

SATURDAY AUGUST 30, 1930

Again trouble getting breakfast. One of the officials at Wiley took us to the best cafe in town. Could get nothing. Had no fruit, eggs, bacon, or bread. Had to go out and buy them. Called for poached eggs on toast and was brought pork chops on toast. Had to tell the people how to prepare them.

Flies were also bad. If there is one thing that makes the South distasteful, it is the great difficulty in getting food.

Immediately thereafter, I called on Dr. Dogan. A small, pot-bellied, jovial man about my complexion. Interested in our work. Took a set of books immediately. Has fine sense of humor. Told me he had set of old maid daughters he wanted to marry off. One of the daughters was nearby when he made the remark. Naturally, she blushed. He told me that he heard us last night and was about to call down and tell us to stop our noise but thought that we might be proposing to some of his old maid daughters in order to get them off his hands, hence, refrained from doing so. Told me to be sure to stop in to see him upon my return from Shreveport. He gave me a list of addresses of people there whom he thought would buy. Among them were Prof. Brown, the principal of the High School there, W. S. Carter of the Knights and Daughters of Tabor, G. C. Williams, a prominent undertaker, and others.

On the way to Shreveport, we passed numerous Negro farmers and laborers coming to town where they massed their wagons or autos for buying or selling. In all manner of conveyances they came. Some came by auto from Fords of ancient vintage down to respectable looking automobiles; others came in wagons or carts. Still others trudged along on foot. Some of the wagons had been made into rentable carryalls in which sat the entire family on seats, the women in their gaudy red or other fantastically colored dresses and the men in their best coats and trousers. Others came in mule-drawn carts piled high with fluffy white cotton carrying it to the ginneries. I saw many of these sights. It was interesting because it was novel to me. These people lived for Saturday. They go to town, gossip, meet friends, buy, sell, get drunk, spend their money, and return home. I can recall Mr. Dogan's telling me that one can see every type of Negro in the market place at the square on Saturday and that these people are so near to the simian that they lack only the posterior elongation.

I saw several instances of Negroes at work. An all-Negro crew in one case was at work on the Texas and Pacific railroad with a white boss over them. In a large lumber mill at Waskom, Texas, Negro men were employed. They were also employed in some of the ginneries. We also passed several Negro farms. They embraced from 15 to 20 acres, I should judge. Most of the houses which were mean and unpainted were empty. The occupants had gone to town.

The Texas road to the border of Louisiana left much to be desired. It was bumpy and uneven, and the pavement covered only a part of it. When the Louisiana border was reached, however, much to my surprise, a concrete road newly laid stretched before us. The speed limit was 35 miles. Not knowing whether they patrolled, I obeyed the traffic injunctions.

We reached Shreveport about 2:30. Here is located an immense refinery of the Standard Oil Company. The very air is heavy with the odor of oil. In fact, the prosperity of the town is due to the Standard Oil Company.

On Texas Avenue are some Negro businesses and offices. The doctors' offices, though housed in an unsightly building, were clean and well appointed. The drug store underneath, however, was the worst I have seen. There was little stock and the place was so filthy that when I asked the proprietor whether he had ice-cream, I was gratified to have him answer in the negative, for I could not have eaten it there. The best office building is the one owned by Dr. Powell (Sol) in Hotchkiss Street.

I met several interesting persons but the most outstanding one was Mrs. Frances Smith, a widow of a Dr. Smith. She lives in a large white house with a beautiful garden at the corner of Pierce Avenue and Hotchkiss Street. She has the finest library of any Negro home I have yet visited. She has everything it seems—books on law, a huge medical library, books on literature, essays, poetry, novels, philosophy, science, astronomy. Everything that one might desire in the line of books, she has. Her husband has been dead five years. She knows John R. Lynch, the former Negro Congressman from Mississippi. He used to stop at her father's house when a boy, she informed me. Her folks gave him meals when he could not feed himself. She told me of his being forced to leave Bay St. Louis and flee to New Orleans. He was trying to organize the Negroes in Mississippi in order to help them to vote. The whites resented it and threatened to lynch him. Hence his flight.

Mrs. Smith's family, too, was quite prominent. Her father was Collector of the Port of Goldboro, Mississippi, now known as Bay St. Louis. Her father's commission was signed by President Grant. Her mother was postmistress there and her uncle was the keeper of a light[house] between Bay St. Louis and New Orleans. She also told me that the home in which she lived was virtually built by slave labor. It is 89 years old. Has been renovated, however. The house is historic for it once housed G_____ Allen (Louisiana). Judge [James A.] Cobb of Washington Mrs. Smith knows well. Her husband persuaded him to go to school. She told me to inform him when I returned to D.C. that I have seen Franky E. Ross, daughter of Pinckney C. Ross. Sold her a set of books. Took them both for herself and niece.

From here went to Dr. Powell's office to see Poe. Had to wait for Dr. Powell. In the interim saw school teacher and others to no avail. Brought Poe back from Dr. Powell's. Latter cried broke. Money tied up. Patrons have no work. Called upon several people. One Rev. Stanley, I thought I had sold. He squirmed out of it, however, by crying broke. He is an A.M.E. and the bishops and presiding elders get the graft, therefore, he might have been telling the truth. Called on a Rev. Luke Allen. Not interested. Went to dinner at a Mother Smith's. Again, the same old story, four starch foods as vegetables, corn, sweet potatoes, blackeyed peas, and rice. No lettuce, tomatoes, or greens. Terrible. Dinner cost 30 cents. I could not eat it.

Went to call upon a Miss Davis, daughter of the N_____. Charming little lady. Marylou Davis was her name. Talked to her for a while. Left. Came back to Marshall at eleven o'clock. Wilkey sore because I sold Dr. Dogan set of books. LaGrone sold four sets. Ate watermelon. Retired about 12:30.

Sunday August 31, 1930

Uneventful day. Wrote in diary, also letters, before breakfast. Called upon the Dogans. Had fine conversation with Dr. Dogan. Asked my opinion of Negro schools. Told him I ranked Wiley best of all [the] church schools. That is from the point of view of physical equipment alone. The school has a nice administration building, a beautiful girls' dormitory and several other well constructed buildings. It has a chapel. The girls' dormitory would do credit to any school. The rooms are fairly large, well furnished, with clean baths and toilets. Miss Dogan (Blanche) took us through it. There could be additional showers on each floor, however. There is only one now. The dormitory houses about 250 girls. They exceed the boys here. The library is fairly well equipped. It also has an interesting collection of Negro books by both white and Negro authors. The campus is spacious, occupying both sides of the road. In front of the administration building stands a beautiful little fountain, which, with its flowers and well cut grass inside a cement enclosure with a seat on every side, lends an atmosphere of beauty and romance to the campus that Howard and many other schools do not know.

Accordingly I told Dr. Dogan that Wiley would have to be ranked after Hampton, Tuskegee, Tennessee, Arkansas A & M College, Spellman, Petersburg (Virginia State), and West Virginia State. He was grateful to know that I gave it such a high place. I told him that it was only my opinion and then from the standpoint of physical equipment alone. He agreed with me that such travesties on the name of colleges like Morris Brown, at Atlanta a Baptist [African Methodist Episcopal] School, Baptist College at Little Rock, Knoxville College, a Presbyterian School at Knoxville, Tennessee, and even Bishop College here would do well to merge or close down altogether. Baptist College at Little Rock is a disgrace, a misnomer, and an eternal mark of shame upon the Baptist denomination.

Visited Bishop College, a Baptist School. The only decent building is a girls' dormitory. Every other building ought to be torn down. There is no such thing as a campus here. Just a few buildings thrown helter-skelter, hither and yon. While the school, no doubt, served its purpose in the days of individualism, it is certainly high time—and it would be much easier to carry the school if denominationalism could be forgotten—that Wiley and Bishop pool their resources to the extent of forming one large and efficient college for the northern part of Texas. Such an advanced step, however, will require a long time for consummation even in this age of consolidation.

The boys' dormitory at Wiley, where we are staying, is an ancient building. The steps are wearing out. The toilet conveniences are terrible. The washrooms are so dirty and unsanitary, I could not take a bath, and the toilet in such filthy condition that I could not dare to use them. This seems to be an almost general condition among Negro schools. Even at Hampton in James Hall this was the case. Those at Johnson C. Smith and Knoxville College were worst of all, and those at Baptist College in Little Rock were indescribable. Tennessee State College, Tuskegee, North Carolina State College for Negroes, A & T, Morehouse and Arkansas, A.M.& N. College, alone, were above par in this respect. This is one aspect of Negro college dormitory life that sadly lacks attention.

Spent evening with Miss Dogan and Mrs. Williams. Both charming.

Monday September 1, 1930

Labor Day. Wanted to leave early for Dallas. But both post office and banks are closed. Could not leave without cashing check. Therefore, decided to leave at 1:00 p.m. Told LaGrone and Poe to work until that time in order to replenish our very depleted exchequer. Poor Poe has had hard luck. Is broke.

Wilkey and I went to Bishop. Met Mr. [J. J.] Rhodes, the president. A very striking man, tall, dark brown, straight, with just an inclination to become portly. Is bald, wears spectacles. A very engaging man. Told me of his plans for Bishop's development. Has already given up fourteen-room mansion used by former president as home. Converted it into school of music. Says is ranked as one of the best in country for Negroes. I fear that is not saying much. Has renovated an old building formerly used for trades and will utilize it as [a] science building. This is his second year—came here from [a] Dallas high school. Responsible for study of Negro history in high schools there. Put it in while other principals talked about it. Brought Melvin Banks here with him. Latter teaches history. Former classmate of mine.

Asked what he could do to help the cause. Is an enthusiastic supporter. Told him he could take books. Did so. Commended the work. Asked me to return to speak to students on 18th. Told him expected to be in West then. Says Woodson disappointed him last year. Has never spoken about his work in Texas, Rhodes said. Felt someone closely connected should do so, therefore, I, the pupil, must substitute for the master. Promised to come to Wiley on return. Would stop. Dr. Rhodes gave Wilkey many addresses for Dallas. Each one, he said, was a good prospect. Upon leaving, Dr. Rhodes told me he desired to make a contribution. Shocked me. First time anyone has ever suggested such. Told me Dogan ought to do same and that I ought to ask any well-to-do Negro for such support. Did not have contribution card. Rhodes promised to make it upon my return to Marshall. Left feeling it an honor to have met such a fine man. Most interesting college president yet. Is a Yale man. Must revise my estimate of Bishop. Any school with a man at the helm like Rhodes must be reckoned with.

Went to Hall. Wilkey and I waited until 12:45. He (Wilkey) went to see a prospect. I wrote. Phone rang. Young Dogan told me Wilkey wanted me at his home. Came over. Wilkey washing car. Needed it. Has not been washed since I was at Alabama State Normal in August. And we have been in mud and dirt ever since. Polished it. Looked fine.

Waited for boys until 3:30. Went to Dogan's and to Williams's to look for them. Thought they would be at the girls' home. Could not locate them there, however. Talked with Arnetta Williams and sister-in-law. Gave me many addresses for LaGrone in San Antonio. Saw boys going to dinner. Wilkey came to tell me Poe and Lagrone had been making sales. I had been angry but became speedily composed, for I never run away from business. Wilkey told me Hodges wanted to take us to Shreveport. Decided to go.

Arrived Shreveport at 8:30. Hodges drove. Met Miss ____ and Miss Bates. Latter pretty, vivacious, charming. Two girls, three fellows. Miss Bates shows preference for me. Wilkey leaves car and goes to golf course. We rode. Miss Bates interesting. Father dairyman. Has more than sixty cows. Recently lost so much money daughter had to stop school. She worries over it. Promised to try to help her. She likes poetry.

By the way, expect I have earned Miss Davis's undying hatred. Called her, she invited me to her home. But I neither went nor called to let her know why.

An escapade to pleasure Wilkey. Wilkey met some "fancy" girls who offered to sell themselves for $2.50. Told them I would not give them a quarter. Left Shreveport at 2:15. Arrive home 3:45. Dead tired.

8

Texas

On to Dallas, Waco, Austin, and Houston

TUESDAY SEPTEMBER 2, 1930

Beautiful day. Sent Woodson telegram for books for agents. To be sent to [James Cecil] Wilkey (Dallas), [Oliver] LaGrone (San Antonio), and [John Wesley] Poe and Greene (New Orleans). Poe made final sale to Anthony Bledsoe. Big, dark, jovial man has largest home in Marshall. Wife blind; uncle of Jules Bledsoe.[1]

Left for Dallas about eleven. Between Longview and Mineola, some distance from Marshall, saw a mixed group of whites and blacks working in the road. All doing same rough labor. In another group working on the railroads of the Southern Pacific were Mexicans, Negroes, and whites. Just illustrates how Negroes are now forced to divide this once despised work.

The land, as we proceeded, changed from brown to white loam, then to red, and finally back to white. This it continued for a long distance. The soil was like cement dust. It was so fine and light that it burned our eyes and nearly choked us.

Passed through Grand Saline—a small Negro-hating town almost halfway to Dallas. Negroes are warned not to stop there, so Dr. Dogan's son and Mr. Hodges, purchasing agent for Wiley told us. The only evidences of their hatred, however, proved to be a few harmless whistles and calls. Wilkey, however, was so frightened that he actually exceeded the speed limit and

1. Julius C. "Jules" Bledsoe was born in Waco, Texas, on December 29, 1898. He made his debut as a concert singer at Aeolian Hall in New York City on April 20, 1924. The talented baritone was featured in concert, musical comedy, and grand opera in the 1930s.

made me fearful that in trying to escape a mental hazard he might run into actual danger—the hands of the law—and God only knows when or how we could get out of the clutches of these "Crackers."

All sorts of roads were transversed in the course of this trip. Dirt roads, asphalt roads, where one is in eminent danger of overturning every time a car passes, loose gravel roads, concrete, and, finally, a road paved on one side only, the other side dirt. Looks like a man who has half of his hair cut. Such a road was a nuisance, for it meant continual turning out to let cars coming from the opposite direction pass. It was paved on our left.

Just outside of Saline we saw a white woman selling watermelons at a stand. They were grown on her own farm. Cost 10 cents apiece. She cut 5 in order to get 2 good ones for us. Was exceptionally civil. Asked us to sit under the trees and eat them. Brought each of us knives; Wilkey was nervous for fear white men would take umbrage at our sitting there eating and talking to the white woman. Many passed but paid no attention to us. Many of the melons, we were told, were small and dry on account of the prolonged drought. No rain to speak of since April. Yet, few evidences of drought appear in Texas. Fields are green, cotton—most of it—looks strong and healthy. Conditions are much better here than in Tennessee or Arkansas.

At Fruitvale, saw white woman and children picking cotton. There is no corn. It has either been picked or dried up.

At Wells Point, we saw idle whites and Negroes laying around the general store or cotton gins. Gins and cotton oil mills are everywhere. Cart after cart of fluffy, newly picked cotton, driven by blacks and whites, passed us going to the gins. The driver usually sits on the cotton. He needs to over some of these roads. Much cotton already baled was lying about uncovered in yards. No provision for covering it in case of rain.

September is the beginning of the rainy season here. There are miles of cotton, however, not ready for picking. What is being picked is being done more by whites, it seems, than by Negroes.

We now came to the region of the flat lands. Great Plains. From a small rise in the road the landscape stretches interminably before us. Never before have I gazed upon such vast distances. It is a beautiful sight to look about one for miles and miles and see green cotton fields and white farmhouses with the beauty marred only by the ugly tenants' quarters dotting the fields. We passed mammoth cotton fields extending on both sides of the road as far as the eye could see. On one large plantation, all Negroes were working. Men, women, and children of all ages were picking cotton, trailing their large bags behind them. Other men were filling the cart with the newly picked cotton. It was a novel sight to me—a New Englander. The cotton here stands like small trees—healthy, strong, and looks as if it will yield a good return.

The road led into the black dirt section. This soil must be extremely fertile. Again we could see for miles. Church steeples of ordinary heights in towns 10 or 12 miles away were clearly visible. We saw white men using three mule plows in the road preparing an embankment. Again we saw whole families of Negroes picking cotton. None were mulattoes. Very rarely do they work on farms it seems, especially the women. Must be a slave tradition still adhered to. The pickers' quarters are mere shacks thrown up in the midst of the cotton field or near the road. Most have two rooms; many one. The bed is the most prominent article of furniture that can always be seen from the roadside. Cotton, cotton, cotton—it is everywhere.

One sees many different kinds of gasoline here such as Arab, Crystal, Hickok, Simms, etc. This is an oil country, and on several occasions, we could see oil wells in the distance.

This is naturally a cotton growing country. Texas leads in this respect. Forney is a town of cotton gins. In one place there were seven in a row. Whites perform this work. We saw no Negroes working in them. This was once a Negro job. However, that time apparently has passed. All the railroad laborers whom we saw were Mexicans. They have largely taken this work away from Negroes in the Southwest.

The narrow bridges here are not only exasperating, but dangerous. The road is sometimes from 1 and ½ to twice as wide as the bridge. One only sees them in the South. They are one-way bridges, when by making them three or four feet wider, they could accommodate two-way traffic and safeguard the life of the motorist. May bear witness to more or less serious accidents. From an elevation in Mesquite, a small town about twelve miles from Dallas, we could see the skyscrapers in the latter city. As we entered Dallas, whites were working on bridges. No Negroes. The road was terrible. We have seen the famous ten gallon hat become quite common to us here in Texas. Everyone wears them. The outskirts of Dallas were imposing. Entered on Second Avenue. The street designation here is good, although they are named. The block number is given along with the street at intersections.

Much manufacturing here. Passed Show Case Manufacturing Company —largest overall factory in the world—mattress company, furniture factory, bottling works, and others.

Also passed the beautiful Exposition building.

Went to post office. Received two cards and letter from [Harry] Hipp. Tells me my letter to Rosenwald Fund was answered. Scholarship already allotted. Holding my letter for Mr. [George R.] Arthur, pending his return to office. Had expected many other letters. Disappointed. Perhaps they have been returned to senders due to my delay in reaching here.

Go to new Y.M.C.A. Best equipped building yet for Negroes. Has everything—fine swimming pool, basketball, volleyball, handball, and baseball courts, drying room, best bath conveniences, assembly halls for men and boys. Fine rooms with steel desks, etc. Mr. Stewart, frat brother, in charge. [It costs] $1.00 a night to stay there. Boys could not pay it, therefore, I went with them to Hotel Powell where a Dr. Hamilton directed and took us. Secured rooms for $1.00 apiece, two in a room. As usual, Poe and I stopped together.

Was tired. After dinner washed and filled car with gas and oil. Played and beat Wilkey [at] a game of golf and retired about 8:45 in order to be ready for trip to Austin, tomorrow. I shall leave Wilkey here. Pick him up on my return from New Orleans.

Dallas Negroes leave much to be desired upon first impression. Seem to be unprogressive. Wilkey and maid.

Wednesday September 3, 1930

Left Dallas 6:00 p.m. Wilkey, fresh from the arms of his "ammorata," leaned over the balcony of the hotel to get final instructions. Told him to work Dallas, then Fort Worth, informing me of his movements and accomplishments. I would write him at post office.

Drive to Waco was uneventful. Stopped just before leaving Dallas. Bought two oranges and two apples. Did not stop nor leave seat until I reached Paul Quinn College in Waco, 109 miles away.[2] En route there, saw the most beautiful and the vastest landscape I have ever been privileged to see. The land was so flat that one could see for miles and miles on every hand. So illimitable were the distances that the very land seemed to merge into the sky. It was grand, inspiring, mighty.

The only crop here is cotton with a little patch of corn separating the field. Diversification seems to be unknown. In most cases Negroes are the cotton pickers. But in an alarmingly large number of cases, great fields are being picked by whites. Whole families are in the fields, from the grandmother

2. Paul Quinn College, an African Methodist Episcopal Church school, was founded in 1872 in Austin, Texas. After operating there for five years, the school was moved to Waco, where it operated as a trade school. A college site was acquired in 1881, and the college celebrated its formal opening in 1882. The enrollment in 1927 was 177, and the faculty numbered seven members. Michael R. Heintze, *Private Black Colleges in Texas, 1865–1954,* 21; U.S. Department of the Interior, Bureau of Education, *Survey of Negro Colleges and Universities,* 856–65.

and father to the little tots. In other cases, both whites and blacks work side by side. This was the case near Alvarado, near Midlothian, and Hillsboro. In the many gins that dot the countryside, Negroes work only a few. Most of the workers I have seen were white. In the oil wells it is different. Saw Negroes in but one gin. That was near Waco.

Arrived there at 9:30. One hundred and nine miles in 3½ hours. Pretty good time. Roads fairly good. Stopped at Paul Quinn to see President and Prof. Bozeman. School disappointing. Only two buildings, girls' and boys' dormitories. The latter combining the administration building and library. Is wretched inside. Chapel has cement walls. Never been plastered. Shows inability of A.M.E. Church to maintain schools. Could do so but money is squandered. Dean Mohr, the principal, is a garrulous individual without the bearing or mien of a college professor. Looks more like a pool room buffer. Is a Chicago man. Told me of a Southerner who was going to thrash him because the school owed him a debt. Mohr defied him, paid him, and warned him never more to appear on the campus. His wife is the sister-in-law of Charles S. Johnson. Met Bozeman, a friend of (Oliver) Crump, (a former Howard classmate of mine from Kansas). (Crump) visited me last year (when I was sick). Bozeman is leaving. Will teach in Dallas. Socialized too much. Took us to breakfast. Before going met Zeister Steptoe of Baltimore, daughter of pastor of Bethel A.M.E. Will teach in San Antonio this year.

Told boys to work doctors in business section here. Do it in one hour. Will leave at 12:00. Good breakfast at Anderson's Cafe.

While boys worked, I interviewed Negro farmhand and laborers on employment situation. Mexicans have greatly cut Negro working opportunities. They are everywhere. Keep small stores, groceries, fruit stores, barber shops, etc. One sees them everywhere working on railroads. They do not overtax themselves either. They live in colonies. Chiefly, occupy a higher social position than the Negroes. Will not mix with them. Whites generally will not miscegenate with them.

There is very little work here for Negroes. Nearly everyone tells me that. A laborer told me that the chief reason for this is that the Mexicans, by underworking Negroes, are taking many employments out of their hands. For instance, it was said by a farmhand that now a Negro will receive only 60 cents a hundred for picking cotton because of the Mexicans' competition. Hence, nearly all the picking about Waco is done by Mexicans. The colored, I was told, get most of the service work in homes and hotels here, however. No Negroes work on the streets. According to Mr. Rather, a laborer, not a Negro has swept the streets in Waco for 20 years. White men do that. Collect garbage, too. Negroes furnish most of the labor in the building trades, such as hod carrying and the like. Too heavy for Mexicans. Dislike hard work. Most of the railroad labor, however, is in their hands. Porters on trains are Negroes, however. There are very few skilled artisans among Negroes here. There are one or two bricklayers and very few carpenters. Nearly all the gins use whites. In the oil mills, however, because of the hard and disagreeable work, Negroes are largely used, but the hard times have caused many of these to be displaced by whites. Now the forces are well mixed. Said my informant, white men are doing things here that they never have done before.

Sold three sets of books in Waco. Each of us sold one. I sold President Mohr. Order not to be sent until October 21st.

Left for Austin at 1:30. More gorgeous flat country. Beautiful landscape stretching for miles about us. Nature paints on a vast canvas here. Texans ought to think big thoughts. Their surroundings are so limitless. Know the reason they are characteristically laconic. The mighty stretches of territory devoid of humans impel them to silence. Nature is so grand and vast about them. Everywhere one sees cotton going either to the gins or baled cotton going to the warehouses. In mule and horse drawn carts, in passenger cars and trucks, this commodity is transported. I saw piles of cotton seed newly separated from the cotton. I saw oil mills in operation and farmers hauling away the oil pressed from their cotton seeds. The resulting cake makes food for cattle or this is treated to make fertilizer.

Arrived Austin at 5:00 p.m. The state capitol here is the most beautiful I have ever seen. A replica of the national capitol at Washington. The grounds are magnificent. They constitute a large, lovely park, in the center of which sits the capitol itself. It is made of brownstone.

Went to Samuel Huston College.[3] A fairly nice school. Larger than I imagined. The principal, T. R. Davis, was not in town. Met Mr. Brewer, the Dean. By the way, Mr. Davis has gone to Tennessee State and Dr. [Willis J.] King, an Oxford graduate, succeeds him. Think King is a minister. God help the school. The school itself sits on a hill. Has several fine buildings. Can't compare with Tennessee State College or Arkansas A.M.&N., however. Rather with Wiley but a little below it.

Stayed at Mrs. Goins, wife of Reverend. Cost 75 cents each. Poe is broke; that means I shall have to pay his. Would leave me with $1.50, and must go to Houston in the a.m. Oh, by the way, LaGrone began a foolish argument in Waco as we were leaving. Wanted me to drive to San Antonio and leave

3. Samuel Huston College, named for Samuel Huston of Marengo, Iowa, was founded in 1900 by the Methodist Episcopal Church. In 1927, the faculty numbered twelve members, and the enrollment was 201. See U.S. Department of the Interior, Bureau of Education, *Survey of Negro Colleges and Universities,* 836–56.

him there. Told him I was in a hurry to get to Houston, that it would cost the same regardless whether he worked San Antonio or Austin first. He threatened to leave San Antonio untouched. Told him to do so. Could quit too. He calmed down.

Poe wouldn't eat dinner. Claimed he felt nauseated. Don't believe him. Feel he did not want to impose upon me. Begged him to accompany me to dinner. Refused. Still contended he was indisposed. Perhaps. Yet as long as I have, he has. Ought to know that. He is my friend. Bought ice cream for Mrs. Halbert. Magazine for myself and Poe. Retired at 9:30 after getting the lady to deduct 25 cents. Wrote Woodson before. Leaving at 5:00 a.m. tomorrow for Houston. Anxious to begin work there.

Thursday September 4, 1930

Left Austin at 6:30 after giving LaGrone instructions to work Austin and then San Antonio. Will pick him up there. Reached Prairie View, about 112 miles from Austin, about 10:30. This is the seat of Prairie View State College for Negroes.[4] There is nothing here but the school. Largest Negro land grant college—1,450 acres. Some fine buildings, but they are thrown up helter-skelter and the vast and flat acreage upon which the school sits will never be utilized to its fullest to afford it any idea of beauty. If a campus is developed at all it must be apart from the buildings or must be enclosed by an entire set of new buildings. Such a program is improbable in the near future.

Met Dean Austin, head of liberal arts school, Mr. Reeves, whom I met at Alabama State Normal and who teaches education, and Mr. Southern, a good friend of Zeister Steptoe. Poe had a message for her.

Mr. Reeves introduced me to Mrs. [Virginia] Banks, wife of the President, W. R[utherford] Banks. He is in Galveston attending an institute. Very pleasant home, rather large. Mrs. Banks told me that there is already a large interest here in Negro History. Used to have a program during the entire month of February. Negro History celebration now lasts for seventeen days. Became boresome. Has many of our books here; sure, however, husband will take more. School opens next Thursday, September 11th. Wants me to return to speak. Promised her I would.

4. Prairie View State Normal and Industrial College, now Prairie View State University, was established as the land-grant college for African Americans by an act of the Texas Legislature in 1879. The college enrollment in 1927 was 559. The faculty of thirty-seven members consisted of thirty-three college instructors and four high school teachers. U.S. Department of the Interior, Bureau of Education, *Survey of Negro Colleges and Universities*, 796–810.

Now I met Mr. Southern, a frat brother. Took us to much welcome dinner at the cafeteria. Good meal. Told me about and pointed out to me the hospital, new mechanical building. They have resident nurses here, two resident physicians at the hospital and a pharmacist, all paid by the state. The administration building, sorry to relate, is an old stone structure. The boys' dormitory is fair; so are the toilet accommodations.

Left Prairie View at 1:30. Arrived at Houston at 2:30. About 48 miles. Saw the greatest distances on all sides yet experienced. For miles and miles flat almost treeless plains. About 40 feet above sea level. So flat is the country that we drove 46 miles with only one partial turn in the road and 22 3/10 miles with no turn at all. Exceeded my experience in the West in 1927, when we went for about 10 miles in Ohio and Indiana.

Reached Houston at 2:30. Met Dr. [Joseph Leon] Peacock, [Joseph G.] Gathings, Davis, and others. First two classmates. Latter brother of Marylou Davis of Shreveport, Louisiana. Had lots of fun after they had recovered from shock of seeing us. Gathings doing well. Practicing two years. One of the best Negro surgeons here. Davis secured us room on Darling Street. We don't like it. Can't change for we are broke. I have had to see Poe "go," poor fellow. His money ran out at Waco.

On the way to Prairie View we had an occasion to realize just how critical is the employment situation here. We picked up two Negroes who hailed us for a ride. Were going to Brenham, Texas, looking for work. They had left San Antonio more than 100 miles back and had walked it when they could not catch a ride. I was told by them that farmhands are being paid $1.25 a day without board, $1.00 with board. Wages are low because the Mexicans are underworking Negroes. Told me that Mexicans are doing nearly all the cotton picking. Get from 75 cents to $1.00. Wages cut by cheap Mexican labor. All the railroad work, they tell me, is done by Mexicans. Although they "loaf" on the job and will not exert themselves, they get the work. The Negro loses because his standards of living, low as they are, are higher than that of the Mexican. Road work, I was told, is done either by whites or Mexicans. The latter cook in the hotels, too. Whereas a Negro, one remarked, will demand $25 a week as a hotel cook, the Mexican will do it for $15. Consequently, he gets the job. Mexican women are also doing much of the work as servants and cooks in private families and are freely employed as chauffeurs. The only work that they will not do that Negroes labor at is hotel work such as porters, etc. That is still in the hands of Negroes. Skilled Negro workers, they told me, are very rare about San Antonio. In the cotton gins about that city all white labor is used. The Negroes do the dirty work in the oil mills. The employment situation for Negroes, therefore, I was told, is serious, and Negroes are rambling idly about from town to town seeking work; while those displaced farmhands from the rural sections also crowd upon the towns, increasing the group of unemployed and lowering the already low wages here. I myself have had laundry done in Marshall, Texas, for 45 cents which would have cost $1.80 in North Carolina.

Saw my first large group of cattle. About 100 cows and steers being driven to a new pasturage between Austin and Brenham. They were in [the] charge of two cowboys. One was a Mexican. They are excellent riders, I am told. Later on I saw a cowboy sit magnificently astride his horse as it shied at the approach of our auto. Backed him into a ditch and I feared would throw him over and crush him but he displayed his mastery by regaining control of the frightened beast.

Went to a party last night. Could not enjoy myself because of lack of money, and, moreover, did not have suit pressed. Felt very self-conscious. Met a Mr. L____, who teaches at Prairie View. Told me salaries are very low. Range from $80 to $120 a month and teachers must board themselves and pay room rent. Get less than in city schools here. Maximum $1,600. That is minimum for whites. Three senior high schools here, Miss Scott, a teacher, told me. One Jr. College. Poe became enamored of a Miss Newton, Fisk student. Could not blame him. Her complexion was a treat to the eyes. Retired after writing, about 12:30.

Oh, yes! Received two letters from Woodson. Told me he received requisitions for *The Rural Negro.* Sending them to New Orleans. Sending blanks as I ordered. Wants to know what is being done with them. Angers me when he asks whether we are distributing among children. Mentions the fact that we must be having fine time with ladies judging from letters coming to the office. I shall write him and give him an equal amount of sarcasm in return. This trip is netting me nothing financial. It is being done by me solely because of publicity given the organization. He cannot see that, however, or else every other little thing bulks so large that it obscures his vision. It is such petty things that will impel me ultimately to sever connections with him and tell him to go to hell.

9
Texas
Houston

Friday September 5, 1930

Rose at 6:30. Wrote in diary until 7:30. Dressed. I had 73 cents. Ashamed to meet the landlady because we could not pay her. For breakfast, sat in car and ate a few grapes and remainder of graham crackers I had bought last night. Got gallon of gas. Reduced exchequer to 15 cents.

Called on [J. H.] Harmon. Keeps store on West Dallas Street. Sells dry goods, etc. Disappointing to me. Had told me it was a department store. Yet it is an effort in a field entered into by very few Negroes. Is married. Eloped. Wife [Cornelia Routte] very charming and hospitable. Cashed a five-dollar check for me, took me to his bank.

Told me employment situation here is bad. Twenty thousand Negroes out of work. General depression [the] cause. Says Houston has become second largest city in the South and the largest in Texas. Ship canal has taken priority in shipping from Galveston. Latter dependent upon cotton for hugh volume of trade. Oceangoing ships can now come into the interior and load on this staple, which formerly had to go through Houston to Galveston by rail. Most of Galveston's trade now is that which comes from the far western or southern part of Texas. It has been totally eclipsed as a port by Houston. And to think that before the ship canal was constructed, the volume of Galveston's trade was second only to that of New York.

Harmon took us to dinner at the New Day Cafe, following his wife's failure to prepare lunch for us at the store. Like most women, she desired to show up to best advantage and have us take dinner with her Sunday. The proprietor of the New Day Cafe, Smith, has succeeded in driving out of business two Greeks who thrive upon Negro trade. The result is he has a great quantity and variety of food. No quality. I did not enjoy my dinner, for neither the place nor the food attracted me. It is patronized chiefly by laborers.

Came by the Pilgrim's Life Insurance Company's building on West Dallas. An imposing office building. The most beautiful owned by Negroes I have seen. It has even a unique style of architecture. I must add, too, that the Odd Fellows also have a fine building on Milam Street. I had been trying to get to Galveston all morning. But being without money, detained me. Gave [John Wesley] Poe money to pay our room rent. We are going to leave the place where we now stop. Don't like either the tenants, landlady, or the location of the room.

Returned to Harmon's store after filling car with gas and oil. Was ready to leave for Galveston. Mrs. Harmon telephoning told me she had a prospect for me. Tried to put it off till tomorrow that I might go to Galveston. Could not. Therefore, sent to a Mr. V. C. Henry, a railway mail clerk. Has a fine home on Shepherd Street. Told me Negroes' economic plight here is terrible. One-third out of work. Street work done by whites. Once in a while, Negroes can be seen driving garbage wagons, but that is infrequent. Says track gangs are nearly all white and Mexican. Told of coming into a town where railroad bridge was under construction. All laborers white. Informed me Mexicans have so hurt Negroes that about San Antonio, wages are terribly low and Negroes have little or no work. Only labor which Negroes have real hold on here is loading and unloading ships. Work heavy and in the sun. Whites and Mexicans dislike it. Negroes well paid. Sometimes can make $12 a day. Irregular, however. Depends upon ships entering or leaving. Told me Mexicans have taken railroad work because Negroes dislike the hot sun. Mexicans can stand more. I countered that the Negroes had been enduring the heat until quite recently. I considered it a case of cheaper labor by the Mexicans whose standards of living are lower than the Negroes just as theirs is lower than the whites (generally). Henry bought the books. Told me he was usually a hard man to sell. Took me to see Mr. [R. J. C.] White, another railway clerk. He duplicated the order after I had moved him to buy the books for his son. Asked me, upon Mr. Henry's suggestion, to come speak at the meeting of postal employees tonight at the Odd Fellows Hall. About 9:30. Felt I might be able to sell something. Promised to be there.

Called upon Mrs. Johns, secretary of the Y.W.C.A. A fine woman. Y in the Odd Fellows Temple. Very attractively furnished. Mrs. Johns knows many people with whom I am acquainted, including Vernon Johns, Gladys McDonald, Miriam Atkins, Ned Pope, and others. The latter, now engaged in social work, has been here several times. Comes two or three times a year. Told me Y.W.C.A. expects to build within the next few years. Need building badly to care for social problems here. Mrs. Johns is interested in starting a Negro History Club. Wants me to speak here at Houston upon my return from New Orleans. She and Mr. Carter Wesley—lawyer, newspaperman, etc., whom I met last night—will sponsor it in connection with a Reverend [C. A. Pleasant]. I am to see them tomorrow morning. Mrs. Johns took a set for the Y.W.C.A..

After dinner, [I] wrote Woodson. Referring to his sarcasm in respect to the use made by us of the subscription blanks, I said: "I am at loss to understand your very excellent sarcasm in this respect. If you expect that for every subscription blank which leaves the office a corresponding order will enter the office, then I see that you know nothing about practical selling in the field. Since you are ignorant of this fact, let me enlighten you. Some people when interviewed by the agent do not find themselves in a position to buy at that time. Some do not intend to buy. However, they will ask that we leave a blank which they will forward to the office with the initial deposit before the sale ends. And we leave them. If this may be called distributing blanks or souvenirs for juveniles then we plead guilty. And it shall continue until you order otherwise, since we are interested in arousing the curiosity of these people as to our work even if we are not able to sell them. You ought to know what a subscription blank in the hands of an interested person means when a book on Negro History or some kindred topic is needed."

Referring to his ironic statement concerning our advertising the office through the fair sex, I wrote: "Yes, the ladies are advertising the office. And we are having a lovely time. My love letters kindly hold until my return that I might pick out the lady who offers most fiscally!!" I felt better after writing him this letter. Someday he may learn how to deal with people but I fear death will cut short its consummation.

Returned home. Dressed after waiting ¾ of an hour to get into the bathroom. Nice home. Terrible street. Spoke to railway mail clerks. About 12 present. Sold three sets of books. Mr. [Johnny] Walls, the president, will take a set today. Pleased with the day's work.

From the meeting went to dance. Saw no one who interested me until Miss Johnny May Newton introduced me to a Miss Ella Robey. Both girls are beautiful. Miss Newton's skin is a thing of beauty to behold. Shall call Miss Robey today. Is school teacher here. Bishop graduate. Returned home at 12:45. Miss Bates gave me a slice of excellent watermelon. Retired about 1:20. Houston, I believe, will be a good town.

SATURDAY SEPTEMBER 6, 1930

After breakfast this morning, I set out to find Mr. Carter Wesley, who had promised to arrange a meeting for me there next Sunday. It is so difficult to find one's way about Houston that I actually passed his office several times without knowing it. He is a man of many diversified interests. A lawyer, real estate man, publisher, insurance man, among others. A graduate of Northwestern, and he is only a young man. About 32 or 35, I should judge. Introduced me to a Mr. [George] Webster, Mr. [J. Alston] Atkins, and the entire office force associated with him. Made a fine publicity man for me by telling them all about my work.

Tried next to sell them books. Mr. Webster squirmed out of it by pleading lack of time—he had to prepare the payroll, go to the bank, and so forth. Then failed, perhaps deliberately, to be available at 2:00 p.m., at which time he had promised to see me. Mr. Wesley, after the expenditure of much persuasion by me, finally succumbed when I appealed to his ego. Told him his name enrolled would induce others to do likewise. Must send order in November $9.98 C.O.D. Mrs. [Clara] Workman, formerly a school teacher in New Orleans [and] now head of one of the departments in the insurance company, took a set to be sent October 5. From there went to the Pilgrim Temple to see Prof. [James] Ryan. Found him in the most beautiful colored-owned building that I have ever seen. A fine golden-colored brick building, triangular in shape, standing at the apex of West Dallas and Bagby streets. Is four stories in height, has roof garden also. Its interior amazed me, for here was a real attempt at beautification such as few other Negro-owned buildings can boast. The very lifts of the steps were decorated; the walls were inlaid with white marble and granite. The elevators, too, were the roomiest and most elaborate that I have seen in any race building. There were stores, of course, on the first floor—one a white pharmacy.

I told Mr. Ryan, who is also secretary of the Pilgrim Life Insurance Company, how much I admire the structure and how I ranked it first among those I had seen. Thanked me and told me there must be resident in the same some truth, for several people who are qualified to know had told him the same thing. He is a short, stoop-shouldered man rather thickly set with a large head sitting upon broad shoulders. His complexion was brown. He seemed to be an inveterate smoker, puffing on a long cigar during our entire interview. His straw sailor sat on the back of his head.

Told him of my mission. Recounted the gist of the books to him. He bought.

Went back to Odd Fellows Building. This is also a fine structure on Louisiana Avenue. Clean, too. Could do nothing there. Went then to Bastrop

Street after securing directions from Miss Henry. Found Mr. [Johnny] Walls. Had been expecting me. Is mailman, president of the Postal Employees' Alliance of Houston. Medium height, looks like an Indian.

Told me several things of interest respecting the Negro postal employees here. Said post office was rotten when he entered 12 years ago. The old-time Negroes had made it difficult for a young, intelligent colored carrier to get a job. Were hat in hand. Took all manner of abuse and would remove caps when going into office buildings. Tried also to keep young Negro out. White superintendent would not take an intelligent colored man. Preferred more ignorant who were more pliable. Walls got in, however. Organized the Postal Employees' Alliance and fought to break the power of the old Negroes and to bring in men who were eager for promotion through efficiency rather than merely holding their jobs through their obsequiousness and loss of manhood. Refused to take off cap when entering office building. Considered it part of uniform. Like soldier. Whites tried to prevent his delivering mail in business district. Failed.

Alliance, through his persistence, caused a shake-up in the office here two years ago. Succeeded in bringing the post office inspector to Houston from Washington. The result of his investigation was the dismissal or demotion to carriers of all the supervisors and even of the superintendent himself. Inspector congratulated Walls.

Told me that Negroes could have had a post office supervisor, but none was qualified. W. E. Scott was the only Negro so fitted but he, unfortunately, was addicted to drink. There was a fine opportunity for a Negro to gain such a position, for of all those fired, according to Mr. Walls, not one had the necessary qualifications for the position.

There are in Houston now, Mr. Walls informed me, more than 100 Negro mail carriers. This is more than half of the total force which stands at almost 200. In contrast to this imposing showing, there are only eight Negro carriers in San Antonio, the second largest city in the state, none in Dallas or Fort Worth, and none in Waco.

This is not because of prejudice, according to Mr. Walls, but largely because of the inclination of the Negro to follow the line of least resistance, afraid of little resentment of whites. Complained they could not get applications. If such were so, they could be secured with ease from New Orleans or Washington. The chief reason is they do not take the examinations. If they pass among the first three, they would stand an excellent chance of getting on if many took the exam. Where only a few take it, of course, such a consummation is minimized. An example of mass examination taking was described by Mr. Walls when he told me that as soon as examinations are announced, the Alliance gets the examination blanks and distributes them among the Negroes. At the last ones held, 1,400 Houston Negroes took them. Of these, 600 passed and nine were put on as carriers.

Walls has already manifested his worth to the service by a suggestion of his which, when adopted, saved the post office the services of more than 200 substitutes for 3 hours in getting out the extra heavy Monday mail. Where they had hitherto worked 5 hours on Monday delivery, he had them come in 2 hours on Sunday and arrange the mail. The postman, thus saved this trouble, had nothing to do but deliver. The superintendent congratulated him upon his suggestion. Told me he also asked the superintendent for Negro supervisors. Latter told him it would be hazardous for him to do so since there were none when he came. Promised to give Negroes monopoly in carrying the mail. Walls threatened to hold him to his promise. Says another vicious practice among the whites in order to keep the Negro from promotions is to give them freedom to break rules, wink at it, then to hold this as a club over their heads when they seek higher positions. The Alliance seeks to correct this by persuading the carriers to observe the rules. Walls even attacked the superintendent about it. He is a very interesting talker and impressed me as a hard and conscientious worker. Sold him books. Said he would not be without them since he had children.

From Walls, called on Rev. Pleasant. Most active minister here. Told me meeting could be held at his church next Sunday, September 15, at 3:00 p.m. Bought books, $9.98 C.O.D.

Went to Y.W.C.A. to see Mrs. Johns. Had gone. Waited for me until 4:00 p.m. Carter Wesley gone, too. Waited, trying to get in touch with them over the phone. Failed. Called on Prof. [J. T.] Fox, head of junior college here. Thinks Howard finest school in country. Graduated in 1904. Friend of Dean [Oliver W.] Holmes. Houston has three colored high schools. Only city in South in this respect. Teacher must have degree to teach in grades here. Fox kept me talking an hour. Bought nothing.

These streets in Houston are terrible. This applies, of course, to the Negro sections. They are unpaved and most of them are as narrow as alleys. They are almost death to automobile tires, with rocks just dumped into holes and even on the surface. The section around George Street is terrible. Sanitary conditions are bad. Water in many cases is outdoors; so are the toilets. The same can be found in all the wards. The homes, of course, vary from fine brick or frame structures to hovels. All in all, the Negroes are more progressive here than anywhere else in Texas. They have a dry goods store, pharmacies, insurance companies, a newspaper, two fine office buildings, grocery stores, a large theater, gasoline stations, etc. There are about 80 physicians and about 15 dentists.

There is a fine school system, the city is well churched, too well perhaps. There is an amusement park for colored and several dance halls. There is no exclusive society here. Houston is too young and democratic.

Wanted to go to New Orleans early today. Poe, however, has sold nothing. Holds me up. I believe he is doing more socializing than anything else. Can't carry him much longer, for I too must live.

Negroes, due to the lack of employment, are steadily converging upon the cities looking for work. Today we met a young fellow from Santa Fe, New Mexico. Had been doing well upon the ranches nearby shearing sheep at 70 cents a pound for the wool. Sister persuaded him to come to Houston. Jobless for weeks, finally found work as hod carrier. Hard work. Such laborers get 40 cents an hour. In this case, much of this went for car fare, which is 10 cents here.

To add to the glutted labor market, whole families of swarthy, dirty-looking Mexicans in Ford trucks, touring wagons, or whatnot, have crossed the border and flocked to the cities, displacing Negro labor by their willingness to work for wages varying from one quarter to one half. Yesterday I saw several streams of these Latin Americans coming into town. Today I saw several other parties bivouacked near the Negro business district. They were being taken in hand by a white planter to pick cotton. Entire families will do this work to the detriment of the Negro cotton picker. Mexicans don't mix with Negroes.

Sunday September 7, 1930

Wanted to leave for New Orleans today. Had so many checks only. Poe broke. Didn't feel like traveling that way. Tried to find Mrs. Johns to make final arrangements for talk next Sunday. Not at Y.W.C.A. Went to her home. Finally met her returning. Took my pedigree (vita), so to speak, for write-up in paper. Wrote letter for me, which I dictated, to [E. E.] Oberholtzer, school superintendent, asking him to give me chance to speak to Teachers' Institute next Saturday. Enthusiastic worker in cause. Gave me names of Mr. [C. W.] Rice and others. Went to see Mr. Carter Wesley. Took information for write-up in paper. Will take up collection. Needed. Cashed $4 check. From Wesley's went in search of dinner. Thelma[?] Scott failed to heed our hints, took no books. Went out to Mrs. Barnes's, Poe's former sweetheart in third ward. No meal here. Will take books next Sunday.

Returned to town. Ate first meal at 6:00 p.m. Home.

Called on Mrs. Henry. Spent most enjoyable evening of trip. Artye Meka Henry.

Monday September 8, 1930

Up at 7:00. Determined to sell sufficient books to get to New Orleans. Ate at 8:00. Went to see C. W. Rice at Pilgrim Building. Interesting. Knows economic conditions in Texas. Says within ten years Negro will not be able to get a decent job in Texas. Negroes losing not only because of general depression and fact that whites will not tolerate Negroes working while they are idle but, also, because of Negroes' failure to refine their efficiency on job. Unreliability, etc. Arranging mass meeting for me for Tuesday evening. Wants me to speak on economic conditions of Negroes. Around 6:00. Wants me to speak to Teacher's Convention at San Antonio in November. Promised, if they would bear expenses. Will run write-up for me in papers. Promises to take orders for considerable number of *Negro Wage Earner.*

From him, went to Mrs. [Ella] Wall's. Interested. At school. Will take books Sunday. Wants me to speak to Institute. Told me to get in touch with Mr. Cunningham. Called upon Mrs. W. L. D. Johnson, principal of Blackshear school, while Poe called upon Dr. Johnson. Mrs. Johnson interested. Will take set and try to persuade school to do same. Called on Dr. Martin, druggist. Will take set Saturday. Joe Gathings promises to start [others] buying by taking all of books, so to speak. Will pay me $4 after which I shall refund. Not psychology. Went then to get check cashed. Terrible time finding banks. Missed Mrs. Terry. Poe failed to find Prof. [E. O.] Smith.

Left for New Orleans at 3:00 p.m. Passed ranches, rice fields, sheep farms. Cows, hogs, pigs, sheep, horses—all grazing in road. Dangerous to traffic. Passed vast rice fields. Also fig orchards. Across Neches and Sabine rivers. Great lumber district. Saw large warehouse filled with railroad ties. Arrived Beaumont [at] 6:00 p.m. Negroes hard put for work here. Refinery.

[No entries were found for September 9–11.]

Friday September 12, 1930

Met President [James P.] O'Brien of Straight College.[1] Elderly, white. Grieved because he was not asked to speak at Miss ____ Weller's[?] reception

1. Straight University was founded in 1869 by the American Missionary Association, the missionary agency of the National Council of the Congregational Church. In 1915, to reflect the true scope of the institution's work, the name was changed to Straight College. It consisted of a four-year college, a two-year junior college, a high school, and an elementary school. In 1927, the total enrollment was 396 students, of whom 129 were in the college and 230 in the high school. The similarities of purpose, mission, and organization between Straight College and New Orleans College led to the merger of the two institutions in 1935 to form Dillard University. U.S. Department of the Interior, Bureau of Education, *Survey of Negro Colleges and Universities,* 371–81; and Brawley, *Two Centuries of Methodist Concern,* 293–98.

last night. Then added: "I am getting tired of the fact that we white people identify ourselves with colored people only to have them draw the line."

Straight has two nice wooden buildings. Tony Lafon School in rear. Took order. Paid cash.

Went to New Orleans University.[2] Three large brick buildings. Old. . . . President [O. E.] Kriege, white. Says Woodson uses too much ink. Style wretched. Personality creeps in. Can't get service at [Association] office. Mail still comes in name of former president, despite fact that he has written Woodson about it.

Sitting in Arcadian settlement. Married Indians and Negroes. Dark people. Look something like Portuguese or Italians.

[No entries were found for September 13–14.]

Monday September 15, 1930

After breakfast called upon Dr. [B. J.] Covington, who had given me his card yesterday and asked me to call upon him. An elderly dark man of medium build. Resembles my uncle. Told him so. Marveled but remarked it might be possible, for his father was sold south from Virginia and had no recollection of any relatives. Frequently did happen in slavery. Congratulated me upon my speech of yesterday. Thought it was extremely informing. Gave me cue to ask him about the books. Told me he would have to consult his wife and daughter. The latter is a well-known pianist, [Ernestine] Jessie Covington.

I remarked that the Houston Negroes had the best potentialities for development of any group of Negroes I had yet seen in the South. Told me he agreed but that there were some things which nullified to some extent these advantages. For instance, he never drives with his wife if he can help it, neither does he ride with her on the streetcar, because he feels that the Negro is so prone to be insulted by any person with a white skin that it is impossible for him to be a man in the presence of his women. To resent such an insult as any husband, father, or sweetheart would, would be tantamount to suicide. Just last week, he told me, a rich Negro woman

2. In 1873, the Methodist Episcopal Church merged several educational institutions to establish New Orleans University. By 1927, the school enrolled 838 students: 309 in the college, 399 in the academy, 56 in the grade school, and 74 in other divisions—including a nurse training program through Flint-Goodrich Hospital. U.S. Department of the Interior, Bureau of Education, *Survey of Negro Colleges and Universities*, 262–70; and Brawley, *Two Centuries of Methodist Concern*, 267–92.

driving a fine car was ordered by a policeman to take her car off Main Street and leave it on Milam Street (Negro district) where the "niggers" belonged. She was infringing upon no law. Took the officer's number and reported it to the Chief of Police. A citizen's committee of Negro men also waited upon the chief to the same end. All the satisfaction they received, however, was that he would investigate the matter. Later it developed that he did not know who was on duty there at that time. It is such things as this, according to Dr. Covington, that make the tenure of the Negro so insecure that it is equivalent to sitting on a volcano. One never knows when an eruption will occur. If he could secure reciprocity from the state of Illinois, he stated that long ago he would have left the South. But an examination is now required of all the older physicians and he feared he could not pass it.

Called upon Dr. Forde, a West Indian physician. Regretted he could not subscribe. Introduced me to his friend, Dr. Roett, a fellow West Indian. The latter is tiny. I daresay he weighs no more than 100 pounds. Was much interested in the books, especially *African Myths,* for his son. I would not stop at that, however. It was the set I desired to sell him. Told me to come back tomorrow morning after he had consulted his wife. I always fear this excuse. The wife in such cases usually kills the sale. Then, too, if the man is writing the check, he ought to be able to decide for himself and make his wife a present. However, I shall return.

Went to the Y.W.C.A. Met Miss [Marie] Jefferson, Miss [Marion] Hill and Miss ____. Very charming ladies. Reassured Mrs. Johns that she should not feel badly about yesterday, since she had put forth every effort to make the meeting a success. Told me that the teachers were absolutely uninterested. I knew that. Said she called many personally, inviting them to the meeting. They retorted that they knew everything about "niggerology." No one could tell them more. God help them. Most of them are Prairie View graduates, which means that their education is relatively meager.

Tried to see Mr. [O. R.] De Walt, the movie man. Too busy. Would see me tomorrow at 2:00 p.m. Went, thenceforth, to find [Henry Lee] Moon and Poe. Was to meet them at Harmon's at that hour. I arrived 10 minutes late.

Went to Bill Jones's filling station. Interesting old man who spoke at the Democratic Club meeting Sunday. Is a "race" man. Patronizes colored exclusively. Paid a white doctor $12 just to taste the medicine a Negro physician was prescribing for his wife. Negroes had advised him to get a white doctor, said Negro physician was killing his wife. To appease them he secured the white doctor. Told him of Negro physician and medicine he had prescribed for his wife. Asked whether Negro doctor had administered proper treatment. White doctor tasted medicine. Told Jones he would have prescribed same. It cost Jones $12.00, however, to have the medicine tasted, but it confirmed his faith in the Negro physician. Told also of the arrest of his son on flimsy murder charge in Michigan. Friends advised him to get white lawyer. Others admonished him to let son hang. He did neither. Secured colored lawyers, Harold Bledsoe, classmate of mine, and his partner. His boy was acquitted, and once more his confidence in his race was vindicated. So staunch a race supporter is he, that he lost twenty-five cents a case on soda water in order to patronize a Negro soda water manufacturer. That was during the time he kept a store. Most interesting man. I could have talked to him indefinitely. Promised to come to hear me speak tomorrow night and to take a set of books. Introduced us to his daughter who came up at that moment.

From Jones, called upon Professor W. L. D. Johnson, principal of Blackshear School. Was registering students for junior college. Could not see me until tomorrow morning at 7:30. Promised to take a set then. Dr. Martin at the drug store, who promised to take a set and pay cash last Saturday, pleaded an unexpected financial obligation. I grinned, but got him to consent to my sending him a set $9.98 C.O.D. on October 1. He may take them and then he may not.

En route to dinner met Miss Jefferson and Miss Boozer, Y.W.C.A. workers. Chatted with them about 15 minutes. Miss Boozer is charming.

After dinner I had an engagement with a Miss Gladys Davis, to whom Mrs. Harmon had introduced me. Poe had to get a haircut before going to see Miss Newton. The upshot of the matter was that Moon had to take me to Miss Davis, a school teacher, then return for Poe and take him out to Miss Newton's. Moon was supposed to return for me. After spending a few hours with Miss Davis, who proved a charming companion, I returned home by trolley and foot. When I reached home, Moon and Poe had already arrived. They expected I would be peeved, but I came in laughing. They had gone for me, but were told I had departed about ten minutes ago.

Tuesday September 16, 1930

Pretty full day. After breakfast called upon Dr. Covington, father of Jesse Covington, well known pianist. Told me his wife wanted but one book. Ended by selling him a set. From there went to Dr. Forde's office. In the interim, I had sent Moon and Poe away in the car with instructions to meet me at Harmon's store on West Dallas Avenue at 2:30. Jotted down couple of topics at Dr. Forde's office, while Miss Landy, his office girl, smiled and chatted with me.

Called upon Dr. Roett. Brilliant West Indian physician. Is smaller than I, thank heaven. Asked me to return at 6:00 p.m. On my way downstairs, met Carter Wesley and [James] Nabrit, who had sponsored the meeting for me Sunday. Took me to dinner at Y.W.C.A. Nabrit, who had been dean at Pine Bluff School (Arkansas A.M.& N. College), told me Howard paid biggest salaries.[3] I replied that Tennessee State did. Informed me he had been offered $3,000 to teach Political Science at Howard. I doubted him. [Ralph] Bunche, a Harvard M.A., took the position [in 1929] for only $1,800 a year. Salaries at Howard are and have been low, comparatively speaking, on account of the relatively small appropriation for such in the federal grant. We argued to no conclusion.

After leaving Nabrit, was called by Mr. De Walt, the colored theater owner, who sat at a table behind us. Had been trying to get an audience with him for almost two weeks. Invited me to come to his office. Has the best theater in the South owned by Negroes. Took me through it. Is large, well-decorated, and has latest sound recording equipment.

Spent two hours talking with him although both of us pleaded busy. He told me of the precarious economic position of the Negro, his difficulty in finding jobs, and commented upon the utter levity with which the Negro viewed his position. He was laughing while Rome burned, dancing while his very economic structure crumbled beneath him. De Walt considered the Negro teacher almost hopeless, unconcerned with Negro History and its benefits upon the children. Most teachers, he added, assume a know-it-all attitude while the children who come under them seeking inspiration, instead are crushed by the vicious propaganda and theories circulated about Negroes in the textbooks. Told me of failure of Standard Life Insurance Company. He was a director in the ill-fated company. Had also a bank and trust company, as well as the insurance company. At first board meeting De Walt said he warned against the evil of interlocking directorates at the head of which were bishops, including Bishop [John] Hurst (now deceased). Seeing that the same directors were at the head of the banking and trust company and the insurance company, he tried in vain to have it changed. Also protested successfully against directors coming to Atlanta to meetings at expense of company. Had three directors' [meetings] reduced to one. Company distributed dividends of 20 percent before it was able. When the

3. James Madison Nabrit, Jr., earned an undergraduate degree from Morehouse College and a law degree from Northwestern University in 1927. He left Arkansas A.M. & N. College in 1930, and, at the time of Greene's visit, he was practicing law in Houston. Later, he became secretary of Howard University. He also served as dean of the Howard School of Law, and, in 1960, he became president of Howard University.

crash came, it was the result of poor business management. Moon told me later, [Robert R.] Moton tried to save it. Influenced Rosenwald to do so. Told Rosenwald $250,000 was needed. When latter sent experts there, they reported that $500,000 was necessary to save it. Rosenwald then withdrew his support.

Mr. De Walt subscribed, although he had two of the books. Substituted two. Asked me to be sure to call upon him when I again returned to Texas. A fine man. Good business acumen, yet never attended a business school. A graduate of Prairie View.

I phoned Harmon. Asked him to tell Moon and Poe to meet me at dinner at 3:30. Called upon Mr. [Charles Hosewell] McGruder, Grand Secretary of the S.M.T. or something (a fraternal organization) [United Brothers of Friendship]. Took a set. Referred me to the President, Mr. Robinson. During a long talk, he told me that he knew Maude Cuney-Hare, the author of *Antar of Araby*. Robinson was a good friend of her father, Mr. [Norris Wright] Cuney, who, he added, excelled as a politician and speaker in Galveston, Texas. However, he regretted his inability to subscribe. Pleaded lack of funds. Later I called upon Mr. Davis, of the same order. A very humorous man. Kindly and interesting. Sold him easily. Said I made him part with his money quicker than any other person he had ever seen.

Went thenceforth to Dr. Roett's office. While waiting for him, the mother of his office girl, who goes to Fisk, came in. Tried to sell her. Gave me the old answer: "will see you later."

When Dr. Roett was available, he told me he could take but one book—that was *African Myths*. That was letting him off too easily; therefore, I stayed with him until I persuaded him to write a check for $4.00 initial payment on a full set. He has a boy and I played upon that knowledge.

It was now 6:30. Rushed to eat dinner. Did so in ten minutes. Poe and Moon had already eaten. Rushed home. Had to jot down notes, dress, and get to the hall in one hour. On my way home, as will happen when one is in a hurry, we suffered a flat tire. Delayed us fifteen minutes. Arriving home, jotted down a few notes, changed shirt, and hurried to the hall.

Arrived. Found crowd disappointing. Spoke more than an hour. Topic: "Present Unemployment Among Negroes: Causes and Remedies." Was applauded. People thought it was wonderful. I felt as if I had done fairly well.

C. W. Rice, the head of the Colored Laborers Association, also spoke. He sponsored the affair. Is an eloquent speaker, very emotional. Would make a good preacher. Is heavy, dark, and of medium height. Wanted me to go from church to church here with the speech I delivered. Told him I had no speech. Rice asked me to speak at Teachers' Convention at San Antonio, in November. He is trying hard to save jobs for Negroes here. Has a task on his hands. Dr. Shadowin, a pompous man, sporting a goatee, spoke and read letters purporting to give the people confidence in Rice. They were from a Houston banker, a Galveston merchant, and the Texas and Pacific Railroad. Rice is very long winded. Talks so much he ruins a man's speech. Gave me $6.00. Said the crowd was small. I shall speak no more, however, without setting price in advance. Moon had to leave to keep engagement. Poe and I came home. Moon was still out at 11:30, when I retired.

Wednesday September 17, 1930

Immediately after breakfast, I called upon Dr. Shadowin to secure his order for a set of books. The worthy doctor does not have as well equipped an office as Dr. Covington, Forde, and others. Pleaded broke after congratulating me upon my speech. Persuaded him to let me send him a set of books $9.98, C.O.D., by October 1st. There is always more than one way of getting these fellows.

Went over to Carter Wesley's office in the International Longshoreman's Association building. Is progressive young man. Scarcely 32. Interested in insurance, newspaper, and financing company. Wanted him to cash checks. Not in. Saw Mrs. Workman. She had a letter already written to me with a money order enclosed. Gave me the $4.00 instead. It was welcome. Got Mr. Webster, the assistant editor of the newspaper, to subscribe. Had promised to take a set Saturday before last. Took one after much coaxing. But $9.98, C.O.D.

From there we stopped by Mr. De Walt's, the movie owner. Told me that after my speech last night, business and professional men should pay all of my expenses. Invited us to attend his theater gratis. Also invited me to stop with him whenever I visited Houston.

We left Houston about 3:00 p.m., after pulling a deal with a filling station man, whereby I secured a fairly good tire to replace one that had been badly worn. The proprietor asked $1.50 difference, but I "jewed" him down to $1.25. Think I got the better of the bargain. Hope I did, at least.

Now to take stock of Houston. A big sprawling city—largest in Texas, second largest in the South. The total population about 300,000, of whom approximately 70,000 are Negroes. Latter form the most enterprising and most appreciative group of race people in the South. Some idea may be gleaned by the subjoined jottings:

NEGRO BUSINESS: There are about eight colored gasoline filling stations, one finance company, several chain drug stores and independent drug stores, several insurance companies, beauty shops, two hat shops, one dry goods store, ten or more groceries, one soda water manufacturer, several ice men, several fruit dealers, and a theater. The busiest Negro lunchroom is here. It is called the "New Day."

SCHOOLS: Houston has the best colored school system in the South. There are about twenty schools, including three senior high and one junior college. They are all large, airy, brick or adobe buildings. This is especially true of the Phyllis Wheatley High School, which for sheer artistic beauty surpasses any colored school that I have yet seen, even Dunbar High School in Little Rock. There are more than 400 Negro teachers, nearly all of whom have degrees. Indeed, now no person can teach, even in the grades, without a degree. This fine system is due to the efforts of Mr. Oberholtzer, who is Superintendent of Education for the city, and who formerly held that position for the state of North Carolina.

LIBRARY FACILITIES: Houston has the largest colored library in the South. What it needs is a younger and more energetic librarian.

AMUSEMENTS: Most of the recreational facilities include the dance halls, miniature golf courses, pool rooms, etc. The best Negro theater in the South is owned by Mr. De Walt.

POLITICS: Negroes can vote here, but many will not pay poll tax to avail themselves of the privilege. This is a common fault. A movement is on foot here under the auspices of the Negro Democratic Club to correct this. If Negroes could vote, it would go far toward correcting the many inequalities under which the Negro labors.

LABOR: Most of the Negroes are engaged in common labor such as stevedores, laborers in factories, filling stations, garages, porters, janitors, etc. Most of the women are domestics. Some men and women work in laundries. But Negroes are hard pressed economically, for whites are driving garbage wagons, cleaning streets, waiting in hotels, acting as doormen, working on road construction, and on railroads; in short, doing all sorts of work that Negroes formerly did. C. W. Rice has Negro Houston fairly well aroused over this situation; but, in general, although thousands of Negroes are out of work, they laugh, dance, and drink corn whiskey while their economic foundation is crumbling about them. To add to their economic woes, Mexicans are coming in droves and taking their work from them. About 10,000 to 15,000 Negroes are unemployed, I am told.

RACE RELATIONS: Very good here for a Southern city.

10

Texas

Completing the Canvass

Wednesday September 17, 1930 (Continued)

Galveston

Arrived in Galveston about 4:40 p.m. Had to cross from the mainland to the island upon which Galveston is built. A beautiful sight across the water as we sped over the bay. The city is beautiful. Wide streets with stately palm trees in the center lead into the city. It is very well laid out, the streets being either numbered or lettered.

Work is scarce here for Negroes. Work at the wharves has been reduced due to the competition of Houston as a port and the lower dock rates at the municipal piers there. Then too, Mexicans, Italians, poor whites, and others, are taking this work more and more from the Negroes since the depression. Port Arthur, Beaumont, Corpus Christi, and Orange all are cutting down Galveston's once vast commerce, due to their development as ports, and reducing jobs for Galveston's Negro laborers correspondingly. Most of the latter are dependent upon loading or unloading boats chiefly with cotton. There are huge warehouses and cotton presses here. Negroes, I was told by a Negro janitor, have been driven out of the hotels. Whites have their places. I had a chance to verify this statement during a drive along the beach. Not a Negro was seen in the hotels as waiters or bellboys.

Tried to sell Dr. Mosely books. Passed the decision on to his wife. Convinced her easily. Failed to see him, however. Was called out on confinement case.

After dinner called upon Professor G. W. Gibson, the principal of the high school. Lives in a white neighborhood on the main residential street of the city. An elderly man, about 75. What a wealth of experience and knowledge he has! Told me he heard Wendell Phillips speak at Wilberforce University in 1877. Went there as a student in 1876. Bishop Lee taught him. Later, Lee became president of the school. He knew Maude Cuney-Hare well. She is author of "Anter of Araby," which appears in *Negro Plays and Pageants.* He taught her. Mr. [Norris Wright] Cuney, her father, was a personal friend of Professor Gibson's. He was Collector for the Port of Galveston under President Harrison. Was the biggest Negro in Texas. Few excelled him in handling white men. He was also one of the greatest forces in organizing Negro schools. Active in organizing Negro labor. He also organized the Cotton Screwmen's Association of Galveston. Made it possible for whites and blacks to work together on the wharves. When he died, said Mr. Gibson, more white men followed his funeral cortege than ever has occurred here for either black or white. He died about 1897. Lived on Avenue J, a few doors from Professor Gibson. Latter invited me to speak to his students tomorrow morning. I promised to do so at 8:30. Left very much impressed with him.

After securing a room at the Orlando Hotel (God help us) where we paid just 50 cents for the night, [Henry Lee] Moon and I went down to get a view of the Gulf at night. We drove along the boulevard that borders the gulf. The city is protected by a sloping sea wall about 12 feet high. All along the beach were imposing and picturesque hotels, most of them of Spanish construction. The colored people also have a dance hall and a few homes fronting the boulevard. But just as the pavement usually ends where the Negro section begins, just so were the beautiful lights on the boulevard discontinued in front of the Negroes' property. In the white hotels, all the help we saw was white.

After driving along and watching the swashing waves of the gulf from a distance, Moon and I walked down a pair of steps until we sat just above the huge rocks against which the relentless waves rolled and broke unceasingly. The water was beautiful. It was bewitching. There was no moon and the white-capped billows, starting afar out on the black water, appeared like a great light in the distance. Then suddenly they took shape and began their surge landward. As they rolled nearer they seemed to stretch out lengthwise at a furious pace, until they reminded me of legions of enormous snow-white horses galloping madly down the gulf only to swerve and pour their foaming, undulating forces toward the shore. But terrific as were their onslaughts, the unmovable rocks met their countless charges, received their tremendous impact unshaken, and hurled their watery ranks backward, broken now and reduced to a fine spray. There was something in the relentless courage and tenacity of the water that seemed to grip and hold me. I remarked to Moon that, though these same waves now retreated again and again like beaten gladiators, they would return with greater force for the next onslaught and continue to crush against these rocks until, ages hence, they would ultimately triumph by reducing these seemingly irreducible crags to fine and shimmering sand. Both of us left with a deeper appreciation of the spiritual and with a more assured conviction that after all, despite the various appellations He may bear, there exists a greater One than man somewhere, regardless of his nature, who rules wisely over the destinies of us mortals.

Thursday September 18, 1930

At 8:15 I was in the office of Principal J. W. Gibson at the Central High School, where I was to speak to the student body upon some phase of Negro History. The school is a large white stone building and makes an imposing appearance from the outside.

While waiting for the assembly period, Professor Gibson told me some very interesting things about himself. These were reinforced by certain certificates and commissions hanging on the walls of his office.

In the first place, he served as Consul for Liberia at Galveston for 29 years. He was appointed by President McKinley in 1901, August 12th. His commission from Liberia also hangs on the wall and bears the signature of President [Garretson Wilmot]. He was also a four-minute speaker during World War I and bears a certificate of honor from the federal government and a letter of congratulations signed by President Wilson. It bears the date of November 29, 1918. This letter commends him for his valuable services during the war. Mr. Gibson also has the dubious honor of having been the only man to "whip" Jack Johnson, former heavyweight champion of the world. Jack was formerly a pupil of his, went as high as the fourth grade, but would go no further. Mr. Gibson said he had to whip him for fighting, the very field in which he was to rise to world renown. Told me that he regretted doing so many times, for he might have crushed his pugilistic talent.

It was now time to speak. Addressed about 600 students. They gave rapt attention. Perhaps I did well, for one of the teachers, congratulating me afterward, told me that I must have been a Lincoln [University in Pennsylvania] man. They are noted for oratorical ability, which I sadly lack. Mr. Gibson told me that I could have held them there all day. I felt encouraged because I know it is difficult to keep the attention of high school students when one is speaking to them. I know how boresome it was from my own high school days. Professor Gibson tried to persuade me to stay in town to speak at his church Sunday, but I told him it was impossible. He then subscribed to a set of books for the school library.

His next act was to show me through the school. First we went to the library. It is called the Rosenberg Library, in honor of Harry Rosenberg, a Swede, who came to Galveston in the 1850s, became a slave owner, and amassed a large fortune. Left $500,000 for a library for whites. Negroes and friends fought to gain appropriation from the bequest for a Negro library. Were successful enough to secure a school library, which is open also to the public. Mr. Gibson is in charge. Naturally, it is small and inadequate for the demands made upon it. The chemistry and physics laboratories are well fitted out. The laboratories were in the finest condition possible. I went with Mr. Gibson through the carpenter shop, the sewing department, domestic arts department, and the like. All made a fine impression upon me. Left Mr. Gibson with regrets, for he is full of historical facts.

Went to post office, where I sent a report to Dr. Woodson. Sent largest number of orders yet—19. [John Wesley] Poe sent 15. Ought to be heartening to Woodson.

Before leaving Galveston, we rode around the sea boulevard. Beautiful view of the gulf. Saw Fort Izard with its big guns mounted to protect the coast. Also saw smaller batteries. The whole city is on an island that commands the entry to the Southwest.

Insofar as Negro labor is concerned, Negroes are finding difficulty here securing employment. In a laundry here, I noticed that only on the hot steam processes were Negroes used. White girls and men performed the other work. Whites do the hotel work, collect garbage, and clean the streets. We saw Mexicans working on the railroads. The longshoremen's work is divided among Negroes, Mexicans, poor whites, and Italians. The Negro longshoremen are partly organized. Negro business is negligible here as compared with Houston and other Southern towns. The people ascribe it to the unusual freedom enjoyed by the Negroes which tends to retard economic striving among them.

Left Galveston at 12:30. Arrived in Houston, after an uneventful ride, about 1:40. It seemed as if we would never be able to get out of Houston. The city occupies an incredibly large area. It is difficult to enter, to find one's way about, and to leave. Roads are not posted into town. Names of streets, indicated on curbs, are outside the line of vision for the motorist, hence exasperating when a stranger tries to find his way about.

Passed Rice Institute with its vast and beautiful campus. It is noted for its track men.

We gained an excellent insight into the labor struggle between the whites and blacks here, for even farm labor is being rapidly taken away from Negroes. En route to San Antonio, we were accosted by a white man just outside Houston who hailed us thusly: "Say Uncle how far are you going?" I replied just a short distance, not wishing to accommodate him on account of his rough appearance. Asked him where he was going. Told me he was going to pick cotton, or to do anything that he could find. This statement caused me to reflect all the more seriously over this problem, for full well I understood that the entry into these jobs by poor whites meant the corresponding displacement of Negroes. Work is exceedingly scarce when this happens.

We also passed Mexicans in droves. These people migrate from the border cities of Mexico in search of employment in the cotton fields, on the railroads, or in domestic service. Whole families were in motion in Ford trucks or in wagons. Near Richmond, what I supposed at first to be a truck full of cattle turned out to be a family of Mexicans with the children peering through its boarded up sides and dangling their tiny hands through the openings. In many cases they had paused for a rest, either under a tree, along the road, or in a vacant field. Some of them traveled with all their meager household effects. Most of them had mattresses only. Near Richmond we passed migrating Mexicans in covered wagons and could discern mothers suckling their babies as we passed. It reminded me of frontier days. There are so many of these Mexicans about Richmond that we were informed by a white man that part of this town had taken the soubriquet of Little Mexico.

We saw many interesting sights. One was a vast ranch. At least it was vast to me. Large flocks of cattle grazed contentedly in the green fields. In addition, we saw large hay fields where enormous stacks of hay were drying. This was the first time on the entire trip that I had seen hay being made in such quantities. We also crossed the Colorado River at Columbus, a small town about midway to San Antonio. Passed rye, wheat, and oat fields, too. At another time we had to stop to allow a large herd of cattle to cross the road. They were being driven by dark, mustached, sombreroed Mexicans. They rode as easily as if they had been bred to the saddle.

Had trouble with the car about fifty miles from San Antonio. Developed that it needed oil. Strange, and we had just had it changed yesterday.

Moon nearly frightened us stiff by the manner in which he negotiated curves. Many times I feared that the car would overturn. He uses his brake for every turn instead of slowing down. On right-hand curves he was terrible. Was quite relieved to take the wheel myself.

Arrived at San Antonio about 8:30 or quarter of nine. Entrance to the city is not imposing. Disappointed me. Tried vainly to find Williams's Drug Store. Could not locate Mrs. Williams. Finally had to go to a rooming house on Mosquito [Mesquite?] Street, owned by one Mrs. Banks. She has a fine home with excellent accommodations—shower, bath, etc.—at 75 cents a night. She told me one Mr. Ned Pope, among other prominent people, had stopped here during the summer. He is a good friend of mine from New York City. Promised to give me his address.

I should add that the Negro business district is East Commerce Street, and, as usual, one has to cross the railroad to get to it. It is a continuation, however, of the chief business street of the city. Two sets of railroad tracks, the Kansas and the Texas and Pacific, cross the city. Negro business here is small in volume.

Retired, hoping to leave for Mexico at 5:00 a.m. Did not wish [Oliver] LaGrone to know that we were in town for I did not wish to take him along. Does not fit in and might tell me about it later.

Friday September 19, 1930

Left San Antonio at 7:00 a.m. Went through Mexicans' quarters on Laredo Street. Saw very few Negroes there. Everything smacked of Latin America. Black-haired men, women, and children; stores—grocery and fruit—bearing Spanish inscriptions; even the odor was foreign, something akin to that unmistakable Italian odor in my hometown, so common to sections inhabited by Latin peoples.

After leaving San Antonio behind for fifty miles or more, we came into the badlands of Texas, mesquite, cactus, and sagebrush on every hand. The land is arid; vegetation meager and stunted. Whole areas are untenanted. The only means of farming here is by irrigation. And here I saw, for the first time, crops grown under this system. This was in progress about Dilley and further on toward the Rio Grande River. We were now in the mesa or tableland regions. A new road is being built from Dilley to Encinal, but not a Negro was working on it.

Mexicans appeared everywhere. Indeed it seemed that we were already in that country. They owned most of the farms or worked as farm laborers; they performed the labor on the roads and the railroads. Others were traveling with their families toward the cotton areas of central Texas. For this the Ford of ancient vintage was employed. Little children were packed into these carry-alls like animals. We passed many of them with the children peering through the grating of their temporary moving prisons like sheep going to the slaughter. These Mexicans are friendly and called out greetings to us or gazed at us as if we were curios.

Reached Laredo at 10:50. Had trouble with the car. Just barely was able to limp to a garage. Mechanic diagnosed trouble was due to bad distributor points and broken motor spring. Cost $4.00.

Laredo is almost a Mexican city. [It is] just across the river from Nuevo Laredo, Mexico. Very little prejudice here. The reason is that very few

Negroes live here. Indeed they are so rare that people stare at us. The streets are terribly narrow. Spanish, as well as English, adorns the signs and business houses and one beholds hundreds of beautiful dark-skinned, black-haired Mexican girls, many of whom cannot be distinguished from Negroes. They have so reacted to minimize prejudice that the whites allowed us to use their toilets and to go into their offices in order to drink from their water coolers.

Since we could not use the car, we walked across the bridge over the Rio Grande. The river itself is very narrow and at this season of the year is almost dry. Before crossing the river, each of us exchanged $2.00 for its equivalent in Mexican currency. We received four pesos and twenty centavos. One American dollar is worth two pesos and the twenty centavos, equal to ten cents in our money, was given as a bonus for exchanging the money on this side. The transaction took place at a Mexican money broker called a "Ganbia." The border is not fortified. Only United States customs officers and a few soldiers stand guard on the American side. They said nothing as we passed. On the other end, however, we expected to be held up by the Mexican immigration and customs officers. We escaped such, however, although everyone driving automobiles had to submit to having their car and effects carefully scrutinized. The Mexicans are very courteous.

There is a vast difference between Laredo, Texas, and Nuevo Laredo, Mexico. The streets are unpaved! There is no sewerage, and the only things that carried a thoroughly American air were the traffic lights and electric sign boards. We decided to eat our breakfast in a Mexican restaurant, and thus partake of the food of the country. We dined at the Cafe Mejico. The soup was thin gravy, the vegetables not well cooked, the steak was tough, the macaroni absolutely tasteless. And the bread frijoles [tortillas], God help me, appeared to be just flour and water rolled out extra thin, something like a pancake, and cooked on top of the stove. Was not even brown. Could not eat them, but brought two away as souvenirs. Cost us one peso (25 cents). Gave the fellow a 10-cent tip.

Our next move was to visit the market across the street. It held many varieties of fruits and vegetables that were utterly foreign to me. Everybody had something to say to us, and *buenos dias, amigo, companero,* etc., greeted us on every hand. They recognized us as strangers and therefore gullible. And everyone wanted to sell us something. Bought nothing, however.

Engaged an old Mexican hackman to drive us about the town. Wanted 25 cents a half hour at first. "Jewed" him down to treinta [thirty] centavos (15 cents). He took us to the beautiful park, one that would do credit to any in America, and to the most beautiful bathing house and swimming pool I have ever seen. It is open from 5:00 to 2:00. The Mexicans count their time and hours from 1 to 24, a very sensible method. We Americans could learn much from their system. We had our guide take us to the post office. It is a very small affair. The postmaster could speak no English and in my halting Spanish, I had difficulty in making him understand that I desired just cards and stamps. Post cards and stamps that correspond to the plain American penny post card cost cuarto centavos (or 2 cents American money). A letter costs 10 centavos (5 cents). Strange to relate, we bought up all the post cards and all the cuarto centavos stamps (2 cents) the post office had. We bought, even then, only 20 of each. It was laughable, for such could not happen in an American city or town.

Went to a night club. A slick, handsome Mexican introduced us to some beautiful Mexican girls. We danced. Then the Mexican offered us our pick of the girls, who were kissing us and making suggestive and seductive movements as we danced. We could have our choice for dos pesos ($2.00) [$1.00] for an hour and cinco pesos ($5.00) [$2.50] for the night. We broke out of the girls' embraces, gave them a tip, and left.[1]

Saturday September 20, 1930

Ate breakfast at Hotel Hamilton in Laredo, Texas. This time we did not dine in the kitchen, but at a table prepared for us in the banquet hall, looking out onto a beautiful patio. The sun was just rising and flooded the attractive Spanish courtyard with brilliant light. Service was excellent. For once I could get anything I ordered. I paid for it, however, for my breakfast cost me $1.15. Left Laredo with many regrets.

Passed through the same arid lands filled with mesquite, cactus, and sage. Little vegetation. Very few towns. Very sparsely peopled. I stopped to pick some prickly pears as souvenirs. Also a cactus leaf. Got my hands full of thorns from them.

Frightened fellows twice. Once nearly turned over car trying to get back on the road. When we arrived in San Antonio I turned into South Laredo Street so quickly that I nearly ran into two cars which, under their drivers' urge, scattered in both directions. Made the trip in four hours and 15 minutes. The first 37 miles in 45 minutes.

[Went to our lodging place], cleaned up, had suit pressed, and went downtown.[2]

[No entry was found for September 21.]

1. The final paragraph is missing from the entry in the diary notebooks, but Greene included it in a draft of a transcript he made.

2. The entry for September 20, 1930, is in a small notebook and is missing from the main notebook diary.

Monday September 22, 1930

Milner with us all day. Went to Douglas School. . . . Made speech in assembly hall.[3]

Tuesday September 23, 1930

Rose at 6:30. Half an hour later than I had intended. Upon awakening, I was dreaming that a horde of Japanese, who had invited me to their country, had attacked my home, and in the bloody encounter that followed, I had crawled under the bed. It was an old wooden affair and after getting under it, I found that the supports for the springs held me fast and I could not extricate myself. Meanwhile, the Japanese were torturing me with knives. 'Twas a relief to wake and find that it was all a dream.

Bade Mr. Milner farewell. A fine chap. Hated to leave him. Has been of inestimable service to me. I promised to write him. He can never fail as a businessman, for he sells himself.

Left San Antonio at 7:30. A fine town. Mexicans make up the majority of the 200,000 people. About 16,000 of them are Negroes. Not so progressive here as they are in Houston. Yet they have best colored library in the South. Have also a fine dining hall and a large auditorium.

[Additional Notes from Small Notebook]

Met Dr. W. L. Turner, author of *Under the Skin in Africa.* Teaches our text at Sam Huston College.

Told me of movement to build language for Liberia that won't be English. Are *Americanizing* instead of *Christianizing* the Africans. Trying to stop it. Would not have missionary work stopped.

Saw two all-Negro street working gangs at Austin. Mexican (whole families) migrating through Texas in search of work.

Mr. C[harlie] wouldn't allow us to use toilet at Austin. Passed buck around from one to another. Mr. C[harlie] (all whites) picking cotton between Austin and Waco. Here one sees nature at its greatest beauty.

Filling station man passed buck about toilet.

Arrived Waco about 8:30. Went to Paul Quinn. Met the Dean. Told me attendance so small, may have to lessen school term and have school six days a week.

Met Mr. Jackson. Teacher of history. We stayed in teacher's dorm. Cotton growing everywhere.

3. This entry is from jottings in the small notebook.

Wednesday September 24, 1930

Saw Dr. Hood this morning at breakfast. Wanted to talk to students. Matron Mrs. Jones told me school had only 50 students. Latter must pick cotton to help pay expenses. Ought to close school in my opinion. Dining room located in basement. Unclean. Had breakfast: water (warm), egg, salt pork, and toast.

Dallas

[James Cecil] Wilkey came into the Y.M.C.A. grinning. Said he had sworn to kill me. Was going to buy gun. Had written and telegraphed everywhere. Waited a week. Met Mr. [L. Virgil] Williams, head of [Booker T. Washington] high school. Fine building, but too small. Wilkey spoke to Parent Teachers Association last night. Sold three sets of books. P.T.A. took one set for school. Negroes starting ____ company here in Dallas.

White men on trucks and work with broom and shovel cleaning streets in Negro district of Dallas. Negroes play at gas station as we buy gas. Drove 32 miles in 40 minutes. Seventy-one miles in one hour and 37 minutes. Drove entire distance without pause. Mexicans clutter roads. Work in fields. Whites, too. Negroes to great extent excluded.

NEGRO BUSINESS: Dry goods stores. Watkins Dry Goods store, largest one situated on Hall Street. Deals in ready-to-wear clothes. Several drug stores. Several gasoline stations. Candy stores, fruit stands. One miniature golf links owned by colored. Those owned by whites dying down.

RECREATION: Have park, swimming pool, tennis courts, volleyball courts, etc. Have community center. Theaters owned by whites. Can go to only one theater, [the] Majestic, owned by whites. Three clubs, Y.M.C.A., beautiful pool, etc. No Y.W.C.A. Expecting to build one soon.

SCHOOLS: Only one senior high school. System can't compare with Houston.

CHURCHES: Plenty.

LABOR: Mostly common labor. Filipinos replacing Negroes in hotels and stores as porters and the like. Mexicans replacing them in common labor. Ten Negro contractors. Colored electrician. Building laborers. At some hotels, Negroes replaced as bellhops. Negroes again replaced them (Hotel Adolphus).

DOMESTIC SITUATION: Bad. Children neglected because mothers have to work.

En route to Sherman, passed Southern Methodist College in Dallas. Earlier saw Texas State Teachers College at San Marcos.

Wilkey tells me of one Dr. [J. W.] Anderson, a Negro millionaire. He made money in real estate. Owns property in Los Angeles, etc. Bought no books, however. Gave Wilkey $5.

Passed beautiful Memorial Park.

Green cotton on one side of road. Brown corn stalks in other fields.

Looks like fall here. Fields, except cotton, turning brown. May be result of drought. Negroes picking cotton. Beautiful scenery approaching Sherman. Fine concrete road, after traversing turtle back highway. Saw Sherman fifteen miles in the distance.

Sherman, Texas, prosperous looking city. City Hall on square. Still unbuilt. Entire front torn out. Evidences of fire still visible. Cannon fronting it. Work has been started upon tearing down remains. Negro quarter was burned also. Had drug stores, groceries, restaurants, barber shops, etc., in white district. Moved now to Negro district.

Five thousand Negroes in Denison. Common labor in their hands. Mexicans work on railroad. Whites and blacks in service. One doctor and one dentist.

Fine roads in Oklahoma. Dirt roads best yet. Concrete, too, for greater part of remainder of distance from Madill to Ardmore. Latter is city where Oklahomans crossed border to lynch Negroes.

Arrived in Ardmore, Oklahoma. LaGrone met Ragsdale, undertaker. Directed us to Mrs. Allen, 622 E. Main Street. Negroes have businesses on this street; drug store, lunchroom, etc. Met Miss Miller. Had to pay Poe's bill. I have $5.50. Moral tone of town seems low.

11

Oklahoma

Thursday September 25, 1930

Left Ardmore, Oklahoma, at 6:30. Negro girls and women going to service. Ardmore pretty city. Has four-story hotel, beautiful Presbyterian church. Saw Negro bellhop in hotel. Beautiful concrete road stretching for miles before us. Landscape undulating. Sparsely settled. Saw pecan trees growing wild. Much grazing. Little diversification. Cotton and corn. Saw cotton being taken to gin in carts. White women working in fields. Overalled. Price of gas rises. Eighteen cents a gallon here. Eight-and-a-half cents in New Orleans. In Texas, ranges all the way from 13 cents in Houston to 17 cents in Dallas. Passed stone monument on highway stating road was built by prison laborers under governorship of Gov. Trapp. Reprehensible, ought to be prohibited. Yet may act as a deterrent to crime.

Rolling country. Many of the hills divided. Passed limestone rock of "Ordovician Age." Strange rock formations for miles. Grass and few stunted evergreen trees attempting to grow here. Passed ranch—my first sight of one. Beautiful stretch of scenery equalling in vastness that of Texas. Sloping, scantily clad hills and vales looming for miles and miles before us. Saw cattle grazing on brown stubble forcing its way up between the stones. Saw beautiful Turner Falls tumbling over the rocks nearby. Windy and cool this morning. This entire section seems to be a vast series of sugar loaf rock formations. Very little vegetation. Rocks later give way to swirling verdant valleys watered by beautiful creeks. Passed consolidated district school. Passed vast alfalfa hay field. Alfalfa was cut and baled in the field. Done by reaper and binder.

Saw white men, women, and children picking cotton. Wide, green valleys stretching for miles. Numerous oil wells outside Oklahoma City. People from Texas, Arkansas, and Arizona migrating there with household goods. Whole families in autos and trucks. Others walking. Fields of oil wells. Agriculture more diversified here—oats, wheat, corn.

Arrived in Oklahoma City at 10:00 a.m. Busy-looking city. Odor of oil everywhere. City shows signs of newness. All kinds of enterprises and businesses. Mixed indiscriminately on S. Robinson Street. Groups of tall buildings on W. Grand and N. Robinson streets. Also Main Street.

Some Negro business on W. Second Street: Men's furnishings, newsstand, drug store, funeral parlors, billiard halls, cafes, shoe repairing, women's wearing apparel, newspaper *(Black Dispatch)*.

Professor [Inman E.] Page is the principal. Entered Howard 1868, went to Brown University. Graduated from Brown in 1876. He and classmate [were the] first two colored graduates. Became clerk for General [O. O.] Howard (after whom Howard University, Washington, D. C., is named). Page helped him wind up affairs for Freedman's Bureau. Turned findings over to War Department.

I spoke to the high school students and teachers. Must have interested them for they paid rapt attention. Mrs. Brown, music teacher, told me I gripped them. Encouraging.

Later, found Page experienced interesting career. He delivered class oration at Brown University in 1877. Vice President of Lincoln Institute, Jefferson City, [Missouri,] under a white president. For 18 years served as principal of Lincoln. Turned out white teachers. Replaced them with Negro teachers. Twenty-four years later called back and took leadership of Lincoln. Oklahoma City officials would not let him stay. Made such attractive offers (1921–1922 [left Lincoln and came] here and [in] 1922–1923 [back] at Lincoln Institute) would not let him stay at Lincoln. Brought him back here. Succeeded at Lincoln by present incumbent (Dr. [Nathan B.] Young).

In Oklahoma City, one of the hotels has supplanted Negro bellhops by whites.

Went to Langston University.[1] School visible from distance of more than six miles from road. Beautiful road.

1. In 1897, the Territorial Legislature of Oklahoma established the Colored Agricultural and Normal University of Oklahoma, Langston University, as the land-grant school for African Americans in Oklahoma. Inman Page, whom Greene met in Oklahoma City, served as the first president of the new institution. In 1927, the enrollment was 240 students. The faculty consisted of twenty members, nine of whom also taught high school courses. U.S. Department of the Interior, Bureau of Education, *Survey of Negro Colleges and Universities,* 457–70; Schor, *Agriculture in the Black Land-Grant System,* 142–44.

School a revelation to me. Has a fine lot of buildings, fine administration edifice, new dormitories for both men and women, and laid out in accordance with some preconceived plan. Must rank with Pine Bluff, Prairie View, and others. Best evidences of planning in its layout. Unlike latter.

Met President [Z. T.] Hubert again. Plain man. Has been president three years. About 50, I should judge. Member of a famous family. Told me librarian would take care of books. I could not find her. Met "Zip" Gayles (teaches English, also football coach), Hamilton, and other frat brothers. Ate dinner in dining hall. Good food in pleasant surroundings. Contrast to Paul Quinn.

Left in a terrific sandstorm. Blew dust in clouds across treeless plains. Common here. Novel to me. At one time feared it would overturn car. Beheld an inspiring natural phenomenon. Sun hidden by such thick clouds of dust that it appeared "whitish." Looked like the moon obscured by clouds. Could peer at it without its blinding the eyes.

Arrived at Oklahoma City at 10:35. Spent time trying to find accommodations. One woman wanted to fight me almost, because I asked whether the bed linen was clean. It was dirty. I asked her to replace it. She flew into a rage. Had been drinking. Most Negro hotels here are houses of ill repute. Four other hotels were so filthy, or so open in their catering to transient couples, that I refused to stay there. Finally accepted least of evils. $1.00 a room. Paid for two fellows. Left me with $3.00. [James Cecil] Wilkey is broke. [John Wesley] Poe and [Oliver] LaGrone sold five sets apiece today, I heard.

Friday September 26, 1930

Left Oklahoma City at 7:30. Wilkey hit a car. No damage. I lost my briefcase and books. Returned to Oklahoma City from Edmond to find them. In vain. Met Dr. Whitby, staunch supporter of work. Had read of us.

Interviewed Mr. Wells, Secretary of Education for Oklahoma, Mr. Hadley, and Mr. Duke[?]. Latter tells me of plans for colored education, its obstacles, and progress. Is a Georgian. Asks my opinion of Langston. Feels I ought to leave books there on exhibit. Would do better, in his opinion.

On to Tulsa. Beautiful roads. Wide rolling plains. Diversified farming—corn, peas, wheat, oats, hay, etc. Reminds me of the Midwest.

Oil wells are everywhere. One just a mile from Main Street in Oklahoma City. Yesterday an oil well was discovered, yielding more than 80,000 barrels a day. Wells are scattered all around in Oklahoma City. Seventeen miles from Tulsa the whole countryside was dotted with wells and storage tanks. In Drumright, oil wells were even in the backyards of houses. The latter frequently are huts, showing the unexpected oil boom. All the surrounding hills were lined with oil wells. Many refineries here. Passed Sinclair, Texaco, Consolidated Oil Refineries, and also Tydol. Hundreds of oil wells in operation. Prairie Pipe Line Company, ____ Petroleum Company. Gas burning. Wasteful. Agriculture is forgotten. Oil tanks everywhere. Oil wells everywhere. Approaching Tulsa. Entire country is oil rich. LaGrone tells me that [an] 82,000-barrel oil gusher in Oklahoma City is owned by Negro. That is, the land. White oil company has leased it. Negro gets one-eighth of the flow as royalty.

Car gave much trouble en route. Everything goes wrong at one time. Lost my books, briefcase, diary, am broke, have $1.78, and auto is on the blink. Mechanic at Langston worked on it. Told us the steering apparatus needs repairing. Cost 75 cents.

Tulsa

Arrived in Tulsa at 7:30. Went to Century Life Office. Manager, Mr. Wheeler, called Hotel Small. Asked $3.00 per room. Finally went down to $2.00. Refused it as fabulous. Told boys no Negro hotel was worth that much per night. Mr. Wheeler took us to Hotel Small. Expected to see fine lobby. Small, etc. Astonished to find plain water keg in hall with common water pail to catch waste water.

Mr. Small told me that he experienced the riot horror of June 1, 1921, when Tulsa's Negro section was burned by a crowd of infuriated whites. He was suffering from appendicitis. Whites forced him and others to come out of buildings with hands above heads. Assured them they would not be hurt. Even helped him to carry out things. Put them in a field. Then fired homes. Negroes and whites fought one day.

Saturday September 27, 1930

More than 3,000 Negro maids in servants [service?], over 1,000 [male?] servants and butlers employed here. Whites not making much inroads here. Did few years ago when K.K.K. was in power. Frightened some Negroes. None has gone back. Tulsa great oil town. Negroes work in oil refineries, except there are none in oil fields. In oil supply factories, Negroes may drive a truck or be a porter. Common labor: 70 percent done by whites, that is, street cleaning, railroad labor. The Paving Company, largest construction company in Oklahoma, employs 50 percent whites and 50 percent colored. White garbage collectors. Negro has contract to collect and dispose of human filth. About forty Negroes in municipal employments. Fifteen policemen. Have one motorcycle cop, four plainclothesmen, ten patrolmen. Negro can arrest a white man. M____ says he was on the force himself. Arrested whites. Racial feeling not strong. Mr. ____ told me that not a Negro received a nickel for his property loss here after the riot in 1921. Told me every building in this block was burned to the ground. Corroborates statement of Mr. Small. Not a penny of riot money collected.

Steinberg Drug Company here employed more than fifty Negro boys. Forced to let them all go, I was told, because of stealing.

Mr. Tyler told me of cemetery, Crown Hill. Eighty acres. Beautiful place. Owned by whites. Lots sold by Negroes now. White businessman, high powered salesman, failed. Mr. Tyler succeeded him. Doing fine. Took Negroes to put it over.

Mr. ____, a Massachusetts man, tells me he has a Negro, Bert Hayne, employed as a superintendent in his oil wells. Thrifty, dependable. Building home. Has farm he rents. Told me also of biggest ranch in world at Kingsville, Texas. Twenty miles from front gate to ranch front door. It has 1,200,000 acres. Excoriated exploiting Negro ministers. I agreed with him.

Some Negroes are chief engineers in extracting gasoline from gas. Fifteen percent of gasoline comes from this source. Gas is condensed under pressure and cold. Treated with naphtha. Has higher gravity and lower vaporization point. Therefore better for gasoline.

Dr. [P. S.] Thompson, druggist, tells me that the Tulsa riot was led by city officials—the mayor and chief of police. Latter had to leave the country. In Mexico now. The mayor has been in retirement ever since. Showed me picture of devastated area stretching from Arch[er] Street north to Standpipe Hill and from Hartford east to Boston Street. Not a house or building standing (85 blocks burned). Said thirty Negroes and more than 100 whites died.

Dr. Thompson told me Negro uses ballot here to extort concessions from city. Seven precincts out of one hundred entirely Negro. Have just recently secured a hospital, municipal center, library, park, and a police precinct where Negroes arrested may be booked, admitted to, or refused bail without being carried uptown. Balloting entirely controlled by Negroes.

Whites fooled Negroes during riot. Told them all to go to convention hall or ballpark and they would see that they would be taken care of. Negroes did so. Whites then took furniture, looted homes, and burned them. Took Negroes' effects. Later in the fall, many Negroes even found their furniture or clothing in white homes. Mr. [H. O.] Abbott of Tuskegee found all of his furniture in a white home.[2] Secured a warrant. Recovered

2. Upon reviewing these entries, John Hope Franklin informed the editor that Abbott attended Tuskegee and once worked there. Abbott was a printer.

it. Mrs. Ferguson did the same. School teacher found white woman wearing her suit. After the Negroes found they had been fooled, they began fighting. Corner Greenwood and Archer was a bloody ground. Armed Negroes on church tower ran whites from machine guns on hills. Two hours later, whites found it out. Then riddled church.

There are several good Negro schools.

BOOKER T. WASHINGTON HIGH SCHOOL: Only 132 children in the school system when Mr. [Ellis W.] Woods took charge of it 18 years ago. Now 3,200; 400 in high school.

[SCHOOL] CLINIC: Dental clinic excellent. Day hospital wards for boys and girls. Medical clinic also a revelation. Tonsils removed each Wednesday. Every conceivable apparatus.

GEORGE W. CARVER SCHOOL: One of the most beautiful and best equipped yet seen. New one-story building. Fine cooking room. Sewing room with electric sewing machines. Beautiful grounds. City spending $140,000 in equipment for building.

Passed first high school; small yellow frame building. Mr. Woods had it built eighteen years ago. Four rooms and office.

Jake J. Simmons of Muskogee. Scofield Building. Organized the first Negro Royalty Company of Oklahoma with authorized capital of $100,000 on September 14, 1927. Mr. Hickman of Tulsa, Negro royalty broker.

Poe tells me that a Dr. [Tollie] Harris informed him his people were never slaves. Lived in Atlanta. Father practiced medicine before the Civil War. Invited General Sherman to dinner.

SUNDAY SEPTEMBER 28, 1930

Spoke at A.M.E. Church. Mr. [Simon] Berry has largest bus company and service station. Has $110,000 in equipment. Hires thirty-two men. Mr. Berry taught auto mechanics at West Tennessee College. Went to Dodge plant as porter. Rose to bench workman. Animosity of white workers caused him to quit. Began as taxi driver. Started in May 1919. From that time no white man has ever touched his car mechanically. Bus Company had fight. Tulsa Street Railroad Company and others infringing upon its territory. Operating upon six-month permit. Fight. Put vote to people for franchise. Mr. Berry entered in competition to vote for 15-year bus line. In October 1928, Berry won, receiving greater number of votes cast.

MONDAY SEPTEMBER 29, 1930

Things were critical financially for us today. None of us, save Poe, had any money. Or rather, I should say the latter was the only one who acknowledged such. LaGrone claimed to be penniless, but we all believed that he was withholding from the fellows. He is peculiarly unethical. Expects one to "carry" him when "broke" but as soon as he gets money refuses to recognize his obligations. We ate, therefore, a very meager breakfast in order to lessen the strain on Poe.

Went to see Mr. Tyler. Referred me to his wife [Judith?]. Promised to take a set at the meeting tonight. Saw Mr. [Theodore] Baughman, editor of the *Oklahoma Eagle.* Is a big jovial man of German extraction. Looks to be wholly white. His entire plant, then the *Oklahoma Sun,* destroyed in riot of 1921. Ruined him. Started it anew, only to have Dr. _____, who claimed that he could pay the debts of the paper, take it over. Failed. Baughman then started the present *Oklahoma Eagle.* Publishes a clean paper. No scandal headlines. Wants write-up of us.

Went to Dunbar School. Enormous plant. Professor Hughes is the principal. Have recess all the time. One class always is open under physical education director. Unique. Latest one-story school.

Next went to Booker T. High School. Professor Woods unable to preside at meeting tonight. Suggested Dr. [B. A.] Wayne or Dr. Crawford. Referred me to the librarian for books. Received an order for six. Had three of the set.

Had first act of discourtesy. Professor Woods had one of the teachers take LaGrone and me to the cafeteria to get lunch. Regular hours were over, but being strangers and guests of the school, we expected, as had been done in other instances, that the dietitian would waive the rule and accommodate us. Instead of that, without apology or even the civility which one would naturally expect in such a case, she told us abruptly, "We have food, but the dinner hour is over." With that she turned on her heel and walked away. I was dumbfounded, but then I had been told that such things were to be expected in Tulsa.

Sold Mr. [Clyde] Cole, assistant principal. Also sold Mr. [A. J.] Lee, a science teacher now teaching Negro History. Is enthusiastic over the subject. Tulsa is the third Negro High School teaching Negro History. Here it is compulsory. Mr. Lee had prepared a syllabus for the class in order to hold their attention. The text, *Negro Makers of History,* he finds too juvenile for the senior high. *Negro in Our History* is too advanced. Wants to publish syllabus in mimeograph form for teachers' use.

Sold the Y.W.C.A. Mr. Jackson, the undertaker, referred me to his wife [Eunice]. She wants them. Both promised to see me at the church tonight.

Trouble now to find suitable master of ceremonies, someone to introduce me. Mr. Carter could not. Has several meetings. Suggested Drs. Wayne and Crawford. Called both. Dr. Crawford accepted. Need someone to prepare way for me. Everyone tells me Dr. Crawford is capable.

After dinner, revised my notes for the speech. About 50 people at the church when I arrived at 8:30. Started to speak about 9:00. Dr. Crawford failed to give me the send-off such as C. W. Rice in Houston or Milner of San Antonio gave me. Yet, I held the attention of the 200 people who attended for an hour and ten minutes. And small wonder, for what I said, although common, was vital. Mr. Jackson told me it was marvelous. Mr. [W. L.] Hutcherson told the audience that they should have given me 10 times as much as they did. But the audience, although appreciative, was poor. Most of them were unemployed laborers. Some were in overalls. Not so many of the business and professional element came as I expected and as promised to attend. The honorarium amounted to $3.85. Curiously enough, this labor situation is patent enough to these people so much so that much I said was commonplace.

One man even so remarked to Hutcherson. But the very commonness of it militated against the Negroes devoting to this problem the attention it merits.

Oh, yes, I mentioned Jackson's undertaking business as he desired me to. Promised to take books if I did. Will see him this morning. Mrs. [Jean] Goodwin congratulated me heartily. Told me she had never heard such a speech. Disagreed with me in one instance only and that was where I counseled the Negro to stop building segregated businesses only like Poro Skin Whitener or hair grease. Pleaded with them to develop general business all people could patronize even as the Jew has done. She feared Negroes would lose monopoly on hair and skin preparations. He has already lost that. Invited me to speak to her class at Booker T. Promised to do so at one o'clock. Mr. Goodwin extended me an invitation to dinner at 4:00 p.m. Accepted.

Mr. Hutcherson, Y.M.C.A. secretary, took me in hand afterwards. Wants a story of 500 words concerning my speech for the newspaper. Also told me that Saturday he attended a luncheon and dinner downtown given by white Y workers. Was treated cordially. Whites had wives there, too. Also showed me a letter from the Interracial Conference to attend a series of traveling investigations on the Progress of the Negro in the South in November. The entire party of whites and blacks will travel by pullman chartered by the conference. Hutcherson is undecided whether he can attend. The expenses will exceed $136.00.

Upon arriving at the hotel, found note from fellows to call Mrs. [Carrie Booker] Person. Did so. Fellows came for me with ladies. Took us to restaurant. Ate chili con carne for the first time. Girl, Miss [Ernestine] Neely, made it. Afterwards took Miss Yvette Davidson back to Sand Springs, five miles from Tulsa. Teaches there. Parents reported to be very wealthy. Live in Muskogee. Sand Springs greatest manufacturing town in Oklahoma. Has box factory, wood factory, castings plant, oil refineries, furniture plant, and many other industries. Town founded by one Mr. Page. Virtually owned it. Now dead. Miss Davidson told me it has one of the most beautiful parks she has ever seen.[3] About 15 colored teachers there. Have high school there, too. Returned one o'clock.

The fellows told me that LaGrone had gone home. Said not one word to me. Asked them to meet him in Muskogee on Wednesday morning. What a cowardly, base act. He was in my debt about $20.00 and sneaked home like a common thief in order to avoid paying his just debts. He cannot plead the fact that he did not see me, for he and I were together until after 3:00 p.m. As long as I shall know him, I could not employ him, neither could I recommend such a person for a position. It is appalling to believe that a college man would crucify his honor and his name for just a few paltry cents.

TULSA: School pay was all year round. Get check in June for three summer months.

LABOR CONDITIONS: Common labor done mostly by whites. Garbage collecting too. Work on street railways divided. Roads also. Negroes do most of building labor.

Tuesday September 30, 1930

My first act this morning was to borrow LaGrone's books and call upon Mr. S. P. Berry, the keeper of the finest service station and garage owned by Negroes and operated by them. He also owns a bus line. Commended him for his fine enterprise as before. Told him unconsciously I had mentioned his business last night and urged its patronage by Negroes. Told me of lack of race consciousness among our people—many of them. Would pass his garage to have cars repaired by white shop, when they have money, then come to him asking credit when they are broke. Sold him easily.

Next to Mr. Jackson, the undertaker. Congratulated me upon my speech. Had to go to court. Told me to see his wife at 410 North Elgin Street. Fear [he] is giving me the "run around," as we term the attempt of a prospect to dodge us. Made engagement with him this evening. Called upon Mr. Donaldson and Mr. Tyler, theater manager and real estate operator (cemetery), respectively. Both out. Went to the high school to speak to the

3. John Hope Franklin, in reviewing these entries for the editor, questioned the contention that Sand Springs was the leading manufacturing town in Oklahoma at that time. Franklin pointed out that Page was white and that blacks were permitted to visit the park one day a year, perhaps two.

little tots in the adjoining grade school. Met Miss Algerita Jackson, charming teacher.

Mrs. [Jean] Goodwin, who had invited me to speak, was surprised to see me. Felt I would not have time. Told her as busy as I was, I could not forego an opportunity to tell these children something about their past.

The proceedings of the assembly amazed me. There is a platoon system here, and an assembly period for different classes every hour. Here the pupils conduct their own exercises with class president, secretary, treasurer, etc. They are thus taught self-expression and self-confidence, and also obtain the experience of public speaking in this manner. They likewise exchange views. At any rate, once they had assembled, a little boy 8 years of age called them to attention, had them repeat the Lord's Prayer after him, snapped them into attention, and had them salute the flag while the teacher stood on the sidelines and I faced them petrified with astonishment. After singing the Negro National Anthem (God forgive both me and my race) he ordered them to sit down. They did so with as much dispatch as soldiers.

Mrs. Goodwin then introduced me. I spoke for about 15 minutes. No man could have desired a more appreciative audience. I told them facts about the Negro in Africa and entertained them with tales from *African Myths*. Then the teacher asked whether they had any questions to propound. Did they? They just bombarded me with queries, and intelligent ones, too. This is more than any adult gathering has done on the trip. And I must confess that had I not read, comparatively speaking, so much on the Negro, their confidence in me would have been utterly shattered. They asked how the Africans lived, fought, went to school, what kind of clothes they wore and why, the nature of the climate, the resources, whether the Africans had presidents or kings, why the white man owns much of Africa, and a host of others.

Mrs. Goodwin and Miss Jackson were elated. The children went out beaming. They shook my hand and asked me to come again, thanked me. I felt encouraged, elated that I was able to hold the attention of these children. Both Miss Jackson and Mrs. Goodwin implored me to return if I possibly could at 2:30 to speak to another class. At first I decided I could not, but the greater urge to disseminate the history of the Negro among these children overcame me and I promised. These children were from the fourth to the sixth grade.

It was now two o'clock; therefore, I utilized the time by calling on Mr. Carter of the investment corporation [Inter-City Finance Company]. Sold him very easily. Told him of my experience at the school. Thanked me so much for my interest in the children. Told him this was the most novel experiment I had seen.

My greatest surprise yet came upon my return to speak to the class. When after the preliminaries I waited to be introduced by Mrs. Goodwin, the teacher, something astonishing happened.

A little girl ten years of age rose, faced the class of seventy pupils, and in a manner that would have done credit to many a grown man or woman introduced me to the class in the following manner. "Boys and girls we have with us today Professor Greene. Professor Greene is traveling through the country in the interest of Negro History, and he is going to tell us about the boys and girls of our race in Africa and in other places. I take great pleasure in introducing Professor Lorenzo J. Greene."

I was too dumbfounded at first to move. When I finally rose to my feet it was difficult to find words to commend the class in general and this little girl in particular. Never had such an experience been mine, and I spent almost three minutes congratulating her. As at the other hour, I spoke about 15 minutes and reserved the rest of the time for questions. This second audience of children was just as attentive as the first. They leaned forward in their seats in rapt interest, unwilling to lose a single word. And how they plied me with questions. I enjoyed it, and both the pupils and I were sorry when the dismissal bell rang. Like grown men and women, as they passed by me, they congratulated me and shook my hand. Never have I been more gratified nor more satisfied with three quarters of an hour's toil.

Mrs. Goodwin and Miss Jackson showered me with their thanks. The former told me that last year she was assigned the assembly work and told to teach it. There was no guide. Therefore, she has the children instruct themselves, with her lead of course, in ethics, citizenship, health, cleanliness, and Negro History. It was the most interesting experiment I have ever witnessed in education. And for our children, it is invaluable, for it tends to instill in them that confidence that we as a race are so sadly lacking and so vitally need.

Went to Mr. Goodwin's for dinner. Wrote part of report of Monday night's speech for Mr. Hutcherson, Y.M.C.A. secretary, who wants it for the paper. Mrs. Goodwin is an attractive and young matron. Her husband conducts a haberdashery. I should state that my talk to the pupils brought me two orders—one from Miss Jackson and the other from Mrs. Goodwin. She gave me the address of Mrs. [E. O.] Proctor, her sister, at the Y.W.C.A. in New Haven, Connecticut.

Rushed home. Poe and Wilkey out. Knew they would be raving. Writing on report for Hutcherson as they entered. Complained about my not leaving earlier. Told them I would not leave penniless. Poe protested that by staying in Tulsa an extra day, he had spent his money. I told him I had done the same on the road when no one had anything and that whenever gas, oil, or repairs stared them in the face they looked to me. Therefore, it behooved me to remain here until I did sell something. They were silenced, but not convinced.

Finished report. Wrote about 5,000 words. Told Hutcherson in a note to take what he wanted and to forward the original to me in New York. Met Mr. Hickman in the lobby. Just returned from Sapulpa. Congratulated me on the meeting of last night. Went with me to find Mr. Hutcherson. Instead met Mr. Carter. Talked with him for a while. Told me [that] on my return to Tulsa he would have a surprise awaiting me.

While talking, I heard the most gratifying news that had reached me in some time. A man approached, whom Mr. Carter introduced as Mr. Lewis. He shook my hand vigorously—too much so—and asked: "Is this Professor Greene?" I replied, "Yes." "My daughter spoke about you," he returned. "Did you not speak at the school today?" I replied affirmatively. Then he told me that his little daughter had told him that Christopher Columbus did not discover America. "Who told you that," he asked her. "Mr. Greene," she returned. "Well, who did discover America," he queried. "Africans did," replied the daughter. "Negroes, our people, Mr. Greene told us, hundreds of years before Columbus." The father had been amazed. I was gratified, and the result of the girl's enthusiasm was the sale of a set of books to Mr. Lewis. He added that he now would have no peace unless he discussed the African and the history of the American Negro with her. It was his daughter who had read the minutes and led the singing at the second assembly I visited. She is 11 years old.

Back to the hotel. Met Lawyer Twine of the firm of [W. H.] Twine and [Pliny] Twine and [Chauncy] Twine of Muskogee. Frat brother. Told me there are 16 Negroes who are lawyers in Muskogee, all doing well. Rich Indian and Negro clients and constant litigation over oil well and claims keep them busy with big cases. Everyone here knows of the case of the firm of Chandler, Turnage, and Wesley, in which the latter two made more than $100,000 in cold cash in a case for a Negro client, Ingram, then left and went to Houston. Many Negroes have extensive holdings, Twine told me. Before Oklahoma reached statehood, the U.S. allotted lands of 100 acres in size to Negroes and Indians. They were not to be sold. Came statehood. Oil was found. And the whites, in order to get this valuable land, removed the restrictions upon the Negroes which forbade the disposal of their land. Naturally, many Negroes who had been given stony land sold it eagerly only to have oil discovered in this supposedly worthless soil. Hence the buyers became millionaires, in many instances overnight. Those few Negroes who still retained their land also became rich when an oil strike was found.

In order to get the Indians' land, however, a subterfuge had to be resorted to. The Oklahoma legislature declared the Indian a white man and forbade intermarriage between them and Negroes. In this manner, whites could marry Indians and inherit their oil lands, while the Negro was legally debarred from the same privilege. Then murder, kidnapping, fraudulent leases, and even unauthorized tapping of oil lands gave rise to many suits between whites, Indians, and Negroes. Lawyer Twine told me that just last summer he had searched the country for a Raymond Jackson, who owns large oil properties and who had been missing for nine years. Large oil firms employed him, paid all expenses and a handsome salary.

Went to the drug store. Mrs. Ferguson congratulated me on my speech on Monday night. Told me that ministers ought to give me their hour on Sunday morning and let me preach. Mr. Evans [. . .] said all present agreed with me that the Negro should stop building so many churches and fraternity (lodge) buildings and invest this money in some sort of gainful enterprise like a cotton mill, hosiery factory, or the like. They likewise felt the need of getting away from segregated businesses. From there we went to Africa and they also agreed with me that Christianity was ruining the Negro there. Mrs. Ferguson told me I ought to continue this work for the entire year.

Felt constipated and feverish. Drank bottle of citrate of magnesia. Back to the hotel. Twine will go with us to Muskogee in the morning. Expect to leave at seven o'clock tomorrow.

Wednesday October 1, 1930

Passed Barnsdale refinery where first oil refinery in the world was opened in 1860. Mr. Twine tells me 40–50 Negroes in Boley, Oklahoma, are worth $50,000. Own one of the best gins in South there.

Muskogee: Laboring work divided. Negro business in white section.

Stopped in Taft. Negro town. Everything owned by Negroes here. Ford garage.

Muskogee: Has a fine residential section for Negroes. Especially North 11th Street.

Luther Manuel and Mr. [T. J.] Elliot, oil millionaire and merchant, respectively, live next door and across the street. Mr. Elliot's store finest one I have ever seen. Business 50 percent white. Carry John B. Stetson hats only. Up to $50. Two thousand men and boys' suits, more than 2,000 women's garments and dresses. Only people in town to carry boots for $30 and large, wide-brimmed hats for $30. Eighty percent white or Indian trade.

Got into this business years ago. Uptown white merchants finally backed down off it. Could not sell them. [A] white came in to buy hat as I stood at counter. Salvation of Negro race.

Met Mr. Jackson, father of famous Raymond Jackson for whom search has been instituted the country over. [Raymond is the] missing owner of valuable oil land in Seminole field. Father told me they brought an imposter into court today who claimed he was his son. Of course, he denied him. But then, whites go to any length to wrest their valuable oil properties from Negroes. Has been to Africa, too.

Met Lawyer Turnage of firm of Chandler and Turnage. Just a young fellow. Harvard grad of 1927. Doing big business here. Handling famous Ingram case where millions are at stake. Told me of intimidation at trial town of Wetumka where a white walked into his office, stuck a gun in his side, and ordered him to give up the case and get out of town by noon of the following day. Turnage admitted he was frightened, but bluffed the white bad man by telling him he would give him until the next day at noon to shoot him. Told district attorney about it. Latter offered to protect him. Bought gun, practiced shooting. Next day, white called him at 11:45. Told him he had 15 minutes to leave. Turnage replied he had fifteen minutes to get him, and if he did not, he would get him. That whatever happened, he was going to try the case. Did and won it. Told me they handled business in the thousands of dollars. Could see it. Took over Wesley's and Wilkins's business here with Chandler.

Took me for a long drive through Taft, etc. Introduced me to some Negroes. Discussed everything. Played cards later. Saw beautiful Vets Hospital.

R. C. Woods, once Woodson's field agent, took me to the fair. Poor fellow could not invite me to dinner. On the verge of starvation, I hear. About to leave here. Woods told me that whites formerly did street cleaning and garbage collecting. The new administration gave Negroes some of the work here.

Thursday October 2, 1930

Met Mr. L_____ of the *Muskogee Lantern*. I gave him a write-up.

Chandler and Turnage: Best law office I have ever seen operated by Negroes. Have a suite of four rooms; long-distance telephone; private dictaphone; steel filing cabinets; loose-leaf notebook filing system; electric adding machine. All receipts filed.

Merchant Tailors: Work 7–8 tailors in the fall. Four regularly. In white section. Best Negro tailor shop I have seen.

Bought tires. One new and a secondhand one for a spare. These, with gas and changing of oil, left me with $6.00 and Wilkey with $2.25 to make a 500-mile trip to St. Louis. Decided we would have to stop in Kansas City to secure funds.

Felt aggrieved over the manner in which the group has broken up. [Noble] Payton and LaGrone took French leave—deserted. Now Poe departs—my friend and the only man on the entire trip, save Payton, with whom I could converse. He goes to Little Rock to see his fiancée. I hated to see him go. Will meet me in Chicago on Monday.

12

En Route to Chicago

FRIDAY OCTOBER 3, 1930

Wilkey and I left here [Muskogee] about 12:45. Drive over 100 miles of dirt road. Alternated with driving. Stopped in a store about 20 miles North of Vinita[, Oklahoma]. 'Twas 5:00 o'clock. Hungry. Stopped in a white lunchroom. White woman made us sandwiches and coffee. She served it to us on a tray in the lunchroom. No one noticed us.

Arrived in Kansas City. Saw thousands of idle Negroes, some lying about on the grass asleep. The population here is about 390,000; 40,000 Negroes.

Kansas City

LABOR: Most Negroes work in the packing plants. Have lost jobs more so than whites. Much is to be ascribed to the fault of the Negro worker himself. Mexicans doing most of the railway labor. Three-fourths Mexicans on street railways. Saw whites collecting garbage. Nearly all whites in these occupations. Nearly half of the building trade labor is now done by whites. When Mr. [F. S.] Smith [Paseo Department, Y.M.C.A.] came here seventeen years ago, he said, all were Negroes.

COMMON LABOR: White men do yard work. Hotels changed to whites. Baltimore Hotel: Negroes can't get in except in kitchen. Losing out in domestic service.

BUSINESS: Negro business small. Have grocery, drug, one haberdashery, one shoe store, and two florists. Fire Department (Negroes). Booker T. Hotel; best lobby of any Negro hotel yet seen. Has 50 rooms—$1.25 and up, with bath $2.00; per week $5.00. Has a repair shop. Negro newspaper *Kansas City Call*. Mr. [C. A.] Franklin, proprietor. Sam's Taxi Company, 14 cars,

28 uniformed chauffeurs and employees. Negro theater could not prosper, closed. Flying school, closed. Large Negro garage. Also barber shops.

We crossed the river to Kansas City, Kansas. It is a great industrial section. Has large packing houses (Armour and Fowler). Also Chevrolet plant.

Picked up a white man just outside of Kansas City. Brought him to Jefferson City. Was broke. Apologized. We assured him he was our guest. Don't know how he took it. Promised to meet us at the capitol tomorrow to go to St. Louis with us.

We arrived in Jefferson City, Missouri, at 7:30 a.m. The capitol is beautiful. Small town. Population about 18,000. Lincoln University sits on a hill. Called on President [Nathan B.] Young. Greeted me cordially. Gave us every hospitality. Ate supper and chatted for long while. Gave us the guest room.

Beautiful scenery all the way from Kansas City.

Saturday and Sunday October 4 and 5, 1930

The strain of the past day told upon me so that I was unable to awake before six o'clock. And we were supposed to pick up "Charlie" (a white man) at the capitol building at five. I pitied him out there in the cold. And "broke" too.

Decided to remain until 6:20 for breakfast in the dining room. Coach [Eric W.] Epps took us over. The dining hall is in the girls' dormitory. Is fair. The meal, however, was wretched—Post Toasties, one sausage, and bread. There was coffee or milk. It even proved unappetizing to me, low as my finances were. I had two dollars. [James Cecil] Wilkey nothing.

The school has fine potentialities for development. It is situated on a hill overlooking the city. There are some fine buildings, all of which are substantially built. The physical plant, however, cannot compare with Tennessee State, Langston, Arkansas A.M.&N., or Hampton. The girls' dormitories and the men's "dorm" are fair buildings. The administration building is poor.

However, a million-dollar building program extending over a period of ten years is now in progress. Already a new administration building and a new domestic science building are in process of erection. The campus, despite the fact that the school is situated on a hill that rises more or less abruptly, is beautiful. Especially in this time of year. The slopes of grass are well kept. Trees, shrubbery, and a golf course also add to its interest and beauty. The enrollment, according to President Young, is 200. The school has an excellent faculty and pays them well. There are 14 men and women with M.A. degrees here, out of a total of 22 teachers. Those having no such degrees teach in the high school.

Left the school about 7:45. Very appreciative to President Young and his wife for their hospitality. Could not find the president. He had not risen. Sleeps late on Saturday.

Went to the capitol to find our "white friend" ("Charlie"). Did not see him, although we drove around the building. Both of us were awed by its beauty. It is an exact replica of the national Capitol at Washington, D.C. Sitting on a bluff in the center of the city, overlooking the lordly Missouri and surrounded by a beautiful park, with cannons pointing their sinister noses at an unseen enemy from the river. This state capitol, in my opinion, in beauty must be ranked next only to that of the state of Texas in Austin.

Failing to find "Charlie," we decided to leave for St. Louis only to pick him up at a gasoline station on the way to Route 50. Had we taken Route 40 as we desired, we would have missed him. The only reason we did not go that way, which is concrete in its entirety, was our lack of the wherewithal to pay the toll across two bridges en route.

"Charlie" was certainly elated to see us. He had waited for us since five o'clock. I knew he was angry, peeved, and exasperated. But beggars must ever suppress their feelings and instead of complaining, he fawned upon us. Poor fellow, he must have been penniless. Told us he would never forget our kindness.

The scenery en route to St. Louis was very impressive. Time after time, as we journeyed through the picturesque Ozark Mountains with their rolling steeps clothed in blue mist, we could survey the country for miles. On one occasion, we reached the summit of a peak, and far below and before us stretched a rolling plain where farmhouses and neatly kept or newly plowed fields stood in deep contrast to the multicolored slopes of the mountains that rose behind them upward, upward, upward, until they lost their green, brown, and crimson colored summits in the low-hanging clouds of blue haze. Several placid rivers also flowed through these rustic masterpieces of nature. Chief among them was the Osage River, which slowly meandering through a still-verdant valley, wound its peaceful, sunlit way onward, lending such charm and restful beauty to an already lovely spot that the eye of an artist would have gazed enraptured upon it as the inspiration for a master creation. As "Charlie" remarked, who can doubt the presence of an all-pervading Deity when the puny human tears himself away from the "ant-hill" creation of man and goes forth to feed his soul by contemplating the grand, vast, and majestic creations of God?

"Charlie" left us at Union, about 43 miles from St. Louis. Took our names. Thanked us profusely and promised to send us something to Washington, D.C.

The entry into St. Louis was imposing. Wide streets, business, and hustle, giving it all the earmarks of a large city. We went to the Y.M.C.A. on Pine Street. Very fine building here. Large, clean, and with wholesome atmosphere. Mr. [Ottaway Owens] Morris is the manager. Ate in the cafeteria. Cost me 62 cents for the meal. Much too costly. Left me with 38 cents.

Went to Peoples' Finance Corporation to see Arnett G. Lindsay. Woodson had recommended him to us. Bank was closed, he was there, but would not admit me. Left note under the door telling him who I was.

I canvassed on Jefferson Street where much of the Negro business is. Just wanted to make one sale in order to get enough gas to get to Chicago. Few professional men were in their offices. Most of them had either gone to the ball game or were listening in somewhere else over the radio. Those who were in would purchase nothing. Some, like Dr. Centre, were even discourteous. Walked away with a curt "no."

Did meet an interesting man. Lawyer Inge—a friend and supporter of Woodson. Entered Hampton in '71 and was graduated before Booker T. [Washington]. Went to Oberlin in 1876. Heard Wendell Phillips speak several times. Was a member of the first Hampton student singers in 1873. Not in a position to buy books now, however. Interesting to talk to. Got more than $4.00 worth of information from him.

Found Wilkey at the Y.M.C.A. Had made $2. But we could not get to Chicago on that amount. Then too, we had not eaten and there was gas and oil to buy. Determined to find Arnett G. Lindsay. He is head of Peoples' Finance Corporation and a good friend of our cause. Found him at his home on Cote Brilliante. About my height and color. Believes industrial banking is the safest and most desirable form of finance for Negroes. Have too little business to support regular banking institutions. I quite agree with him. The Peoples' Finance Corporation, he told us, was the first organized by Negroes in the country.

Asked him about Negro businesses. Told me that St. Louis could not compare with Chicago, yet it was making strides. There is a large cab company, owned by a Negro named Richard Kent. He operates 75 taxis and Negroes patronize them. Negroes not only own the championship Negro baseball team of the world, but also own the park, which is fitted for night baseball. [G. B.] Key and Kent own the latter. In addition, there are several dry goods stores, millinery shops, haberdashery, and of course, the usual grocery and drug stores and gas filling stations, too. Negroes are finally, within the last few years, going into this lucrative field. I, myself, observed many of the small enterprises, especially on Jefferson and Pine streets, which are the Negro business centers. Lindsay saved our lives by taking the *Rural*

Negro. He had everything else. Dinner was about to be served. I listened with eager expectation for the invitation, which, unfortunately, was not forthcoming. Yet, he will never realize what that $2.65 meant to us.

Mr. Lindsay gave us a list of names whom he believed not only would be interested in the books, but also would be financially able to take them. Yet all, like Mr. Frank Williams, either had them or were unable to take them just now. Others were not at home. We tried, fruitlessly, walking up and down, until about 10:30. At this time, we entered a grocery store. The proprietor seemed to be profoundly interested, but after looking at the book and reading parts of it, for more than three-quarters of an hour, told us that he did not have the time to look at it as he would desire. I was too impatient and hungry to reply. This sale with its $1.20 deposit would have given us $5.00 all told and enable us to eat.

Instead, we decided to leave with $3.85 between us. Luckily, gas was comparatively cheap. 13½ cents. We crossed the "free" bridge over the Missouri [Mississippi] to East St. Louis, Illinois. This was the scene of the fatal race riot in 1917, when 150 Negroes were killed by whites. The town is dark. The Negroes and whites all look degraded and the whole atmosphere reeks with the possibility of something about to happen. Then too, the trains here constituted a distinct menace to life and limb. They cross the city in every direction and at every angle. Once we found ourselves almost caught between the angle of two moving freight trains. And there was not even a gate nor a red light to warn the motorists. We were glad to get out of town. My dinner consisted of one 5-cent hamburger sandwich. Wilkey ate two. Could not afford to spend any more money for food; needed it for gas.

It was cold and we had nothing but a rain slicker, which the one who was not driving tried to cover with until his turn at the wheel came. Railroad crossings were everywhere. Once I almost ran into a moving freight train. I did not see it. And the road had an endless series of sharp curves, such as I had never before beheld. This was Route 4. Saw an enormous coal mountain before we arrived at Springfield. It seemed to rise out of nowhere. Saw other mines, too. The capitol at Springfield was very imposing. Almost as much so as the one at Jefferson City. Outside Springfield I ran off the road. It frightened me later, for both of us could have been killed. But the road had been built for just such an emergency at this point, and a section of the guard rail [had been] removed at the very bend in the curve. It was all that saved us, for I was traveling 55 miles an hour. And Wilkey never even awakened.

By dawn (6 o'clock) we had driven only 145 miles and were still further than that from the city. I drove and made 50 miles in one hour. Wilkey then took the wheel and drove 62 miles in jig time. I then took the wheel again and, keeping it between 55 and 60 miles per hour, we reached the city limits of Chicago at 9:10. Outside of Springfield we had gone into a nice lunchroom adjoining the filling station. Wilkey had 15 cents. I had 40 cents. Each of us got a cup of coffee and a sandwich.

Arrived in Chicago about 9:36 a.m. Wilkey said that his brother would be able to keep us. Took me there. First he had moved. We finally found him at 4101 South Parkway. And in what a predicament. Penniless, out of work, and expecting us to help him. At first glance, God forgive me, I did not like him. He looked rough. Had a cut on his face as if received by a razor in a brawl. Then he was too garrulous. Impressed me as believing he knew everything. And in what surroundings! I was filled with such disgust that I immediately set out for my "frat" house. Unfortunately, however, no one was there. Could not find [Frederick H.] Robb at the "Y" and finally was forced to return to the house. Went from there to Pilgrim Baptist Church to meet Reverend [Junius C.] Austin. [I] knew if I could get an opportunity to talk to his congregation, my worries would be at an end. Tired and sleepy, I drove up before his great stone edifice, formerly a Jewish synagogue. Waited in his office for him. Choir and ushers came in, sang, and prayed. I sat while they stood singing and praying. Felt like a fish out of the water.

Reverend Austin, a small man, entered. Inquired of me my business. Told him I had written him from Tulsa, Oklahoma. Oh, yes, he remembered. Had communicated with him a little late, and his program was filled. At least it was filled for this morning, but he advised me to come in and sit in the pulpit. I could not do so without first going to wash up, shave, and put on another suit. I went home for this purpose.

On my return, Reverend Austin was just ending his sermon. Believed in theatrics, posing with bent knees and outstretched forefinger. My, but what a vast audience he had to inspire him to ascend to rhapsodies of oratorical eloquence. Three thousand people before and all around him, gazing intensely upon the man that they had come to have inspire them, hanging on to his every word, greeting his fiery and fervent outgushings with equally loud and fervid "amens," rising with the pitch of his voice, descending as he lowered his tone, rocking as he rocked and, in short, blending their persons even as one with him. And he, cognizant of their weakness, and knowing full well the strings of their collective hearts, played marvelously upon them. It was oratory—captivating, seducing, entrancing, formidable as the sea's billows, which swept everything before it and consumed all it did not sweep away. It caught and held me, made me to gaze in astonishment at the power of the spoken word. I yearned to have just ten minutes with the same audience. I felt the urge to speak, to say something to arouse them to another pitch of frenzy, only this time on Negro History. But it was not to be. A Miss Davis, a slight missionary from Africa, had previously been scheduled to speak. She did so in a clear, soft, musical, almost childish voice, telling of her struggles and progress in Christianizing the Africans. She was rewarded by a substantial collection, taken up in a wastepaper basket. Austin asked each one to give her a dollar, and many was the dollar that fell in the plates as they passed around. I might say that Austin takes up his usual collections in wastebaskets. I myself saw half a dozen such receptacles, nearly three-quarters full, sitting almost before the pulpit.

I shook hands with Austin after the service. Sorry he could not give me a chance to speak. Told me, however, he would try to do what he could later in the week. Vainglorious, very susceptible to flattery.

Returned to the Wilkeys' place, going first to the Y.M.C.A. Wanted to locate Fred Robb, a home state boy and Howard University classmate. Not there. Could find no one at the frat house. Went to Wilkey's sister-in-law's, who was to have cooked dinner. Did not do so. Gave Wilkey a dollar to take us to a lunchroom. I desired to go to the Y.M.C.A. The older Wilkey vetoed it. Oh, he is so different. His level of values are so much lower than mine that it was almost impossible for me to restrain myself from crying out against him. For dinner I took some kale and rice, with cornbread. It was wretched, but it kept the wolf away. I determined to get out of Chicago as soon as possible.

I went back to the Wilkeys'—the eldest. Went to sleep for two hours. When I arose, the Wilkeys had gone out. Folks were playing cards in the dining room. Liquor was freely flowing. Judging by the carefree speech and actions of the people, it did not take me very long to realize what sort of people I had fallen among. One woman even openly stated that it was getting cold and that she had to find a "sweetie" who would give her a home for the winter. Shocking, yes. But then body and soul must be held together and such immorality is just as great a reflection of unfavorable and low economic opportunity as it is traceable to inherent moral looseness. I played cards for a while in order not to create the impression which I felt.

Went out shortly to mail a card to [John Wesley] Poe. I told him I was leaving in three days. Walking down 50th Street between South Parkway and Michigan Boulevard, I was surprised to find a large Negro auto service station and garage. It was as large, but not as pretentious, as that of Berry's in Tulsa, Oklahoma. Was gratified to see it.

Finally found some fellows at the frat house. Met Karleen there. Friend of mine and [Harcourt A.] Tynes's. Had lived with me at Howard Manor. He loaned me a dollar. Is a salesman. Could not get a job on the boats as he had anticipated. Walked over to South Parkway with me. I stopped in Walgreen's Drug Store at 47th and South Parkway. One of the largest drug stores in the country and is wholly run by Negro clerks. Only the manager is white. I was astonished. Negro girls and youths make up most of the staff. The patronage is nearly all Negro. I was uplifted. Saw in it a chance not only for a rise in quality of Negro labor, but also a splendid opportunity for Negro youth to learn the intricacies of business.

Arrived by midnight at the Wilkeys'. The people who were not drunk were dancing. I danced several times. One couple—a beautiful woman about 25, mother of a small child—retired to a room. The man paid $2.00 for the privilege of the room and $1.50, plus a goodly quantity of bad corn whiskey, for the woman's body. Shocking, yes, but these people must live. I only regret that I was thrown into such an environment where I am even ashamed to tell anyone, whom I may meet, where I am staying. In another room lives a girl, her paramour, and a sister about 19, all of whom have lately come from Mississippi. And Wilkey's brother has been intimate with the landlady. I went to bed; that is, Cecil and I took Wilkey's bed, while he slept in the dining room. I was out of sorts with everything and everybody, especially Tom Wilkey, whom I could not endure.

13

Hard Times in Chicago

Monday October 6, 1930

Our first concern was what to eat for breakfast. We had 25 cents and three persons must be fed. I suggested a box of oatmeal, a loaf of whole wheat bread, and a pint of milk. The Wilkeys acquiesced. The elder brother—God knows, I cannot endure the man—went to the store for the provisions. I intended to do the cooking, but appeared to move too slowly for Mrs. Collins. She cooked the oatmeal, therefore. It was abominably prepared. Hardly cooked, although the quick cooking variety. Ate considerable of it, drank some milk, ate bread and butter, and departed full, but far from satisfied with my breakfast.

My first stop was at the office of the Chicago *Whip.* It is located on the second floor of the Phythian Building on State Street at 37th. It is the largest building I had ever seen owned by Negroes. It is eight stories in height and covers almost a square. It reminds me of other great office buildings with its rows of elevators. The only contrast is only one is in operation.

Met Mr. [Joseph D.] Bibb. Young man, although bald, about 38, I presume. He is large and very fair. Pleasant. Extremely glad to see me and to hear of my travels throughout the South. Told me he wanted me to meet Mr. [Arthur C.] MacNeal, his business manager. Congratulated Bibb upon his campaign to open up jobs for Negroes in white business houses here. Told me that it was only a local panacea and perhaps could not be applied to any community indiscriminately. It comes about by the concentration of many white businesses in the heart of a Negro section. Bibb's slogan is "Don't spend your money where you can't work." Through it he has opened up more than 3,000 jobs for Negroes. Asked me to come in to see him at 6:30 to tell Mr. MacNeal about conditions in the South.

Went from Bibb's to the *Chicago Defender* Building on Indiana Avenue at 33rd Street. Met Mr. [Robert S.] Abbott, the owner, a short, dark man about 53. Was very busy. He asked an assistant to take us through the plant. I was interested in the Linotype machines. They are almost human in their operation. As one white operator commented, they do almost everything except talk. They were invented by [Ottmar] Mergenthaler, a German. After working on the patent for seven years, the idea having been conceived in a dream, he was finally successful in 1903 in realizing his ambition. The shock of his own success drove him insane. Whites operated all the Linotype machines. This is in marked contrast to the *Norfolk Journal and Guide* plant, where all such work is done by Negroes. My guide informed me that these workers must belong to the union and that the union distributed these several men around to the various jobs. The same whites, he added, taught one colored fellow. He is in charge of the makeup department. There are 85 employees. All of the mechanics are white. Negroes do not belong to the union.

It was fascinating to be shown the processes by which a newspaper is prepared. All this was explained to me by my guide, even to the operation of the huge Goss machines, one of which occupies almost half of the plant and which takes several men to operate. The capacity of this machine is 32,000 papers folded each hour. The entire circulation of 250,000 can be run off in a few hours.

Next, I was introduced to Dewey Jones, the city editor. He was so struck by my observations on the trip that he asked me to write an article for his paper. I promised to give it to him tomorrow.

I went to Wilkey's brother's home. Listened to the radio. Wilkey's brother told me last year he stood in line with 3,000 men trying to get a job. Finally sent out in Morgan Park at Christmas time to deliver mail as an extra. He nearly froze. Tells me that to find a job is almost impossible here.

Listened to part of game. I went down to the "Y" to see Robb. I could not find him. Returned to Mrs. Wilkey's. She took us to a restaurant on 51st Street. Took vegetable dinner as the cheapest way out. Found a roach in my corn muffin. Luckily, I had finished eating. It almost nauseated me.

Went to the *Whip* office at 6:10. I failed to find Mr. MacNeal. Mr. Bibb was busy in another office. He came in later. Apologized profusely for my failure to meet Mr. MacNeal. I had seen both, but neither of us recognized the other. Bibb brought me home. Asked me to come to the office tomorrow at 11:00 a.m. to meet MacNeal and McKinley.

Went over to see Major [John R.] Lynch. He looked a trifle thinner than he did last February. Sat wearing a coat sweater and heavy overcoat, although it was not cold. He remembered me. Told me he had just sent Woodson an article to controvert some of the propaganda in Bowers's *The Tragic Era.*[1] Said the latter had not even mentioned his name in connection with affairs in Mississippi during Reconstruction.

He told me that he had been instrumental in enabling [L. Q. C.] Lamar, a Democrat, to gain a seat in the Senate by so arranging the Congressional Districts of Mississippi to give the Democrats a majority. The Democrats in a committee had waited upon him for this favor, the assembly having delegated to him the power to cut up the districts in accordance with his desires. He did so. [James G.] Blaine and Lamar both entered Congress at the same time—about '74. A contest arose in the Senate as to whether Lamar should be seated. It was claimed that his election was fraudulent. Blaine championed him with the theory that any duly elected representative arrived with the credentials from his constituency and was entitled to a seat. Blaine won. Thus, it became a question not of preventing a man from being seated, but of putting him out of his seat once he possessed it, which obviously was a more difficult task. Blaine also fought against the Federal Bill for Civil Rights. That too, was defeated.

In 1884, Blaine received the Republican nomination for President. He was apprised of his nomination by Lynch himself. Blaine asked Lynch, "What about Mississippi?" Lynch told him it was doubtful. Blaine felt that because of his fight in behalf of Lamar, the latter would swing Mississippi in his favor. Lynch warned him against Lamar. Despite this, however, Blaine still believed Lamar would vote for him. But the former disappointed Blaine, and Mississippi went Democratic and Blaine lost the election.[2]

Lynch had more to tell me, but was interrupted by a client. I promised to see him tomorrow.

Tuesday October 7, 1930

The Wilkeys prepared a breakfast of eggs, oatmeal, liver, coffee, and bread and butter, while I worked on an article for the *Chicago Defender.*

Reached the *Whip* office only to find that Mr. MacNeal, Mr. [Ira DeA.] Reid of the Urban League of New York, and Mr. [Albon L.] Foster of

1. Claude G. Bowers, *The Tragic Era: The Revolution after Lincoln,* 1929.

2. This account is somewhat at variance with that in John Roy Lynch, *Reminiscences of an Active Life: The Autobiography of John Roy Lynch,* 94–97, 204–7, and 283–87. At the 1872 session of the Mississippi Legislature, Lynch was Speaker of the House of Representatives. One task facing the legislature was to increase the congressional districts from five to six. The question was whether the Republican majority would redistrict so as to have Republican majorities in all six districts or establish one district with a Democratic majority. Lynch drafted a bill giving the Democrats one district. This was the district that sent Lamar to Congress. This paved the way for his later election to the Senate.

the local branch of the League had waited there to see me. Mr. Bibb called Mr. Foster and advised that I see him. He also told me that he was instrumental in opening up 250 positions for Negro butchers in stores. Commendable.

I walked to the League office in a driving rain. Met Mr. Foster. He called Mr. [Earl R.] Moses of the research department to listen to my experiences and observations. All were keenly interested. Mr. [H. N.] Robinson also came up and listened while I related the condition of the Negroes on the farms, in domestic and personal service, and in other occupations. I asked Mr. Foster what he thought about a meeting on unemployment for Sunday. He thought the time a little short. Believed, however, that he could get the De Sables Club together. Returned to the *Whip* office. En route stopped at Pilgrim Baptist Church. Could not find Rev. Austin in.

Returned to Urban League. Met Mr. [Alonzo C.] Thayer, who is in charge of the industrial department. Estimates number of Negroes out of work at 10,000 here. I believe number too low. Prehaps he means those who *would* work. Did not seem in favor of meeting. Suggested a meeting be held first at which time a solution could be worked out. Antagonistic to the *Whip*'s campaign. Said so in essence. I believe the Urban League is afraid to sponsor a meeting. Asked my purpose. What other purpose could I have except to disseminate information and to earn thereby sufficient money to get out of town? He referred me to Mr. [Irwin C.] Mollison, an attorney who, he added, was president of the Association's branch here.

Mollison's office is in the Loop district. Young man, very fair. Looked with disfavor upon my speaking. Thought it might compromise the Association. Told me the unemployment situation here had created factions, each of which feels convinced it had the panacea for the labor ills of the Negro. The Urban League, of necessity, since its income is derived from capitalists, counsels caution, and asked that economic bars be let down to the Negro because he is efficient. On the other hand, the *Whip* contends that such will never come to pass (and I must to a great extent agree with them) without agitation. Two hostile camps have, therefore, sprung up in Chicago, each striving to solve the problem in its own way and each unable to find any common ground for action.

Mollison felt that the *Whip*'s campaign contained inherent in it the germs of its own defeat. Thought it unwise. Disclosed its deformities as the following:

1. It would provoke reprisals. Already, he said, pastors and other public men have been told by laborers that their jobs have been taken from them by the *Whip*'s campaign.

> 2. Violence, suicidal; provokes violence. The Negro cannot afford to engage in any test of strength economically with the white race. The latter might shut him out of all pursuits.
> 3. It sets up segregation. If Negroes contend that wherever they spend their money they should work, the whites might apply the reverse of this and state that where the Negro does not spend his money he shall not work. The Negro would then be in a terrible predicament.
> 4. Provocative of racial clashes. Typified by that which took place in this city two weeks ago, when Negroes, armed with picks and shovels, drove the whites off a track-repairing job in a Negro section here. A riot was averted only by DePriest and a police captain. Bibb may have unleased a juggernaut that he cannot stop, Mollison believes.

Mollison also told me that MacNeal and not Bibb is the guiding genius of this campaign. He feels that MacNeal is a fanatic; raved because Negroes patronized Goldberg's Drug Store which refused to hire Negroes. Also chided Mollison for patronizing Louis's[?] Drug Store, which hires no Negroes, instead of Walgreen's, which does. Mollison said he invoked the doctrine of personal liberty.

Mollison tried to get the Negro History Club together to have me talk to it, but it could not be arranged. Asked me to speak to his Economic Club tonight at 8:30. Will meet at Lawyer [Herman E.] Moore's office on South Parkway. Assured me that my hearers would be few, but interested. I promised to do so.

Walked from 43rd Street and Wabash home in a driving rain. Feet wet. Wilkey and his brother out. Thank God. Latter is unbearable to me. Effects the mannerisms of a big "towner," although only one year removed from the country. His humor is not only stale, but irritating to me. He is too familiar.

Went to dinner at Smith's Cafe on 47th Street. Hungry, yet had only 60 cents. Had to pour over the bill of fare until I could find something within my reach. Could not, so therefore, took vegetable dinner. It cost 50 cents. Had to leave when the waitress was not looking, for I could not tip her. Forced to walk eight blocks in the rain. Drenched. Almost decided I would not go to Moore's office. But then I had promised to do so.

I arrived at Moore's about 8:15. Mollison arrived about 10 minutes later. After a little preliminary business, they introduced me, or rather Mollison did. Told me that they adjourned at 9:00 sharp, even if the speaker was in the midst of a sentence. I began talking at 8:45. Finished at 9:50. Wesley, a lawyer, told me it was the best discussion of the Negro unemployment problem that he had ever heard. Mollison said he could not stop me, it was so interesting. He told me I was the only speaker who had ever exceeded the time limit. I was grateful. After many congratulations lasting until 10:35, Mollison wanted to take me to a show. I felt it was too late, however. Was tired. Desired to go home. Yet we sat in the drug store and talked for more than an hour and a half.

Mollison is a man of many activities. He has a forum, economic club, is deacon of a church, editor of a church paper, and also has a large law practice. Tells me he is marrying shortly. I assured him he would have to curtail many of his activities. He told me that he had great expectations. Has foresight. Noted that men like Abbott, [Anthony] Overton, and others have no one to carry on their work. Most of them are childless or their sons are worthless. Mollison and those of his Economic Club are preparing to take their places. Told me they discussed Binga's failure long before it happened. Gave me a card of introduction to Mrs. DePriest, the daughter-in-law of Oscar DePriest, his sister, and a teacher at Wendell Phillips High School. He told me that she would introduce me to the principal, who would give me permission to speak to the students at the school. I thanked him and left him at 12:30.

Wednesday October 8, 1930

Rose at 8:00, after spending an abominable night. These two Wilkeys were all over me. At one time they had me lying on the extreme edge of the mattress, with one foot dangling over the side. They roll, toss, and tumble, and the younger one takes on the shape of an "S." I have not been used to this and God knows if I were able financially I should have left Chicago long ago. I have just refused, however, to cash another personal check in order to extricate these fellows from their predicament, and Wilkey's brother had the temerity to ask me when I expected to leave. I told him as soon as I secured gas money. Asked if I would leave him here owing three weeks' rent and the money that he has spent for gas, etc? Of course he straightway had to admit that he and his brother had utilized the car since our advent here. I told him that as soon as I made a sale and could pay my just debts I was leaving Chicago. I did not come here to pay his debts. Will not carry him.

Now for breakfast. Grapes, doughnut, and coffee, with a small piece of cheese. For the first time in my entire trip I have been called upon to eat such a meager breakfast.

Went with Wilkey to see Dr. Mansefield. He is interested in books. Promised to take a set on Friday. Will also invite about 20 others to his office. Have me speak to them. Told me at least 20 will subscribe. God grant they do. Told me if I knew anyone else who was interested to invite them.

From there I stopped at Wendell Phillips High School. Met Mrs. DePriest. She is a junior high school teacher. The school, itself, is too small to accommodate the students. Hence, a double row of portables takes care of the overflow. In one of them, Mrs. DePriest, a pleasant, brown woman of 35 or 36, taught. She greeted me affably and expressed delight in her brother's sending me. She took me to meet Mr. McCarthy and Mr. Williard. The latter, a small, white man about 52, did not incline to favor my speaking. He told me that several times Negroes have spoken from the platform and their speeches have rankled both the whites and some of the blacks there. Last year, he said, Reverend Austin had brought a man there whom he recommended highly. The gentleman in the course of his address, however, caused both himself (Mr. Williard) and Reverend Austin to squirm mightily on the platform. From that time on he swore that no more Negroes would speak to the students.

I assured him, however, that my talk to the students would be free from anything that smacked of propaganda. He told me to make out an outline, and if it met his approval, all well and good. I also informed him that I meant to speak on the Negro only from the point of view of his achievements and contributions to civilization, preparing my remarks by a succinct account of the Association for the Study of Negro Life and History, its origin, purposes, and achievements.

Williard was satisfied when I showed him the outline that nothing I would say could possibly arouse resentment. However, he still was not inclined to let me speak. He asked several of the colored teachers whether they knew me. Of course they did not. Two of them knew of or affected to know about the Association and, therefore, remarked that it would be all right to permit me to speak.

Still not wishing to commit himself, Mr. Williard took me to the dean of the school—Mrs. [Annabel Carey] Prescott. She, I learned later, is the daughter of Bishop [Archibald] Carey. She decided it would not be expedient to have me speak on an entirely Negro subject. The colored students might feel that since they are about 95 percent of the student body they were having things foisted upon them which they would not get if they are attending Hyde Park or some other high school. She also felt that there was a certain undercurrent among both students and teachers which, every now and then, caused a ripple upon the surface and which might be exaggerated by such a special Negro assembly. I remarked in answer to her first point that Negro children ought to be glad to hear about the exploits of their race and that they ought to feel proud to have these contributions made known to them in the presence of white teachers and students. White students, too, enjoy it as I know from my experience, not only in New York but also in the South.

To her second contention, while I admitted that under no circumstances would I knowingly or willingly be party to any action which would fan racial prejudice here, I did not feel that anything I would say could be taken in any different light than the recitation of facts on English or Greek history, which such as a visitor from these countries might bring to the students in a talk.

Mrs. Prescott then replied that the Chicago schools were now facing a crisis as to whether there should be separate schools because of the voluntary segregation practiced by Negroes in herding together in residential districts. (Wendell Phillips is surrounded by the black belt of the South Side). She feared, therefore, to bring in anything in the nature of a segregated talk which might foster a dual school system.

I assured her again that nothing I would say could possibly be construed as favoring segregated schools, hating as I do any and every form of segregation. In fact, I would a thousand times forego the opportunity of speaking to the students if such a culmination would result therefrom. I therefore told her that under no consideration would I speak. She considered it best not to, but informed me that there was a history club at the school, consisting of some 90 members. Suggested that I return later in the fall and speak to them.

I took my leave, but could not help feeling that both Mr. Williard and Mrs. Prescott were insincere. The former had passed the "buck" to Mrs. Prescott in order that it might not be said that a white principal had refused to grant a Negro an opportunity to bring a message to a high school student body, more than 90 percent of which was colored. For Mrs. Prescott, if she was sincere, she was wanting in vision. If not, then she lacked the courage to allow me to bring to those Negro children the thing for which their very souls are starving. Mrs. DePriest, whom I met before leaving, concurred with me.

Went to the *Whip* office. Mr. Bibb felt that the Urban League could have arranged a meeting for me, if it desired. But was afraid of conflicting opinions on the problem. Evidently he doesn't think much of Mollison. He asked me why I wanted to go all the way down there to see him. Told me Mollison is fighting him. How well I know that. Advised me to see Turner [probably Arthur Turner, president of the National Negro Chamber of Commerce] and others about books then return to see him.

Turner was out. Dr. Charles Thompson, who had been so widely recommended to me, and who is president of the De Sables Club, could do nothing for me. Lacking in ready cash was the reason he gave. I called upon Mr. [Sheridan A.] Bruseaux, head of a detective school. He advised me to call upon him at 11:15 a.m. tomorrow. Would talk to me then. Dr. [Benjamin] Bluitt and Dr. Diggs were not in their offices. I met Miss Viseau, an Algerian girl, stenographer for Dr. Bluitt. Very informing. Talked with her a long time. Well educated, cultured, and refined.

From there I called upon Mr. Jones at the *Chicago Defender.* Gave him my article. Told him to take what he wanted for his paper, but to give me a second copy. Also showed me a letter written by a Mr. Cunningham from Meridian, Mississippi. He writes upon the entire Negro problem in the South, from the point of view of his own experience in Mississippi. Enumerations almost worthless, except where he mentions fact that lodges leave their money lying idle in banks instead of putting it to work building factories, etc., in order that they might hire their own boys and girls. Shall see Jones tomorrow afternoon. I saw the great Goss press machine running off the *Chicago Defender.* The page begins as a huge roll of blank paper and comes out at the other end printed, folded, counted, and ready for sale at the rate of 30,000 per hour. It was marvelous to behold.

Called upon Mr. J. D. Stamps of the Victory Life Insurance Company. The company has its own building (the Overton) three stories in height on State Street near 35th. It is a fine looking edifice. Mr. Stamps is well acquainted with Woodson and, unfortunately for me, had nearly all of the books. He told me, however, that he would introduce me to the Reverend L. K. Williams [pastor of Olivet Baptist Church] today in an endeavor to see whether I could get a chance to speak to his congregation on Sunday. I am to meet Stamps at 11:00 a.m. tomorrow.

Went back to the *Whip* office where I finally met the fiery MacNeal and his henchman, Mr. Porter. MacNeal told me of his fight to win Negroes jobs. He also recounted some of his struggles. He told me that most of the opposition comes from within the Negro group. The *Defender* fights him; so does the Urban League; so does Mollison's organization. Then he told me that despite the fact that they are struggling to secure jobs for Negroes, many show lack of appreciation after receiving them. Told me of placing 941 in jobs and that only 14 wrote in and thanked them. The others never even informed them they were on the job and the *Whip* had to call the employers to find out whether the persons sent had actually reported and been put to work. This information they keep for their files. Another girl, working in a store adjacent to Woolworth's before which they had set pickets and which was under a boycott, actually went into this forbidden store and made a purchase. On coming out she was accosted by a picket whom she told to "Go to hell, she would spend her money where she pleased." Boycotts are always dangerous for they infringe upon personal liberty.

MacNeal then showed me a list of letters from manufacturers in the Midwest in reply to questionnaires that the *Whip* had sent out relative to the number of Negroes employed, the kind of work done by them, and whether they expected to hire more of them. A threat was also enclosed in the form of a circular stating that a campaign was on among the Negroes of Chicago to spend their money only where they can get a job. Replies from Quaker Oats, Kellogg's Corn Flakes Company, Cracker Jack Company, and others gave some information. Few Negroes are employed by these plants, however. I think here the *Whip* is overstepping its bounds, for suppose the white employers of the West invoked the same sort of retaliation. They would then drive the Negro out of the iron and steel mills, cooper mills, quarries, off railroads, from laundries, and a host of other industries. I hinted the same to MacNeal.

He was interested in what I had to say concerning labor conditions in the South. Did not know that the Mexicans were making as much headway as I had reported. He felt that there was some concerted effort on the part of white employers to freeze the Negro out of jobs. I did not find that to be the case in the South.

Promised MacNeal I would see him again before leaving town.

Lest I forget, reprisals have already been directed against the *Whip* by white patrons of the newspaper who are out of sympathy with the *Whip*'s program. For instance, Mr. MacNeal told me that they had lost several "ads." One was just withdrawn yesterday that was worth $800.00. Although he hated to part with such an asset, Mr. McNeil asserted that consistency forced him to tell the former patron to take his "ad" and "go to hell." Then, too, he informed me, sudden calling in of notes and the demand that unpaid bills be settled immediately and a number of other embarrassing annoyances beset them on every hand. This comes from the white, but he assured me that his most relentless enemies are the Negroes themselves. Mr. MacNeal, in my opinion, for doing a fine work in one respect by exposing Negroes to practical business experience and training and taking their minds off menial labor alone, is certainly to be commended. So long as he does not cause a showdown between the whites and Negroes he is safe enough. The Negroes, themselves, will be the gainers to an inestimable measure. But let the whites employ the same methods against the Negroes, and God help them! Pitiful as it is to admit it, the Negroes here, and everywhere else, are still very dependent upon the charity of the whites for their very existence; for we are seekers after jobs, and the whites have in their power to dispense them among or withhold them from us.

Wilkey made a dollar somewhere and we ate in a lunchroom on State Street. Could not enjoy my rice, cabbage, and cornbread for the flies. I must get some money. Am not feeling well either.

There is an outlook, however, which may mean something to the exchequer. About five o'clock I approached a Mr. McGhee, Grand Master of the

Missouri Masons, whom I had been told was presiding at the nationwide convention of this order. I told him of my work and asked that he grant me a few minutes tomorrow to speak to the "Shriners." Mr. McGhee, who was robed in all the splendor of his organization (fez and pennants, apron, sword, and the like), told me he would be glad to give me the opportunity. Advised me to see him tomorrow morning at 10:00 a.m. He also promised to see that I secured an honorarium. It was the most encouraging news I have received since my arrival here.

Wilkey took an ignorant girl from Mississippi into our room. They stayed about three hours. God only knows what occurred.

THURSDAY OCTOBER 9, 1930

Wilkey and his brother left at seven-thirty ostensibly to get gas by taking two girls who live in the apartment to work. I could not see the logic in their doing so, remonstrated with them, but since gas was needed and I lacked the wherewithal, let them go. I waited for them until 9:30, then I left very much irritated at their failure to return. I had had nothing to eat.

Went to the Pythian Temple. Arrived at 9:50. Waited for Mr. McGhee, who was to allow me to speak to the Masons. I visualized a good meal as the result of my efforts. It was not to be, however. After waiting an hour, Mr. McGhee informed me it would be better to come back about 2:30 or 3:00 p.m. Left, disconsolate, nursing a fever and feeling as if I were afflicted with the grippe.

Went to the Victory Life to see Mr. Stamps, who was to take me to meet Reverend L. K. Williams. Met him just as we arrived at his church. A dark, unimportant-looking man. Told us without stopping that his assistant pastor would make all arrangements. I met Reverend Branham, a bright, intelligent-looking man about 42. He regretted that he could not find an opening for me Sunday morning. Told me, however, that I could speak at the B[aptist] Y[oung] P[eoples'] U[nion]. He felt that perhaps he could get a good crowd there. Disappointed here.

I returned to the Victory Life office. I noticed that not a dark girl was employed here. All were very pretty girls, ranging in color from yellow to almost white. Whether this was done deliberately, I do not know, but I expect so. It cannot be possible that the only girls equipped for clerical work are mulattoes. And if such is the case, then those of our race afflicted with colorphobia are responsible, for they have discouraged the black girl from taking such training when she realizes the futility of securing a position except when no lighter-skinned girl is available. This company does not have as many employees as the Atlanta Life, North Carolina Mutual, or the Century Insurance companies.

Mr. Stamps had a young woman to present me to Mr. Overton, who is the head and founder of this insurance company and the beauty preparation company, which manufacturers *High Brown* toilet articles, and also the head of the Douglass National Bank. He was in conference with a bank examiner as I walked in. I surely expected to see a man of imposing build. Instead, he is as short as I, somewhat heavier, though, stooped-shouldered with a tired look in his eyes. He is a man about 62, I judged, of medium brown complexion, affable, and exceedingly unassuming. He congratulated me on the work I had been doing for Woodson and the Association for the Study of Negro Life and History. I had just complimented him upon his creative genius in building up three fine business institutions. He thanked me. Told me he was deeply interested in our work, but could not do anything for us now on account of the bank examiners being present. They would be here for a week, he said. No doubt he is very anxious since banks are failing all about him. Told me he could give me plenty of time next Tuesday. However, I shall have left here by that time.

I went over to the Binga Arcade Building to see Dr. A. Wilberforce Williams. Not in. The arcade must take first rank as the most beautiful building owned by Negroes. It is of white marble, beautiful, modernistic architecture about six stories in height, on the corner of State at 35th Street. It stands as an imposing monument of the imbecility of the attempt by Negroes to run banks without previous business training and experience and lacking in that foresight required by bankers to be able to detect (dog-like) the trend of business conditions the country over. [Jesse] Binga—short-sighted, bull-headed—kept investing in real estate (depreciating real estate, at that) until, with the building of the Arcade, he found himself laden with frozen assets in the form of buildings that could not be rented, for State Street had lost its priority as a business center for Negroes to 47th Street. Then, unable to unload, the crash came, and the greatest Negro financial institution that the race has yet built and operated in America, an institution with a national reputation, went down, carrying with it the savings of thousands of Negro depositors. But, greater still, it crashed in its wake the confidence of thousands of Negroes in the ability of Negroes to operate such institutions. The bank is closed now—a silent reminder of Binga's folly—while small crowds of Negroes, whose life savings have been lost, peer pitifully at its iron gratings. They will be lucky, I was told by Mr. Jones of the *Defender,* if they receive 20 cents on the dollar.

I stopped in Congressman DePriest's real estate office. Outside I saw my old friend Morris Lewis, his secretary. Greeted me uproarously. Lewis asked me, was I the man from Washington, D.C., whom the newspapers were raving [about] over here? Said they told him he and the Congressman should see me by all means. I was glad to see him. He was just inspecting a broadcasting machine, which plays music (both classical and jungle). The machine itself is hidden in a large, covered top truck which is plastered with campaign propaganda for DePriest, who is seeking re-election to Congress. The entire South Side is fairly littered up with stickers, posters, handbills, and other campaign literature. I had to congratulate Lewis on the vast scale upon which DePriest operated. He then told me that it cost $1,200.00 to hire the music machine for a month. After talking over several matters, I asked Lewis to get in touch with Reverend Austin for me. He tried. Could not reach him. Sought to communicate with Reverend [Harold M.] Kingsley. He was out of town. Asked him what about Binga's failure. Told me frozen real estate investments. He is in hiding now. A warrant has been issued by the Elks for his arrest, and even his wife now is suing him for a divorce. It seems that all the woes of the universe fall on the hapless head of a man when he is down. In the case of his wife, it is sheer treason. She should be his comfort, his rock, his solace now, instead of deserting him. Such is life, however.

I left Lewis, promising to return about 4:30. Went to speak for the Masons. After waiting an hour and a half—until four o'clock, with a splitting headache and suffering from hunger—I was told that Mr. McGhee could not secure an opportunity for me to speak to them. This news was crushing, for I had not eaten all day. Moreover, I was ill and desired to get some medicine or else see a physician. I left to return to the Binga Arcade.

On the way, I was sorely tempted to put my "frat" pin in pawn, for a couple of dollars in order to get the wherewithal to eat. Overcame it, however. Finally caught Rev. Williams in. A very intelligent and refined man. Also widely traveled. Just returned from the Riviera this summer. Interested in the books, interested to a high degree in my travels and observations. Asked about treatment in the South at the hands of whites, the labor situation of the Negroes there, and many other such kindred queries. Faint and sick as I was, I answered them. Could not purchase the books, however. His savings, like so many others, were tied up in the Binga State Bank debacle. Told me to take care of myself. I was too valuable to the race to die.

I was about at the end of my physical resource when I called upon Dr. Turner. He encouraged me, however, by subscribing, although I was forced to make several substitutions. I received his check for $4.00, which I immediately rushed downstairs to the *Whip* office, where Mr. MacNeal cashed it for me. I went immediately to the Y.M.C.A.—weak, sick, and hungry, as I was—and ordered dinner. The dinner was well-cooked and appetizing, but I was too unwell to eat it.

Walked home and went to bed. Wilkey and his brother came in about an hour later. I was burning with fever and aching terribly. Wilkey was exceedingly kind to me. Did not want me to get up to go to the drug store for some castor oil, as I had planned. Told me to remain in bed. He brought me aspirin and some quinine, which I took. Then about 10:00 o'clock he came in with the castor oil, which he had had mixed for me at the drug store. It was a terrible dose, but I "downed" it, sucking a lemon afterwards. About twelve o'clock I must confess I felt a little better.

Then something astounding happened. Wilkey's brother came to the room, sat on the bed, and asked me how I felt. I answered a little better. Then he told me of the manner in which the landlady made her money—namely, by selling booze and renting rooms to couples. I had surmised this, now he had confirmed it. Then he told me that there was a couple who wanted to go to bed and, since he had not paid his rent and the landlady had an opportunity to make $2.00, she wanted to give them this room, because it was bigger. I could go out to a smaller room, which was used by Mrs. Clark and her husband. (God forgive me for as slovenly and loose as she appears I certainly did not relish lying in her bed.) I was amazed. He asked me whether it was all right with me. And in my helpless condition what could I say? Nothing but yes, because it was a demand rather than a request. Even then Mrs. Collins, the landlady, was waiting outside the room door with linen and the couple, like two animals, were also not only waiting, but clamoring to get in. I was sick, mortified, angry, for Wilkey and I would have paid for our lodging irrespective of his brother's delinquency.

Well, I got up, but found I was so weak I could scarcely stand. When I started out to the other room I found that it was not yet ready for me and while it was being prepared, I nearly fainted. Only seating myself saved me. Then Wilkey, who was lying on a couch in the dining room, and who all along had been ignorant of the proceedings, asked me whether I felt so good that I had got up. His brother then told him that the landlady had taken the room and was changing me to another one. Then Wilkey performed. I did not know he was that loyal to me. He excoriated his brother for abetting such a thing. His only excuse was that he had asked me and I had consented. Wilkey could see through that. He cried out that he would have paid the woman tomorrow, but that to move a sick man around for a whore was abominable. And while they argued again I nearly fainted. I tried to get to the bathroom because of the violent action of the castor oil. Some one was there.

When I finally got in Mrs. Clark nearly knocked the door down trying to seek entry, although she knew I was in there. Truly nothing had ever disgusted me or embarrassed me so much in all my life. She stood there knocking, shaking the door, and calling "let me in." When I finally came out, she looked at me and said "excuse me."

After going to bed in her former room, I was not even permitted to stay there. Wilkey's brother came in to ask me whether I desired to sleep in the dining room where there was a day bed and consequently more air, because of two windows. It did not require the brain of a seer to perceive what was meant. Therefore, I was moved again. Wilkey grumbled and fussed about it until he fell off to sleep.

During the night the castor oil must have exerted an unprecedented action on me, for the first time in my life an accident happened. All signs were well removed, however, when the other people rose. But as long as I live, I shall never forget this night. It was hideous, yet not necessary; for I could easily have secured some money.

Friday October 10, 1930

This morning dawned very inauspiciously for us. In the first place, Wilkey's brother and the landlady had an argument over his back payments. Both contended that the one was trying to "skin" the other. Then Wilkey lost his temper when Mrs. Collins told him that we owned her $5.00 and railed against her for putting us out of the room last night, and especially because I was sick at the time. She contended that as long as we had paid no rent in advance the room was not ours. Then Wilkey logically contended that since she took the room at will, then it had never been rented us. The argument assumed boisterous proportions. Mrs. Collins, talking so fast that she was almost unintelligible, raised her voice and began to use strong language. Then the older Wilkey entered the fray saying that since he rented the room, all arrangements should have been made through him. She told him he had paid nothing of what he had promised to pay. Had he paid, that probably would have been the proper procedure; namely, to have let him take care of our lodging—we of course, paying him. But although I kept silent, I could not see where this rent-gorging woman should receive twice her usual remuneration from the one room. Of course that of Wilkey's brother would, no doubt, adorn the debt column.

Wilkey and I packed our things to leave. His brother—whom God knows I wish I had never met—asked us in a frightening tone, whether we meant to leave him there. I asked him where he was going. With me? Good heaven, no! His own brother propounded the same query. He answered that he thought he was going with us. I asked whether he had money sufficient to rent another room. He answered negatively.

Then he wanted to know whether he was to go with us to Washington. I replied that I could not countenance or be party to his going away while owing just debts. Tried to show me why he was not indebted to Mrs. Collins. Told me everything, except that he had been intimate with her, which released him from any obligation. Told him he had better remain there. We would call for him on Saturday.

Wilkey promised to pay Mrs. Collins for the rent. Went to his sister-in-law's to get her to intercede for him to get a check cashed at her bank. She is a fine woman. Actually got up, dressed, and went to the bank with us. I had a check dated October 10th which she cashed. It was from a school teacher at Alabama State Normal School in Montgomery, Alabama.

Upon returning, Wilkey and I bought breakfast. Axie, his sister-in-law, cooked. We both felt like new men to feel a little money in our pockets. Buying at the store and cooking breakfast also saved money.

Went to Mr. DePriest's office. Mr. Lewis tried to get in touch with Reverend Austin, but again he could not be located. Hardest man in town to try to catch. Went to the *Chicago Defender* to get a copy of my article. It was not ready. A young fellow, [Barfoot] Gordon, had not begun to type it. Promised to give it to me at 1:00 p.m. tomorrow. Wilkey took him home. I went to DePriest's. Latter not in. I returned to the Associated Negro Press. Met Mr. [Claude] Barnett. I talked with him about conditions in the South. He asked me to give him a story of about 500 words covering travels. He knows Woodson personally. Feels it would help the cause. Promised to do so and see him tomorrow. He had to hurry to catch a train.

One of the most hopeful tendencies of the present unemployment situation is the comparative rapidity with which Negroes are turning to small independent ventures, like popcorn, fruit, vegetables, hot dogs, tamales, and other such commodities. In most instances, they are pushing carts laden with vegetables. Others vend one commodity only such as grapes. I saw a very old man offering these for sale on Indiana Avenue at 36th Street today. Others on State Street, Wabash, and the side streets can be seen with oranges, apples, potatoes, or a selection of these commodities on homemade carts reminiscent of the Italians of the North. Still other Negroes are selling wearing apparel on the streets. Today a Negro accosted me on 47th Street to buy some neckties from him, which he carried in a long box strung about his neck. When one contemplates the rising new labor psychology of the Negro when he is faced by actual destitution, one almost rejoices that he is being forced out of his lowly employment. This may be the means, perhaps, of bringing forth a small independent class of entrepreneur. Then too, this business training is invaluable. Others should follow their example, for one can begin with a dollar's worth of merchandise. The ultimate result of all this labor upheaval may react to make our group less menial-minded, to feel that something better awaits them in the matter of employment than "waiting," "portering," and the like.

Wilkey met me at the Y.M.C.A. at 5:00 p.m. Had dinner there. Would have secured some rooms there, but the price was prohibitive. Wilkey caused me to be embarrassed by misinterpreting the price of the rooms as given him by the clerk at the desk. He told me we could both be accommodated in one room for $1.50. Upon the strength of that, both of us signed only to have the clerk render us a bill of $3.00 for the room and 50 cents deposit on the key. I was taken aback, but hastily apologized, claiming I had been misinformed by the error of my colleague. Then, from 7:00 until 9:00, we tried every hotel in Chicago for Negroes, with the exception of the Vincennes. We also went to several of those superb houses on South Parkway where a room for rent sign was displayed. These people, however, would not take us as transients. They said they rented by the week only. As one bone-sucking woman said: "I don't rent no rooms by the night."

Finally we came to Mrs. Wilkey's to wash up before going to speak at Dr. Mansefield's. He had invited me since Tuesday to speak to some of his friends and club members at his office. I wanted to get a suit pressed. Time would not permit it so Axie let me press the trousers in her bedroom. By the way, I had almost forgotten that she informed us that her husband told her to have us take a room here and that if we did not have the money to pay, he would do so. Were we overjoyed? I should say so. The elder Wilkey is a much better fellow, morally, I believe, than his two brothers.

After getting dressed, tired and sleepy as I was, we hurried to Dr. Mansefield's office, only to find that neither the doctor nor anyone was at home. His office was dark; the windows were open. He may have gone to bed. At any rate, it was a pretty scurvy trick. I could have put the time expended to far more profitable use.

Wilkey told me that while getting out of the car today, he was suddenly told to "stick 'em up." He turned about to see himself gazing into the muzzle of three pistols, held by policemen. The police believed he might have stolen the car. After quizzing him, however, they allowed him to depart.

SATURDAY OCTOBER 11, 1930

While Wilkey's sister-in-law cooked breakfast for us, I hastened to see Reverend Austin. The worthy divine was preparing his sermon and was not to be disturbed, his secretary informed me, because it disturbed his train of thought. That is remarkable for a colored minister, for most of them are so devoid of any such thing. In this case, however, the gentleman might be pardoned since he is somewhat above the average Negro minister in intelligence.

I met Barfoot Gordon, a young man on Dewey Jones's staff at the *Defender* office. Promised to have my article typed by one o'clock. He had a long talk with me on the ultimate solution of the Negro's problems. I held that the ills of the race were economic fundamentally, and all his disabilities—social, political, and otherwise—flowed therefrom. Gordon, like so many others, Du Bois, in particular, felt that the leverage of the ballot constitutes the only hope of deliverance for us. Of course, we arrived nowhere. Such discussions never do.

At one o'clock I returned. The article still was untyped. He took a story from me verbatim. Told me the other was too valuable to waste as a newspaper article, but would make a fine story for a magazine. He suggested the *American Mercury.* The style of the thing, however, made me balk. I don't like the idea of writing things in sensational style. Gordon wanted to help me get it out, that is, he would attend to its style, etc. Then he would have certain articles drawn up, and have the story of the economic position of the Negro in the South published in the *Mercury.* Of course, he desired something for his pains. We would get it out tomorrow. He also promised to take me to a Mr. Sellers, whom he claimed would buy all the books we publish. He would take me tomorrow at 4:00.

Although I had promised Gordon to work out the story with him, the knowledge of his being a student still, plus the fact that my friend [Emile] Holley has had more training in the work, made me a little reticent about giving him the article. Decided to think the matter over, especially since I did not believe justice could be done to it as hurriedly as we proposed to turn it out.

Met Mr. Regruder, a lawyer. Told me 33⅓ [percent] of all the working colored people of Chicago were out of work. He did not include idlers and loafers. While sitting in a car on South Parkway, which is lined with beautiful homes tenanted by Negroes, I asked how these people were faring with their dwellings, which many were trying to buy. He told me any number had lost their homes through the viciousness of a second mortgage that really does not exist. A house worth $20,000, is quoted to a Negro at $40,000; he must pay $20,000 before he secures any equity in it at all. Then many times, he wants to borrow on what he has been led to believe is a $40,000 proposition and the banks refuse to treat with him because he has nothing. Many, therefore, have lost their homes through foreclosure. Others, who rent these palatial homes for $150.00 a month, are themselves unable to pay such high rentals and, therefore, are forced to resort to taking roomers (nearly every house on South Parkway displays its "rooms for rent" sign in the window). Still others convert their once exclusive residences into gambling dens, beer and whiskey parlors, and immoral houses. They must live, and sometimes I am at a loss whether to censure or to pity them. How many times have I had women and girls to accost me on the streets here offering themselves for sale from 50 cents up. It happened the first night I arrived and still goes on.

Barfoot Gordon introduced me later to Mr. Dunlap, the head of the National Association of Colored Waiters and Hotel Employees, who has just opened a school where colored waiters and other domestic workers may learn the three Rs, and also foreign languages. The lack of an understanding of the latter, according to Mr. Dunlap, between mouthfuls of food (he was eating his dinner), is largely responsible for Negroes losing their jobs as waiters in the best hotels. They are unable to take orders from foreigners and unable to read foreign dishes when they appear on the menu. It is a commendable and an extremely timely effort.

Again I went to Reverend Austin's office only to find him out again. But this time something occurred that might be construed as extremely fortuitous for me. An elderly gentleman, who was also attempting to see the Reverend, told me that it was very difficult to find him at home. I replied that he seemed busier than Dr. Woodson. The gentleman beamed at the name. He told me he was acquainted with him. He then told me that Woodson had informed him of some works which he was going to publish on the Negro. I then told him of my connection with Dr. Woodson and of the books already published, some of which I had with me. The gentleman, Capt. [John] Fry, he called himself, asked me to come to his home. He took me next door, looked at the books, and decided straightway he wanted a complete set. He said he would give me a check on Monday. Told me to come to the Appomattox Club, at 3632 South Parkway at 10:00 p.m., that he would speak to the president, Mr. Louis Johnson, and arrange for me to speak. I was elated and thanked him heartily.

Wilkey came in a little after my arrival. He wanted to use the car to keep a date. I refused him. He had the temerity to suggest that I use a trolley. Absurd.

At 10:00 p.m. I was ascending the steps of the Appomattox Club. It is a palatial building of three stories, built of white stone. Its atmosphere bespeaks dignity, refinement, and leisure. Mr. Johnson, the president, was expecting me. He greeted me very cordially. Asked me to be seated while the business meeting opened. It was punctuated by the successive interruptions of one Mr. Porter—a small, middle-aged gentleman, with a lock of hair à-la-Heflin (only Heflin's is straight)—who leaped to his feet every now and then to wax eloquent now upon the duty of every member to preserve the club by paying his dues, despite the hard times, and then again to make a speech in favor of Judge [Albert B.] George, who is running again for office. By the way, Porter even took the introductory speech out of the mouth of the president and really presented Judge George himself. The president, rather flabbergasted, sat down. It seemed prearranged to me.

Judge George, whom no one would ever take for a colored man, rose. Politician-like, he said he would make no speech, nor covet the vote of anyone because they were members of his club. Then in keeping with his kind, he made a most powerful talk in behalf of himself, even giving the most minute details of how to vote for him. He is a very good speaker. Told the members he was the only elected Negro judge in the country. I know of Judge [Edward W.] Henry in Philadelphia, but according to George, the latter is only a police magistrate and is appointed like Judge [James A.] Cobb of Washington, D.C. Still, I must verify George's statement.[3]

This club has a varied program. Between each talk there was a musical selection. Now came a song and dance by a very clever girl. She was warmly applauded.

I was introduced. The president bungled the introduction. He made me a book agent. My fault, for I ought to carry cards. Talked about 20 minutes. Must have impressed my hearers, for they crowded around with congratulations. And what was more important, I sold five sets of books. I could have sold more, but the hour was late and I could not write them fast enough. It was a life saver. Judge George, himself, congratulated me. Told me I was doing a splendid work.

Telegraphed Dr. Vernon Johns of Lynchburg Theological Seminary. I asked him to arrange a meeting, that I would arrive Wednesday without fail. Chicago has such a bad reputation, that no longer can one use coins in the telephone boxes. Slugs are now used instead. When I remarked to the druggist that this did not even occur in New York City, he retorted: "Hell, you New York fellows are honest." I retired about 1:45.

Sunday October 12, 1930

I was awakened at 10:30 by Wilkey coming in. Claimed he had met a friend who took him to a party and afterwards he had spent the night at his home. I was skeptical, but reprimanded him because of possible injury to his health.

3. In any case, George lost in the 1930 Republican primary. In New York City, however, two African Americans were elected judges from judicial districts on the Democratic ticket. See Harold F. Gosnell, *Negro Politicians: The Rise of Negro Politics in Chicago,* 88–89.

Went out to his aunt's in Maywood to breakfast. At the intersection of Michigan Avenue and 33rd Street, Wilkey failed to stop at the boulevard sign. Neither did the other drivers. Yet, a cop hailed us. We stopped. He told us he was going to take us in. Wilkey pleaded he did not see the sign. Of course, that was no excuse, as the officer speedily told him. Asked us whom we knew in town. Told him I knew Abbott of the *Chicago Defender* and DePriest, among others. Pretended not to know Abbott and retorted DePriest had nothing to do with him. They were looking for graft and only decided to let us go when we told him that we were trying to sell books. Also informed him Wilkey was a student. Another cop had come up by this time. Between them they evidently realized we had nothing, therefore, allowed us to depart. It was purely an attempt to fleece "scared" niggers, nothing more. I would have allowed them to arrest me first.

Passed the opera house, the civic theater, and Al Capone's hotel, en route to Maywood. Had a very fine time there.

Rushed back in time to address B.Y.P.U. meeting at Reverend L. K. Williams's church. Reverend Branham, however, had made no arrangements. A Mr. Spikes had me speak to the senior section. They were very attentive. In the adult section, their program was so extended I could not be worked in. Sorry I stayed in town. Went to a Mrs. Watkins, who is a friend of Wilkey's. Here we were given a good dinner, after which we played whist. Mrs. Watkins and I bested Mrs. Green and Wilkey.

Arrived home about 11:30. Wilkey took the car on pretext of going down to the garage where a friend of his was to give him a new tube. He arrived home at 4:30 a.m. I am more determined than ever to take him away from Chicago. Lest I forget, his aunt tells me that under no condition should I take Wilkey's brother with me. Told me his laziness and big talk would embarrass me. I shall follow her advice.

[No entries were found for October 13–15, 1930.]

14

Return to Washington and the Cleveland Convention

THURSDAY OCTOBER 16, 1930

Rose at 4:00 a.m. It was warmer here than what I have been given to expect. [James Cecil] Wilkey was for remaining in bed until 8:00 or 9:00. I vetoed that, of course. We drove Medders back to the "Y" and left Cincinnati at 5:10. I clambered into the back seat of the car, rolled up in a blanket, and slept while Wilkey drove. I first saw to it, however, that he was upon the main highway.

When I awoke it was 8:30, and we had gone exactly 64 miles. I was very disappointed, for I hoped to have traversed at least 100 miles in that time. Wilkey told me he was forced to make a series of detours, had crossed several mountains, and that he had been faced with a road of loose gravel most of the way.

I relieved him while he slept and drove 70 miles to Portsmouth, Ohio. The scenery was beautiful. The woods and the mountains were resplendent in a riot of colors—gold, brown, green, yellow, crimson, and others. At Ripley, we stopped to buy a tube. Got a secondhand one for 40 cents. It was a lucky strike. We stopped in a white restaurant to get breakfast, but the flies were so numerous, that I took only a bowl of bran flakes and milk. Wilkey eats—flies or no flies. He took eggs and hamburger. He is broke and the expense for breakfast, bed, and for the remainder of the trip to Lynchburg must devolve upon me.

Outside of Ripley—that is, before coming into the town—I saw several Negro farmers. This is a unique sight in the North. Their farms were very small, but well kept. Most of them showed the industry of these people who had cleared the mountainside and planted crops there. Ripley is in Brown County, just across the Ohio from Kentucky. This county contained a goodly number of Negro farmers as far back as 1828. Many ran away from their master; others were liberated, and settled here; still others were given land by benevolent whites. The Ohio Antislavery Society Bulletin for 1838 speaks of them. Many, no doubt, are their descendants. There are also a number of colored mechanics here, a Negro painter told us. In Ripley, unlike Cincinnati, both races attend the same school and I beheld a sight that reminded me of my school days, and one I had not seen since I left New York—namely, white and colored girls going to school together.

It would be impossible not to mention the beautiful Ohio as it meanders placidly past Ripley and, in fact, as we followed its gorgeously colored banks for miles from Cincinnati. It shimmered like a glistening sheet of highly polished silver as the glancing sunbeams struck its placid surface, only to be reflected again as from a mirror. Here and there an island, resplendent in its autumnal raiment, showed itself, which gave the impression that nature herself in some of her amorous moments had created a miniature paradise in the center of this lovely stream.

The entire trip now led over a succession of mountains. And to hinder our progress, the road was exceedingly dangerous because it had been freshly covered with tar oil. From West Union to Portsmouth, the entire road was as slick as glass. This not only obtained on the level stretches, what few there existed, but even the slopes of the mountains were similarly covered, and consequently slippery. I certainly could not imagine why any sober thinking individual, much less the highway commission of a great state, would jeopardize the life, limbs, and property of motorists by offering every inducement for an accident. With only one brake effective, each time I would apply it the car would skid, even on a dry road, and one can easily imagine what would occur on a mountainside rendered slick with oil. I was almost afraid to make the descent of some of the mountains. Once I thought both of us were lost. I tried to apply the brake and the machine skidded out to the embankment. I could almost feel myself plunging down the side of the mountain, hundreds of feet below. Luckily, I righted the car none too soon. Poor Wilkey, asleep, knew nothing about it. I told him about it later and he shuddered.

Between Huntington and Charleston, West Virginia, a new road is being built. And although large numbers of Negroes live in this section, not a Negro was employed. All the work was being done by whites. Nearer Charleston, where another gang was at work repairing another highway, every man was white.

We picked up a white man outside of Huntington and gave him a lift to West Virginia State College at Institute, West Virginia.[1] Told him we would meet him at seven o'clock the next morning at the state capitol in Charleston, and we would take him to Lynchburg. He is from Binghamton, New York, and seemed to be a pretty decent chap. His name is Bentley. He told us he is trying to locate a friend.

I met John W. Davis, president of West Virginia State College, whom I had met on several occasions before. Dr. Woodson was instrumental in getting him his position here. Davis is a good friend of the latter. He was glad to see us and put me up in a guest room with fine accommodations. The school is progressive, and has several splendid buildings. There is one still in the process of being constructed. The school has one of the best administration buildings I have yet seen. The campus has some potential beauty; trees and shrubbery have just been planted. The buildings are arranged fairly well.

A few hours later I was introduced to a Mr. McKenzie, a teacher of History. He promised to call on me at 8:00 p.m.

Went to dinner. It was abominable: beef, tomatoes, lettuce, and bread. Ye Gods! I would have been ashamed to offer that to a guest. And such was the teachers' fare. Met Harrison, a Howard man, with whom I had a long chat.

After dinner I wrote in my diary for a while. Two teachers, McKenzie and [D. P.] Lincoln, came to see me. McKenzie is big, black, and effeminate, with a kindly rather than scholarly appearance. Lincoln is smart in dress, small, clean-cut, and suggests the student and the scholar more. He uses such English mannerisms as "upon my word." Both of them are fine men; both are M.A.'s, but McKenzie is well on the way to his doctorate at Columbia University. We discussed the advisability of Spanish as a substitute for German, since the field of the Negro in Latin America is relatively untouched. We all agreed upon the choice of the former language. We then discussed possible examination questions, historians, research possibilities, methods of teaching history, and the like. Lincoln is going to our annual

1. The state legislature of West Virginia established West Virginia Colored Institute in 1890 as the land-grant institution for African Americans. The school formally opened in 1892, and in 1915, the name was changed to the West Virginia Collegiate Institute, now West Virginia State College. Carter G. Woodson was offered the presidency of the school in 1919, but he declined and recommended his friend John W. Davis. When Woodson was fired from his position at Howard University, after a disagreement with the president, Davis employed Woodson as dean of the college department at West Virginia State. Woodson remained there from 1920 to 1922. U.S. Department of the Interior, Bureau of Education, *Survey of Negro Colleges and Universities,* 625–39; Jacqueline Goggin, *Carter G. Woodson: A Life in Black History,* 52–58.

meeting of the Association for the Study Negro Life and History. I told him I might come by for him. I promised to write him. Was very much impressed by both men. They were amazed at the information I had concerning the Southern Negro and his economic problems.

After they left, I took a good warm bath and retired.

Friday October 17, 1930

After breakfast, I went to President Davis's office to thank him for his hospitality and to bid him farewell. Was not in. Went to the library. There I found Miss Drain. Charming, winsome. Spent one hour behind the stacks conversing with her. Returned to Dr. Davis's office. He told me the librarian would order all books published by us the school did not already have.

I could not get the car started. The battery was dead. Had a long talk with Mrs. Davis while waiting for the car to be fixed.

[No entries were found for October 18–24, 1930.]

Saturday October 25, 1930

Went to the office at 10:20 a.m. Woodson seemed sarcastic in his greeting. He wanted to know whether I had become "Doctor," "Professor," or what, in Lynchburg. Equally sarcastic, I told him I had. Said he wondered what had become of me. I told him there was no need to write when there was nothing to report.

Felt the campaign would go, but stated that return packages were eating up the profit. He said that the office was receiving two sets of books back each day. One came while I was there. It is his own fault. Told him in the beginning he ought to include postage. Persons will not bargain for one thing and then pay another, even if the difference is twenty-five cents.

He wants someone to go to Cleveland to the meeting. I told him I would go. He asked if I would take Wilkey. Told him yes, but in reality, he is just for company only. He does not fit.

He told me that [S. W.] Rutherford wants someone to make a survey of Negro unemployment in Washington. He had asked Rutherford to give it to me. I may accept it, may not. I would rather write a pamphlet on Negro unemployment in the South, its causes, and remedies, and sell it. Woodson then told me to have the car put in shape for the trip to Cleveland. I took it to a Ford service station. Will cost $15.76. Woodson gave me $20.

From there I went to see Bertha [Baylor]. I bought six pairs of lisle socks for 75 cents en route.

Monday October 27, 1930

Ate breakfast in the beautiful Phyllis Wheatley Association Cafeteria in Cleveland. This splendid nine story building is the culmination of the struggles of Miss Jane Hunter to found a center for Negro girls independently of the Y.W.C.A. . . . It is beautifully furnished, and doing a real service, unlike many colored Y.W.C.A.'s, by catering to the type of girl who most needs uplifting—the homeless and the working girls.

Met several interesting and "distinguished" people at breakfast. Among them were Dr. [Pezavia] O'Connell, of Morgan College. A fine, elderly man, and an engaging speaker, but not so impressive as a scholar. I also met Mrs. Lucy Harth Smith of Lexington, Kentucky, one of our leading enthusiasts in the work; Professor Luther Porter Jackson of Virginia State College, Petersburg, Virginia, a history teacher and also a research man of no small ability; President [Rufus Ballard] Atwood, head of Kentucky State College, at Louisville[?][Frankfort], Kentucky; and several others.

After an enjoyable breakfast—Woodson paying the bills—we took Mr. Jackson to his lodging house. We were supposed to meet Woodson and the others at Cleveland College, Engineers Hall, where the Board of Education is located. We went downtown but were unable to locate them. Returned to the Phyllis Wheatley Association, where we passed Mrs. Smith in company with one of the white members of the Board of Education.

The balance of the day was spent in efforts to find Woodson, or in an endeavor to type two write-ups for the Associated Press of Chicago, Illinois, concerning my speaking in Lynchburg on unemployment, and also Negro History.[2]

Woodson came into the Phyllis Wheatley about 5:00, wondering what had become of us. We told him we had gone to the engineers building. He replied that, he stated the Board of Education would be the meeting place. Everything usually goes wrong, chiefly because he thinks he says or does what, in reality, he intended to say or do.

2. *Norfolk Journal and Guide,* November 15 and November 22, 1930, carried articles from the Associated Negro Press reporting on two speeches Greene made at the Virginia Seminary at Lynchburg, Virginia. His first presentation, according to the release, "refuted many accepted but erroneous theories concerning the Negro. He dispelled the notion that the Negro had his beginnings in slavery by narrating the rich heritage of the Negro in Africa before the destruction of the great Negro kingdoms there following the beginning of the slave trade." His second presentation was more controversial. He called for African Americans to stop building churches and to channel the money released into more productive channels. He said that the church leaders—the clergy—were "primarily interested in their own self-aggrandizement."

The banquet in honor of visiting delegates proved a huge success. The toastmaster, Dr. [Charles H.] Garvin, was just ordinary; no speaker at all. The Mayor of Cleveland, [John D. Marshall,] a short pudgy fellow, praised the Negro sky-high in welcoming the Association to the city. Boasted that this was one city where Negroes actually receive a "square deal." Mrs. Wilkinson, a white woman who sat beside me, assured me, however, that such words were only a political gesture calculated to win the Negro vote in the coming election. According to her, Negroes are given no such opportunity here economically, politically, or otherwise, which would approach the equality suggested by the Mayor. I knew as much myself. The City Manager, a Harvard graduate, was more imposing. His welcome, while not flamboyant, at least appeared sincere.

The response was very ably delivered by a Mr. Lincoln, a young teacher of history at West Virginia Collegiate Institute. He really surprised me.

The great treat of the evening, however, came from Dr. Woodson. In this setting of nearly 150 or 200 persons, half of whom were white, spurred on by the many attestations of interest and pride in the work he was doing, and keyed up, no doubt, by the realization that despite all of his trials, disappointments, and the lethargy of the very group in whose interest he was pouring out his life, Woodson delivered the greatest effort of his career. In my opinion, he could never rise to greater heights than on this night. Beginning in his usual sarcastic manner, he ran through the necessity of studying Negro History, told of the efforts of some Negroes to hush up their own past because it would attract attention to the fact that they are Negroes; recounted others who don't want to hear about it, because they are ashamed of their color. He then narrated the disabilities—social, economic, and political—under which the Negro lives here; showed how it was interwoven with the ignorance of his past; and touched briefly the achievements of the Negro in Africa and America. He ended with a stirring, eloquent, and thrilling plea for justice to the Negro in all spheres, because of his rich heritage and his ability to do the same things as the white man.

Whites as well as blacks hung on his every word, and the acclamation with which his speech was received ought to have been full compensation for him, even if the rest of the meetings should prove failures (which I am sure they won't).

I met a Miss Carver of the Negro Welfare Association here. A very charming lady. She wants to see me to talk over the unemployment situation with her. And I want to see her, too. I also met a host of other people. Miss Wilkinson, of the Friendly Inn Settlement, became interested in my work and invited me to dinner on Wednesday at 6:00 p.m. in order that we might talk things over. A Miss Jacques was with her. We discussed any number of things concerning the Negro while at the table. I promised her I would accept her invitation.

From the banquet we went to a festival of Negro music at the Mount Zion A.M.E. Church. Here a soprano, Miss Myrtle Wiggins, sang gloriously. She held her audience spellbound by the ease and grace with which she performed. She is a small, thin, dark woman.

Luther Porter Jackson of the history department of Virginia State College then spoke on Negro music. It has, he said, two outstanding characteristics:

1. Universality of appeal:
   (a) Goes to the heart because it comes from the heart.
2. Historic value:
   (a) Fosters racial pride.
   (b) Outlet for anguish of heart in slavery.
   (c) Enables Negro to live.

Jackson treated his subject fairly well. He read his paper. He is no speaker at all. A Mr. George M. Edwards gave a delightful rendition on the violin. Mrs. [Cleota Collins] Lacy, head of Lacy's School of Music, then sang. She was the typical artist. In fact, her personality alone would have been sufficient to win her audience. She is as beautiful as she sings. Her interpretation of the "Sailor's Return" was marvelous.

I met Miss Wiggins, Dr. Hall, Mrs. Lacy, and a host of other people after the musicale. Dr. Woodson, Mr. [Walter] Dyson, and I all agreed that the first day of the meeting had gone over big. I was very happy for Woodson's sake.

Tuesday October 28, 1930

After breakfast we went to Cleveland Hall, where the first of our regular sessions was to take place.

We heard two fine addresses. One by Professor Newell N. Puckett on "Religious Folk Beliefs of Negroes and Whites." Showed that basically there existed no difference in their beliefs throughout the South. He had little new information. . . . However, Puckett took high ground for a Southerner. He is from Alabama, and speaks monotonously, in addition to his Southern drawl. He definitely is no speaker. A fine discussion followed.

Following him came Dr. [T. Wingate] Todd of [the Brush Foundation and Western Reserve University]. He spoke with a distinct Irish brogue. His subject was ["An Anthropologist's Study of Negro Life"].[3]

3. See "Proceedings of the Annual Meeting of the Association Held in Cleveland, Ohio, October 26–30, 1930," *Journal of Negro History* 16 (January 1931): 1–8. The papers delivered during the meeting were published in this issue of the journal.

Wednesday October 29, 1930

Dr. Woodson spoke on Haiti in the place of Dr. Holley, a native of Haiti. Holley was to speak on conditions in that country, but failed to appear.

Professor [Newell L.] Sims of Oberlin then spoke on "Human Relations." The main objective, he pointed out, is to get the Negro accepted into American society.

Sims went on to state that the problem of racial adjustment groups is the super-problem of our age; that at present domination by one group and subordination by the other is the status between whites and blacks; that segregation destroys the psychological result of any unified effort to solve the problem. The races, he contends, have drawn farther apart since emancipation, all of which tends to breed disharmony. To offset this, Sims believes that better techniques will be found in cooperation between the races instead of segregation. Use of such will bring about harmony, predicated upon equality. The amount of goodwill between races is limited, he went on. Unfortunately, only a small group of whites are interested in race adjustment from an ethical point of view. And it does not compromise their religion, either. As for democracy, it remains to be seen how many can invoke the doctrine of equality among unequals. Yet it makes a better appeal than Christian ethics. But every democracy is failing. (Not only failing, it has never been implemented.)

Self-interest, he went on, is doubtlessly stronger. There are few who don't seek their own safety first. Our safety as a nation depends upon eradication of vice, disease, and poverty, in all groups of the social order. Many would not risk doing this, however.

All devices mentioned, he said, will not eradicate the evil. It seems we have made "Get who may and keep who can," our law of life.

In reply to Sims's reading of the Negro Business League's figures on potential employment of Negroes in business, my view is that Negroes can't develop separate economic systems here.

For the American Negro, Sims went on, there is a New Beatitude: Let him who is discriminated against, discriminate in turn.

Nor is interracial cooperation the answer for, as Jessie O. Thomas of the Atlanta Urban League humorously put it, Negroes do the "co-ing" and the whites the "operating."

Dr. Woodson, seeing that the discussion had run into economic lines, designated me to lead it. I spoke of the futility of the Negroes' trying to match force with force with the white power structure even in the economic spheres. I referred to the boycott. Boycott is a dangerous weapon. We, as a race, are not powerful enough to wield such a ponderous weapon. It may slip from our grasp and crush the wielder. I referred to the Chicago

Whip campaign with its slogan, "Don't spend your money where you can't work." What if whites countered with "Don't hire Negroes where they don't spend their money"? Again, I cautioned against the erection of Negro businesses separate and distinct from whites, such as Professor Sims hinted. It can't be done. We don't even have a monopoly on our own skin whiteners and hair straighteners. We must develop a business or businesses that can attract the patronage of all groups. I discussed, also, the dismal labor outlook among Negroes, stressing the vanishing racial lines in occupation due to increasing unemployment. Negroes are being displaced in farm work, domestic service, hotel work, common labor, and in the trades. I answered several questions apropos of the Negroes in the oil region of Oklahoma, their wealth, etc., calling attention to the Negro lawyers in Muskogee, and the large oil properties owned by the Negroes there.

People applauded me. Gordon H. Simpson, reporter for the *Norfolk Journal and Guide,* renewed his request to chat with me before leaving the city.

I took Dr. W. O. Brown [of the University of Cincinnati], a young chap who made such a glowing speech last night, to luncheon at the railroad station. Had a delightful chat with him. He is a Texan, born in a little town between Houston and San Antonio. Of poor white stock, he grew up among Negroes and liked them. But like many others, had to respect the mores of the South, and looked condescendingly upon the Negro. I asked him what would his mother say if she heard him pronounce such sentiments. He retorted that she had been converted. It is the type of Southerner such as Brown represents toward whom Negroes must eventually look for their salvation here in America.

Later Woodson read the minutes of the Annual Meeting of the Association for the Study of Negro Life and History. Two things especially bothered him:

> 1. How to introduce Negro history in the schools.
> Obstacles:
> The main obstacles stemmed from the Negro teachers who believe that nothing should be said about Negroes and from whites who believe that Negroes have made no contribution to civilization.

Comes now a report on how to introduce a course of Negro History in the schools.

Mrs. Smith: Stated she got no cooperation from Miss Cromwell. However, she offered the following suggestions:

> 1. Have a course of study in Negro History for both white and colored schools. The outline could be worked out, giving subjects taken from the

texts. Negro History should be introduced in the grades. Teachers could dramatize African myths, etc.

2. Dr. Cromwell felt that Negro History should not be introduced until entrance to college. Professors Bye and Donald Young felt that was too late. Mrs. Evans suggested that Negro History, sociology, and achievements in correlated fields ought to be mentioned in connection with general topics. Professor Dyson suggests a syllabus be made for the schools.

A motion made by Mr. Howell [of Lincoln High School in Kansas City] that a committee be selected to report on the matter next year.

Mr. [Harry E.] Davis seconded the motion. The motion passed.

Report read by Mr. [J. H. B.] Evans.

Motion made by Mr. Davis and seconded by Mrs. Smith that the report be adopted. Passed.

Dr. Woodson discussed research, educational, and informative aspects of the Association. He cited the need to find properly qualified Negro men for universities as teachers.

It was moved, seconded, and passed, that the rules be suspended and that the administrative officers be re-elected for the ensuing year.

Moved and seconded and passed that the report of the Executive Council specifying that the following persons be submitted to replace either deceased or inactive members: A. Clayton Powell, of New York; Davis of Cleveland; and Professor A. M. Schlesinger of Harvard were elected.

Mr. Evans suggested we dramatize the thing that the Negro has done rather than the man. For example, he cited Benjamin Banneker, who helped lay out the Nation's Capital of Washington, D.C.

Thursday October 30, 1930

President R. B. Sims [of Bluefield Institute] spoke on the "Negro in Literature." He showed that Negroes have influenced American and European history since the beginning of the Era of Discovery. Diaz, a Negro, he said, is recognized as the national poet of Brazil. Portuguese language, in crossing the ocean, according to Costa, virtually doubled itself because of its contact with Negroes.

In short, Mr. Sims made a fairly good presentation of the Negro in literature.

Dr. Gilbert Jones of Wilberforce followed. He had twenty minutes, but took too much time for his introduction. Further he was full of apologies, which were out of place. Beginnings ran into the florescent [fluorescent?] stage.

Mrs. Sargent Smith, librarian, was the next speaker. Her thesis is that the American Public Library is unique among the libraries of the world. It stands for democracy. In the North maybe, but what about the South?

When Negroes came to the library here, some got foreign books, they also obtained foreign interpreters, or translators. She objected to "You people." Why not say Negro. It would sound better. Some of the valued library assistants are now Negroes. Suggestions: Write simple books on the Negro. Dr. Woodson can't see it.

Mr. Davis says that the Brownies' Book started by Du Bois a few years ago was a step in that direction. Failed for lack of support, as Woodson stated.

[No entries were found for October 31–November 14.]

15

Pennsylvania, Delaware, and New Jersey

Saturday November 15, 1930

Left for Harrisburg at 9:30, after sitting down to an enjoyable breakfast by Mrs. Fox. She virtually allowed us to stay at her home gratis, because the $2.50 that we paid apiece for ten days was a big joke to me. She did us a favor.[1]

The Ford sputtered going up a hill en route to Harrisburg. Fearing a repetition of the trip to Cleveland, we stopped at the nearest garage and had it fixed. Cost us $2.50.

Stopped in Altoona. Few Negroes here. Met Dr. [Ulysses] Wharton. Friend of Woodson's. Just recovering from paralytic stroke. Occurred in June. Getting along fine. Can't use right leg normally. Has large practice among whites. Naturally, lives in a big brick house [and] has two cars. Stressed the fact that he drives to church in Washington in his Packard, while his wife runs down to Baltimore in her car any time. Has son at Andover Academy. Advised us against going to Harrisburg. Told us steel mills were in bad shape there.

Went nevertheless. Arrived 7:20 p.m. Dr. Wharton had told us to get in touch with Dr. [Charles H.] Crampton here. Did so. But the white patients streamed in so fast—there were a few colored—that we went to dinner, knowing full well that it would take him almost 3 hours or more to wait upon those who were there. He has two large waiting rooms, and they were filled.

1. No diary entry or correspondence was found that gives any clues as to where they were leaving. Since they remained there ten days, they were probably in one of the larger cities, such as Pittsburgh, between Cleveland, Ohio, and Altoona, Pennsylvania.

Crossed the street and called upon Dr. [H. T.] Vernon, a dentist. Advised us to go to [the] Jackson home for food and lodging. We did. Very nice place. Mrs. Jackson, the proprietor, introduced us to Miss Annie Lee Hill. Pretty dark girl. Girl [is the] Reserve secretary at the Y.W.C.A. here. Told us she hates Harrisburg. Spends most of time and money going to New York. Impresses me as one who loves amusement and plenty of it. Is just a modern girl. Tells us everyone here wants to interfere with everyone's business.

Takes us to see Rev. [C. F.] Jenkins of Second Baptist Church. Young man. Friend of Vernon Johns. Is also very intelligent. Could not have me speak at his church tomorrow. Very sorry, but even then a student whom he had invited to come to preach was there. Took me next door, however, to Rev. [D. A.] Scott, a youngish black fellow with blotches on his face. Would be glad to have me at night. Jenkins then took me to Steelton, 3 miles away, to see some pastors there. One was in bed and couldn't be awakened; the other has booked a preacher from Philadelphia.

So foggy I could hardly see to drive. Returned to Rev. Jenkins's. He then sent me to Rev. [W. L.] Johnson's. This divine, however, was just preparing to start a revival at his church and did not want anything to interfere. Told me that he knew all about the problem. Felt the Negro had to suffer before he can be brought face to face with his problems. Said all these hotels here still have Negro waiters. Unique among northern cities.

By the way, [James Cecil] Wilkey embarrassed me beyond measure at Dr. Jenkins's. Sprawled out on the sofa with his head hung on one side, he virtually asked the Reverend to lodge him and intimated that he did not have money to pay his way. I am a student, he said, and I can't pay the $2.00 which is asked at [the] Jackson home. I had to rudely tell him that it would be better to thrash that matter out with Mrs. Jackson; that it did not and could not concern Rev. Jenkins.

Arrived home. He went to another hotel to see about a room. There the landlady wanted $5.00 a week apiece. I went to see it. Smelled of cabbage and looked so bad I could not consider staying there. Came back. Planned to give Mrs. Jackson $2.50 the first night, then find a cheaper place in the morning.

Then there was the car. Could not be parked on street. Took a chance and did so. Retired tired out.

[No entries were found for November 16–19.]

Thursday November 20, 1930

Left Harrisburg this morning. Peculiar city. Most Negroes have no race consciousness according to businessmen. Yet best city for books since I left Houston, Texas. Interesting in several ways.

LABOR: Have all hotels' waiters, etc. Some men work in R.R. shops and other factories, especially in Steelton. Women in domestic and personal service.

SCHOOLS: Separate for primary grades. Both races in same junior high and high schools. Students complain of discrimination. Want separate system.

CHURCHES: Have three intelligent pastors. Jenkins, Johnson, and Sedgust[?]. Jenkins wielding largest influence.

BUSINESS: Very little. One good drugstore, Marshall's. Five grocery and meat stores (Roland). Best pool parlor, barber shop, lunchroom, etc., I have ever seen (Strother's). Very good hotel. (Jackson's).

Before leaving, [I] stopped at Mrs. Temples. Met Stella Scott. Pretty and has fine personality. Went to Carlisle. Small historic town location of Dickinson College and home of John Dickinson.

Saw my friend Harlan Carter, head of school. Worst behaved children I have ever seen. Are utterly incorrigible. Girls made eyes at me while I talked. Only 12–14. Carter tells me some are common prostitutes. Carter himself has hard task to hold himself in check.

Schools for Negroes here [are] bad. Toilets on outside. No water to rinse urinals. Stench terrible. Met Rev. J. J. Robinson. Had dinner with him. Wilkey went to Harrisburg to bring up Stella and Hortense [Temple?]. Pageant given by Chambersburg group fills church. People excited to high spiritual pitch. I spoke. I grip them. Perhaps it is Stella who makes me do so. But they are moved, and they applaud me again and again. Rev. [J. H.] Slade of Harrisburg invites me to his church. Then comes the buffoonery. Rev. Robinson—in an effort to prove he is an orator—steps out, raises his voice to the heavens, gets the people crying away, then, while everyone's mind is fixed on heaven, suddenly thrusts them back to earth with, "Let's go downstairs and eat." Drove home with Stella in my arms.

FRIDAY NOVEMBER 21, 1930

Left Harrisburg about 11:00. Arrived [in] York around 12:00. Went immediately to the office of Dr. George Bowles, the leading Negro physician here. Not in. Went to his home. Mrs. Bowles, who did not have the courtesy to invite us in, told us that we could find the doctor in at 1:00.

From there I called upon Mrs. Armstead, the sister-in-law of Miss [Louise] Armstead, the school teacher of Harrisburg. Could not accommodate us. She told us of a Mrs. [Ida] Grayson who kept lodgers. Concerning the books, [she] advised that I return when her husband was home. She is very pleasant.

Did not like rooms at Mrs. Grayson's. Charlotte Hotel, where Mrs. Bowles had referred us, looked so uninviting that I would not even consider staying there. Instead, I went to one of the schools on South Pershing Avenue where I was told a Mr. [Henry W.] Hopewell was principal. The school was small and unattractive as well as uninspiring.

Mr. Hopewell, I found, was a frat brother. Very kind and anxious to help. A Lincoln University graduate. He knows Carter at Carlisle; Anderson at Howard as professor and others. About thirty-two years of age. He has either a wooden leg or else his left leg is so stiff that he is compelled to drag it. Introduced me to teachers. One, Miss Johnson, said she was not interested. The Misses [Florence and Mary E.] Turner gave different reactions; one was going out of town, yet was interested. The other said she was not interested; so said Miss Carter also. Poor things, they cannot see the value of such things.

From soliciting among the teachers, I returned to talk to Mr. Hopewell's class, 7b [grade level?]. They listened, exceedingly attentive, unlike the pupils at Carlisle yesterday. So gripped were these students that many, or about half the class, remained in at recess to copy from the blackboard the facts and names I had put thereon concerning Negro History. Both Hopewell and I were very gratified.

Mr. Hopewell then took me to the old high school, where a play was being enacted by children in the third and fourth grades. I was so very favorably impressed by the mistress of ceremonies, a little girl of about ten years of age, that I asked who she was. I was informed by a gentleman who sat beside me that she was Helen Armstead. To my surprise, I found it was Mrs. Armstead's daughter. She conducted the play and introduced the supervisor of schools and Mr. Hopewell with just as much assurance and clarity as any adult, and better than many.

Mr. Hopewell took us to a Mrs. Harris, [at] 455 South King Street, where we not only secured a room, but also board. We promised to call for him at 6:30, at which time he would take us to see some prospective buyers.

In the meantime, we called upon Reverend [Thomas E.] Montouth, a Presbyterian pastor. Has a community center in connection with the church, on the first floor of his home. The schools are abominable here, he told me. There is now a movement afoot to add three more teachers to the grammar school, then to bar Negro children from the white junior high school, thus permitting them to attend the senior high school only. And the Negroes sit supinely by and allow it to take place. The Negroes, we were told, at one time attended the white schools, but later agitated for separated schools. So says Mrs. Harris, who lived here all her life. Now Negro children living next door to a school have to go a mile or more to a colored school.

There is a peculiar labor problem in York. Although this is one of the leading manufacturing cities of Pennsylvania, very little opportunity is given Negroes to work in them. In the factories, with the exception of a few molders, all the Negroes who do get in are unskilled laborers. Most of them are porters, janitors, truck drivers, teamsters, etc. This is also a non-union town. Hence, Negroes are kept out by the native whites, who formed 93 percent of the population in 1930. Despite the fact that more than 5,000 women are now employed in the factories, not a single Negro woman is hired. Most of them work in service.

I met Dr. Bowles. He flatly refused to take the books. Interested, however, and he told me to send them in February. I told him he would have to pay full price. He wrote me a check. Then began to talk. Interesting. He told me Dr. Greene, of Knoxville, Tennessee, had lost everything in a bank crash there. Dr. Walker and son, of Asheville, North Carolina, had both gone stark crazy. Forty-three banks had failed in Arkansas last week. Sixty-three throughout the South. The Negroes are hard hit. I went from Dr. Bowles to a Miss Johnson, who lives with a Miss Craig. I sold the former, and Wilkey failed with the latter. We went to Mr. Armstead's. Told me pointedly that he would take nothing, that I could save my breath. I told him he ought to buy a book for his child, who had thrilled me by her superb conduction of the exercises at the school during the afternoon. He replied he was already doing so. I asked him whether he refused because he did not want to, or could not buy the books. He told me flatly he did not want them. I thereupon asked him if he would allow me to present a book to his daughter. Acquiesced. Hopewell, Mrs. Armstead, and Wilkey were apprehensive lest even fisticuffs be indulged in between us, but nothing of the sort happened. Armstead is only a bluff, ignorant chauffeur. It is a shame that such a man must be saddled upon such a progressive woman as his wife. (I presented and autographed for her a copy of [R. T.] Kerlin's *Negro Poets and Their Poetry [Poems]*.[2] Her pretty face lighted up as she thanked me, after reading my prediction that she was destined to do great things.)[3] Took Hopewell home after another stop. His wife was just getting in from a club meeting. Both are excellent people and friends.

SATURDAY NOVEMBER 22, 1930

Mrs. Grayson tells me of $5,000 Metropolitan Endowment Policy. Could be turned over as collateral to help education of children. Thought she would

2. R[obert] T[homas] Kerlin, *Negro Poets and Their Poems.*

3. These sentences were added by Greene to a draft transcription he made in later years.

do so for her boy. Lions and Rotary Club sponsoring it. Draw color line. Mrs. Grayson saw Mr. Stribes of Lions Club. Latter told her he regretted to say it was true. Left York about 4:00 p.m. Arrived D.C. about 8:15. Saw Bertha [Baylor]. Called [Bushrod and Lillian] Mickey.

Sunday November 23, 1930

Saw Bertha and Mickey. Went to show with latter at night.

Monday to Saturday November 24–29, 1930

Uneventful, slept late in the morning. Woodson told me Tuesday that survey of Negro unemployment might not go through. And I had typed questionnaires on Monday. Woodson wants me to make survey. Sent [John Wesley] Poe $25 on Monday to come from Gary, Indiana. Cannot endure Wilkey longer. [Ernest] Bacote came down on Wednesday night. Took dinner with him and Vickie [Victoria Bacote] on Thursday.

Had several letters from Emile Holley. My check of $11.00 to him had come back. He was quite upset about it. Sent him a money order for $13.59—$11.00 plus $2.54 protest charges.

Saturday November 29, 1930

Left Washington about 6:00 p.m. Before doing so, however, went to Howard Manor. Called on Elois.

[No entries were found for November 30–December 2.]

Wednesday December 3, 1930

Wilmington, Delaware

Called on Dr. [Samuel G.] Elbert. Fine man. Referred me to Mr. and Mrs. [William Henri] Pipes.

Mrs. Pipes tells me that the Board of Education of Chester is preparing to feed all school children. Will give them two meals a day. I asked what methods should be followed. Will give as many gallons of milk as needed. Women's Century Club has been providing milk. School board there has been a political football. Chester [was] called Upland in William Penn's time. Historic. Have nice junior high school. Inadequate. Mr. William K. Valentine [is] principal. All Negro schools old [and] inadequate, will begin to build later. Installed Negro as automobile mechanic. Children being taught in church.

Mr. Pipes is an alumnus of Lincoln and Howard universities. The first Negro to matriculate in medicine at Temple University. Studied pharmacy. First and only commissioned notary public in the U.S. of our race. Ran for Assemblyman in 1920 and won. Told not to come to legislature. Went to Recorder's Office. Was chief chemist at Douglas. Assistant resident physician.

Mrs. Pipes [is] Wilmingtonian. [She was] educated here and in Philadelphia. M.A. from Wilberforce. Studied law. Taught first in Maryland at 16. Took extension courses etc. Kept house and took vocal lessons, too. Singer. Led Bethel Church choir for 30 years. Taught at Chester for 30 years. Taught every grade to junior high. Principal of grammar school for 20 years. Specialized in primary work. Had model primary department. . . . Trained teachers from Normal Department. Stopped teaching after marriage. Asked to return after four years. Taught under Professor Thomas. Returned under solicitation of president of the board. Had boys ranging from six to thirteen. Looking for strong teacher. First married teacher to reenter system.

Created first colored playground in Chester. Largest in Chester. Began in 1910. Carried on fourteen years. While there in 1910, Mr. Wilson gave up principalship. Selected by the board as principal. Did not apply. Inaugurated cooking and sewing [into the curriculum]. First one in Chester [to do so], white or black. Supervisor stated that he would start it and, if successful, would put it in other [schools] (Harvey School). Now in all. Divided work and put Mr. Thomas at head of junior high. Put Mrs. Pipes at Watts school. Has 20 teachers. Sent no less than sixteen classes to senior high school.

Vice Chairman of Black 5th Ward and State Central Committeeman of the state of Delaware, Charles Colburn [is also] Chairman of Colored Union Republican Organization. Took active part in campaigns of Harding, Coolidge, and Hoover.

Dr. [J. A.] Stubbs: No Wassermann [tests for syphilis] taken of Negroes here until 1925. More work going on in this health center than any in the city. Four health centers, two when it started.

Mr. Marshall Skip told me that he tried to rent building from Ezron Church. Matthews, Board of Securities, then asked him could he move next week. Next thing he knew "Jew Joe" had come up from Front Street (the Coast) and rented it. Church owns property at 9th and Walnut. Escheated to it.

Chester, Pennsylvania

Go to Chester. Old city, founded 1682. Goodly number of Negroes.

RESIDENCES: Mostly fair and of brick. Many homes in newer sections on ill-graded streets. No sidewalks, no gutters; houses new, however.

SCHOOLS: Three—Watts, McKay, and junior high. First two old and too small to accommodate students. Watts school built in 1876. Segregated schools for primary and junior high. All go to same high. Schools antiquated with exception of junior high. In contrast are the white schools, most of which are new. The Larken[?] school and the high are built of imposing white stone. No equality in equipment where there is dual school system.

LABOR: Many people out of work because of slackness in steel factories. Hit Negroes hardest. Board of Education feeding students twice a day. Whites working on streets. A few Negroes work in oil refineries at Marcus Hook—Sinclair and Pure Oil.

BUSINESSES: Virtually no Negro business here with the exception of a pool parlor and funeral parlor. Mr. Hunt owns the latter. Is very representative.

PROFESSIONAL CLASS: Consists of doctors (7), dentists, and teachers. Most of the latter are well equipped. All normal school or college graduates. Some have master's degrees, others are working toward them.

CHURCHES: Like every colored community there is an oversupply of churches. Baptists, A.M.E., M.E., and A.M.E.Z., as well as store fronts.

MORALS: Pretty bad here. School teacher tells us there are some parts of the town below 5th from Central Avenue where she fears to go even with an escort in a car. Whites and blacks approach her.

Met and spoke to the teachers at Watts school. Through the intercession of Mrs. Pipes, I was able to secure about $20 worth of business payable tomorrow. God grant it may materialize. Poe would not remain.

THURSDAY DECEMBER 4, 1930

At nine o'clock this morning I arrived at the Howard High School where I was to speak to the students. It is a beautiful school, with a corps of some 35 teachers and approximately 600 students.

Did not speak until 9:20. Spoke for twenty minutes. What I said and the way I said it must have interested the students, for they paid strict attention. Mr. [G. A.] Johnson, no doubt, revised his estimate of Monday when he doubted whether I could hold the attention of students. Miss Redding, one of the teachers, congratulated me as I passed and remarked that it was very well done. It was encouraging.

I had no opportunity to contact the teachers, however, but Mr. Johnson assures me I could see them tomorrow. Met Miss Sarah Strickland, one of the teachers here. She told me that the Branch Association was meeting in Philadelphia on Saturday evening and that it would be well for me to attend. Decided I would.

Went to breakfast at 11:00 a.m. From there got the battery, which had been recharged. The cost of that, together with new tires, amounted to $3.50.

Off we went then to Chester. Poe drove for a while. He did well. Arrived at Chester at one o'clock. All the teachers, with the exception of Miss Hall, took the books as agreed. The latter finally did so, but only because I accepted a postdated check. Mrs. Pipes, as usual, was just fine. She, however, felt indisposed today.

Can't understand Mrs. [Sarah] Pride (Woodson's cousin). Seems interested. Yet is a widow and certainly not attractive. Wants me to call her when I come to Philadelphia. Miss Fontaine, too, is interesting. Miss Valentine took only one book as she had originally planned. In all, I collected almost $32. Mrs. Pipes, however, paid me $9.98 cash for her books.

Mr. Smith told me that the white librarian desired to see me about the books. Went there. She was out, but her assistant assured me that they could give me an order. Am to see her at 4:00 p.m. tomorrow. Oh, lest I forget, on account of the Teachers' Institute today I was prevented from seeing other teachers, because of the fact that classes were dismissed at 2:00 p.m. Took four of the teachers there. Strange to say, white and black teachers meet together, though the schools are separate.

Returned to Wilmington at 5:00 p.m. After dinner went out to interview Mr. [William J.] Winchester, who had been referred to me by Drs. Elbert, Stubbs, and others. A great black hulking man. Witty. He told me he thought I was bringing him money, when lo and behold, I was looking for it. Has a good job in Recorder's Office, but won't take the books.

Came back, met and talked with Mrs. Barnes, who teaches at Howard High, yet goes back and forth to Columbia University in New York, every weekend, working for her doctorate degree. Just wanted to talk, however, not to buy books. Did virtually nothing today. Merely collected old promises.

FRIDAY DECEMBER 5, 1930

Went to Chester, arriving at noontime. Proceeded to the McKay School, of which Mrs. Greene is principal. An old inadequate unimposing building so reminiscent of the schools I used to know when I was a boy. Has six rooms. Teachers were at lunch when I entered. Most of them had their lunches brought to school.

Spoke to them for twenty minutes. One subscribed outright. She was a Mrs. Moore, the wife of a pastor here. Gave me only $2.00, however. Mrs. Greene, the principal, told me that she has four children and that her husband has been out of work for some time. Could not subscribe. Another who desired the books greatly for her son has no husband and is supporting four children. Still another, a Miss Saunders, a saucy little thing, told me that she would read those of her uncle—Mr. Valentine—the principal of the junior high school. All were interested, however.

Before leaving, one of the teachers requested that I send the books to her $9.98 C.O.D. Agreed. Another teacher then called me to do the same thing. Brought away 3 orders therefore.

Went to the Booker T. Junior High. Secured Mr. Valentine's order. Told me he has been principal here for 16 years. Also informed me of the teachers who came to his school in order to do their practical work in teaching. Remarked that Temple University requires 100 hours; University of Pennsylvania 75 teaching hours. Has a large number who have done their practice work at his school. Commends them highly. He had his ups and downs. Once had to go to court and plead the case of a teacher when a mother was trying to "crucify" her. He won it, too.

From Booker T., I went to the A.M.E. Church. Two classes are held here due to overcrowding in the school. There I met Miss [Faye] Knight, a young, attractive teacher, also a Miss [Maybelle] Wilson. They talked to me of different things for over an hour. School teaching went a-glimmering. They wanted me to stay in Chester a while so that they might entertain me. They took me to the library, at least Miss Knight did. There the white librarian, who is extremely desirous of starting a Negro section in the institution, subscribed for a set of books. Coming out of the library, I found Poe waiting in the car. We took Miss Knight home and returned to Wilmington.

A sidelight on the desperate economic plight of Chester Negroes was gleaned by the inability of Miss Knight to purchase the books. Her entire family of five, she stated, are dependent upon her earnings. Her father has been out of work for months. Miss Wilson, too, is doing the same thing and, in addition, sending a sister through normal school.

Went to speak at the Garrett Center at 8:00. Upon my arrival, I found the place dark and closed. There was a notice in the window, however, to the effect that Professor Lorenzo Greene, Negro labor expert, would speak on unemployment. The hour given was 9:00 p.m. Dr. Stubbs had told me 8:00 p.m. I was furious, for I could have spent this time to advantage otherwise. And yet I was moved to mirth, for had the meeting been scheduled for 8:00, either the audience or I would have been tardy. Seeing a light in the church across the way, I went over and met a Rev. Stevenson, a big, healthy looking, well-fed minister. He formerly pastored in Washington, D.C. He told me that Attorney [Julius A.] Redding is the first and only lawyer of our race to be admitted to the bar in Delaware. His admission came through political "pull," engineered by Mr. [Charles] Colburn through Senator Daniel P. Hasty. Redding, whom I have met, is a Harvard University graduate. His father is a mail carrier. Rev. Stevenson asserted that so potent is the Negroes' political balance of power here that "if they remained at home during an election, the state would go Democratic; or if they voted Democratic, the state would go to that party likewise." But by joining with the white Republicans, they swing the vote to the G.O.P. This was news to me, for I entertained no idea of the Negroes' political power here. Yet I had been told that several Negroes hold responsible political offices, such as Mr. Pipes, Mr. Winchester, Dr. Elbert, and Mr. Colburn.

The Garrett Settlement now being lighted up, I went thither. Three or four people had gathered. The place itself was cold and the interior resembled one of the settlements in the Bowery. I waited, cursing under my breath, until 10:20 p.m., when finally Dr. Stubbs arrived, expressing profuse apologies for his delay. Naturally I turned it off as of no moment. I could not afford to manifest my exasperation, for he held $9.98 for a set of books, which I was very desirous of obtaining. I spoke an hour. The people seemed interested, what few were there. It is a shame, however, to waste such good information upon empty benches. Dr. Stubbs, speaking to me after my talk, said he wished that everyone in Wilmington could have heard it. So did I, especially that they might have manifested their interest and pleasure by an honorarium in keeping with what I had dispensed. I am getting sick of eternally speaking for nothing. People take advantage of my enthusiasm. But it is the cause. I presume it is my destiny to give unstintingly to this work. Why should one enter any field if he is not willing to give his all?

Saturday December 6, 1930

Wilmington, Delaware

This morning I received six sets of books from Woodson's office. He stated in his covering letter that I had failed to send certain monies for books to the office; that such was our agreement. I became so wrought up that I was of a mind to return at once to Washington, [and] tell Woodson to take the car and "go to hell." But there was Poe, whom I had persuaded to come along with me. I could not leave him in the lurch; therefore, I said nothing. Together we sent Woodson $35; I remitted $13.98; Poe almost twice as much. Only in case the subscriber paid the entire amount in cash or check to the agent would we handle any funds belonging to the office. Yet his letter stated that Wilkey had sold twice as many books as I. Further that I must change my procedure and not keep the money belonging to the office "as I had done this summer." He had, in fact, virtually branded me as a thief. God only knows what would have happened had he told me that to my face, for whatever my shortcomings and they are legion—I at least strive to be honest. I would not barter my honor and reputation for a few pennies. I wondered whether Woodson was trying to so anger me that I would give up the work; for, in the closing paragraph, he intimated that if I continued to attack the church, I would have to do so as a freelance. That would be evident to anyone. He probably was "quaking in his boots" because Rev. R. R. Wright, Jr., of Philadelphia replied to a statement I had made concerning the church, which Woodson believed might cause Negro ministers to withdraw their "support" from the Association. I believe John R. Hawkins, who is president of the Association, is behind this. He is also financial secretary of the A.M.E. Church and a political leader. My temper quickly subsided, for I knew that I had forwarded to the office whatever monies were due. (Our agreement was that the books would sell for $9.98 a set: the salesman would collect his commission of $4.00—the balance was to be paid by the subscriber C.O.D. upon receipt of the books. Eighty cents of each sale by my colleagues was to come to me as compensation for my efforts in speaking to groups, which made it easier for the other salesmen to secure orders. It was the accumulation of about $64.00, sent back to the office for me last summer by the men from our Hampton campaign, which caused Woodson to mistakenly accuse me of keeping money belonging to the office. He refused to allow me a commission on the men's sales, so the matter was dropped. Nevertheless, the entire responsibility for the campaign: car, lodging, boarding, and even the laundry of the salesmen, was mine in case they could not meet their expenses.)[4]

As for the church, I did not give a "hang" whether it kept on mulcting the people or not. It could only do so until Negroes opened their eyes and refused to be "milked" any longer.

Now about Woodson himself. He is the most arrogant, scornful, and depressing person I have ever been associated with. He has a virulent temper, but does not like to see the same manifested by another. He is puffed up with his own importance and deprecates that of everyone associated closely with him. He possesses a humor which rankles, instead of warms, a wit which makes me wish to strangle him at times. Then, too, he reminds me of a politician. He has no honor. Like a reptile, he is sly [and] mole-like; he works underground, undermining his victim, until the latter is ready to step upon the hollow earth to his downfall. The case of Dr. [Charles H.] Wesley is still fresh in my memory. His word is like thin ice—easily broken. I refer

4. This section was added in later years when Greene made a draft transcription of this entry.

here to his promises to me concerning the *Negro Wage Earner.* He will make mistakes and then place the blame on his subordinates. He has absolutely no regard for the feelings of others, but seems to believe that he has a God-given right to vent his spleen upon anyone. He can brook no subordinate position. He must be the ruler; he cannot share power; enemies he makes in profusion, who either abstain from supporting or else hinder the work. He doesn't seem to care. His whole nature has been warped, bent, [and] blasted, I believe, by an unfortunate love affair. Since that time, he seems to revel in ascertaining the extent to which he can irritate others.

I do not believe he has one true friend in the entire world. He has countless acquaintances, thousands of admirers, but like Bismarck and others, he is not loved. He belongs to that group of mortals who, unloving and unloved, are prized because they possess some unique attribute that the world desires. What a shame! That Woodson is of this temperament renders it impossible for him to inspire younger black scholars to perfect themselves in Negro History with a view toward taking his place when death or infirmity shall cause him to relinquish the helm.

Went to Chester. Poe sold two sets of books. I called upon a Miss Dorothy Wilson who took me to see several people. A humorous incident happened while we were awaiting the arrival of Reverend Bond. I happened to notice a very odd ring on Miss Wilson's finger. She was sitting beside me on the divan, so I unceremoniously slipped it off. While I was holding it in my hand, the minister entered. Shooting a quick glance at the ring, his face beamed as he asked, "What can I do for you, my children?" (He was an elderly man.) When I began to mention the books which I had, his smile changed as he added, "Oh, I thought you wished to see me about something else." Once outside, I told Miss Wilson that she had had a narrow escape, for the minister verily believed that we had come there to be united in holy wedlock.

Took Miss Wilson home. She played and sang for me. Does both well, from an amateur's point of view. I rewarded her with several kisses, which she yielded freely. I took my leave, promising her that I would visit her while in Philadelphia.

Returned to Wilmington, for I had to see Mr. Gunby[?], the undertaker. He was not home. I took dinner, after which I dressed and left for Philadelphia. A cold rain was falling. Poe, at first, did not wish to go. Finally decided that he would take Miss [Betty] Forrester to movies in "Philly," and I could come after them following the close of my meeting.

We stopped in Chester for Miss Forrester—a very charming girl and an old flame of Poe's. What a time we had finding Dauphin Street! Arrived there. Poe and Miss Forrester, who had reached Philadelphia too late to attend a show, declined to come in.

It was already 10:20 when I entered the house and the club had virtually despaired of my reaching there. They had called Miss Strickland, but were unable to reach her. My host was a lady of middle age, very refined and gracious. She had a finely appointed home. There were some 20 members of the club present. The president, whom I later learned was Dr. DeHaven Hinkson, was just concluding some remarks concerning an address by one of the members, Mrs. Sadie Pace Alexander.[5]

I was introduced and asked to speak. In truth, although I had not the slightest idea of what to say when I rose, the environment, the interest manifested in Negro History by the group, and the expectancy with which they all looked forward to my coming, so inspired me that perhaps I surpassed myself. At any rate, a Miss Chase (a school principal) remarked that Dr. Woodson could not find a better disciple to disseminate his work. The congratulations came so thick and furious, that perhaps they were sincere—at least some of them. Miss Chase asked me to go—if possible—to Camden tomorrow and talk to a sorority, under the headship of a Mrs. Paul, which group was meeting at the Y.W.C.A. These persons were about to start a Junior History Club. I promised to go.

The result of my speech here was two outright subscriptions and several promises to take books when I come to Philadelphia. A fine collation was served after the business meeting.

I endeavored to persuade the lovers to come in, but although half-frozen, they still declined, which meant that they had to sit another half hour. As we drove home, both were in good humor, Miss Forrester stating that she would never forget tonight for it meant a new experience for her. I retired at 1:45, absolutely fatigued.

Lest I forget, when we paid Mrs. Murray, our landlady, tonight just before we left, she seemed like a totally new woman. How a little money does affect the disposition of mortals!

Sunday December 7, 1930

After breakfast, I started for Camden. Arriving there about 2:10, the sorority was awaiting me. I met Mrs. Paul, a beautiful and extremely fair

5. Sadie Tanner Mossell Alexander (1898–1989) was a member of the prominent Mossell family of Philadelphia. She attended the University of Pennsylvania and became the second black woman to receive a Ph.D. and the first to earn a doctorate in economics. In 1923, she married Raymond Pace Alexander and, after earning a law degree from the University of Pennsylvania in 1927, entered the practice of law with her husband. They enjoyed long and distinguished careers in law and as crusaders for the rights of African Americans. See Hine, *Black Women in America,* 17–19.

woman, who introduced me to the group. My talk so intrigued them that we were able to get rid of two sets of books without effort. I also received another invitation to speak to the high school Junior Negro History Club on Monday, December 15th.

We ate dinner at Horne and Hardat's Automat on Market Street near 15th Street. To a great extent, it is self-service—a nickel or dime in the slot and you get everything from cereal to desserts. The average person does not realize the extent to which such inventions are rapidly taking work out of the hands of the laborer. I was interested to note that both whites and blacks of both sexes worked here in about equal numbers. They do everything from cooking to acting as bus girls and boys and waiting on the guests.

Later we set forth for Dover—a trip of more than 60 miles over excellent roads. After one leaves Wilmington, there are no more cities in Delaware—just a few towns of which Dover, the capital, is the largest. And its population is only about 7,000.

We first called on Dr. Henry, the Negro physician there. His wife told us he was out of town. She greeted us cordially, however, and had us sit while she called her husband's nephew, Dr. Charles King, a dentist, who lived next door.

What a surprise when I found to my astonishment that he was a former classmate of mine at Howard University! Henry told me [that] he has been practicing here for three years. Is married, but his wife is working at the Census Office in Washington, D.C., in order to help make ends meet. We asked him where we could get lodging for the night.[6]

He took us to a Mrs. Cannon on Division Street. She has a fairly decent home, but no furnace. There is a Negro-owned hotel, we were told, but is located in an undesirable section and likewise has no central heating. We decided after a lot of "hemming and hawing" to stay at Mrs. Cannon's, who charged us 75 cents each a night. The room was heated by an oil stove, which gave forth an insufferable stench common to them.

Dr. Henry then took us to Rev. [S. J.] Horsey's [Whatcoat] M.E. Church where I was invited to speak. I spoke for ten minutes. The pastor said later that had he known I was bringing such a message, he would have been glad to have given me the entire hour. And he might have done so with profit, for all he was doing was making a great bluster in the pulpit, but saying

6. This entry is confusing. Greene did not say so, but Henry must have returned while they were waiting. A Charles Alexander Henry, Jr., received a degree in dentistry from Howard University in 1926. In the 1960s, he was still living in Dover, Delaware. No Charles King is listed in the Howard directory. See Frederick D. Wilkinson, ed., *Directory of Graduates: Howard University, 1870–1963*.

nothing. Nonetheless, I believe he could preach a fairly nice and interesting sermon, but he was giving the people what they desired. A Mr. Hardcastle asked that I see him tomorrow, that he would take something then. I shall certainly do so.

Monday December 8, 1930

Dover, Delaware

SIZE: Less than 10,000, about 1,000 Negroes.

BUSINESS: Virtually nil, with exception of tailor shop and two or three poorly equipped lunchrooms and barber shop.

SCHOOLS: Very good. B. T. Washington Grade School has eight rooms. [It is a] fine brick building, [with] ample room for playground. Gift largely by T. Coleman Dupont.

PROFESSIONAL: One physician, Dr. Henry. One Dentist. About ten or twelve teachers. All normal school or college graduates. Well trained. Principal, Mr. [S. Marcellus] Blackburn, seems not to be as well trained, cultured, or commanding of respect as my idea of principal should be. Seems to be person easily tractable to whim of whites.

LABOR: Most of Negroes work in domestic service in the winter. In spring, summer, and fall many leave housework for the farms and orchards. Delaware is a great truck farming and fruit growing state. Besides quantities of tomatoes, sweet potatoes, corn, cantaloupes, etc., peaches, apples, pears, and strawberries flourish. Mrs. Cannon's mother told me that she has grown varieties [of strawberries] of which thirteen will fill a quart basket. This is also a great canning state. And in season—when the tomatoes, corn, peaches, and other vegetables and fruit are ripe—many Negroes leave their service places for work in the canneries, lured thereto by higher wages. Later when the canning season is over they return to service. There are several canning factories in Dover that we personally observed. Others we saw scattered throughout the state. Negroes worked with whites on the street and drive trucks and wagons.

RACE RELATIONS: Good. The Duponts have done much for Negroes in the way of schools. Give every Negro over 60 years of age a pension of $8 a month as long as they live.

CHURCHES: Have seven churches, less than 1,000 Negroes, one church for less than every 150 Negroes. Rev. Horsey only one I met. A preacher of old stripe. Yet good speaker.

Went to Booker T. Washington School. Spoke to children. Fine school. Teachers will see me tonight. Went out to State College.[7] Fine school. One

7. The State College for Colored Students of the State of Delaware, now Delaware State College, was established in 1891 by an act of the Delaware General Assembly. Although

fine building $65,000. Dr. [R. S.] Grossley, president. Hoped he would invite us to stay there. Didn't, however. Poe eager. Went back to ask him to direct us to place in town. Told us to see Henry. While there, he called. Would accommodate us at the school. Put us in guest room. Just ordinary house but was warm. Took dinner in dining hall.

Bailey, frat brother, invited us to men's club. Went there and played cards.

Previously had gone to see teachers. Had not arrived. Went to see Miss Gibbs. Missed her. Arrived home at 1:50.

[No entries were found for December 9–10.]

Thursday December 11, 1930

Mr. Turner, hotel owner. Camden, [New Jersey,] 100,000 people, 88,000 white [and] 12,000 Negroes. Churches—Negroes 36, whites 25. . . .

Mr. Grundy says that his great grandfather was sent to Africa 87 years ago. Was past pastor of Eziah A.M.E. Church. Buried under there. Bells tolled when he left. Said Africa was not a fit place for Negroes. Church (Eziah M.E.) 150 years old, celebrated two weeks ago, Rev. Dickerson [pastor].

Dr. Stubbs "jews" me down to $9.00. He and wife started Garrett Settlement 20 years ago.

This afternoon went great guns. Sold all teachers at Smyrna, four. Mr. Wray, principal. Unimposing as principal. All took small sets. Went to Middleton. Sold all three teachers large set. Mrs. Henry, principal. Looked timid to extreme. Five DuPont schools. Poe elated. I too. . . .

Friday December 12, 1930

Delaware

Hoped to repeat success of yesterday. Went first to Marshalltown. Principal short, black, bowlegged man. Old Uncle Tom type. Did not even have the courtesy to tell us his name. Took nothing. Saving for Christmas.

From there to school in Newport. Mrs. Mulley, middle-aged woman, principal. Called in teachers. Sound interested. Too near Christmas. More impressive type of teacher than the man at Marshalltown. Four-teacher school.

---

founded as the state's 1890 land-grant college, under provisions of the second Morrill Act, in 1926–1927, State College was still largely a high school and junior college. That year, there were 144 students in the high school and only nineteen in the junior college programs, which consisted of the normal school, agriculture, and home economics. U.S. Department of the Interior, Bureau of Education, *Survey of Negro Colleges and Universities,* 148–56.

Now to Newark School. Mr. Richards, globe-trotter principal, cultured, refined. Bachelor who is impressed with the importance of his position to the extent that he refused to allow us to contact his teachers.

[No entry was found for December 13.]

Sunday December 14, 1930

Rose at 12:00. Ate no breakfast. Tired from late hour getting in this morning. Went to dinner at automat to please Poe. Returned, tried to find the Keene girls. Failed. Wrote Woodson [and] told him I never intended to pay 80¢ to office. Trying to bull me. Shall do so no longer. Went to Wilmington to speak. Left Poe in Chester with Betty Forrester. In Wilmington, church almost empty. Minister bellowing at top of voice. You must love Jesus. Talking to benches. Felt like going home. Was seen first. Could not with decency leave. Spoke 5 minutes. Time wasted. Failed to see either Miss Knight or Wilson in Chester. Returned for Poe. Time and money thrown away.

Monday December 15, 1930

Rose late. Cold, and I was tired. Read quite a deal of Cellini's autobiography.[8] Salacious in part but only reflects 16th-century Italy. Man was genius, master artist, murderer, adulterer, intriguer, soldier, and a score of other things.

Went to Camden about 3:00 p.m. Spoke to high school boys and girls. Attention not as good as I desired. Hampered my speaking. Disappointed myself. Teachers and students considered it o.k., however.

Took Miss [Florence] Holcombe to Moorestown. Met Mr. Branch, principal, and a Mrs. Wauble who seemed inclined to strike up an acquaintance. Returned after dinner at Williams's Restaurant in Citizen's Hotel. Good meal. Ate so late could not sleep at night. Failed to receive list of names from Sarah Pride. She forgot about it no doubt. Read quite a bit from Cellini before retiring.

Tuesday December 16, 1930

Another cold day. Late getting breakfast, for this work keeps me going so, night and day, that unless I rise late in the morning I find it difficult to receive adequate rest.

8. Benvenuto Cellini, *Autobiography of Benvenuto Cellini.*

Cold as usual. Called upon several persons in North Philadelphia. Were not in, however. Called at the branch Y on North 43rd Street. Would telephone me regarding order. Don't expect to hear from them.

Could not find Mr. Williams at home. Dr. Manley not in, either.

Received letter from Woodson. Came down off high horse. Asked what matter did it make whether or not 80¢ was sent in. Of course, none. Yet if such were the case why did he assume such a tone in reference to it so as to cause me to send him a threat of giving up the campaign? This leads me to believe that he can be smoked out of his blustering attitude if met with equal bluster and firmness. Mother wants me to come home for Christmas. Anxious to do so but hate to go empty-handed. My wish has been to visit home laden with presents for everyone. Can't do so this year, however.

Wednesday December 17, 1930

After breakfast, realizing that very little can be done here during the day, Poe and I went to movies. Poe played host. Saw "Abraham Lincoln," a fairly good presentation. [It] covered too much ground, however, and the ending was too abrupt.

Returning to the hotel I went out to North Philadelphia. Everyone upon whom I called, however, was out. After dinner, was fortunate to find Mr. Williams at home. Reminded me that although he and Dr. Hinkson had intended to take the set together, in case the latter did not, he himself would. Asked me to find out what Hinkson desired. The physician wanted only one book. He gave me the names of several persons, however. One of them, a Mr. Mason, I sold immediately, though at first he reminded me of so much ice.

Returned elated to the Y.

Thursday December 18, 1930

While shaving this morning, Poe brought me two copies of the *Negro Wage Earner,* my book, which Woodson has practically appropriated for his own. The cover is beautiful, jade green, with the authors' names in gold. The jacket, however, is a vile bungling of incongruities. In the background is a factory; in the foreground a Negro wearing a collar and a tie and arrayed in a business suit. Woodson's idea, no doubt, and perfectly correct because it is his.

Now for the most infamous of assumptions and fabrications; so wholly has Woodson taken to himself the credit for the book, that all he waives responsibility for is the collecting of the information—and not even all of that. All the correcting, supplementing, and reduction of the data to literary form are, he states, his. This is an *infamous* lie. I myself not only collected the data, but also put it in virtually the exact form, with the exception of a few expurgations, in which the book now stands. When I left on the bookselling campaign, the page proof read: Lorenzo J. Greene, *The Negro Wage Earner.* Whatever corrections were made, moreover, were carried out by me under his supervision. And as for his supplementary data, there is not an idea of Woodson's in the entire book, save the inconsequential statement that some Negro farmers worked for white planters during weekdays and labored on their own farms on Sunday and holidays in order to make ends meet. This practice was to show one means of the increase in Negro farms during the transition period, from tenant farmer to farm owner.

When I left in July, the book was ready for its final printing. All corrections had been made on the page proof. To think that he would offer such a monstrous misrepresentation to the world is amazing. But as I remarked in a letter to him in September, little more can be expected from a person devoid of a sense of honor. Woodson never held a high place in my estimation, but now my regard for him in every respect, save scholarship, has sunk to its nadir.

As to the book, it contains some mighty errors, chiefly because Woodson did not know its contents. In his fine art of expurgating, he has made a laughing stock of himself. Where I stated that 90–95 percent of the Negro steel laborers in Pittsburgh were unskilled in 1917, Woodson cut out the remainder of the paragraph, left the above dangling in midair, then two or three pages later the statement is made and proved by Census figures that about one-third of all Negro laborers in factories were doing work "requiring greater or less skill" (334). Then, too, his monumental ignorance of how space was to be allocated in respect to the different topics is evident when he stated in the catalogue announcement that, since most Negroes worked in domestic service and on farms, more space would be devoted to these occupations. That is just what I did not do, for I purposely devoted more space to the other occupations.

After breakfast I went to Lawnside, New Jersey. This is an all-Negro town. The mayor and all the officials, with the exception of the solicitor, are Negroes. It was formerly an underground railroad station maintained by Quakers. It is a small place of about a thousand souls. Negroes have some fine homes here. There is no industry, however, which makes the further development of the place rather dubious. This lack might well be applied to all Negro towns.

The school is an imposing looking building. There are eight teachers. Mr. Kelly the principal, albeit a Philadelphia man, looks more like a farmer. I was graciously received by him, thanks to the introduction given him beforehand by Miss Holcombe, who had heard me speak in Camden.

Spoke to the teachers. The result was that six out of eight promised to take books. Had to reduce the deposit to $2, however. Spoke to the upper classes—5, 6, 7, 8. Did definitely better than in Camden on Monday. Visited all the classes and spoke. The attention was wonderful even in the kindergarten.

Returned to town. Poe had already eaten. Took him out to see Mrs. Lena Trent Gordon. Very intelligent. She works in the Department of Labor of the state. Took nothing but told me much (which I already knew) of her trip south with the interracial committee. She waxed enthusiastic over Montgomery, Alabama. Yet that city is doing nothing. Birmingham would excite one's admiration far more. Not to speak of Tulsa, Muskogee, and Houston. But it was her first trip south. As investigators they did nothing; for, in Montgomery, Mrs. Gordon told me, everything was prepared for them. That accounts chiefly for my refusal to accompany the committee south. We do not investigate in that manner. While Mrs. Gordon talked, Poe was sitting in the car freezing. Asked me to take him to the Y. Had to take Williams's books, however. There I was kept by Mrs. Williams, whose words gushed from her lips as endlessly as the waters falling over Niagara. She told me many interesting things, however, concerning their trip to the coast. Poor Poe sat out in the cold for 45 minutes longer. I finally got Mrs. Williams's check in my hand then set forth for the Y. Wrote Woodson and sent several letters to other persons also.

Friday December 19, 1930

Acquiescing to Poe's suggestion that we could no doubt pick up some business in the small Jersey towns, we left for Moorestown after breakfast. They have a nice school here, though in comparison with the white school it is poor indeed. Miss Branch, the principal, seemed to lack that facility of introducing me to the teachers in order that I could talk to them for a few minutes with some prospect of favorable reaction from them. In truth, to some of the teachers she did not introduce us at all.

Still, I showed them the books. But the librarian, a short, officious looking person assured the teachers that within the school, city, or county libraries they possessed the books.

[No entries were found for December 20–21.]

Monday December 22, 1930

Dr. Harry Barnes, only Negro otolaryngologist recognized by the American Board of Otolaryngology, attended University of Pennsylvania, University of Paris, and University of Bordeaux. . . . On staff of Jefferson Hospital. . . .

Picture of French students and professor of University of Bordeaux, sixteen nationalities, Dr. Barnes only American (1924).

Dr. Moure, head of faculty at University of Bordeaux, cured Alfonce. Latter born a deaf-mute.

Most interesting sight yet. Funeral supply manufacturing company. Owned and operated by Mr. W. L. Tooks, 1043 S. Colorado Street. Only two others. One in Waycross, Georgia, and the other in Memphis, Tennessee. Gets lumber by carload lots. Makes mouldings. Employs nine persons, five have families.

[Tooks] was carpenter. Held high position in Navy yard. Later started making furniture. Victrola cabinets, etc. People paid so irregularly he gave it up. Bought a casket, took it to pieces, and put it together again. Began nine years ago to manufacture them. Jewish manufacturers stopped wholesale lumber merchant from furnishing mouldings. Bought machine. Now can make anything.

[No entries were found for December 23–31.]

16

At Home in Connecticut

A Working Interlude

THURSDAY JANUARY 1, 1931

I am at home in Ansonia, Connecticut. This is New Year's Day. Awoke at 8:30. All of us are more or less tired today, for we went to bed late. My cold seems to be improving. At least I can talk.

Took Helen (Notis) to see my former sweetheart, Gladys (Hamilton Campbell), who now has four children. Poor Gladys! She is broken and so young! Her name recalls those blissful, fiery days of early youth. She is about 26, but looks to be 36. She, who was a model of ripe, rounded maidenhood, is now toothless, sunken-jawed, flat-breasted, and surrounded by a brood of four boys. She has little interest in life, and has ridden but once on a train. God, what if I had married her! And Floyd, her brother! Saw him and didn't know him.

We went downtown. I introduced Helen to Mildred Boone, a friend who virtually runs Bristol's Drugstore on Main Street. From there we went to my sister Emma's, where we were invited to dinner. The meal was enjoyable, although my sister kept me on "pins and needles," fearful lest her temper directed against her poor, henpecked husband might explode to embarrass Helen. Everything passed off well, however, thanks be to Allah!

I went downtown after dinner. Brought back a box of chocolates for Helen from the McQuade's Drugstore, where I formerly worked. Went to church. Froze while a Stamford Negro ranted. I spoke five minutes. People interested. Returned home. Whole family, except Careatha, came. Uncle (Tom Coleman, a retired grocer) and (his wife) Aunt (Cora also came in).

Played whist (and) danced. Aunt Cora and I proved unbeatable. They left at 2:30 a.m. Took goose grease and whiskey for my cold.

Friday January 2, 1931

Ate breakfast about 12:00. Helen cooked part—made toast—I poached eggs. She eats so little. Poor thing! She has eaten so much turkey, I believe she will never want to see another for a decade.

Went downtown to see some of my white friends who had been inquiring about me. Visited copper mill. (Thomas) Molineaux, the superintendent, who wanted to see me (was) not in. Met Tom Kneen, master mechanic of the machine shop, where I formerly worked, before and during the summer of my college days. (He) embraced me on the street. Took me in wire mill. Fellows cheered as I entered. Wiped grease off hands on overalls and waste to shake my hand. Made me feel like weeping. Kneen then took me to my old "home," the wire mill machine shop. Told me I was honored, for strict orders had been issued to allow no one to visit the shop during the holidays. Another ovation awaited me. All work ceased. For an hour and a half I chatted, shook hands, and received congratulations. Had to wash hands before leaving. Must send a book to the office here.

Stopped by (Anthony) Corsella's, attorney, former high school classmate. Enjoyed 15 minutes with him. Told me that Jimmie (Vincent) Impelliteri, another classmate, is now Assistant District Attorney for New York City. Rushed home. Took Helen to Shelton to visit (the Mr. and Mrs. Thomas) Andersons, old friends of family. I am their son, they say.

Back home. Went to Aunt Cora's to play cards. Helen and I played rather successfully.

My cold is improving. But I can get no rest. Have not gone to bed before 2:30 a.m. since coming home. I took more goose grease and whiskey. Nasty dose. I go to bed.

Saturday January 3, 1931

After breakfast I called upon Molineaux at the copper mill. Praised me. Extolled my book, *The Negro Wage Earner.* Told me he has always been friendly to the Negro. It's true. No color line in his mill. Gives Negroes any work they can do. Even now, he stated, he had his eyes on a young Negro worker whom he expected to advance. Will look over *The Negro Wage Earner.* Thinks he will buy it.

Picked up Dad. On the way home, stopped at the Manufacturers' Club. Sold John Sims (a friend of the family) $10.98 worth of books. Collected $5.00 for myself. Afterwards went to Derby, [Connecticut,] where Lillian, my sister, works. The cook and Marion Santos (née Austin), sister of a dear friend, Irving Austin, bought sets. Promised to send $2.00 next Thursday to me in Philadelphia.

Back to Ansonia. Stopped in to see (Edward) McQuade, the druggist, for whom I formerly worked. Seemed as proud of me as if I were his son. Perturbed because I refused to share his rancor toward Catholics. He feels they will bring the country to ruin. Doctors Wilmot and Parmelee, white physicians, also congratulated me. Wilmot feels medicine is gradually becoming a non-paying profession. Went to Boones' (Mildred and Maude). Did not try to sell Mildred (a former high school classmate and now bookkeeper at Bristol's Drug Store).

Arriving home, found Crockett there. Had given Dad $4.00 deposit on books.

After dinner, (my sister-in-law) Lillian had invited some friends in. Mother made pineapple ice cream. Charlie (my brother) and I froze it. Got ice off street. Lena and her white fiancé came down from Plainville. We played cards and danced. Had nice time. Helen tired out. We all went to bed about 5:00. . . . We leave for Newark at noon. It was certainly difficult to leave home after a week spent with my family. I hated to part with my parents, both of whom seemed to be in such happier spirits since I came home. I assured them, however, that I would return near the middle of the month. They want me to return and rest for a month. Such darling parents. No person ever had better.

Left at 12:05. Stopped to bid farewell to my sister Emma. The day was beautiful, warm, with snow melting everywhere. The roads were dry. Ride to New York uneventful, save for a puncture near Stamford. Took the 125th Street ferry to New Jersey, for brakes were not working well enough to drive through the downtown traffic in New York City. Regaled ourselves by reflecting over our pleasant visit home. Tired out when I reached Helen's home in Newark.

Called Ernest (my good physician friend, Dr. Bacote). Wanted me to stay with him. Helen invited me to stay at her home. Did. Sat up until 1:30. . . . She gave up her room for me.

Monday January 5, 1931

Was awakened by Helen knocking at my door at 7:00. When I came downstairs, breakfast was served for me. While eating, Helen came in—no one else was present—and presented me with a prolonged farewell kiss. It made me forget the food. I told her, however, I would take her to her office. Left her home with some trepidation. Did not know what her parents would ultimately expect. Might prove embarrassing to Helen. Took her within a block of her office. Hated to leave her.

Get books from Bacote. A Negro, Bryant, was in bed with him. Don't see why he allows him to hang around. Not the type. Laughed at my staying at Helen's. Left for Jersey City at 9 o'clock.

Picked up [John Wesley] Poe, who was in a position where it was well I arrived. Mrs. Upperman, wife of his friend, arrayed in kimono and bath robe, had been endeavoring to lead him on. Poe told me so later on.

Drove to Philadelphia in rain. Pump on the car stopped working near Lowry, New Jersey. Cost $1.50. Arrived Philadelphia at 3:30. Slept until 6:00. Ate. Retired at 8:30.

Lorenzo J. Greene in 1936. *Lorenzo and Thomasina Talley Greene Papers, Western Historical Manuscript Collection–Columbia.*

Aunt Emma's house, Ansonia, Connecticut. *Lorenzo and Thomasina Talley Greene Papers, Western Historical Manuscript Collection–Columbia.*

Aunt Emma (Greene) Solomon. *Lorenzo and Thomasina Talley Greene Papers, Western Historical Manuscript Collection–Columbia.*

Emma (Greene) Solomon and friends, Ansonia, Connecticut. *Lorenzo and Thomasina Talley Greene Papers, Western Historical Manuscript Collection–Columbia.*

Family and friends in Connecticut, c. 1940. *Lorenzo and Thomasina Talley Greene Papers, Western Historical Manuscript Collection–Columbia.*

Edna Gaines, 1941. *Lorenzo and Thomasina Talley Greene Papers, Western Historical Manuscript Collection–Columbia.*

Greene and Helen, Newark, New Jersey, 1924. *Lorenzo and Thomasina Talley Greene Papers, Western Historical Manuscript Collection–Columbia.*

Lorenzo J. Greene in 1980. *Lorenzo and Thomasina Talley Greene Papers, Western Historical Manuscript Collection–Columbia.*

Carter G. Woodson, founder and director of the Association for the Study of Negro Life and History, in middle life. *Courtesy of Janette Hoston Harris.*

Rev. Vernon Johns. *Courtesy of Jeanne Johns Adkins.*

R. Nathaniel Dett, c. 1941, musician and composer.

James Madison Nabrit, educator and lawyer.

Rev. Junius C. Austin, c. 1927.

E. Franklin Frazier, c. 1927, sociologist and educator.

Rev. Lacey K. Williams, c. 1927.

Rev. Richard R. Wright, Jr., c. 1927.

William Jasper Hale, founding president of Tennessee State Agricultural and Industrial State Normal School (now Tennessee State University). *Courtesy of Tennessee State University.*

Lois Mailou Jones, artist. *Courtesy of Lois Mailou Jones.*

Samuel W. Rutherford, president of the National Benefit Insurance Company, Washington, D.C. *Courtesy of The Associated Publishers.*

Mordecai Johnson, c. 1927, president of Howard University, educator, orator.

Perry Wilbon Howard, c. 1941.

Emmett J. Scott. *Courtesy of Donna M. Wells.*

John R. Hawkins, president of the National Negro Republican League and of the Association for the Study of Negro Life and History. *Courtesy of The Associated Publishers.*

Charles W. Florence, president of Lincoln University, Jefferson City, Missouri. *Courtesy of Page Library, Lincoln University.*

GROUP NO. I

Eight Valuable Books for $9.98

PAY REPRESENTATIVE $4.00

	Mailing Price
HISTORY	
THE NEGRO IN OUR HISTORY, C. G. Woodson	$4.25
NEGRO MAKERS OF HISTORY, C. G. Woodson	1.65
HISTORY OF THE NEGRO CHURCH, C. G. Woodson	2.65
AFRICAN BACKGROUND	
NEGROES OF AFRICA, Maurice Delafosse	3.15
ESSAYS	
EVERLASTING STAIN, Kelly Miller	2.65
DRAMA	
PLAYS AND PAGEANTS, Willis Richardson	3.15
POETRY	
NEGRO POETS AND THEIR POEMS, R. T. Kerlin	2.65
FOLKLORE	
AFRICAN MYTHS, C. G. Woodson	1.10
	$21.35

PURCHASER'S FIRST PAYMENT RECEIPT

I have today collected $........ as first payment
on combination ....
on group ....
It is clearly understood by the subscriber that a second payment of $........ is to be made upon receipt of books.
Representative ....
Date ....

THE ASSOCIATED PUBLISHERS, INC.,
1538 Ninth Street Northwest Washington, D. C.

This balance includes postage

Received from:
Name ....
Street and No. ....
Town .... State ....
Balance .... as part payment for
group ....
combination ....
Representative .... Date ....
The undersigned agrees to pay the balance $........ upon receipt of books.

Special Combinations

Combination	Title	Total Price	Sale Price	Pay Agent	Remit to Office
A Books on Africa	Negroes of Africa; Company Royal Adventurers Trading in Africa; Extracts from Records of African Companies; African Myths	$6.45	$4.50	$2.00	$2.50
B Books for Ministers	History of Negro Church; Negro in Our History; Negro Orators and Their Orations; Negroes of Africa	$14.30	$7.00	$3.00	$4.00
C Economics	Negroes of Africa; Negro Wage Earner; Rural Negro	$9.05	$5.50	$2.00	$3.50
D Books for the Home	Negro in Our History; African Myths; Negro Makers of History; Negro Poets and Their Poems; Negroes of Africa	$11.90	$6.50	$2.50	$4.00
E Books for English Teachers	Plays and Pageants; Negro Poets and Their Poems; Negro Orators and Their Orations; African Myths; Everlasting Stain	$14.80	$7.50	$3.00	$4.50

Order form used by Greene and his companions on the bookselling campaign.

17

Back to Philadelphia

TUESDAY JANUARY 6, 1931

Rose at 10:20 quite refreshed. Without breakfast, went to Verona Beckett's school. Took [John Wesley] Poe. Made a fatal mistake of eating first. Mrs. Taylor, the secretary, introduced us to a Mrs. [Edna] Gaines, an attractive teacher. Made appointment with her after lunch, but wasted too much time there. (It was) 12:40 when we went upstairs. Mrs. Beckett, the plump but jovial principal, told me I had five minutes to interview the teachers. Preferred to return tomorrow noon.

Mrs. Taylor told me of her club meeting tonight. Suggested I see members individually. I proposed meeting them in a group. Agreed, although she told me it was to take place at Gray's Ferry, New Jersey. (She) could not direct me. Promised to take her there. Told me she lived halfway to Trenton. Made no difference. It is the cause. Promised to call me if she could find someone who knew the way.

Stopped by the Berean School. Conducted by the Berean Presbyterian Church. Vocational. Met Miss Yergan, sister of Max Yergan. Interesting to talk to. Brother [is] missionary to Africa. Told me she desired me to address her group of girls. Invited me to come to her home, also. Informed me more than 100 girls and fellows attended the school—both vocational and secretarial work. Promised to take books before I leave city. Poe, meanwhile, had waited a half hour in the car. He went to a school, promising to return in twenty minutes. I sat in the car for an hour, freezing, awaiting him. Returned and, Poe-like, swore he had been gone no longer than a half hour.

Returned to "Y." Called on my cousin Almira, who lives on Addison Street. Recently married for the third time. Now has four stepchildren.

Very devoted to them. Nice home. Met another cousin, Helen [McClellan], about 24. Remained for dinner.

Mrs. Taylor had called. Asked me to be at her home at 7:30. Took me an hour to reach there. Fine girl, however. Jovial personality. Took two other girls to meeting. Went to other end of the city (for them). Talked to club for ten minutes. Sold one set. Did not have to take girls home, thank God!

Oh yes, policeman accosted me for leaving the car in front of the Y.M.C.A. all night. Not allowed to park on street. Meant leaving car in garage, $3.00 a week.

Wednesday January 7, 1931

Rose late. Ate a hasty breakfast and rushed out to the Field School. What luck! Mrs. Edna Gaines started the ball rolling. Took $6.50 worth of books. Told me she was intensely interested. Asked me to get in touch with the president of her sorority and arrange to speak to the members on Saturday night. Gave me names of prominent whites, also. A little, funny-looking teacher, young but dressed so old-fashioned-like, took a set. Will bring $4.00 dollars tomorrow. Then, after waiting until the close of school, Mrs. Taylor and Mrs. Singleton took sets outright. Mrs. Okomoto also took a set. Deliver Singleton's on Saturday. Others promised to see me tomorrow. I leave in high spirits. Best day since coming to Philadelphia. Left school about 3:45. Finished for the day. Poe came in. Had done nothing. Funds getting low.

Woodson sent letter telling us more books are being sold now than at this time last year, despite the depression. In fact, selling twice as many. And what we sell is not included.

Receive letters from Helen (Notis) also. Could not cash check of Mr. Faronce; dated on legal holiday, January 1. Went to dinner at the Horne and Hardat Cafeteria, due to Poe's anxiety to avoid Miss (Frances) Williams at the Citizen's Hotel. Desired to read something light. Went to Liggett's Bookstore. Bought Giovanni Papini's *Life of Christ.*[1] Poe bought Vandercook's *Black Majesty.*[2]

Returned. Read 100 pages before retiring. Poe read entire book. Papini has an inimitable style. Makes Christ more understandable than the Bible: glosses over any reference to Christ's divine origin. Is eulogistic, rather than critical. We should expect that in a man recently converted from atheism to a fanatical believer.

I felt rather elated over the day's work.

1. Giovanni Papini, *Life of Christ.*
2. John W. Vandercook, *Black Majesty: The Life of Christophe, King of Haiti.*

THURSDAY JANUARY 8, 1931

Spoke at Durham school, Mr. [Clarence] Whyte, principal, at 9:00 a.m. Talk must have interested pupils. They gave splendid attention. Teacher congratulated me and asked to see books. Mrs. Bowes and a Mrs. [Ethel Hedgeman] Lyle promised to take sets. Sold the secretary and left a set in her office.

Called upon Mr. [Wayne L.] Hopkins, executive secretary of the Armstrong Association, about 10:00 a.m. to ascertain whether he had arranged for me to speak to luncheon club next Tuesday. Had not. Told me speakers had been arranged for. Desired me when entire hour could be allotted to me. Felt my message too important to be hitched on to another's speech. Told me about meeting of Pennsylvania State Council at Cheyney on Saturday. Asked me to go. Felt it would be inspirational as well as profitable. Told him I would.

Went to the Fields School to resume order-taking from teachers. What luck! Secured orders from Mrs. Freeman (who politely told me at first she would take no books), Mrs. [Bessie F.] Brown, Mrs. [Katherine B.] Anderson, the dietitian, and Mrs. _____, the sewing teacher. All these are taking books outright. Mrs. Freeman's are being delivered tonight. All the teachers here seem to be fired by emulation. It is helpful to both of us. They get the books; I am able to exist.

Rushed back to the "Y." Meet Poe. He has been able to do nothing. I lent him another dollar. Lend him one this morning. Makes $5.00 now he is indebted to me. Has allowed Francis Williams, the innocent and utterly unsophisticated daughter of the hotel owner where we take our meals, to intrigue him into taking her to the movies.

Sent Woodson $28.85. Also telegraphed for books. Called Reverend R. R. Wright, Jr., in order to get books from him. Not in. Call to see him at his office. Is man who replied to my article on Negro church. Accused me of attacking it. Did not mention it during our conversation, however. Yet, the atmosphere was a little charged. Could get the books tomorrow at noon. Went to Almira's, to meet girlfriend of Helen. Former did not come. Played cards.

FRIDAY JANUARY 9, 1931

Arrived at the Durham School at noon. I found a note from one Thomas Wallace Swann advising me to get in touch with John Drew of Darby, Pennsylvania. Also found that Mrs. Lyle had given her check to Mrs. Bowes as deposit on set of books. Met Jimmy Waring's cousin, (Mr. Waring) taught me German at Howard. Liked books but not in position to buy.

One Mr. Lewis wanted books but desired to have substitutions made. Did nothing here.

Went down to *Tribune* office to see Mr. Swann. Not in. Returned to the Durham School. Swann, by good fortune, was in the office. Greeted me cordially. Seemed anxious to assist me in work. Would take me to Darby. Told me to call on Dr. [Charles A.] Lewis, Broad and Lombard streets. Gave me note to him. Advised me to go there before my trip to the Fields School. Since I had to collect $13.98 at the school, bethought it wise to make sure of the certain, rather than speculate with uncertainty. Went there, collected money, and was astounded to have a teacher gently reprove me for not having shown her the books. She was a Mrs. [Malvina] Burns. The result was I am to deliver her a set tomorrow morning.

Back I went to Dr. Lewis. No one there. Found Swann at the *Tribune* office. Told me he would come to "Y" at 5:45. Tried to get books from Wright. Could not until after 8:00. Poe couldn't get them. Was going to Sharon Hill (Pennsylvania).

Swann took me to Darby. Drew, a blustery, loud-mouthed man, irritated me by his crudeness. Kept hat on. Profanity also galled me. Was obscene. Respected neither mother nor housekeeper. Took books, however. Has two grown boys. Retired businessman. Sold bus line between Landsdowne and 69th to Pennsylvania Railroad for $250,000.00 cash. Waging campaign to persuade Gold Star Mothers from taking pilgrimage.[3] Waxed long and eloquent over it. Kept me talking until 9:50. Got away. Rushed to church at 20th and Dauphin to get the books. Unable to. Janitor did not know where they were. Called Wright. Promised to have them for me at 9:00 a.m. tomorrow. I went home tired out. Swann promised to go to Cheyney with us tomorrow. Am to meet him at 8:00. Object to sell books.

Saturday January 10, 1931

When I reached Swann's hotel, he had gone to breakfast. [Swann is] an indomitable little man, near-sighted, half-blind, unkempt in attire, but an

3. When Herbert Hoover became president, he inherited a program approved and funded by Congress to send the mothers of soldiers who had been killed in World War I to Europe. Congress authorized the secretary of war to make arrangements for the Gold Star mothers' trip. Secretary of War Patrick J. Hurley, an Oklahoma segregationist, assumed this responsibility. Hurley arranged for white Gold Star mothers to travel to Europe on navy ships, but the black Gold Star mothers had to travel by commercial steamers. African American leaders called upon President Hoover to order that the black Gold Star mothers also be transported by navy ships. Hoover, however, refused to do so, and he refused to make any public statement on the issue. See Donald J. Lisio, *Hoover, Blacks, and Lily-Whites: A Study of Southern Strategies,* 235–36.

amazing talker with wide grasp upon affairs. He made me promise him last night that if he spent Saturday with me helping me to dispose of books, I would write up a pamphlet on the Negro Gold Star Mothers. Got books and delivered them. Swann then sold two sets for me, one in Media and one in Philadelphia. Both to Reading brothers. One a printer and real estate agent. Owns a street of houses in Landsdowne. Other [is a] county detective in Media.

Arrived Cheyney at 12:30. School surprising to me. Buildings substantially constructed of stone, well laid out. An air of refinement and dignity pervaded it.[4]

The meeting was about to close its morning session when we entered. There were several people whom I knew. Jimmie [James] Waring, principal at Downingtown was one of the first. Exclaimed was it possible he had taught me (German at Howard University)! (I also met) Carrie Pickens [Parks?] of New Haven, Connecticut, and Washington, D.C.; Grace Coleman of the Department of Labor of Pennsylvania; Wayne Hopkins of the Armstrong Association; and others. Met also Mr. Laterly, minister and professor at Lincoln University in (Oxford, Pennsylvania). Alice Dunbar Nelson, wife of Paul Lawrence Dunbar, flaxen-haired, superbly built woman, who in her youth must have been the heart's desire of many a burning swain. Met the Biddle brothers. But the deepest impression was made by Dr. Leslie Pinkney Hill. He is the most impressive Negro college president I have yet met. Intelligent, critical, cultured, refined, a challenge to those who feel that the Negro cannot evince all the social and intellectual amenities and virtues of the whites.

The conference: It was a bombast of words, based largely upon the contention of E. Washington Rhodes, Editor of the Philadelphia *Tribune,* that the Negro church had really done nothing to elevate the Negro socially. A Reverend Logan hotly defended the church. I hear he does not preach a fiery gospel. How to keep youth in school was another problem. How to stimulate Negro business was another. How to bring about cooperation between church, school, families, and social agencies was the real crux of the discussion. Yet all groups seemed to be set against one another, or felt itself called upon to defend its raison d'être. Nothing tangible was accomplished. Met Archdeacon Phillips. Fine old man. Religious radical. Man after my

4. Cheyney Training School for Teachers, now Cheyney University of Pennsylvania, was founded in 1847 by the Society of Friends. The Pennsylvania state legislature authorized the purchase of the school in 1921. At that time, Cheyney became one of fourteen normal schools operated by the state of Pennsylvania. During the 1926–1927 school year, there were ninety-two students in attendance. U.S. Department of the Interior, Bureau of Education, *Survey of Negro Colleges and Universities,* 654–64.

own heart. Remained to a social. On way home, Swann took me to see Dr. Adkins, uncle of Jessie Adkins (a former Howard University classmate of mine). Extolled (Vernon) Johns. Bought nothing.

Sunday January 11, 1931

Went over at 10:30 to get Swann. Found him asleep in a dreary, sunless room at the Roadside Hotel on 15th Street. Told him to come to my place. Paid for his breakfast. Had already had mine. By the way, he stipulated that I pay for meals yesterday at Cheyney. Did so for he had made $10.40 for me. Swann brought the letters to my place. He had the raw materials sent to Drew by Negro mothers who had refused to make the pilgrimage. Of the 251 Gold Star Mothers eligible to go, 25 refused outright, due to Drew's entreaties that they would be relinquishing the vital principle of equality of all citizens of the United States regardless of race if they accepted the trip under Jim Crow conditions. The effort is noble. Drew is far seeing. Drew wrote a letter to Hoover in which he accused the latter of placing his stamp of approval upon governmental segregation. Through his Acting Secretary of War, Hoover replied that it was for the interest of both groups. Worked all day, due to the garrulousness of Swann, to put [letters from the Gold Star Mothers] into literary form. Met Drew at 12:30. He was elated with them. Swann was elated with it. I do the work; Swann receives the credit. It reminded me of the *Negro Wage Earner,* where Woodson robbed me of the credit.

Monday January 12, 1931

'Twas snowing when I rose today. Supposed to see Swann at 2:30. Went to Durham School to get orders, if possible. Met a Miss [Myrtle] Glenn. Attractive. Will take set tomorrow. Went to see Dr. Lewis to get his subscription. Poe had sold him. Lewis is intensely interested in work. Wants to put money into selling agency. I had been thinking of the same thing. Must talk it over with Lewis. Believe he is a higher type of man than Swann. At least he is not a politician. Has an enormous library. Wanted me to make his office my headquarters. Would have me write to popularize Negro History for average man, in order to put over program. Rich Quakers will back idea. Guarantee me $10,000. Sounded intriguing. Promised to see him again. Took *The Negro Wage Earner.* Went downtown to look over some suits. Nothing I liked. Returned to *Tribune* office. Swann not there. Went to the Y, then to dinner. Poe had gone to show. Nothing sold today. Felt tired out. Meant to retire at 8:00. Claytor came in and talked until 9 o'clock.

Tuesday January 13, 1931

Swann was in the Citizen's Hotel when I walked in today. Greeted me with little show of affection. Irritated because I had failed to keep appointment yesterday evening. Told him it was a case of trying to take care of certain affairs which were important to me. Swann introduced me to Dr. [Nathan F.] Mossell, a tall, tired-looking man of 72, who is head of Douglass Hospital. Married a descendent of Joseph Bustle, Negro who was the first to make plans for the bridging of the Delaware River. In difficulties with hospital now. Could take nothing.

Swann, garrulous as ever, took me to see Dr. [James Augustus] Trotman. Is West Indian. Graduate of the medical school of the University of Paris. Has a splendidly appointed office and fine library. Bought $15.00 worth of books. Left Swann (and) went to Durham School to collect deposit from Miss (Myrtle) Glenn. Was to meet Swann in 15 minutes. Spent almost an hour engaged in charming tête-à-tête with Miss Glenn, who stated she liked to look at me, whereupon I retorted, it would cost her a quarter. Asked me to come to see her tonight. But, I am going to the opera tonight to see *Siegfried*. Offered to take her, but she declined, saying that she did not know me.

My fine conversation was suddenly interrupted by Swann, who had been waiting in the car for me. Made excuses and left hastily for the Luncheon Club, where the most prominent Negroes were gathered. A Reverend [Edgar C.] Young made an exceedingly stimulating address on Negro uplift. Swann's purpose was to introduce me to everyone present. He did so and several persons told me to see them tomorrow. Sold nothing more today. J. Max Barbour proved a fizzle. Swann did not want me to quit for the opera. Told him I would let nothing stand in the way. He made me angry. I fear I shall have to cut adrift from him, for I cannot be bossed. I know how much time I shall allot to this work and not for mere money will I finish wrecking my health. Bought Swann's dinner, although I did not want to. He seems to have no visible means of support. And yet, he tries to make me feel that he is an asset to me. I can do better alone.

Reached the opera just as curtain was rising. Seat $2.00. Performance splendid, uplifting. Breaking of Wotan's spear by Siegfried significant of the supplanting of old age by youth.

Wednesday January 14, 1931

Swann was waiting for his accustomed breakfast at the Citizen's Hotel when I arrived at 9:45. What angered me was that he expected it. Told him that we ought to come to some business arrangement about the aid he would give me. Would not hear of it. Offered him a dollar on each sale. Our first "victim" was Leonidus Allen, a real estate man and delinquent property tax collector. The latter is city job. Interesting man. Told me (his) father was a slave blacksmith. After emancipation (he) never worked a day for a white person. His wife is the granddaughter of Jeremiah Asher, who was born in Hartford, Connecticut. Was active in the Underground Railroad before Civil War. Chaplain in the 6th Regiment of U.S. Colored Volunteers. Enlisted December 24, 1863. Died in service July 27, 1865. Pastored Shiloh Baptist Church on Eleventh and Lombard streets before enlistment. Built church in Yorktown (Virginia). Also went abroad. Cousin of wife, Kit Asher—grandson of Jeremiah Asher—[is] a detective in Philadelphia. Say he has caught more murderers and killed fewer people than anyone on the force. Allen says that D[aughters] [of the] A[merican] R[evolution] is trying to get the Negroes' property around Yorktown to transform it into national shrine. Sold him eight books. Will collect $12.98 from him on January 29.

Went to see Rev. [Wesley F.] "Pop" Graham, Baptist preacher. Is reputed to be one of richest men in Philadelphia. Also philanthropist. Established first Negro industrial insurance company in the United States. Daughter, Ottie, classmate of mine. Married. Saw her. Wants me to come over on Saturday. Pop Graham will see me on March 1. Spending money now feeding people. Went by and sold Rev. Young. Took $14.98 worth of books. Sold Mr. [Walter W. H.] Casselle, the undertaker.

Went to Media to meet Judge McDade and sell him. Latter trying vice ring in Delaware County. Heard my first trial. Remained in court an hour. McDade fine, upright fellow, fearless. Told me he was determined to clean up the county. Will kick him upstairs, if he does, Swann told him. Asked us to come back later when he had more time.

Went to Darby. Failed to sell the Scotts. Had dinner at Drew's at 8:15, past my dinner hour. I'll feel it shortly. Had long argument with Drew about my relationship with Woodson. Also on Lincoln. Returned to the "Y" at 11:45.

Thursday January 15, 1931

Was chagrined early this morning to find that the laundry did not have my clothes ready, despite the fact that they had been there a week. Took one shirt in disgust because I had to. Swore I'd never bring anything else there.

'Twas dreadfully cold. Did not have time to eat breakfast. Drove about eighteen miles to Riverton (New Jersey). Left Philadelphia at 9:01. Reached Mr. (Albert) Johnson's place at 9:51. He took me to the school. Was so cold I was shivering.

Both white and black pupils and teachers had come together at the white school. The superintendent, Mr. Taylor, reminded me of a farmer, which no doubt he was. There were some 350 to 400 children present—the majority of them white. I told them some of the many achievements of the Negro, not in isolated fashion but in relation to similar contributions of other races and nationalities. I merely placed the Negro in the picture with all other groups. Everyone seemed to be pleased. The white superintendent and the principal, Mr. Bryan, took me to their office and had me relate much more to them than I had told the children. Whites are so thirsty for knowledge that whether their pride is hurt or not they value information for information's sake. Therefore, they took two sets of books.

Went down to Mrs. [Carolyn] Kibble's school, where Mr. Taylor directed us to see some of Mrs. Terry's artwork done by her pupils. It was marvelous paintings done by these boys and girls depicting the evolution of transportation. Congratulated me on my talk. Said it was wonderful because it was not boastful and gave no offense. Mrs. Kibble, likewise, was profuse in her congratulations. Said she wanted to see me. And I wanted to see her. That was my main reason for coming to her school.

The preparation for lunch at the school reminded me that I had not eaten. Mr. Johnson, therefore, took me to his landlady's—he works for a rich Quaker—where he prepared lunch. His son came in while he was congratulating me on my talk at the school. Later, his nephew took me back to the school to see Mrs. Young, who wanted books. Talked to her children for about ten minutes. Gave them a cactus leaf I had brought with me from Texas, near the Mexican border. Mrs. Young was touched. The kiddies were interested.

However, I was anxious to see Mrs. Kibble before she left. Chided me gently for failure to keep engagement with her before Christmas. She had telegraphed me. Told her weather was too bad. Invited me to dinner. Told me to come as early as I chose.

Mr. Johnson took me several places, but failed to get an order. Went to Moorestown to find out whether meeting had been arranged there. Told no. Returned to Mrs. Kibble's. Had been awaiting me for more than an hour. Told me I was mean to her. Young widow has two children, three and five. Splendid little fellows. She is very attractive. After dinner, talked (and) danced. Enjoyable time, interrupted by Mr. Johnson's coming for me.

Sold Mrs Young. Spoke to the club members. Young people seemed interested. Mr. Johnson's niece took set. Club took eight books. Gave them for $2.00 apiece. Will let me know next week (whether the members will take more). Left for Philadelphia at 11:10. Tired out. Arrived home at 11:50.

Friday January 16, 1931

Attacked by such pains in my back this morning, while taking Poe to West Philadelphia, that I had to quit and go to a doctor. Couldn't walk. Could hardly breathe. Went to Dr. Trotman. Told me I had pleurodema, sort of rheumatism in the muscles. Prescribed liniment. Told me to have hot towels applied, then dried and rubbed well, morning and night. Could not do this at Y. Went to my cousin Almira. Put me to bed. Oh, those hot towels. How I squirmed as she applied them. Rubbed me well and put me to bed. Had dinner in bed. Another hot application before bedtime. Kids enjoyed my agony under the hot towels. Just wanted to see Helen for some reason. She had warned me against just such.

Saturday January 17, 1931

Got up this morning for breakfast. Almira, my cousin, nurse, doctor, etc., gave me no application because of my avowed intention to speak to the AKA sorority tonight. Read *If Winter Comes,* or at least most of it.[5] Yesterday, I read *Black Majesty,* the story of Christophe, the second emperor of Haiti. What a dizzy rise! From a slave working in the fields, to a bootblack for a French Officer in Comte d'Estaing's expedition to the United States in 1779, to slave master of a Negro, to second in command under Touissaint L'Ouverture, until finally, after the death of Dessalines (The Tiger), he came to rule more than one-half of Haiti. Poor Christophe. Mighty as he was, he could never sign his full name. But he was proud; he strove to make his people proud, and, thus, he built the greatest citadel in the New World. The creation of his own brain, brought to fruition by black artisans (under the mulatto engineer, Besse), and perched imposingly 3,000 feet above sea level, (San Souci was) a masterpiece of engineering genius that rivaled the marvelous pyramids of the Pharaohs. And when his empire was crumbling, when his own death seemed imminent, even the craven would take heart to see him fling his paralyzed body on the floor, drag it to a cabinet, take a pistol therefrom, and send a golden bullet crashing into his brain, while a blood-thirsty mob howled even in his palace for his life. A fitting end for this astounding character.

Went out, despite the entreaties of Almira, to dress for the AKA talk. Laundry not ready. Letters from Mrs. (Edna) Gaines and telephone call from Mrs. Jergan. Talked to sorority. Members were intensely interested. Sold no books outright, but I feel they will materialize. One member said

5. Arthur Stuart-Menteth Hutchinson, *If Winter Comes.*

a teacher remarked (that) never had she met a person who could rattle off Negro History like one could the multiplication table.

Took another hot toweling and rubbing. Retired at 10:00.

Sunday January 18, 1931

Awoke at 8:30. Continued reading *If Winter Comes.* Shows the complete wrecking of any number of lives because of the inability of the hero to arrive at any definite conviction. Felt like getting out today. Being kept in is extremely irksome. Yet, I suppose it is best I do so. No doubt Swann feels I have disappeared. But he is too garrulous. Makes me sick!

Took another terrific toweling after breakfast. Believed the skin would be burnt from my back. Felt better after it was over. Almira is a jewel. Her husband, too. Spent the day lolling about. Played a few games of checkers. Wrote in diary for awhile. Find it difficult to keep inactive. Just must read or do something. Almira says that Mrs. Gardner and Mrs. Moseley, slaves of Jefferson Davis, (are) living in Hall's Hill (Virginia).

Monday January 19, 1931

Another day passed in virtual idleness. How it grates upon me! Poe came over about 10:00 a.m. Told me Mr. Albert Johnson had called from Riverton to inform me he had sold two more sets of books for me. Told me that additional interest has been stimulated there.

Went over to the school (Durham), ostensibly to take a book to Miss Connors, but in reality to chat with Miss (Myrtle) Glenn, a charming little teacher. A Mr. Hawkins was chatting with her as she lunched. Yet we discussed the opera, letter writing, and a medley of other things. Saw and sold Mr. Sears, the physical education teacher, a set of books. Mr. Whyte, the principal, tells me that the teachers are not to be interviewed except at noontime, and his name is not to be mentioned. I appreciated it. He fears a "comeback" from the office. Feel much improved today.

Tuesday January 20, 1931

Today, like yesterday, was spent in comparative idleness. And yet it is gradually becoming more bearable. Last night the boys with whom I sleep—one is eleven, the other six—kicked like steers. Woke me at odd and sundry moments, doubled themselves like gigantic figure S's and punched their knees in my back, wrapped divers legs about my neck, threatened in their gropings and turnings to gouge out my eyes; in short, made my rest anything but rest. Yet, such is life. But, honestly, I believe I made a better sleeper when I was young.

At noon, I again went to Durham School to collect the balance of the payment from Mr. Lewis. As usual, I saw and tarried with the charming Miss Glenn. She tells me that she loves to hear me talk; gets a kick out of looking at me; finds me so entertaining, different, and a lot of other bunk. Yet, since I am human, it is good to me. Asks me to come see her at home. Promised to see her on Friday evening.

Poe came over. Wants to get a suit and had me cash another $5.00 check for him. God grant it is not like the others. Swears as soon as he gets a suit his sales will double. He is that type. Must be presentable at all times or refuses to go out socially. For that reason, has refused to see one Miss [Alberta S.] Norwood, a teacher who seems to be interested in him. I admire him for it.

The Wickersham Prohibition Commission reported yesterday to President Hoover. The problem is still up in the air. Opposed, like everyone else, to the saloon. It is opposed to repeal and to state or federal participation in the liquor business. Finds fault with present method of enforcement by states and federal agencies, recommends increased appropriations for enforcement, increase in enforcement personnel, abolition of specifications for use of whiskey prescribed by physicians, and several others. The Commission itself was divided in its opinion. Newton D. Baker and Monty [Monte?] M. Lehman of Louisiana recommended repeal; another, Henry W. Anderson of Virginia, advocated government liquor control. The total result of the Commission's findings may lead to an eventual revision of the Volstead Amendment. But this even is a short-sighted measure. It ought to be repealed. The country favors it, as evidenced by the *Literary Digest* poll of last year. The elections of last fall ought to have been sufficient warning.

Played Almira several games of checkers. She beat me at Spanish pool. Can't play that, and play straight checkers little better. Poe came over. Remained until 8:45. Believe he was lonesome. He won at Spanish pool; I at checkers. I am beginning to like Spanish pool.

(Gifford) Pinchot was inaugurated Governor of Pennsylvania today. First governor in the history of the state who has been reelected after having served his first term. Pledges himself to save people from the fangs of power trust.

Felt decidedly improved today.

Wednesday January 21, 1931

After breakfast this morning, I went out to the Berean School to see Mrs. Anderson. En route, got most of my things from the Y. Also stopped by the Fields School to give a copy of *Plays and Pageants* to Mrs. Beckett. Desired *Negro Wage Earner.* Will pay me for *Plays,* etc. Went therefrom to

Berean School. Mrs. Anderson, Directress—widow of the Rev. Anderson and founder of the school—greeted me by name. I felt embarrassed. She had heard me speak to Negro History Club more than a month ago. Had expected me. Yet, hastened to tell me that she could not take books. Flattered her a little, told her I had called to see her before, but she had been ill. She is a little woman about 45, refined, the kind that kills with attention. Saw *Negro Wage Earner.* Embarrassed me by asking who Lorenzo J. Greene is. Took set and *Wage Earner,* too, $5.20 for me. Not so bad for a sick man. Introduced me to Rev. [Arthur E.] Rankin, pastor of the Berean church. Not impressive. Middle aged, very fair. Took nothing. At night, Almira's husband gave me some idea of job discrimination practiced by white workers against Negroes. He was pillmaker at Mumford Chemical Company here. One day all men quit in protest. The foreman told him, "Sorry, I'd take all colored if possible. Can't get them, therefore, I shall have to let you go." He is very depressed about the Negro's chances for work here compared to the South.

THURSDAY JANUARY 22, 1931

Immediately after breakfast I called upon Mr. B. G. Collier, Grand Chancellor of the Knights of Pythias, to sell him a set of books. His office is located in a large building built by the order and used exclusively by the Lodge as offices and meeting rooms. Sometimes the auditorium is used for dances. Yet, such small revenue is insufficient to provide a normal return on the investment, therefore, as in Chicago and other cities, this edifice is really a white elephant on the lodge's hands. Should have been a factory. Mr. Collier was downstairs, so the secretary informed me. After waiting for him awhile, she went down after him. He came up—a small wizened man, in a frayed brown suit. Did not seem any too affable. Told me when I began the object of my visit that the lodge could not buy books because they had no club associated with it. At the Old Folk's Home the people are too lazy to read. Even too lazy to eat. Told him he ought to be interested. Was. But first we chatted about the Negro generally. Extolled Booker T. (Washington). Deprecated (W. E. B.) Du Bois. Feels Kelly Miller great thinker but too cognizant of his powers to become closely allied to whites. Says Negro must "pet" white man until he can get what he wants. Finally, told me he didn't want the books but needed them. Took them. Could have chatted with him indefinitely.

Poe was at the house when I returned. Went out to school. Wanted to borrow $3.00 to get suit. Told him he could get it from me if he did not make it. Almira and I read. Went to barber shop. Really getting quite bald.

And just 31. And women hate bald-headed men. Better marry soon. Almira wants me to. Prefers Thelma. She is a will-o'-the-wisp.

Poe resplendent in new suit, tie, shirt, and socks when I returned. Playing checkers with Almira. Going to see a Miss Norwood. School teacher.

Called Mrs. Gaines about 9:30. Wanted to find out whether she really is married. Interesting to me. Told me she had something to tell me when she saw me. Led me to inquire was it concerning husband? Replied yes. There is no husband. Invited me out to play cards. Went. Very attractive and interesting. Told her how charming she appeared last Saturday. Pleased her. Almira and her husband bundled me up as if I were going to the North Pole. Very fine of them. I returned home at 1:30.

Friday January 23, 1931

Poe came over this morning bringing me a letter from B[ertha?]. Remarkable! Had just written her on Wednesday night. Made me feel like a cad. Told me for two months she had worried about me, fearful lest I had met with an accident, but only to find out later that I had been at home and that Helen had been there with me. B[ertha?] is finding it difficult to secure employment. Yet tells me she still loves me, although I am not "dear" anymore. Went to see Levi Snowdon about books. As Sarah Pride told me, he took nothing. Promised to leave $4.00 at the "Y" for me. But I do not believe it will materialize. He seems to be a climber socially, a four-flusher.

Stopped at the Durham School to catch a glimpse of (Myrtle) Glenn since I had been unable to get her on the phone. Seemed to act a trifle cold, in that it was some seconds before she faced me after I had spoken to her and Miss Connors, another teacher, who sat facing me. As soon as she turned, however, her conversation became just as animated as formerly and, even before Miss Connors, she confessed that never before had she met anyone so intriguing. Told me my presence inspired her to teach her class like "nobody's business." Sold two books to two other teachers.

Returned home intending to rest. Ate some lettuce and drank a glass of warm milk to induce sleep, then retired. Was dozing when Almira announced Mr. Swann. Asked what had happened to me. He had called the "Y" several times. Glad he found me in bed. Did not wish him to feel I was trying to get rid of him, which is certainly what I am trying to do. Showed me paper with articles I wrote on the Gold Star Mothers two weeks ago. Swann's picture appears as the author. How the public is misled. My work, but the public acclaims him, just as Woodson gets the credit for *The Negro Wage Earner.* Swann remained about an hour. Glad to see him depart.

Called upon Miss Glenn at 9:00 p.m. Allowed me to ring twice purposely so that I would not sense her eagerness to see me. Told me reason she acted as she did this noon was in order that I would not detect the joyful expression her face registered upon hearing my voice. I was amazed. Read poetry to her until she asked me to stop because it so increased her great interest in me, so that she could not suppress her emotions without great effort. Swears it is a pleasure just to look at me. She has good eyes. Told of her fiancé at the Medical School of Howard University. Loves him but feels it entirely possible that I might sweep her off her feet. Before I knew it, her father announced that it was 12:30. I made haste to depart. She is small, interesting, with fine intelligence and charm. Why she makes a hero of me, I cannot say.

Saturday January 24, 1931

Poe came over this morning, bringing me a letter from Helen [Notis]. Informs me that the check she cashed for me was worthless. Protests to me against bearing the expense of her sister's children. Doesn't mind supporting her parents. Fine girl, but her family imposes upon her generosity and kindness. She must confide in someone, hence me.

Asked Poe to get me two pairs of pajamas. Laughed. Told me I must be going somewhere. Spent entire day reading. Finished *Life of Christ* by Papini. Gospel made much clearer than the Bible itself. Interpretations, although colored by Papini's views, are interesting. Study of life not conducive to strengthened belief in the divine Christ of the Bible. Did he rise again or was the body stolen? Did Christ actually die on the cross? His legs were not broken to accelerate his end as in the case of the two thieves. Did Christ die or did he sink into a coma? Did he regain consciousness in the tomb, push the stone away and then appear in corporeal form to the amazed women on Easter Sunday? Or did his friend, Joseph, discover that he was not dead and care for him until he was able to leave his home? Or was the body stolen away by his disciples, whose childish faith in him and his promise to rise in three days impelled them to spread abroad the word that he had done so, in order to fulfill the prophesy of their murdered master? Could not the hallucinations of these men easily confuse such figments of the brain as reality? Or was the body taken away by the men of the high priest, Annas or Caiaphas? These are some of the queries that the *Life of Christ* arouse in the reader's mind. Almira's interest has been so whetted that she will read the book.

Called Mrs. Gaines. Invites me to intersorority tea on Sunday afternoon. Told her I must go to tea at Miss Yergan's. Tells me I could make both, then come back and have some fun with her gang. Wanted to, so I called Miss Yergan. Told her I would come to her tea last because it will be from 4:00 to 9:00 p.m. Mrs. Gaines wanted me to bring Poe.

Helen McClellan, cousin of Almira and nurse at Mercy Hospital, came down. Nice looking little thing. Brought a friend (a Miss Yerby). Called Poe. We danced and played cards about an hour. Poe interested in Helen. Took girls home. Miss Yerby very demonstrative. Took Poe to Y. Johnson from Riverton had left message for me. Too late to call him.

Sunday January 25, 1931

Went to an interesting intersorority tea this afternoon. Was guest of Mrs. Gaines. Met Dr. Lewis there. Gratified at seeing me. Fine program. Secured new angle on Paul Lawrence Dunbar. His former wife, Mrs. Alice Dunbar Nelson, told the guests that Dunbar died brokenhearted because the white public would not accept his poems in classical English, but insisted upon his writing in dialect. Only one-third of his works are in dialect but latter are best known, while those in reputable English are his best creations. Mrs. Nelson forceful, interesting speaker, but exotic, sophisticated, and condescending.

Went to Mrs. Yergan's tea. Left Mrs. Gaines at sorority tea promising to see her at 9:00 p.m. Had to speak as soon as I arrived at Mrs. Yergan's. Spoke 10 minutes. People interested. A Mrs. White invited me to speak to the Business and Professional Women's Club of Germantown on the 4th of February. Another wants me to speak in Atlantic City next week.

Returned to Mrs. Gaines. Looked charming today in black velvet. We discussed my trip South until group came. Went to 55th Street to party. I called her Edna, she called me "Rennie." Lots of fun. Told jokes, danced. Plenty of liquor. Edna likes wine. Wants me to promise to go to New York City with her gang on February 20th. Will see Edna on Wednesday. Very interesting, but not type I'd want for a wife. Came home at 2:00 a.m.

Monday January 26, 1931

Sold two copies of *African Myths* to teachers at Durham School. Saw Myrtle (Glenn) again. Asked me to write stanza of poetry on board so that she would have something to remember me by. Called on Dr. Lewis to be examined. Am still far from well. Lewis told me I missed something inspiring, a delegation of East Indians who placed a wreath upon the tomb of (Benjamin) Franklin. Mayor and others participated. Rejoiced because Mahatma Gandhi, the leader of the bloodless revolution against England and the originator and exponent of the unique nonresistance campaign against Britain, was released from prison today. Weighed 97 pounds.

Lewis wants to get started on the Negro History affair for the Chicago Exposition in 1933. Tells me that it would show the great epochs in the life of the Negro in America. Would have largest book world has ever seen. Epochal events (would be) illustrated. (I told him the story should) go farther back, even to Africa. Lewis agreed. Feels I know the subject and that I have the ability to stir up the people. Feels I ought to make myself secure economically. Also counseled me against putting off marriage too long. I shall come in on Wednesday and he will examine me. Tells me I must have actual daily routine.

Tuesday January 27, 1931

Did nothing after breakfast with the exception of calling upon Miss Yergan at the Berean School on 19th and South College Avenue. It was she who gave the tea on Sunday. Her interest in Negro History is so boundless that she really presented the (book) proposition to persons as they came in. Miss Yergan has a very pleasant personality, is brown-skinned, fair looking, about my height and of medium build. A Mr. Wells entered, was introduced to me and the books by Miss Yergan, and ended by telling me he would see me before I left town. One Mr. Leverte Roberts, a real estate dealer of West Philadelphia, was the next victim. He asked me to call him, feeling certain that he would take a set.

On the return to Almira's (where I stop), I experienced a headache, which did not add to the expectancy of the trip to Riverton. Almira tried to persuade me to forgo the drive there. Told her, however, my word had been given. Set out for Riverton about 3:30 p.m. Arrived there, I went straight to Mrs. [Carolyn] Kibble's, an attractive widow and school teacher. She and a Mrs. Young, another teacher, were sitting in the latter's car in front of Mrs. Kibble's home. Carolyn could not get in because her mother was out. Took her with me to East Riverton. Introduced me to several people in interest of books. Got insight into a clash of small-town personalities. A Mr. Williams, prominent upholsterer, nurses [a] grudge against Mr. Johnson because no old folks are admitted to history club. Refused to take books on that account. Gave Carolyn my poetry to read while talking with him. Praised it. Thinks "Out of the Mist" a gem.[6] Had dinner with her. Went to [home of] Mr. Johnson's niece at 8:15. Met him as I stepped out of the car. Had $21.00 for me, three sets and three (copies of) *The Negro in Our*

6. See appendix.

History. Took me to see Rev. Barber, pastor of A.M.E. Church. Arranged a meeting for me on February 8, start of Negro History Week.

Felt sick enough to faint on way back to Philadelphia. Bought bottle of citrate of magnesia. Nettie, Almira's sister, here when I returned. Bigger and older than Almira. Has peculiar disposition.

Wednesday January 28, 1931

Felt much better this morning, especially after the evacuative (laxative) had acted. Almira duns me about eating. Yet I take the biggest breakfast of anyone in the house—two oranges, cereal, two poached eggs, toast, and milk. But my cousin! My, if I followed her advice, I'd either kill myself or grow as big as a whale.

Went to see Dr. Lewis at 1:30. The doctor was not in. His nurse informed me he would be back at 1:30 or 2:00, however. While waiting, I amused myself by trying to ponder over just what he would find wrong with me—my teeth, lungs, heart, or whatnot. Then too, I wondered why he should have taken such an interest in me.

The doctor arrived within a few moments. Again we started talking about Negro History. Again he rose to pitches of passion as he discussed my possibilities and the possibilities of Negro History, especially since I was so closely allied with its leading sponsor. He struck some chords, all unawares, which struck an echo in my own mind. Told me that I might become too big for Woodson and that, through jealousy, ways and means might be found to bring me down to and retain me in an inferior status. Told me that in many cases I would do the work and Woodson would get the credit. I remember only too well *The Negro Wage Earner,* where *I* did the work and *Woodson* received most of the credit. Told me all I needed was someone to place me before the public, to make engagements for me and the like. Sees a great future in the Negro Exposition in Chicago in 1933. I told him that a Negro Lecture Business Bureau might be set up which might aid in spreading the gospel of Negro History. Asked me would I consider his proposition or whether I intended to associate myself permanently with Woodson. My response was that I am interested in Negro History. My life is dedicated to it and whether I continue under Woodson, independently, under some other foundation, is immaterial to me. My life's purpose is to further the Negro's appreciation of himself and all the petty chicaneries, petty treacheries, and dishonesty of a Woodson could not deter me. Talked for two hours. Got no examination. Lewis gave me, notwithstanding, a bottle of tonic and some pills. I'll have to go elsewhere for an examination. This man cannot divorce history from me. It includes my physical requirements with him, I fear. Yet, he insists I must have a health program.

Called Edna (Gaines) tonight. Had a fine chat with her. Bought copy of George Sand's *Intimate Journal.*[7] If anyone knows aught about George Sand, it ought to make excellent reading.

Oh yes, Dr. Lewis intends to present me to the public here as the speaker to deliver the oration on the occasion of the Richard Allen–Frederick Douglass celebration. Took a short walk, then retired.

THURSDAY JANUARY 29, 1931

Spoke at Reverend [Edgar C.] Young's Episcopal Church on 19th and Lombard at 8:30. The occasion was the formation of the Men's Club. Gave them a cross section of Negro History. Seemed to grip them. Marveled Negroes could have done so much. Many stupefied. After listening to me for 25 minutes, held me up by asking questions. Made arrangements for four sets of books during Negro History Week. Reverend Young profoundly interested. It is encouraging, to say the least. Yet, I am anxious to see Edna. Rev. Young told me to see him next Wednesday, that the club would surely take a set.

'Twas 10:35. Felt it too late to go to Edna's. Went anyway. She is quite Bohemian. Waiting for me. Laughed at my protests that it was too late to remove my coat. She appeared as charming as ever in a light-colored silk and wool sweater and skirt outfit. Languid eyes looked tired. Talked to me with closed eyes about her life. Informed me she had lost hope of ever having a home. Yet this desire dominated her entire life. Disappointed twice. Would vow to live for love. Extremely emotional. Feels love—stark, whole-souled love—is all that is worth living for. Is moody. I feel she has experienced such utter destruction of ideals that her mood is largely a defensive mechanism. Indeed, she admitted that she "wore the mask." And is she not the type of woman I desire? Warm, impulsive, moody as an April day, yet one whose soulful ebullitions will inspire me to surpass myself. She made tea. We discussed poetry and thereupon she asked about the poem "Out of the Mist." Let her read it. Liked it but felt that climax came too quickly after having worked up to the crisis. Suggested that the 7th stanza be divided, then expanded after 6th line into an additional stanza. Agreed with her. Promised to rewrite it and submit it to her for approval before sending it to Washington. Talked with her until 1:45 a.m.

7. George Sand [Mme. Dudevant], *The Intimate Journal of George Sand.*

Friday January 30, 1931

Trusting never pays. It is always difficult to collect after one has had goods in his possession for some time. Thus, when I called upon Mr. Allen, real estate dealer and delinquent tax collector, I was told by his wife it would be necessary to call next week. Nothing to do but grin and do so. Was disappointed in Dr. Stanford. Richest black physician in Philadelphia. Bachelor. Money invested in bank and railroad stock. Excuse: budget made up until March 1. Might see him then. Called Mr. Roberts, real estate man. Will see me Monday, 7:00 p.m.

Took Cousin Jane (Almira's mother) to see her physician, Dr. Burden[?] [probably Aldrich R. Burton], about 6:00 p.m. Met a man there who is inspector of maintenance for the Pennsylvania Railroad Terminal. Tells me he is one of the two Negroes holding such positions. Held it twenty-two years. Would not disclose name. Cognizant of his importance, too.

Picked up Poe and Wyatt on way to house. Let them take car and my license. Going to party in Westchester. Dangerous business loaning my license. Then, too, Wyatt, who will drive, drinks.

Saturday January 31, 1931

Planned to get out early this morning and go to the library to get information for Allen-Douglass speech. Prevented by Swann's calling. Was quite excited. Governor Pinchot was in town and Swann, who has his ear, was eager to know whether a meeting had been arranged in Harrisburg, the capital, for Negro History Week. Told him I had written both Mrs. Frazier, Y.W.C.A. secretary, and Reverend [C. F.] Jenkins to that end. (Swann was) eager to receive a reply so that he could inform Governor Pinchot and have him attend the meeting. Advised me to call Mrs. Frazier. Did so. She was not in. Called Reverend Jenkins. He likewise had gone out. Mrs. Jenkins promised to have him call me as soon as he returned. Communicated my findings to Swann. Yet I am loathe to become entangled with this man. How far can I use him before his utility has been dissipated? Lewis says [that] to some folk, association with Swann will discredit me. The same applies to Lewis. Leaders always have enemies. Swann advised my waiting for the Harrisburg call. Decided to do so.

Mr. John Drew called me about 8:00 p.m. after I had remained in all day. Wanted to know whether I could address church in Darby next Sunday on occasion of Richard Allen Day on February 8th. Promised I would. Also promised to ascertain when the local school wanted me to speak to their assembly. Designated February 14th. Drew inquired whether I intended accompanying him to New York tomorrow where I was to speak on the same program with him at the Rev. Lloyd Imes's Presbyterian Church. Replied negatively. Actuated by Dr. Lewis's suggestion that intimacy with these men might be damaging, especially if they sponsor me. No one can do for me here what I cannot do for myself, except to act as publicity manager for me, which would enable me to meet large groups of people and sell books in quantities. Only on this score could Swann be of service to me. I shall tell him so when we meet. Swann called me later from Drew's. Told me Pinchot would be here tomorrow and to call him in case I received any word from Harrisburg. Waited until 11:00 p.m. Failing to receive any communication up to that time, I went out for a walk.

Called Sarah Pride. She was dismayed to learn that I had been in town a month and had not called her. But, poor Sarah, although possessing an affectionate and charming disposition, is so unlovely that one can scarcely become romantic or demonstrative toward her. A splendid girl and has given me no little aid in this work. She is another widow. Lord help me! She is the sixth widow in whom I have been more or less interested. May marry a secondhand wife after all. 'Twould be funny! Yet, firsthand wives! Who hears of such animals nowadays?

Returned home. Retired. Awakened by boy bringing telegram from Reverend Jenkins. It informed me impossible to arrange meeting. Would write later. Disappointed. Had banked heavily upon him.

18

Still in Philadelphia

SUNDAY FEBRUARY 1, 1931

Beginning my second month here in Philadelphia. Would have been more profitable had I not been ill since January 15. Yet interest here is much higher than in any other city we have visited, and still growing. Before breakfast, [Thomas Wallace] Swann called to inquire whether I had heard from Harrisburg. Irritated me to hear his voice. Told him of [C. F.] Jenkins's inability to arrange meeting. Swann told me Pinchot was still in town. Would see me tomorrow. Worked upon and finally finished ten stanzas for "Out of the Mist." Sent them to Frances Williams to have them typed.

Almira's sister Alice and her husband came in. Had just arrived from Chicago yesterday. Is jollier, more natural than Nettie. Has disposition like my sister Careatha. Husband had narrow escape from death when a friend drove into the side of a moving freight locomotive. (Luckily, no one was injured.) Frances, who typed poem, is madly smitten by [John Wesley] Poe. Hearing that I was about to call him from her dad's restaurant, she asked me to let her speak to him. I did. Poe spoke to me later. Wanted to give me hell, but I turned it off by talking about Swann.

Went to Gaines. Edna looked charming in red. Had lots of fun. Played whist and bridge more or less indifferently and danced some hot dances. Met a Mr. Moses, a Hindu working for a doctor's degree in psychology at the University of Pennsylvania. Is a brilliant student. Likes Negroes. Naturally! Oppression makes brothers of us all. Says the greatest bar to Indian independence is the multiplicity of native languages: 326 dialects and 16 languages spoken. Moses wants to learn the American dances. A real flapper, Frances Trusty, a minister's daughter from Elizabeth, New Jersey, was his first instructor. Poor Moses. As one fellow, a physician, said, "She wiggled her body so, poor Moses could not concentrate upon the dance." It was a fox trot. Edna made waffles—chocolate and banana ones. Had hot time. Got home at 2:00 a.m. exactly. A hot bunch. Believe I fell for Vernell Griffin, a charming, intoxicating little friend of Edna's. Believe she is not wholly uninterested in me.

Tried to retire before Almira noticed what time I came in. She woke, however, just as I was about to jump in bed. Foiled my strategy. Supposed to see Swann tomorrow.

Monday February 2, 1931

Before I could begin breakfast, Poe called. Told me that he would go to Camden with me. Borrowed a dollar. Informed him that I would not hear of Swann's canvassing with me. Could only aid me by bringing together large groups of people. Poe agreed. Heckled me for allowing Frances Williams to call him. Poe has stopped eating at her dad's place on her account. Promised to return after breakfast to go to Camden with me. Did not do so. I worked on Allen Day speech. Took Almira and Catherine to Chester with me. Went there to see school teacher, Miss Hall, whose check for $4.00 was returned to me. Missed her. Saw Mrs. Pipes, the principal. She is a splendid woman. Promised to help arrange Negro History Week meeting in Wilmington, Delaware, for next week. Met Sarah Pride. Asked me to take her to Philadelphia. Did so. Almira liked her. Took her home. After dinner went out to West Philadelphia to see Leverte Roberts, a young real estate dealer who wanted to look at a set of books. Persuaded him to take them. Just married six months ago and is only 27. Has [the] only Negro office on Girard Avenue. Introduced Negroes into white sections. Was unintimidated even when whites shot into his home, etc. Has nice home in the making. Made me feel a little sad when he told me that, despite his youth, he had bought the house and furnished it, then married. That is my ideal. I am practical enough to know that to have love without economic foundations is to lay the basis for all sorts of marital difficulties. Roberts invited me out to meet his wife. I shall do so Friday.

Tuesday February 3, 1931

Swann called this morning just before breakfast. He is an abomination. Told my cousin he was going to Harrisburg tomorrow. I don't give a darn. Told her to tell him I was out. Almira went me one better. Informed him that I had gone out at 9:30 and would not return until 10:30 p.m. I rejoiced to have got rid of him so easily. Tried to persuade Mr. Patience at the Y.M.C.A. to take a set of books, but in vain. Put me off until the end of the week.

About noon I left for Camden to canvass some of the school teachers over there. Went to the Whittier School, a large graded institution for Negroes. Its principal, Mr. [Howard Washington] Brown, a man about 40, cultured and refined, gave me every possible assistance. Suggested that I meet the teachers in a group tomorrow at noon. He would call them together. He had bought a set of books for the school in June. Introduced me to some of the teachers and expressed regret that he could not allow me to solicit among them, which practice I understand is strictly "taboo." Asked if I would speak to some of the children in the "platoon" assembly. Assented. The first assembly was composed of girls between the ages of 8 and 12. None of them seemed of normal mentality. (I found out later they were retarded children). Listened attentively. Then the teacher told them they were free to ask me questions. And many of them were quite intelligent, such as: "How do people in Africa live? What do they eat? Do they have schools like we do? What is their religion? Who discovered Africa? Who taught the Africans to build ships?" And myriads of other questions. They wore me out for 35 minutes.

When I ceased replying to their queries, they were brandishing a large number of eager hands to attract my attention for more questions. But I had to disappoint them. They were interested. The teacher was amazed; I was gratified and grateful. Mrs. Jefferson was so enthusiastic that she promised to give a set of books to the Y.W.C.A. Then Mrs. Stratton, a newlywed, whose father-in-law preaches in Tulsa, Oklahoma, next congratulated me. Told me she had never heard of such. Asked if I would speak to her group of boys during the next period, which began immediately. Promised to do so. Then, under the pretext of getting some air, I got a boy to conduct me to the urinal, else I should have been unable to stand long enough to speak. Embarrassed by passing two teachers in the basement near the boys' lavatory, then having the boy blurt out: "There it is, the second door."

Spoke to the boys for twenty minutes. They were a much more intelligent group. One boy about 11 years of age, in particular, asked some very interesting questions, then later told of his reactions to reading an article on big-game hunting in Africa. I was pleased to note that his impressions of Africa had undergone a change. For instance, when I asked them at the outset of my talk what thoughts came into their minds at the mention of Africa, one boy told me he conceived tropical land full of jungles and wild animals: lions, tigers, elephants, and the like. Another—probably the brightest boy in the group—instantly thought of wild, black, half-naked savages with hair standing on end, rings in their noses and ears, fighting and eating one another. I told them about Africa's contributions to civilization along the lines of discovery, exploration, art, painting, empire building, weaving, and many other things. They thanked me individually afterwards. The teachers were astounded. Asked the principal, Mr. Brown, what were the prospects of arranging a Negro History meeting for the Camden public. Thought it a fine idea. Called a minister, Reverend Davis, and to my surprise that worthy, who wanted Woodson, replied that he would have to hear me speak in order to ascertain whether I knew anything about Negro History. It was humorous to me. Mr. Brown invited him over tomorrow noon when I shall speak to the teachers. Promised Miss [Lillian] Goins I would give her a set of books if she could arrange for me to sell ten sets there. She agreed to bring a list of names tomorrow.

Returned home and after dinner went out to meet Sarah Pride at the University of Pennsylvania. Didn't want to go either. Then was disappointed. Waited until 9:25. It was cold and I got angry as h____ sitting there in the cold car. En route home got a bottle of citrate of magnesia and some Ovaltine. The latter is not only a builder but induces sleep.

Wednesday February 4, 1931

Stopped by to see Swann this morning en route to Camden. Poor fellow, he was ill in his dingy, dark room. Told me he was going to Harrisburg to see Pinchot. Wanted to take a set of books with him. Left him a copy of *The Negro in Our History.* Promised to see him when I returned from Camden. Warm day. Reminded me of spring.

My talk to the teachers consumed nearly all the time allotted. There were three preachers there, two of whom had been brought over by Reverend Davis. They just gazed at me with open mouths as I poured forth the achievement of the Negroes in the fields of empire building, invention, history, poetry, music, painting, sculpturing, fiction, and as conquerors. They decided that the Ministerial Alliance would sponsor the program for a Negro History meeting. Named the evening of Tuesday, February 19, for the occasion. Miss Jefferson, the assembly teacher, promised to take a set of books tomorrow. I was secretly pleased at having confounded the ministerial gentry, the best educated of whom were Lincoln graduates. They had come to pass judgment on me. I shall come over tomorrow to see what the harvest in respect to bookselling will be here.

Went to Merchantville, New Jersey, to see Dr. Wilson, the leading practitioner there, whom I had met in Washington, D.C., two years ago. Found that he and his wife were just rebuilding their home, destroyed by fire on New Year's Day. They will have a beautiful home. Mrs. Wilson, while the doctor was busy, took me to the school where an "Uncle Tom" Negro, Mr. Johnson, is principal. After showing him the books, he told me that he would ask the Board of Education to take two of them. Just think of it! Here is an opportunity to get seven books for the price of two, so to speak! And he will recommend two. I was astonished.

Dr. Wilson was glad as well as surprised to see me. Has been kept so busy by "flu" patients that he had to turn me over to his wife to be entertained. She took me to the Camden County Vocational School, where her mother is the head of the cafeteria. The teachers were cooking. Her mother appears quite as dignified as Mrs. Wilson is "flapperish." The school is a large, beautiful, white brick structure, one of the largest vocational schools I have yet seen. Mrs. Lewis deplored the fact that so few Negroes were pursuing the course. In reply to my query as to what proportion of the students were taking the vocational courses, she answered, "A bare 2 percent." And yet cooking, waiting, maid service, and the like, is practically all that the Negro girls can get here. And still fewer Negro boys are preparing for the trades. The white superintendent of schools has interrogated Mrs. Lewis on the same score, especially since farming and handwork was virtually all the Negro man could secure.

Had dinner at Mrs. Lewis's. She has some fine antiques. All furniture in this style. Met a Reverend ____. Between Mr. Johnson and Mrs. Wilson, arrangements will be made for me to speak to the Parent-Teachers on February 26. Mrs. Lewis and Mrs. Wilson will take books at that time.

Returned home. Did not call Swann. Went down to cousin Nettie's, Almira's sister. Played cards. Had some fun but nearly choked because of tobacco and coal gas fumes. Did it to please Almira.

THURSDAY FEBRUARY 5, 1931

En route to Camden, stopped to secure tickets for Rigolletto. All sold with the exception of a few seats in the dress circle. And my tuxedo is in D.C. Embarrassing, for I told Edna on Sunday that I intended taking her. Did not know what to tell her. To inform her that I had waited until the last moment to get tickets, only to find them all sold, would certainly lower me in her estimation. Went to Camden resolving in my mind ways and means of getting out of this fix. Sold only one set of books to the teachers. Lacked the spirit of the Philadelphia ones. Then, too, they have had a half-day's salary deducted from their wages because of unemployment relief. The cultural level of Camden is low and although many of the teachers live in Philadelphia, I fear that the inferior Camden social environment has exerted an unfortunate cultural effect upon them.

The doctors, too, I found unresponsive. Two doctors—[Marcus Fitzherbert] Wheatland and Picou—pleaded lack of funds. I knew that Wheatland, even if he had money, would not be interested in literature. Is a Howard man. Was there during my time. Dr. Bowman, a dentist, took a set, however, but could only pay a $2.98 deposit.

Left Camden. Went to Lawnside (an all-Negro town). Called on the Kentons who are friends of [Ernest] Bacote. Mrs. Arthur came in. Fine looking woman. Bacote knows her (perhaps biblically). Would not live in Lawnside. In their discussion, (that is between Mrs. Arthur and Mrs. Kenton), I learned that there was virtually no business in Lawnside. Only one grocery store, no drug store, no meat market, no furniture or otherwise. No factories. The town is virtually bankrupt. At one time it was feared the school would have to be closed. There is no running water, no gas and when these could have been obtained, the people who owned their homes objected to and defeated the measure. They felt it would increase their taxes, oblivious to the fact that such improvements would add to the value of their property. Two townships, Haddon Heights and one other nearby, which is virtually a residence for millionaires or independently rich whites, have desired at different intervals to incorporate Lawnside. Each time, however, the project was defeated, chiefly out of pride in the fact that this Negro community ought [to] be perpetuated, but from the point of view of the masses, largely on account of the desire to balk the laying of sewers, the introduction of water, and the like. Mrs. Kenton voted against it. She also voted for [Thomas N.] Rivers, as mayor, who was sworn to keep out improvements. Mrs. Arthur rubbed it in pretty strong. Said that the cesspools carried an eternal stench during the summer, and neighbors took a secret pride and pleasure in cleaning out such places, especially when one had company or was giving a lawn party. She vowed she would not live in Lawnside for anything in the world. No business and no cooperation here, therefore make the future of this Negro community extremely dubious.

Called the Mayor to see whether he could arrange a meeting here during Negro History Week. Told me he would try. Asked me to call him Saturday.

Had to figure out some way to break the news to Edna. Went to Pensauken (New Jersey). Called from there. Lied virtuously. Told her mother, who answered the phone, that I had trouble with the car. Would call her daughter when I reached town. Came home. Informed Almira of my dilemma. She is capital. Understood and acquiesced.

Called Edna. Like any woman, she was profuse with sympathy, thinking about me out in the cold. I had to smile. Asked me to come out. I did so. Spent a very enjoyable evening. Looked exceedingly lovely in red. Told me she had planned to wear brown for me because her friends felt it became her best. Talked about a thousand things. Kept her laughing. Told me she liked to have me about her. It is mutual. She has not yet read the poem.

Has not been in the mood. Continues to ask me about going to the sorority dance. Says I must be with the gang. Told her my tuxedo is in D.C. Advises that I go on Thursday and take the gang. Told her I would decide. I could not resist kissing her several times before leaving, but only on the cheek.

Friday February 6, 1931

Went out to North Philadelphia and picked up a check from Mr. Allen, the real estate man. From there returned to Reverend [Edgar C.] Young's church to ascertain whether any of the club members had taken books. Had not. But I sold a Mr. Mousseron[?], the church clerk, and a very talkative individual who gave me a check for $2.00 as a deposit on a set. Is a lay reader. Dr. Young assured me the club would take a set. Asked me to come in on Friday of next week.

From there I stopped at the Durham School to leave a set of books for one of the teachers, a Mr. Branson. The janitor at first refused to admit me, informing me that Mr. [Clarence] Whyte, the principal, had instructed him to bar me because I had imposed upon his good nature in allowing me to come in once for this purpose. I was angry but concealed it. Told him to tell Mr. Whyte it was I. Then the flunky told me I might go to the office. Did not need to for Whyte was talking in the hall. Before he could speak, I told him I had an appointment with one of his teachers. He smiled blandly and assured me it was all right. I delivered the book, secured my $9.98 and was satisfied. Did not attempt to see Miss [Myrtle] Glenn.

Called on Miss White at Brown's Drug Store, 1215 South 17th Street, to find out whether she had secured orders for books for me. She is a pharmacist. Explained that the meeting in Germantown at which I was to speak had been converted into an interracial affair at which my talk would have exerted little bearing upon the business to be discussed. Told me the president of the club, Mrs. [Serena] Vance, however, would be interested. Congratulated me upon the excellent review of *The Wage Earner* in the *New York Times* for Sunday, February 1. She let me read it. 'Twas favorable enough. Considered it a vast collection of material [and] that the situation (was) discussed with candor and detachment. Felt, however, that I exhibited some animus toward the foreign-born element and with some justification. Felt also that the interpretations were weak and that the last word had not yet been said.

Called on three or four other prospects without luck. Returned to house. Went to North Philadelphia at night to collect from Mr. Roberts. Did not have the money. Met his wife, a very charming woman. (Her) mother also interesting.

Returned home about 10:30. Was supposed to go to Sarah Pride's or call her. Did neither.

Saturday February 7, 1931

Today I received one of the most pleasant surprises of my life, something that made me feel that despite all the knavery of Woodson in his endeavor to keep me in the background, I was yet to be vindicated as the author of *The Negro Wage Earner.* This welcome and unexpected news came in the form of a letter which Poe brought me. It was an invitation from the head of the department of economics of Dartmouth College to speak to the senior class on "Labor Relations in America." I was amazed. An honorarium of $50 will also be given me. That, however, is secondary, unimportant. The honor is reward enough. I am to come anytime during the spring semester. I shall go, however, in March, for that will give me opportunities to receive similar engagements from other schools. Poe was elated. Seemed just as happy as if the offer had come to him. Told me from now on I would be a big Negro in his sight.

Both Poe and I noted that although Woodson had read the letter, he forwarded it along with others with no word of comment. Then, too, he has not written me in over a month. Has ignored my order for a dozen copies of *The Wage Earner* and a dozen sets of books. Wanted them here for Negro History Week. He cannot hurt me by his juvenile tactics, for this invitation from Dartmouth brings me just that much nearer my breaking point with him. Just so much more able will I be to stand alone. I desire only the scholarship from him. Then, if necessary, I shall be free to wash my hands.

Poe admonished me not to be too hasty. Reminded me that despite Woodson's trickery and meanness, I owed what little success I had earned to my association with him, to his giving me the opportunity to write the book. I listened attentively. There was much truth in what he said.

Prepared talk for tomorrow at Darby on Richard Allen. Will discuss the founder of the A.M.E. Church as a slave, exhorter, protestor, and builder. He was all that. Likened him to Martin Luther.

Returned from Y, where I was writing, to take Almira shopping. It was snowing. From there got haircut and had brakes adjusted. Did not desire to drive, the way car swerved every time the brakes were applied. Brakes are to safeguard, not to kill one. Cost $1.50.

Took two-hour rest before going to party. Went to sorority meeting where I was to meet Edna. [I] was introduced to Mrs. [Florence S. Johnson] Hunt, wife of the president of the Fort Valley School, Fort Valley, Georgia, a middle-aged woman of medium build. We discussed the educational progress of the southern Negro. Edna was dressed in brown. Did not like her as well as I did in red or black. Introduced me to two girls, with one of whom I had lots of fun.

It was terribly slippery. The roads were like glass. Edna looked aghast when I told her that I had narrowly escaped death on the way here. Crossing 18th and Spring Garden streets, a car going west struck my rear bumper and turned me completely about. What a sensation I had! It seemed as if the entire world had suddenly gone awry, everything was rocking, about to overturn and crush me. By diligent manipulation of the wheel, however, I brought the crazily careening car to a standstill against the curb, facing the way I had lately come. Had a car been coming from the opposite direction during that moment when the car had passed beyond my control, I would have been lost.

Arrived at the party. I found a friendly, well-met group. The hostess was extremely charming and suffusing with personality. And how she danced! It was almost impossible for one to hold her in his arms and still the ardent surgings of his blood that cried out for her. And she enjoyed it! Had enjoyable time. Edna seems to be getting much more friendly and affectionate. Perhaps it is because I was having such a fine time with the other girls. I note, too, that she appears to be more or less crippled. She goes upstairs sideways and very slowly. Comes down in the same manner. It is too delicate a subject to question her about, so I appear not to notice it. She does not waltz, does not dance fox trots. Prefers, perhaps through necessity, slow drags. I don't hate them myself.

Met a Mrs. _____, principal of a school in Harrington, Delaware. Asked me to come down to speak to the Parent-Teachers Association on February 19th. Promised I would.

Took Edna home after taking some of her friends to their various domiciles. Sat out in the car before her house for almost an hour. I knew that she had come to the point where she expected me to caress her. And I did. Could not help it. And what fiery embraces. She kisses like Bertha, Helen, M_____, and any number of other master kissers whom I have known. And her arms entwined about me so tightly that she just trembled each time I kissed her. And those great eyes looked up into mine so appealing and so full of passion that it was with considerable effort that I tore myself away from her. Even then, it was 3:00 a.m. and I had to be in Darby tomorrow morning at 10:30. I went home feeling not a little satisfied that at last she had lain weak and panting in my arms, had returned kiss for kiss and in the rhapsody of her affection had forgotten, along with me, that it was dreadfully cold. I halfway promised to take her to Riverton, New Jersey, with me tomorrow. She seems to enjoy my company. I hers.

Reached home at 3:15 utterly fatigued. Must keep better hours.

SUNDAY FEBRUARY 8, 1931

Awoke at 7:00, caused by Almira's going to work and calling everyone for breakfast at 8:00. I felt tired, certainly not like one who was to deliver the morning address to a congregation. Looked over a few notes on Allen after breakfast to refresh my memory with the cardinal points of his life. Feel my comparison of Allen with Luther will impress people.

Left for Darby about 9:30. Thought it was 10:00 a.m. but the clock was fast. It was a clear day. Thank God! Much warmer than last night, which melted the ice on the roads and made driving easier.

Reached Darby about 10:00. Called on Mr. [John M.] Drew, since I had three quarters of an hour to wait, but that worthy was in bed. I went forth to Mrs. Gates, who sponsored the meeting. She was just beginning to dress. I waited until she was ready. Has a comfortable home. Husband is a dentist; she a school teacher. Is Mr. Drew's niece. Very fine woman. Met the doctor, a young dentist from the University of Pennsylvania. Is equipped with an up-to-date office.

Went to church with Mrs. Gates. Disappointed at first in the size of the church. Also felt depressed at the one or two persons who had arrived when I reached there. Met the pastor, a Reverend Williams, a fairly intelligent man of about 52, small, yet a keen sympathizer with the movement of Negro History. Mrs. Gates suggested that I place books in the vestibule on a table so that the people might peruse them after the service. Did so.

The entire service hour was mine. When I rose to speak, the church was full. I spoke for 40 minutes on the history of Negro achievement in Africa and America, showing the Negro contributions in every field, their importance and necessity and the means of disseminating it. The latter, I told them, could be attained only through the united endeavor of all parties: the church, the teachers, the parents, and clubs. I then descanted upon Richard Allen. When I paused, the minister told the congregation that if it were not Sunday, he would permit the unrestrained response that such a fine address demanded.

Never have I felt so gratified, so buoyed up. Especially when a school principal, one Mrs. Bailey, grasped my hand and exclaimed, "Mr. Greene, for the first time in my life I have felt proud to be black." And she *is* black.

Invitations now (came) to speak to the New Century Club on February 24. They have a Negro History group. Mrs. Bailey is president. The minister was jubilant. Wanted me to come again when he could get everyone in Darby there to hear me. Doctors, wives, school teachers, lowly laborers and their wives, even children crowded about to congratulate me. And then, best of all, I sold three sets of books and two single copies. A high school boy asked me to come over to speak at his high school. I promised I would. Mrs. Gates told me that she had never heard anything like it as she took me to her uncle's for dinner. And Reverend Williams said that he could have listened for another hour.

Took dinner at Mr. Drew's. He is bitter against ministers. Told him he ought to arrange committee to help sponsor his work against the segregation of Negro Gold Star Mothers on their pilgrimage to France. Replied with some heat that he had laid such a proposition before the Ministerial Alliance, but they had scoffed at it. Drew has little confidence in ability of preachers to guide the Negro upward. Are too hungry, he avows. Would sell themselves and group for their own selfish purposes. Dislike to give over pulpit for anything that will take money out of their hands.

Returned to Philadelphia. Met Poe and his lady on 18th Street near Y.M.C.A. Found she was Miss [Alberta S.] Norwood, a school teacher, who, despite her denial, seems to have made a profound impression on Poe. Met her for the first time. Is considerably older than Poe. Must be about 40 or 41. She is not so well-formed, but possesses an engaging personality. I hope Poe won't fall too hard.

Returned home. Almira disappointed because I would not eat. Called Gaines. Asked her about going to Riverton. Tickled to death. Enjoyed ride there. Had to stop en route and rub off the windshield and windows with paper. Could not see through it. Gaines enjoyed it. Bought her box of Pall Malls. I smoke so seldom I never buy cigarettes. Arrived in Riverton. Went to Miss Johnson's. From there went to church. Goodly crowd. Program too long. About seven persons (history club members who were conducting the program) spoke on Richard Allen. Johnson also spoke on him for twenty minutes. Therefore, I considered that sufficient had been said concerning him and told the audience so. Spoke for thirty minutes. Two whites in the rear of the audience grinned as if what I said was pure fiction. Did not mind them, however. After the collection I received $5.00. Mr. Johnson also gave me a check from the Missioner School for a set of books. The people applauded my talk. Many congratulated me personally; one woman told me I had a whole Negro History in my head. I did not feel that I acquitted myself as well as this morning. Edna said nothing. Her eyes spoke. The ride home made me wish it were spring. Edna whispered how much she would miss me if I had to leave this section. I like her but God knows I could never love her. She is intriguing, but I believe her life a little too blasted by disappointment for her to ever have faith in another mortal.

Returning home, she wanted to make coffee. I suggested ice cream. Bought it. Then she was in my arms. . . . Left at 2:00 a.m. She wanted to see me Tuesday. Told her I would be busy. Reminded me how much I meant to her.

MONDAY FEBRUARY 9, 1931

Today it rained as if the very clouds had opened. I was to take Miss [Myrtle] Glenn, a school teacher, for a ride at noontime. Of course I did not go. At 3:00, went to the Y.M.C.A. to meet the gym class of doctors and businessmen to see if I could sell them books. Too busily engaged with volleyball to pay attention to books.

Returned home. Took Almira and her sister downtown, then home. About 10:00, Almira received a call telling her to get in touch with Alice's husband. It meant a job for him as doorman for a white dentist on Market Street. Drove down to tell them about it. On the return, Julius bought some ice cream, while I bought citrate of magnesia, for I had a headache. Meant to go to bed early. Could not, however, until 12:30. Called [James] Waring. Made engagement to speak at Downingtown Industrial School at Downington tomorrow at 7:30 p.m.

TUESDAY FEBRUARY 10, 1931

Had intended to go to Darby this morning. Did not, however. Cold and having speaking engagements for several successive days, I decided to remain in. Did so until 1:00 p.m., at which time I went to see Miss Wagner, head of the history department in the girls' division of the South Philadelphia High School at 2100 South Broad Street. Had previously arranged to see her concerning adoption of books on Negro History for the school. Found her a woman about 45. Very frank and liberal on race question. Interested in the Negro and his past. Trying to change the attitudes of the white students toward the Negro. Told me despite the fact that Jewish students comprise the major part of the student body, many of them expressed their disinclination to ride on trolleys beside Negroes or to live next door to them. Told me one girl felt that it lowered her social prestige to live next door to Negroes. We discussed the economic situation among Negroes, the condition of the Southern Negro, and other pertinent things. I marvelled at her fine grasp of Negro History. Agreed with me that neither race is willing to lay all its cards on the table, even in interracial discussions. Also agreed that the situation and condition of the Negro is a relative thing; that if the Negro were in the same position, he would be just as severe an overlord. Miss Wagner amazed me when she confided in me that, all things considered, were she a Negro in America, she would commit suicide. I had often speculated how whites would feel if our positions were reversed. We would act similarly, no doubt, had not centuries of oppression here schooled, hardened, and inured us to many of the disabilities under which we live and have our being. She took down a list of books for the school. Was elated at the material contained in the books. Advised my seeing the supervisor of elementary schools in order to get *Negro Makers of History* and *African Myths* adopted in the schools for supplementary readers.

Stopped by Dr. [Charles A.] Lewis's. Is still interested in the Negro Epoch affair for the Exposition in Chicago for 1933. Delighted to hear of my invitation to speak at Dartmouth. Offered, if I would remain in Philadelphia, to put me before the public, serving as my publicity agent. Told him I would think it over. Reminded me again of Allen Day. Wants me to speak at the wreath-laying ceremony at the tomb of Allen on Saturday, then at the Douglass-Allen celebration on Sunday.

Returning home, called G[aines] to see whether she and the gang might desire to go to Downingtown with me. Could not locate the gang. Suggested we go alone; that she would enjoy it. I agreed. Did not intend to call her, yet did not care to go to Downingtown alone.

On the way, she told me how happy she was to go along with me. I enjoyed having her with me too, once we had started.

Arrived at Downingtown about 7:30. It is a small school. I saw three buildings as we drove in. Very unpretentious. (The President, James) Waring, wondered whether I was coming. Spoke for about a half hour. The students, ranging from about thirteen to twenty, seemed to be absorbed in what I said. Edna sat in the back of the room to give me encouragement and inspiration whenever I glanced in her direction. I thrive on the knowledge that a woman is interested in me even though it be but momentarily.

After my talk, we went into the modest office of the principal. Waring was formerly my teacher of German at Howard University. Edna met two of her sorors. I met a Miss [Virginia Louise?] Ruffin, a former classmate at Howard. They are teaching here. Sold three sets of books. Got checks for the full amount. Another, Miss Whitfield, and a Miss Ross promised to forward checks.

Left about 10:00 p.m. Delightful trip home with Edna cuddling close to me, whispering words of affection, and I nearly losing control of the car in endeavors to kiss her while traveling at 45 to 50 miles an hour.

Arrived in Philadelphia at 11:00 p.m. Edna made cocoa. Chided her because she scorched it. . . . Left at 12:30. Wished me pleasant trip to D.C. tomorrow.

WEDNESDAY FEBRUARY 11, 1931

Almira called me about 7:30 to inform me that Mr. Drew had made arrangements for me to speak at the high school in Darby. Meant Washington trip must be called off. Both of us were disappointed. Started for Darby at 8:10. Was due there at 8:35. Had to go to the Y for books. En route to Darby, radiator steamed so I feared radiator had frozen at least. It was terribly cold last night. Cold this morning, too. Happily, it wasn't [frozen], for after having a quantity of alcohol and water put in, the escape of steam stopped.

Spoke to about 600 high school students—the majority white. Told them briefly (about 20 minutes) about Negro contributions in all fields in Africa, Europe, and America. The students applauded heartily after I had finished. Mr. Zaner, the superintendent, told me it was wonderful. So did the teachers in charge of the assembly. Drew came in as I was preparing to leave. Took me to lunch with him. Got on ministers again.

Returned to Philadelphia. Sent my aunt a special (delivery letter) asking her to send my dress clothes.

Received no books from Woodson. Have none. Much of the sales that could have been made were nullified because of the lack of books. Wrote Woodson a letter informing him either to send books or declare the campaign closed. I am sick of his procrastination and his ignoring requests for books. I am working for the benefit of the Association, but it can all go to Hades before I shall work and then beg for the privilege of so doing. I wrote in part, "The ignoring of my requests for books has led me to one of two conclusions: either that the Associated Publishers has been blessed with the sale of all of its books or else that you desire the campaign stopped. Whatever it is, please have the courtesy to inform me. I hate suspense, especially in a case of this kind, for we have been embarrassed by lack of books. Indeed it seems that you have deliberately chosen the high point of the year for the sale of books to withdraw the support of the office from the work. Whatever your decision is—and it matters not—advise me and advise me definitely."

Wrote Helen [Notis] and other persons. Send checks and money orders to office for $15.56.

Nettie, Alice, and others came to the house at 10:30, after I had gone to bed. Had to get up to play cards. Could not retire before 1:00 a.m. Must speak in Chester tomorrow.

THURSDAY FEBRUARY 12, 1931

Before breakfast, Mrs. Gates called from Chester. Asked me to speak to her pupils. Would entail my getting to Chester earlier than usual. Wanted me at 11:00. And Mrs. Bailey wishes me at 1:00 at her school. Felt tired, but it is the cause. En route stopped at the Y. Letter from Woodson and check from Miss Ruffin for books. Woodson advises me that the survey of unemployment among Negroes in the District of Columbia has gone through. Wants me to make it in conjunction with Mr. [E. E.] Lewis of Howard. Came at inopportune time. Things just going fine here. Hate to break off now. Was ready for it at Christmas time. Undecided what I shall do. Can make more money in this work. Yet I could add another survey to my record. And then, perhaps, I shall be forced to work under Lewis when I know the economic situation of the Negro. And will I be cheated again of the reward of my labors? Then too, salary! The same under which I began three years ago. Cheapen myself. Wish I had (Harry) Hipp to talk to. I am all up in the air.

Spoke to Mrs. Gates's pupils. Seemed to enjoy it. Mrs. Gates and the other teachers thanked me profusely. A Mr. Bruce will take books next Thursday. The principal may take a set, also. Had lunch. Children get theirs for six cents: oatmeal, lamb stew, salad, bread, butter, milk, and dessert. These are backward children. Supposed to be fitted only for domestic service and handicrafts.

Went therefrom to Mrs. Bailey's school, 5th and Welch streets. Another old and unpretentious building. Does have an assembly hall, however. Mrs. Bailey had invited the assistant superintendent of education and the supervisor as well as other persons. Spoke half an hour. The children, especially those of the 4th, 5th, and 6th grades, must have been interested for many craned necks to hear what I was saying. Another teacher will take books next week when I bring Mrs. Bailey's.

Went to the McKay School hoping I might see Ada Saunders, one of the teachers there. Did not. Went to the Watts School. Saw Miss Valentine. Asked me to take her to Philadelphia. Promised to. Sarah Pride next asked me the same question. Told her I was angry with her because she had "stood me up" last week. She showered me with apologies. Informed me that she waited for a telephone call from me until 12:00 last Friday night. Asked whether I would let her sit beside me on the way to Philadelphia. Told her I'd pray over it. When we did start, although Sarah sat in front, Miss Valentine sat beside me. Ada (Saunders) was waiting at the station. Dark and very attractive. My bandying remarks with her certainly set Sarah on edge, although they (Ada and Miss Valentine) were seated in the rear of the car.

Brought them to Temple University. Took Sarah home. Made me promise to call her on Sunday.

After dinner called Edna. She was in North Philadelphia. Asked me to come for her. Got lost on way out. Met Dr. and Mrs. Jenkins with whom she was meeting. Told her of my desire to have a letter typed. Suggested Vernell Griffin.

Went there. Vernell was not in. Talked with her landlady. Got myself in trouble speaking of the prevalence of pellagra in the South. When asked its causes, I replied that the lack of fresh vegetables and milk was the chief source of it. Remarked that (it is) common knowledge that the South raises few vegetables but confines its efforts chiefly to cotton, rice, sugar cane, tobacco, and some little corn. Whereupon mine hostess was moved to ridicule me, stating that she had lived in Mississippi and that everybody raised vegetables; in fact, that was what most people ate. I stopped talking before such colossal ignorance. Everyone knows that the Southern Negro and the poor white exist mainly upon a diet mainly of cornbread, pork, and molasses. Vernell apologized to me. I laughingly brushed it aside. I showed her the letter I wanted her to write forwarding my acceptance to Mr. (Malcolm) Keir of Dartmouth College to speak to the senior class in economics. She promised to type it immediately.

Told Edna I intended to retire early tonight. Therefore, left Vernell's at 10:30. Edna lives in the next block. Would not go in. Sat in car. Told her of my offer to make Washington survey. She asked what I would do. Told her I was in a quandary myself. We talked about other matters. Told me more of herself: That her husband had left her with an eight-month-old child and another on the way; that another man who worshipped her, and who went to the dogs because she would not marry him, disappointed her in the mess he made of his life. While we talked, while we caressed one another, the time slipped by so until it was 1:30 when I looked at my watch. Told me she would wait to hear from me until 10:00 p.m. tomorrow to see if I will go to the dance. Assured her I would, if my tuxedo came and was not full of moth holes.

19

Philadelphia and Vicinity

Work and Leisure

FRIDAY FEBRUARY 13, 1931

Before I could get out of bed, a special-delivery boy brought my dress clothes. Everything was there except the scarf. Found a broken place in the trousers of the tuxedo. Looked as if it had been mended. Perhaps Glenn (Carrington) did it four years ago when I loaned it to him. Took it to a weaver. Cost $3.00. Went from there to the Durham School. Read poetry to Miss [Myrtle] Glenn. Got so excited after my rendition of "A June Night" that she started stroking my hair. Both she and Miss Connors liked the poem "Out of the Mist," especially the second version. Promised to see Miss Glenn tomorrow night.

Went to the Barker private school. Talked to children. Looked backward to me. Mrs. Barker will take set next week (Wednesday). Ordered also five copies of *Negro Makers of History.* Called upon Reverend [Edgar C.] Young. Wife ill. Will be unable to do anything until next Friday because of failure to see treasurer of the club. Will give me deposit at that time.

This is the night of the dance affair. It has already cost me $10.50. Called for Edna [Gaines] at 11:00. Beautiful in long white dress. She wore no jewelry, no earrings. With her black hair set off by red roses, the color of her lips, her appeal was heightened one hundred fold. Felt like crushing her in my arms. But I remembered that we still had to go to the affair. The dance itself was tame enough. Enjoyed two dances with Edna. Those with Vernell [Griffin] were the best, because of the music and the mood in which I found her. Vernell still attracts me. Miss Cummings, a teacher from Camden whom I had met last week, stood out as the most attractive woman in the place. Of medium height, dark, with smooth skin and clean cut features. Attired in a rose-hued gown that revealed a perfect back down to her waist, she was the cynosure of all masculine eyes. And had I known earlier that I was going to the affair, she would have been my guest. She was visiting Vernell. After the dance, took Vernell and Miss Cummings home. Vernell was in a terrible mood. Lonesome, lovesick, didn't want to go to bed. Didn't know what to do. Felt sorry for her. Finally left them after getting an order of Chinese ham and eggs for her. (She paid for it.)

Edna and I went to the Golden Dawn. Got there about 4:00 a.m. People were about ready to go. No particular fun. Took her home. Sat in the car before her house. She told me what a glorious evening she had spent with me and soon her tantalizing lips melted into mine. God! I had previously told her I did not drink but, lo, now I was drunk, gloriously, heavenly drunk; intoxicated by her nearness, her arms, her lips, her body. With arms entwined about one another we sat gazing into each other's eyes, thinking thoughts and desiring one another from the very depths of our being. It was not to be, however. She told me she could not leave me as long as I kissed her. I replied I could not help kissing her as long as she remained near me. The only way we could leave the car was her promise to give me one last kiss in the vestibule. That, too, was not to be for when she put the key into the outer door, she spied her mother up and moving about in the kitchen. We both laughed knowingly and took leave of one another. . . .

Arrived home at 6:30 a.m. Terribly late hour. Tired out. Almira did not awaken either. Wired Woodson I could not undertake survey until March 1.

Saturday February 14, 1931

[John Wesley] Poe called me before I got out of bed. Left word that two letters had come for me. One came here from a Mrs. Wilson, principal of a school in Harrington, Delaware. Wants me to speak on February 17. I am already booked for that date in Camden, New Jersey. Had arranged to give her the 19th. Must telegraph her.

Letter from Woodson informing me that my complaint was first he had heard about books. "That is the way you do things. You imagine you have done them and then go ahead and say that you have done them." We received the books. That is the only thing which interested me.

In the afternoon went down to the ceremonies at the bier of Bishop [Richard] Allen, who is buried in the mausoleum of Bethel Church. First, we were taken through the building and shown the interesting articles in the Allen Museum. The dress worn during Mrs. Allen's time, the chair upon which Allen sat and his footrest, a jug, a hat, a bonnet, and many other interesting things were shown us by a Mr. Johnson, whose mother belonged to the church and who was born in 1855. Told us also that a station of the Underground Railroad was located there. The pulpit now used in the church is the same one from which Allen used to preach. It is of plain wood, giving the appearance that it was made from a box. The stained glass window reflected the afternoon sun in dazzling array of colors: gold, green, amethyst, jade, and others.

The Historical Society of Germantown, composed of women, laid a wreath on the tomb. Reverend Jones, pastor of the church, made a very fine speech on Reverend Allen. Dr. [Charles A.] Lewis also spoke.

I too spoke. Disappointed myself. Asked to speak tomorrow night at a Douglass-Allen celebration at a Baptist church on Tasker Street. Expect to do better.

Went out to West Philadelphia to see M[yrtle]. Large number of girls. Giddy. Was bored to death. . . . Walked home. She is one of those persons who would be natural but fears to. Is a person of inhibitions. Seems to be wild about me, yet holds herself in leash. No virtue in total abstinence. Moderation is the desirable quality. I admire the girl who can kiss, etc., yet who will go no farther if she does not care to. I don't drink. There is no virtue in that. The virtue inheres in my drinking moderately, never to excess. Don't believe I shall ever bother to see her again.

Sunday February 15, 1931

Spent all day writing up my diary and preparing to make remarks on Allen and [Frederick] Douglass whose joint anniversary celebrations are to be held today. The latter has never been fully appreciated by the members of his group. Two contemporary characters enjoyed such a comprehensive grasp upon the events of the time. An escaped slave, endowed with little formal learning, but gifted with varied and natural talents, a keen analytical mind, a wealth of information garnered from reading and contact, widely traveled, possessed of a moving and persuasive eloquence that prompted his hearers to hang upon his every syllable—Douglass easily took rank as one of the foremost American statesmen of the 19th century. But for his humble origin and identification with a depressed people, there can be no doubt that he would have held one of the portfolios either in a presidential cabinet or filled the position of ambassador to some foreign country for which his admirable qualities eminently fitted him. But on account of his color, he was doomed to nothing higher than the post as minister to Haiti. For us, it is meet that we remember his determined stand against any scheme to colonize the free Negroes whether in Mexico, Haiti, Africa, or Canada; his conviction that the South offered the best field for the ultimate rise of the Negro; his advocacy of women's right to vote; and his warnings to the Negroes to learn trades and hold their jobs by increasing their efficiency to entrench themselves in farm buying, domestic service, and all other employments at that time in their hands, but which foreign whites were already taking out of their hands.

Went to church about 8:00 p.m. The sponsors of the celebration had not yet arrived. The program began about 9:00 p.m. (C.P. [Colored People's] time.) After a lot of preliminaries an attorney, Miller, delivered a eulogy on Douglass. It was stimulating, moving, high soaring, but like all such pieces of eloquence had little meat. A Mr. Love, who had arranged for Colonel [Charles] Young's body to be escorted by a military cortege, next spoke. Mrs. Duckett gave some stimulating remarks covering the Women's Civic League of West Philadelphia. Dr. Lewis then called upon me last. Spoke about eight minutes. Vindicated myself for Saturday's failure. Excelled myself tonight. Showed need for Negro History.

Gave few facts, then interpreted Fred Douglass in the light of what he means to us: namely, that he opposed colonization; felt that the Negro was better off in the South; and his appeal to the Negro to fortify himself in jobs. That the main points of Booker T. Washington's Atlanta Exposition Address of 1895 was largely a popularization of Douglass's ideas, especially Washington's exhorting the Negroes to remain in the South to perfect themselves in the trades, etc. Was overwhelmed by congratulations afterwards. Guess I stole some of Miller's thunder.

Called Edna. Was still at Mrs. Garth's. Needed gas. Had left pocketbook at home. License with it. Embarrassed in church. Had to leave Helen's ring in order to get gas. Reached there (Mrs. Garth's) about 12:00. Edna informed me that the AKAs want me to speak at a tea on May 17. Will pay expenses. Enjoyed myself by telling casual tales to the group. Edna accused me of being dignified and reserved. Felt I did not want her near me. Says everyone feels I am the scholar only. I laughed. Absurd, I am intensely human. Told me she had lost her heart to me. Sounded good for my ego, but again I laughed. But in the car in front of her house wrapped in each others arms. Don't love Edna. Don't even like her especially. . . .

MONDAY FEBRUARY 16, 1931

Today I was so tired, that despite my original intention of going to Camden, I did nothing until the evening. Poe came over bringing two letters, one from Helen N[otis]; one from Howard. Helen wants me to come to Newark for the weekend. Otherwise, she may visit friends in Philadelphia.

Recounts last February. I am in a quandary, for I have promised Edna to go to New York. I'm always getting into a jam. Must pray over it.

Mrs. Wilson from Harrington, Delaware, also sent me a letter informing me that she is expecting me on Tuesday, February 17. Knew it could not be so, for I am scheduled for Camden. Wired her to that effect. We arranged for Thursday, the 19th.

Poe seems to be getting involved deeper and deeper with Miss [Alberta S.] Norwood. She buys his meals. Wants to take him to New York for the weekend and a host of other things. She is so much older than he that he feels quite puerile at times, especially when she calls him "baby." Says he, "I actually feel like one."

After dinner, called upon Helen Hewlitt. Met her at Hampton in 1927. Thought she was better looking. Sold her. Remembered me, too. From there (went) to sell Jewel Porter on the same street. Went therefrom to Mrs. [Florence] Evans on Summer Street, the head of the Business and Professional Girls Club of Germantown. Going out. Met her brother, Orville Evans, city editor of the *Tribune.* Wants to prepare write-up of *The Negro Wage Earner* and run it in the *Philadelphia Record.* Feels it would increase sales of books. Wants picture, also. We planned to get together Thursday in case I did not go to Delaware. Also wants to get me to address Fireside Club in Germantown and another discussion group composed largely of whites. Expenses will be paid.

Tuesday February 17, 1931

Rose at 8:00 this morning. Called Mr. Newman, the proprietor of Holland's Catering Establishment, for appointment. After quite a bit of shifting and procrastination, consented to see me at 3:00 p.m. Took cousin Jane to Alice's on way to the Y. Redeemed ring then went out to [Arthur] Fauset's school to interview some of the teachers. Fauset had gone to lunch, unfortunately. Not desiring to do so without his permission, I left. Tried to find Dr. Whyte. He was not at home, however. Had pictures made. So self-conscious, I feel they will look horrid. (Cost) $12.00 a dozen. Called on Dr. Lewis. Importuned me to think of his proposition. Congratulated me on my talk the other night.

Rushed out to see Mr. Newman. What a spectacle his establishment presents! A beautiful restaurant of marble two stories high on one side. Then across the street a restaurant, a bakery, store, etc. Largest business I have yet seen run by Negroes, insurance companies and Madame Malone's excepted. Newman bought nothing. Told me he was taking on new responsibilities and depression prevented his doing so. Wanted one book, *Negro Orators and*

Their Orations, but could not see $5.00. Showed him the virtue that lay in taking a set. Wouldn't buy. Disappointed me. Next saw Mr. McHenry, fine young fellow and one of the leading men in the establishment. To my queries about the business, informed me it was 68 years old. Rapid expansion in the last three years has elicited envy from whites and jealousy from many Negroes. Whites hate to feel that they are contributing to building up of Negro fortune. Therefore no ostentation, no big cars or luxurious homes are indulged in by either Mr. Newman, Mr. McHenry, or others in charge. Refuse to publish cost of buildings in papers, especially Negro weeklies which would distort figures. Whites were amazed at extent of business and the motley array of workers—German cooks, Negro cooks; Japanese, white, and colored girls. And Mr. McHenry tells me that they hire everybody. Efficiency alone counts.

Returned home. Had suit pressed. Called Edna about 6:00. Informed her that I would take her to Camden. Promised to be ready at 7:30. Wired Woodson for twelve (copies of) *The Negro Wage Earner.*

Was raining terribly when I arrived for Edna. To my protestations about taking her out in the rain, she replied that it afforded her great pleasure to be with me and that the rain only served to keep our affection green. 'Twas a wretched night for romance, unless one and his love had the good fortune to be sitting on a bear rug before a blazing hearth with only the red glare from the crackling logs as light.

Had difficulty finding the church in Camden, besides going some distance out of my way to get to the Camden Bridge. I insisted upon going down Market Street, even against the advice of Edna who knew the way. I insisted upon going down Market Street because the traffic moved faster. Arrived at the church at 8:45. Too early. Few people upstairs.

'Twas the occasion for the installation of the officers of the Ministerial Alliance. I was to deliver the main address. After some delay while the divers divines and their wives assembled, the ceremonies began. Of course, there was much talk and confusion. It was not decided until the last moment who would introduce the master of ceremonies, pronounce the invocation, or perform other trivial, but seemingly important, duties. I sat highly amused through it all, pitying Edna, who sat in the rear of the church.

I suppose about 100 persons were present when I began to speak. I do believe that tonight I rose above myself. Don't know what possessed me. Recounted the exploits of the Negroes in all fields, after showing the necessity for the study of Negro History. Many times the audience broke into applause, especially after my apostrophes to Touissant L'Ouverture, Christophe, Sonni Ali, Allen, and Fred Douglass. I did wax somewhat warm on the latter two and Touissant. The ministers overwhelmed me with applause. One man told me that he could have listened all night. A Reverend Fernandez, who grasped my hand before I sat down, told me was the greatest oration he had ever heard. The women overwhelmed me. I felt grateful that I was able to stir these people. It is something I could not do last year.

Could sell no books, however. These people, due to the lack of employment among Negroes, cannot buy books. Then, too, the cultural level here is so much lower than in Philadelphia. I was embarrassed when I went downstairs to the collation served for the ministers. One of the gentlemen of the cloth persisted in finding out whether Edna was Miss or Mrs. Gaines. I had introduced her as the latter. He kept repeating, "Mrs.?" I answered, "Gaines." "Mrs.?" Again I retorted, "Gaines," until finally Edna, sensing the situation and the embarrassment it was causing me, told the good Reverend that it was "Miss," but that she was a widow. Mr. Flournoy of the Y.M.C.A. asked me to come over to his club Friday at 7:00. I promised. Was given an honorarium of $5.00. Not so bad, but could have better remained at home.

Returning, Edna was as loving as only she can be. Asked me about New York. Told her I would inform her later. After kissing me rapturously for a moment, she suddenly fled into the house. I left filled with both elation and dejection. The former, because of the successful effort to acquaint the audience with some facts on the Negro; the latter because of the peculiar action of Edna.

Reached home about 2:00 a.m. Fatigued.

Wednesday February 18, 1931

Rose about noon. Went to Dr. Whyte's on North 23rd Street. Not in. Went therefrom to the Field School to leave a copy of *Negro Wage Earner* with Mrs. (Verona) Beckett. Talked with her almost an hour. Finally persuaded her to take a set of books. It was a task but I put it over. She inquired whether I had interviewed the librarians here. Replied in the negative. Suggested that I go to the Pedagogical Library on South 18th Street and tell the librarian that she sent me. I thanked her. Did not stop to see Edna, who teaches here. Started back to Dr. Whyte's.

On the way there, sustained what might have been a serious accident. Going North on 23rd Street, a wagon suddenly turned south out of a narrow street. Swerving to my left to avoid hitting the horse, I spied a truck coming out of the same street, but half hidden by the wagon. Neither the driver of the truck nor I saw each other until it was too late. And despite our frantic efforts—mine to speed out of his oncoming path and his to stop—we collided. That is, his front bumper struck my rear right fender almost ripping it off from the running board. Immediately a crowd gathered as we tried to ascertain the amount of damage done. The truck driver acknowledged it was his fault. He was driving a vehicle owned by the Philadelphia Department of Education. Assured me the insurance company would take care of my damages. Thus assured, I went on.

The doctor was not in, either. Went down to Alice's. Brought back articles, beer, etc., for Almira, who had invited a few friends in tonight.

After dinner, called upon Edna. Took me to Dr. Broadus's, a friend of hers. Danced for a while. Returned home. Sat in car for a while. . . . Left her at 2:45.

Tired out and I am to go to Harrington, Delaware, tomorrow.

Thursday February 19, 1931

Got some books from the Y.M.C.A. this morning and left for Harrington, Delaware, to speak. Would have taken Poe, but he did not appear at the stated time; therefore, I left him. Departed at 11:45. Had to go 98 miles. Could not stop in Chester to leave books as I had promised. 'Twas cold and rainy, thus impossible to enjoy the drive. Arrived at Harrington about 2:45. School a frame structure, a DuPont school. Well built, with assembly hall of considerable dimensions. Large playground. But then, that is one of the features of these schools.

Mrs. Wilson gathered the children together, some of them ranging as high as 19 years of age. They entertained me first with singing and recitations. One little girl—I later learned she was 15—nearly moved me to tears as she recited a poem, "Won't You Buy My Matches?" I spoke about twenty minutes. Children seemed interested. Teachers bought no books. A Miss Ryland claimed she had no money; Miss Moore, a tall, impressionable girl, confessed her inability to buy due to the fact that she was just substituting. However, Miss Ryland assured me that they would take something before I left.

There are no eligible men. Makes it precarious for one to enter. (The teachers had a party afterwards.) Mrs. Wilson—she must be 45—and the other teacher, Miss Moore, tall as she was, kept me busy dancing, and quite suggestively, too. Mrs. Wilson was more or less nauseating to me. Danced because it was the polite thing. With Miss Moore, however, it was different. She was soon increasing the pressure of her arms about me while we danced to a slow fox-trot. Then she began to breathe in a laborious manner, started to gasp, and then crushed her lips in reckless abandon upon mine. I finished the dance marvelously wrought up. So was she. Sought to induce her to take a ride, but she declined. She was too well known.

After dinner we went to the school where I was to address the Parent-Teachers (Association). Before going I locked the keys in the car and had to get a boy to take the handle off the door in order to get them. Miss Moore had got out of the car and slammed the door with the catch on.

The parents who came to the meeting were either farmhands or domestics. That is the only work the Negroes can get to do here. They listened attentively to what I had to say. Surprised me, however, by buying a fair number of books, most of which were the *Negro Makers of History,* a dollar and a half book. A teacher took a set. Hardly paid for my coming down here. But these people have little money.

Went back to where Mrs. Wilson stayed. Danced again with Miss Moore, with both of us reacting as we did earlier in the evening. Took her home, where after a profusion of mad embraces, I went to a Mr. Hays's, where I was to spend the night.

There was no steam heat, the house being warmed by a stove. Lay down with thought of the morrow, [and] the trip to New York and its possibilities, to intrigue me until far into the morning.

Friday February 20, 1931

This day marked a radical departure for me in a very vital way. One of my most cherished ideas went overboard—catapulted there by riotous, upsurging emotion and soul-fire that knew no downing.

And yet, it began prosaically enough. Woke tired and cold. Could not sleep. The breakfast prepared for me was such that I could not consume it. All I managed to eat was the grapefruit. The eggs were fried so hard that it would have been suicide to try to digest them; [the] sausage, I knew, would disturb me gastronomically; therefore, I eschewed both. I was so cold, however, that I would have taken some coffee, but it was lukewarm, hence abominable. Paid mine hostess one dollar for her services and left for Chester.

Made good time. Was speeding along at such a rate that I daresay I could have reached Chester in less than two hours. But I was delayed a half hour by a blowout. And it rained meanwhile as the damp, cold air chilled me through and through. In this condition I drove into Chester about 10:45. Went directly to Mrs. Pipes's school, where I secured the $4.00 deposit from a Miss Hall, whose check had been returned for lack of funds. Went thence to the portable school where Miss Bowser, a friend of Edna, teaches.

This schoolroom is in a nursery. Is the lightest, airiest schoolroom for Negroes in Chester. I sat for almost an hour fascinated by the method Miss Bowser used in drilling her pupils in word study. She is a soft-voiced, small, dark-brown skinned girl. Talked her into taking a set of books. She promised to send the deposit to my Philadelphia address by the time I returned from New York. Nice, too nice; reminded me of a pussycat.

Rushed therefrom to the school at 2nd and Fulton streets—the Garthside School. Met again and apologized to Mrs. Gates for my failure to bring her back to Philadelphia during my last visit here. Received order from Mr. Bruce, the vocational arts teacher, but received no money. Like Miss Bowser, he promised to forward it to me in Philadelphia. By the way, he lives there.

The visit proved profitable, however, for I sold a set of books for the school. Collected for them. Went in haste to the school at 5th and Welch streets to deliver books to Mrs. Bailey. Had promised to take a $13.98 worth. Had slept over it however; now she took only set, $9.98. Better than nothing. Another teacher found it impossible to subscribe.

Left hurriedly for Philadelphia, after collecting $12.00 with $8.00 more yet to follow. Reached Philadelphia about 2:00 p.m. Went downtown. Bought underwear, slippers, and lounging robe. Rushed back home at 3:15. And I was to meet Edna at 3:30. There still remained a thousand and one things for me to do. I had eaten practically nothing all day, therefore, in haste, I devoured a dish of prunes and apricots. I had to bathe, dress, pack, go to the Y, have a tire vulcanized, and get the handle fixed on my suitcase.

Everyone helped. Almira started to pack my things. I had just started to bathe when Edna called me. Told her I could not possibly meet her before 5:00 p.m. It was to be on Christian Street between 8th and 9th.

After a deal of confusion, during which I committed the prize act of absentmindedness by leaving my bag, after having it packed. I was ready to leave about 5:00.

Went by the Y to secure more money. Poe admonished me not to marry while in New York. I laughingly advised him likewise.

Reached the appointed meeting place at 5:30. Did not see them as I passed. Went around the block. Felt halfway relieved that I did not see them. Could then give time to E_____ [Helen Notis?] who would feel disappointed at not seeing me over the weekend. Made up my mind if I failed to see them the second time, I should go on with Newark as my destination. However, we both spied each other at the same time. There stood T_____ (Edna) in her fur coat with her face turned a yellowish color by the cold. L_____, on the other hand—with her long, green, fur-trimmed coat—gave the appearance of a miniature Russian cossack. She was not cold. T_____'s (Edna's) feet were. Jested with them by complaining that I had driven past the place several times vainly attempting to find them. Both were astounded. Confessed they had been standing there half an hour. We were off.

I frankly anticipated my little joy. I felt like a man who is yielding up the known for the unknown. And I confess at the time I felt that the weekend could be more pleasantly spent with E_____ [Helen]. Moreover, I realized that I was breaking faith with her, since I had promised to come. But T_____ [Edna]—there she sat after we left Philadelphia with her arm clasped about mine, snuggling closely against me, and firing me with the anticipation of the joy she intended to give me when I reached New York.

I was utterly fatigued. Indeed, after my exertions of the last two days, I had no business driving to New York, as Almira tried to persuade me. Then I was hungry. My head ached. . . .

We stopped at a drug store in Trenton and wasted thirty perfectly good minutes getting hot drinks. T_____ [Edna] promised to stop in Trenton to give me an hour's rest, but I felt equal to going on. It was cold, but the ride was beautiful. Route 1 presents all that the motorist desires: no sharp curves, wide enough for five traffic lanes, and leading through no cities all the way from Trenton to Jersey City. Thought of E_____ [Helen] as I passed Newark. Would have taken girls to my pals, but T_____ [Edna] knew an acquaintance at the Urban League on the same street. Then, too, I had qualms lest E_____ [Helen] should suddenly drop in. Therefore, I went on to New York. Went up the Jersey shore and crossed at the 125th Street Ferry. Reached the apartment at 10:00. It is located on 141th Street. The home itself is not very attractive. There is no elevator and we had to climb up four flights. Pretty hard on T_____ [Edna], especially on account of her difficulty in mounting the same. L_____ met her sweetheart M_____ on the steps. Was just leaving. The apartment itself is furnished in quite Bohemian fashion. My first impulse was to go to Harry's and sleep. . . .

I started to go. My plan being to see Harry (Hipp) in order to have some legitimate place to stop. . . .

Outside the cold air brought me to my senses. Should I return to spend the night with her or should I remain where I was going—at Harry's? Several conflicting emotions surged within me. I needed rest. . . .

I decided to go first to Cap's [Florence Bacote] to see if she had some "vodka." Never take the stuff, but I was down and out, utterly fatigued. Would brace me up. Then too, the trip to Harrington, Delaware, and the sleeping in a cold room gave me a cold. The chief reason, however, was because T_____ [Edna] likes it. I wanted to see her "high," as she styles it. Cap was home. Had no "schnapps." Together we went over to Harry's. I confided in her [Cap] that I had a duty to perform.

Rang Harry's bell an interminably long time. Just about to give up in despair when his mother-in-law opened the door. Surprised to see me. Harry came in stupefied. Of course, he and his wife wanted to make provisions for me to stay. Had to invent the story of Poe's being with me, and that I would stay with him tonight. Finally got Harry aside and confided in him. I always can. He understood. Advised me to leave books and bags there. Took pajamas with me, also toilet articles. Asked Harry for schnapps. Gave me a four-ounce bottle. Harry chided me playfully, telling me women were my eternal weakness—he might have said ours. I did not gainsay him. Told me of a sale on suits going on at John David's and Halton's. Promised to meet him at 12:10 at Gimble's, 33rd and 6th Avenue, tomorrow.

Left him and went with Cap to the Widow's [Mrs. Emma Burbridge]. She was out. Got a half pint of corn whiskey there. I had to ask myself was it really possible that I was buying whiskey? For the first time in my life, I did so. Left the car in front of Florence's. Walked to 141st Street and St. Nicholas Avenue. My coat felt strangely and unusually heavy—whiskey in two pockets, pajama jacket in one, and the trousers in another. Then, toothbrush, powder, etc.

T_____'s [Edna's] girlfriend admitted me. A striking looking woman about twenty-eight or thirty. Slim, medium height, dark, with sharp features and one of the most beautiful profiles I have ever seen in a colored girl. T_____ [Edna] introduced us. Her name is so similar to my nickname that whenever she was called I responded or else looked in the direction of the caller. She usually did likewise. She was regular. Took my heavy coat. I felt quite embarrassed. L_____ was then with her boy. R_____ had hers, and T_____ [Edna] had been awaiting me (her boy had come and gone). I brought forth the vodka, but the folks had decided to eat first. The suggestion embarrassed me, for I had left all my money with the exception of $3.00 with Harry. Confided my predicament to T_____ [Edna]. She promised to see me "go."

Frankly, I desired one thing—sleep. But the others and T_____ [Edna] especially were hungry. I drove to Dominicks on 7th Avenue between 128th and 129th. It is a restaurant owned by whites. Everything used to be served there until the recent investigation of police vice in the city checked to some extent the haziness of the sale of beverages. As it was, L_____ and M_____ took mine. It was served in teacups. T_____ [Edna] took food only. I, too. Lamb chops were good. So was the milk. T_____ [Edna] was cold. Had taken off her woolen undies.

Back to the apartment. Highballs were fixed and served. I actually drank. A new departure for me. Had I not, I should have fainted from fatigue. Told stories until 4:30, when M_____ started to go. R_____'s friend had already left. She returned. L_____ and M_____ went into the kitchen to talk things over while T_____ [Edna] and I reveled in each other's arms. Finally, she began to prepare the sofa, which sat near the windows in the living room. . . .

[Entries for February 21–23 were omitted by editor.]

20

Final Days in Philadelphia

Tuesday February 24, 1931

Rose at noon. [Thomas Wallace] Swann had sent two letters respecting a Crispus Attucks Celebration in Harrisburg. He wanted me to be the principal speaker. Letters from him and Dr. [Charles H.] Crampton. Offering me $25.00 and expenses. I was elated. Wired acceptances to both. [John Wesley] Poe came over. Brought letter from Secretary [Robert P.] Lamont, head of the U.S. Department of Commerce. Letter was invitation from him and President Herbert Hoover to serve on committee to investigate housing conditions among Negroes. Gave me additional cause for elation. I shall accept it.

Ate (and) returned to bed, for I was dead tired. Rose at 5:30. Ate again. Prepared to go to Darby where I was to address the New Century Club. My topic was "Negro Contributions to World History."

There was a good crowd and I was in an inspired mood. I actually outdid myself, especially in my apostrophes to L'Ouverture, Allen, Douglass, and Christophe. The people sat spellbound. The audience overwhelmed me later. I do not recall what I said, but I do know that at times I was gazing into the ceiling as I spoke, for my thoughts were far above these people. I was communing with angels. It was the result of the past few days. I wish T_____ [Edna] could have been there. It was thoughts of her that lifted me up.

Home at 12:00. Almira, thoughtful and motherly as she is, had left a thermos bottle of hot milk and Ovaltine for me. I was grateful. Went to bed. . . .

Wednesday February 25, 1931

Rose late today. Still needed rest after the last few hectic days. It was 10:00 when I went down to breakfast. Called Vernell [Griffin] to inquire whether she would type a letter to Secretary Lamont, Head of the Department of Commerce. I had decided to accept a place on the Negro Housing Committee. Wrote him to that effect. Told him: "I shall be happy to serve in any manner you might care to designate." Vernell—she is such a dear—asked me to bring the letter down. She would type it immediately. Did so. She would accept no compensation. Told me she had to work tonight. I like her very much. But she is E____'s [Edna's] friend. Told her I would leave something at E____'s [Edna's] for her. . . .

Saw Miss (Myrtle) Glenn at the Durham (School). Said she liked me so much that she finds it difficult to maintain her equilibrium when I am about her. I hurt her by remarking that she was a moral coward in that she feared to trust herself. Naturally, she maintained just the opposite.

I returned home. Poe came over. Was elated when I told him of the invitation from the secretary of commerce and the president. Reading it, confessed that he considered it an honor to work with me. In his language I was a "big Nigger." We both laughed. Felt that an error made by Vernell should be corrected by rewriting the letter. Would have it done at the "Y." I let him take it. Invited me to dinner with him and Bert [Alberta S. Norwood] tomorrow evening. Oh, yes, my suit came this morning, $24.50. Did not fit too well.

In the evening, Almira asked me to take her to West Philadelphia. Promised to take her as I went to E____'s [Edna's]. Took Almira to North Ruby Street. Mrs. Allemand, a lodger who accompanied her, looked so strikingly attractive that I had to marvel. Moved me. Promised to return for Almira at 11:30 or 12:00. Arrived at E____'s [Edna's] about 8:00 p.m. Had first stopped by Leverte Roberts's office to collect $12.98. In vain, however.

E____ [Edna] looked more rested than when I last saw her. Seemed as vivacious as ever. We chatted about our trip to New York. She told me yesterday at school she could only think of me. Asked me would I think of her when I returned to D.C. Told her I understood I was to forget her.

Replied that she could not have that happen now. Also discussed with me the apparent jealousy of her New York admirer, who is anxious to marry her and who questioned her as to the fellow who had brought her to New York. Of course, womanlike, she squirmed out of it by devious verbal means. She was late for his engagement. He had gone, leaving her ticket there. She met him at the box office at the theater. He is a frat brother and is also majoring in history at Columbia. Advised her to marry him. Commended me because I understood her predicament. Told me she could confide in me. She had informed me of much of this on Monday. Had argued with him. He had threatened to remain at the apartment until I came. Told her I should have enjoyed meeting him. She felt that the time was not expedient. We chatted until it was time to go to Vernell's.

Arrived there; Vernell evidently was still working, for there was a light in the office. E____ [Edna] got out to call her when just then Vernell opened the window and called that she would be right down. En route home stopped by for Almira. Wanted us to come in. We declined, however. It was then about 11:30. Evidently I had come a little too soon for her. She came out within ten minutes. Introduced her to the girls. Arrived at home. Almira purposely delayed getting out of the car in order to secure a good close-up of E____ [Edna]. I shall be interested to learn her reaction.

Went back to E____'s [Edna's] where she prepared sandwiches and cocoa. At least she started the making of the cocoa, but I actually made it. They told me it was good. I put salt and vanilla into it. Vernell is going to New York for the weekend. I joked with her about the Friday evening after the Delta [Sigma Theta] dance when she seemed disinclined to go home. She left about 1:00 or 1:30.

E____ [Edna] and I sat talking. She made elaborate plans whereby I was to come back to Philadelphia for weekends. She would speak to Mrs. Salter tomorrow in order to arrange for me to interview the teachers at the school of which Mrs. [Marie] Chase is principal. She would take me to Trenton Friday and she would also try to make arrangements for me to meet with a (racially) mixed group in Germantown. I could come back to Philadelphia during weekends and finish business here and in adjacent towns. Then, too, there was the question of a rendezvous. Atlantic City? Yes, she knew some friends there. Asbury Park. Cape May. All were from festive places.

. . . I left promising to see her tomorrow in order to meet several persons. Oh, yes, I met her daughter Barbara for the first time tonight. She is a sweet little thing about eight years of age, slight of build, and giving the earmarks of being quite delicate. . . .

Thursday February 26, 1931

Almira told me this morning that she did not like T____ [Edna]. Felt that I cared more for her than she did for me. Based it upon our conversation en route to the house. I could not very well explain that it really was the opposite. I could not tell her of T____'s [Edna's] confession. I would not have been fair. Said T____ [Edna] looked like a gypsy, especially with the "tam" she wore. Was much better looking than the picture.

Took books to the school today (Williams private school). Collected only $1.50. Called upon Dr. [Edgar C.] Young. Secured $2.00 deposit on set of books for his church. Received letter from Swann deploring the fact that I had disappointed his friends in Harrisburg. Asked me to write him a letter stating that he was authorized to use my name. Wrote such.

Did very little else today. Had blue suit pressed and went to dinner at Mrs. Warwick's. Poe and Bert were there. As usual, I was late. Excellent dinner. Mrs. Warwick makes a fine hostess. Mr. Warwick, somewhat older, seemed more reticent. Cultured, refined. Looks like a businessman or professor.

God help Poe! I fear he is deeply enmeshed in the toils of Bert. She is at least fifteen years his senior. Is head over heels in "infatuation" with him. Adores him for his youth and ability to gratify her longing for sex love. He is drawn to her because she spends money on him, buys food, etc. I wonder how far poor Poe is able to go and yet be able to tear himself away when the time comes. They hung on to each other like two cows, one the mother and the other her first-gotten calf. They mooned and petted so before me that I was so embarrassed it was a relief when the time for my engagement with E____ [Edna] arrived.

For the first time, I had to wait for E____ [Edna]. She came looking as lovely as ever in a black dress with a blue velvet collar (turquoise she calls it). Knows I like it and wears it for me. And I appreciate it. On the way to Mrs. Salter's, she informed me that she had spoken to a Mrs. B____ relative to my addressing a mixed group in Germantown. My response about some triviality concerning her elicited a charming "damn" in seeming indignation. "Here I am," quoth she, "attempting to arrange business matters for you, and you answer me with such a trifling comment." Told me she wanted to convert *The Negro Wage Earner* into a textbook.

Mrs. Salter already knew me. I had spoken to her Negro History Club on December 5. She had been present. Could not sell her books, either. Husband, an insipid looking individual whose sole purpose in life seems to be the task of laughing every now and then, caused me to almost laugh outright when he served notice that he knew all the Negro History because he was born in the South, whereas I and Dr. Woodson had to study it. I could not answer him. 'Twas useless. Met Mrs. Griffin. Played four hands of bridge.

(Edna) asked her to arrange with Miss Chase for me to canvass the teachers at the school tomorrow, or at least to speak to the students. Promised to do so. I am to call her at 8:15 tomorrow morning. If possible, then I shall go out to the school immediately. The school is to be dedicated on April 15. They want a speaker. I suggested Dr. Woodson. After we left, however, (Edna) told me that she would try to secure the appointment for me. I could only kiss her. Here was a woman who would make a man rise. Stopped at a delicatessen store. T____ [Edna] wanted to make cocoa.

It was made by me, however, when we arrived at her home. She complimented me in this manner upon that made by me last night. While so engaged, she came over to me, embraced me, and asked me whether I would wear her sorority pin on my trip South. For a moment, the shock stunned me. Then I answered that I was quite selfish. "What do you mean?" she asked, looking up at me. "I have asked for nothing." "Just this," I replied, "the wearing of a sorority pin by the man usually implies but one thing, an engagement. And it follows that if you permit me, and I accept, the wearing of your pin would it not be but just that I let you wear my frat pin? And I have not yet advanced to that point." She looked at me, clung to me, and said: "I offered you the pin. I asked for nothing in return. If when you are ready to go South you want to wear my pin, it is here waiting for you. But I shall not mention it again." I felt like a cad, for I knew I had wounded her. I finished making the cocoa; she the sandwiches. We then repaired to our accustomed place in the living room. The lights were out, save those in the dining room. . . .

Truly, T____ [Edna] is becoming a problem. She is consuming all my spare time.

Friday February 27, 1931

Called Mrs. Salter this morning at the hour agreed, only to learn that Miss Chase could not permit the teachers to be canvassed, for that was strictly forbidden. Just like her, Mrs. Salter assured me that, if I had gone out there, no doubt I could have canvassed to my heart's content. Surprised at Miss Chase's attitude, since she enjoys a reputation of being an enthusiastic supporter of our work.

Did very little today. Called on a few persons. Returned and played Almira a few games of checkers. Received a letter from Woodson telling me that a commission of 10 percent only was allowed on *Negro Makers of History* and *African Myths.* I was hot and wrote him accordingly. Told him one never knew just what he was doing when working with him. His actions varied so, (that) one was ever at sea. Suggested that he make out a typewritten list of all books, their sale price, and commission allowed. Told Poe to sell no more of these books.

Almira fixed lunch and cocoa for me (to take) on the trip to Trenton. Did not tell her of T____ [Edna]. Met her at the appointed time. Luckily, for once, I was there first. Stopped at a garage and put up the mirror in the car. Had been down since October. Don't know why I have not had an accident due to its absence. En route to Trenton, I told T____ [Edna] I had definitely decided not to go to Newark. One idea now was to go to Trenton and from there to Merchantville.

Reached Trenton about 5:00. (Edna) took me to the Y.W.C.A., where I met Mrs. Edna Stratton, a Pittsburgh woman and friend of Edna's. Charming personality. Gave me names of key people in Trenton: Dr. [C. F.] Scarborough; Mr. [Hilmar] Jensen, head of the Y.M.C.A.; Mrs. Hill, librarian at the high school; and Mrs. _____. Could not persuade her (Mrs. Stratton) to give me an order for books at this time, but she told me that she would take them later. Called and arranged for three of the above persons to see me. Is starting a young people's forum. Asked me to come over and speak to them some Sunday. Told her I was going to Delaware but would be glad to come up. She would write me. Also inquired where she could get someone to sing at a musical sometime in March. I recommended Miss Blake (of Cleveland). Told her that I would have the latter write her. (Edna) visited a friend while I called upon prospects.

Called upon Mrs. Hill. Has all the books in the school library. Not interested for her home. Will take *The Negro Wage Earner* and one or two others, however. Has met Poe. Cannot arrange meeting for him. Attractive woman. Called upon Mr. Jensen of the Y.M.C.A. Young man with engaging personality. Is a great grandson of former Congressman Gibbs, one of the Reconstruction leaders.[1] Tells me prejudice in Trenton is so widespread that one might just as well be in the South. Segregation in schools, theaters, [and] public places. And the most insidious propaganda about the Negro is dished out by Southern professor at the State Normal School here as history. Nothing of uplifting influence here for Negro boys and girls. Over 6,200 Negroes in Trenton, mostly laborers and servants. Depressing in school to hear of whites talk of Negroes. Gave teacher in history a copy of *Negro in Our History.* Changed his attitude. Will try to get books later.

Called upon Mrs. B_____. Did nothing. Yet, she has a number of clubs under her control and is in charge of educational work at the Y.W.C.A. Went to the office of Dr. Scarborough. Young fellow. Sold him easily. (Edna), who had returned, marveled. Said she was afraid to ask me.

My selling blood had been stirred now. Asked (Edna) to wait a while longer if she were not cold. Assured me she wasn't. Dr. Gibbs was not at home. Called on Dr. Morris. Busy, (and I) wouldn't wait.

Started thenceforth for Merchantville. Called Dr. Wilson there to see whether Parent-Teachers meeting was being held. Answer being in the negative, I decided to return to Philadelphia. Knew Edna was hungry. Brought out candy and peanut butter sandwiches. Made her eat them, and finally, after we had almost reached Philadelphia, she consented to

1. Jonathan C. Gibbs was an outstanding black leader in Florida during Reconstruction. He served as secretary of state and as superintendent of public instruction.

drinking some cocoa. Showed me the place where her party was to take place. Intended for me to drive down there, but I passed it before she thought, else she purposely let me do so. I myself rejoiced, for I knew my weakness, and I still felt she would take cold. Made me promise I would return weekends to do Trenton and adjacent towns. Trip was not wholly without profit, and, too, it showed me the potentialities of the place. Told her if I had had my way, we would now be in Newark. She laughed, told me I had called it off.

Reached her home about 10:30. She changed her dress. Came down with . . . dress setting off her brown charms as only it can. We went to an inn on 20th and Bainbridge for dinner. The food was well cooked. I enjoyed it. T____ [Edna] desired fruit salad. Would not take it, however, because I did not desire it. Said she hated to eat alone.

Returned to her home. She told me that she would go to Washington with me Sunday. What would I do with her, I wondered? Yet, I would be tickled to take her, for I desired company. Did not imagine she would drive down and spend $4.00 to come back, just to be with me.

This was our last night together. . . . And it became a memorable one. . . . Home, and so to bed.

Saturday February 28, 1931

The last day of the month and my last full day in Philadelphia. And I shall leave just as I have learned to like the city. And to think that I go back to that most detestable of all places—Washington.

Rose about 9:00 this morning. Had planned an ambitious program. Started for Darby to sell Mrs. Henderson a set of books about 10:00. Stopped at Leverte Roberts's real estate office first to collect $12.98. Was not at home or at office, either. Went to Darby. Mrs. Henderson felt she could not take the books just yet, although she felt that her children needed them. Told me she had never dreamed Negroes have accomplished the numerous things I had recounted. I persuaded her, however, to take the books. Told me she would make her husband understand. Took them outright. Called on Mrs. Blake, mother of Florence who sings so well. She recognized me. Praised me for my speeches here. Thanked me for interceding for her daughter. Told me she is only 18. I believed she was 24 or 25. Goes to Cheyney. Miss Bolding, who plays so well, is studying medicine. Doing so because her parents rammed it down her throat, not because she likes it. Her proclivities run along musical lines. Another case of parents ruining the careers of their children by forcing them into grooves of their own liking. Stopped by Dr. Carrington's. Not in. Dr. ____ not in, either.

Sped back to Philadelphia. Again Leverte Roberts was not at home nor in his office. A devil of a time I've had collecting that $9.98. Went home. Almira fixed me some Ovaltine to take with me. Started for Merchantville about 3:00. Stopped by the "Y" for books. Saw Poe. He was ill. Told me he intended to call on a doctor; feared he was getting the "flu." Informed me that Mr. Johnson had called from Riverton relative to the books that he was to have received. Damned poor cooperation from the office. These books were to have been sent almost a month ago. Told Poe I would take them there tomorrow. Gave me two telegrams. One from Swann telling me that he had made arrangements for me to address the Negro History Club of Harrisburg, Pennsylvania, on Tuesday next. Advised me to wire Mrs. Sarah Wirth Dunston if I could not keep the engagement. Can't understand Swann. Ought to have known I was going to Washington tomorrow. I told him so. Other telegram was from Crampton. Regretted I could not visit them on the occasion of the 161st anniversary of the death of Crispus Attucks. Poe also informed me that he had taken two letters to Almira's for me. Paid me two of the three dollars he owed me. I desired to get a hat. Told me of his difficulty in getting away from (Bert). Don't believe he *will* be able to get away from her.

Left Poe and sped on to Merchantville. Went about five miles out of the way. Met Dr. Wilson. Sold him easily. Collected his check for $12.98. Sold Mrs. Lewis, also. Is the doctor's mother-in-law. Received $9.98 from her. The day's total netted me $13.20. Not so bad. Left Merchantville at 5:35. Promised Almira I would be home at 5:30. Helen was coming down to cook dinner. Reached home at 6:05. Got them all excited when I told them I had already eaten. Almira became disgusted. H(elen) was hurt. Told them I was joking and proved it by eating a big dinner. It was exceedingly well cooked. The pie was delicious.

H(elen) had to go to see Alice. I took her along with me. She is the soft, affectionate type of woman, one who likes to be loved. Emotional, yet lacks the sophistication of E____ [Edna]. We went downtown first. I had to get a hat. She helped me pick out one—a light tan. Also bought a dark maroon tie. Went therefrom to Alice's. Left H(elen) and went to the barber's. Returned for her ¾ of an hour later. Took her home. Could not help kissing her. She enjoys it. Kisses rapturously—so much so that she excited me terribly. Yet, she restrained me.

Took Almira and Helen out to North Ruby Street. While Almira knocked at the door, we petted. No one was home, so I took Almira over to Mr. Roberts. He was not at home. Called back at North Ruby Street. The folks were home. We remained in the car for a while but were finally called in the house by Almira. She got her things and we were off. Went back home, buying ice cream en route.

We ate ice cream and pie, and, whenever we could slip away, H(elen) and I engaged in innocent love-making. I like her—perhaps I like them all. She wants to come down to help me pack tomorrow. I was to have gone for (Edna) at 10:00 p.m. Called her and informed her that because company was at the house, I could not come. She pardoned me, of course. Told me to get plenty of rest for tomorrow. Also notified me of L_____'s desire to go to D.C. with us. Wanted to know when I would leave. Told her about 12:00. She would be ready. Told her L_____ could go. Took H(elen) home about 11:30. Spent very enjoyable time with her. Just my height. Well built. She kisses well. Almira kidded me when I returned.

Sunday March 1, 1931

H(elen) arrived while I was in the bath. Brought a friend, Miss Smith, with her. Is very attractive. Poe called me. I tried to induce him to come over but he was at that moment at (Bert's), therefore impossible for him to leave. It was raining terribly hard. Yet I felt that I would go. As the morning waned and still it did not abate, I decided to go tomorrow. We spent the entire morning petting, laughing, kissing, reading poetry, and alternating with packing. While kissing her as we lay across the bed, I was shocked to see Cousin Jane. What she thought, I know not.

Called (Edna) at 12:00. Told her I would not leave until tomorrow on account of the rain. She was glad, as well as disappointed. Asked me to come out. Told her I had to go to Riverton. She wanted to go with me. A moment after I had hung up, she called and asked me to dine with her family at 5:30. I accepted. (Helen) now wanted to leave at 12:00. Persuaded her to remain until 2:00. Took them home at that hour. Gave (Helen) a *Negro Wage Earner.* Asked me to write her. Also requested a picture. Promised both. She is a sweet girl. Only thing that spoils her is the roughness of her skin.

Went to (Edna's) at 5:30. Irrepressible as ever, she met me at the door with, "I've good new for you. Miss Baxter wants you to come over and get your four dollars." She again wore my favorite dress. It was the last day. Could have embraced her for her enthusiasm evinced in my interest and also for her charming appearance in my favorite dress.

Dinner was enjoyable. Later we stopped at Miss Baxter's (she is the teacher I sold in Chester), where I collected a money order of three dollars from her.

From there we went to Riverton. It was raining, and the fine particles of water clung to the glass so as to almost prevent me from seeing. Arrived at Riverton. I stopped at Miss Johnson's. She was in. Told me she had enjoyed herself so much in New York. Going again at Eastertime. Did not tell her (Edna) was in the car. Miss Johnson asked me to take the books to Mrs. Young, a teacher here, who would deliver them. Did so.

Returned to Philadelphia. T_____ [Edna] made cocoa. We talked and petted and planned. (Edna) intends to keep the book sales going until I return to Philadelphia. She will make arrangements for me to speak at places. Again, she desired to retell those folk tales so that they would be adaptable for children in the grades.

T_____ [Edna] told me she scarcely knew what effect I had exerted upon her. When she first met me it was with the conviction that we should be friends only. But now, she could not imagine just what had come over her. . . .

As I left her, I knew within my soul that the memories of the last ten days would never be erased. They had stamped themselves indelibly upon me. And in the midst of it all, there stood out in bold relief one person—beautiful and, yet, not beautiful, attractive, charming, sophisticated, affectionate, passionate, and inspiring—T_____ [Edna]. She made me like Philadelphia, and she revealed to me a new type of woman.

21

Washington

Preparing to Survey Negro Employment

MONDAY   MARCH 2, 1931

Left Almira's at 10:00. After she had cared for me like a mother, hated to leave her, the children, her husband, and Cousin Jane. My little "wife," Catherine, who is three years [old], had to come to the door to see me off. Almira prepared me sandwiches, made cocoa, [and] gave me enough other food for three or four persons. Stopped by Leverte Roberts. Finally gave me a check for $12.98, but it was postdated for March 12th.

Trip to D.C. uneventful. Went the Conowingo Dam route. Many curves and many little towns. The Conowingo Dam is a masterful creation. The Susquehanna is dammed up and a concrete bridge or roadway crosses below it.

Passed Lincoln University just outside of Oxford. Certainly did not impress me. The buildings that were visible and the campus were unattractive.

Arrived at the office about 4:00. Woodson seemed glad to see me. Had expected me this morning. We talked about the work. Seemed happy to know that I had been able to interest people in the Negro's past. Told me he had declined to send my name to Morgan College for the position as teacher of history because he knew I did not care for teaching. I acquiesced in what he had done.

About the survey. [E. E.] Lewis would take care of the Negro business end of it.[1] All that devolved upon me is to procure information from white

1. E. E. Lewis received his doctorate from Columbia University in 1931, and he was inducted into Phi Beta Kappa while at Columbia. His dissertation was titled "A Study of the Mobility of the Negro Population." In 1931, he was an assistant professor of economics at Howard University. *Norfolk Journal and Guide,* July 18, 1931, 15.

employers of Negro labor. Advised me to get in touch with Lewis as quickly as possible, also to see Brown, the printer, about the questionnaires. Did so. Were not ready. Lewis was not at the university.

(Woodson and I) talked about a number of things. He told me eleven sets of books had been returned from Philadelphia. Complained that no money was being made. Yet, had it not been for such he would have been virtually bankrupt this winter. (Miss Dunlap), the bookkeeper, is [the] authority for this statement. He sees only the black, unpleasant side of the other fellow's labors.

Left the office. En route to Howard Manor met [Thomas] Georges. Came up with me. Tried to get an apartment. But all were taken. Therefore, I asked Rosella [manager of the Howard Manor Apartments] if she knew of anyone who wanted a roomer. She referred me to a Mrs. (Mayme) White in 306. She had a room. Just two women, 38 or 40 years old. Took room, $20 per month.

Met (Bushrod Mickey). Shocked to see me. Outdone that I would think of looking for a place to stay temporarily when I could stay with him and his wife. Asked if I would come to see her. She had been asking about me.

Later, as I started up there, I met her with him on their way to the movies. Asked them what they had to eat. Told me everything was right on the stove. Went in. There was chicken, greens, potatoes, salad, milk, and brown bread. Splendid. (Before I could serve myself, they returned.)

Took them to movies. Just before, however, a knock sounded. Someone to see him. She [Lillian Mickey] told me that my absence had almost driven her crazy, especially during the long summer evenings. Raised the shade and showed me the great, round full moon just rising above the hills over the reservoir. "Every time I see the moon," she said, "I think of you. And B____ [Bushrod] doesn't appreciate it." Then suddenly she seized my hand, squeezed it, and held it to her. I wanted to gasp but stifled it. She looked beautiful, as loveable and desirable as ever. When B____ [Bushrod] returned, she stood gazing at the moon. I was silent.

Tuesday to Saturday March 3–7, 1931

These days I spent in routine work, preparing from the telephone directory a list of names of businessmen and establishments to whom questionnaires will go. Called on (Bertha) [Baylor] on Tuesday. She reprimanded me for not writing her, then kissed me and made up. Has only a part-time job. . . .

On Thursday night I went to see E____. Shocked and surprised to know I was in town. We discussed a thousand things. A loveable little thing. Saturday night I called on the Chambers. Saw a girl there, but did not even remember her name.

The book *(The Wage Earner)* has come in for a lot of criticism, I learn. Doesn't surprise me. In fact, I even rejoice because Woodson's name is there. He felt he was injuring me. (Professor Emmette) Dorsey (my friend and political science teacher at Howard University) told me the New York *Tribune* gave it "hell." Ira Reid ridiculed it in *Opportunity,* the organ of the Urban League. But no one takes Ira Reid seriously. Several other minor reviews I have seen, also. They all see merit in the facts, but nearly all unite upon saying that the interpretations are weak. 'Tis true. But then that is largely Woodson's fault. He rushed the thing through, blocked me at every turn, and read his own interpretations in, in some cases. I have said nothing to him concerning the book, although everyone knows that he cheated me. Dorsey waxed wrathful.

My landlady and her friend, Miss [Violet] Hemsley, went to New York over the weekend. I felt like calling Edna [Gaines] it was so lonesome. Did call E_____. She was not at home, however.

Sunday March 8, 1931

Another miserable day. 'Twas brightened by a special [delivery letter] from Edna. Told me how much she missed me. Is arranging to get me speaking engagements. Has already written Miss Stratton at the Trenton "Y." Glad to hear from her. Somehow I suspected she would send me a special delivery. Just like her. Impulsive, always doing the bizarre, the exotic. It makes her doubly attractive.

Mr. Mickey called me about 9:30. Invited me to breakfast at 10:00. Spent three very enjoyable hours with them. Returned. Called B[ertha]. Told her I would come for her at 2:00 to go to Rosslyn.

Called on Gertrude McBrown, poetess, and Lois Jones, artist. The latter has promised to illustrate my (poem), "Out of the Mist." Did not see her. She was in the kitchen. Showed the revised version of "Out of the Mist" to Gertrude. Preferred it to the former. Left the book with her. Promised to return tomorrow evening for it.

Almost an hour late for B[ertha]. She was ready. Introduced me to her friend. Heating service in the house has broken down and it is cold there.

Cousins Rose and Grace (my mother's cousins) were astonished to see me in Rosslyn. They were well. (Gently) reproved me for failure to write them. Feared something had befallen me. They are the most hospitable people in the world, I believe. After Bertha and I arrived, a mother, stepfather, and three children came in, and they fed all. Still there was plenty left. After dinner we visited with them, [about] the dead and the sick. Miss Annie, mother of Millie, about whom Rabbit [Ernest] (Bacote) and I used to kid Harry [Hipp] during our school days, died yesterday. And her husband, in an intoxicated condition, came over to break the news to Cousins Rose and Grace.

Took B[ertha] home about 9:30. I reached home about 10:30. Mrs. White and Miss Hemsley had returned.

MONDAY MARCH 9, 1931

Spent forenoon on names to whom questionnaires were going. Figured we would need about 2,000. (The printer) finally got them ready and sent them over. Woodson suggested I have calling cards printed. Told him I had already taken care of that. Asked to see one. Disliked them. I then had 1,000 printed at his expense. Perhaps he will like that. Feels that whites will have to make some contacts for us. Felt car ought to be washed and painted. Good. I approved so long as he spends the money. Took it to auto laundry. Got it washed and greased. Cost $1.75. From there I went to Georges's place. Asked him to take me to garage where I could get fender fixed. Escorted me to place on 4th and K. Owned by Negro—that is, Baker, the cashier of Prudential Bank, owns it. Lends money to apparent (person), when in reality he is borrowing money himself. It is none of my business, but such methods are dishonest—if true—and can but lead to bank insolvency and failure. I shall hold my piece.

Arthur, the manager, promises to do job cheaply. Had one wild, thrilling ride for two blocks in Georges's car. Feared it would fall to pieces at any moment. Every now and then, the door would fly open. Glad when I got to my own car. Then I had to return with him. Heart remained in my mouth and, upon alighting, I rendered grateful praise to Allah for having caused his benevolent face to smile upon me and deliver me safe out of imminent bodily peril. Georges laughed at me, but I honestly admitted my fright.

Began reading Spero and Harris, *The Black Worker.*[2] Well written. Approaches problem differently than I did. Concerned with theory.

Called on Gertrude McBrown. Spent enjoyable time with her and Lois (Jones).

TUESDAY MARCH 10, 1931

Cold, blustery. Started upon actual survey. Left blanks with Lewis. Don't believe it will profit me, for he can't reconcile my part of the study—that is contacting white businessmen—with their investigation of Negro business. It is well. They would only bungle matters.

2. Sterling D. Spero and Abram L. Harris, *The Black Worker: The Negro and the Labor Movement.*

Called on Mr. Johnson, secretary of Y.M.C.A. Not in. Later in afternoon, paid visit to United States Department of Labor to see Mr. Karl Phillips, Negro commissioner of reconciliation, in order to get numbers of Negroes in government service. Stout, dark man. Not impressive. Gave me the entire list for United States, then approximate number for District of Columbia. Georgia Douglass Johnson, Negro poetess, is his secretary. I had not seen her for a couple of years and we had an opportunity to chat for a few moments. Did not recognize her for a long time. Had aged so. But then, she has suffered from nervous breakdown.

[Mr. Phillips] gave me list of Negro unions, also, which are affiliated directly with the American Federation of Labor. Asked him procedures to get list of Negro employees in the various bureaus. Referred me to Mr. Brandt of the Civil Service Commission. [He] called him, informed him he would send me over. Mr. Brandt could not help me. No record is kept of employees by race in his office. Not required on application blank. Assured me only method would be to contact each bureau head and thereby secure desired information. Referred me to Mr. Long, assistant director of the Bureau of Engraving and Printing. Will go there tomorrow.

Called again on Mr. Johnson of the Y at office. Compared the figures for District of Columbia civil employees with those given me by Phillips. Felt the latter's total too large. Johnson had figures for departments taken in 1923. Difference of about 2,000 in five years. (Phillips figures were as of 1928.) Felt they ought to be checked.

Got letter from a Miss Stocking, of the Friends Service, who offered aid in survey. Woodson desired it.

To dinner, home, read more of Abe Harris's book. My landlady prepared dinner for me. Very suggestive. I am not attracted, however.

WEDNESDAY MARCH 11, 1931

Called on Mr. Long this morning. He is the assistant director of the Bureau of Printing and Engraving. My object was to find out something respecting the number of Negroes in his department, the kind of work they were doing, etc.

[No entries were found for March 12–17.]

WEDNESDAY MARCH 18, 1931

Going to Dartmouth College

Today must ever hold a unique place in my life for it marked my debut—so to speak—in academic society. This is the day I am to go to Dartmouth. Tomorrow I shall be on trial.

Got up early this morning, or rather Jim [James Greene] called me earlier than was my wont. Saw him off after taking him to breakfast. (He had just driven to Washington from Palm Beach, Florida. Jim is a chauffeur for a millionaire of Scarsdale, New York, who regularly escapes the rigors of most of the Northern winters by taking his wife South for a few months.) The car—a sixteen-cylinder Cadillac—appears beside mine like a dreadnought to a submarine chaser. Bought some things for Bertha, all of which consumed my valuable time. But, then, she deserves every consideration from me.

Returned home. Worked on notes for speech until 12:00, when I rushed to the station to make a reservation on the Montrealer for 2:50 p.m. Stopped at the office. Got $20.00 from Woodson. Back home. I was able to spend another hour on my notes, but no more. En route to the station, I stopped by the office to get a copy of the *Negro Wage Earner* to present to Professor (Malcolm) Keir who had invited me to Dartmouth. Woodson vetoed it. Felt that it was not the conventional thing to do, unless Keir had shown me some extraordinary courtesy. I felt that his invitation would permit me to leave a copy of the book with all due propriety. Did not take one, however, out of deference to Woodson. He took the liberty also to admonish me not to "hang about" the campus after my lecture, reminding me that the food was good at Hanover Inn, intending, of course, that I get the intimation that he had been there. I laughed (with) scorn, informing him that it was my intention to get the next train following my lecture.

Once on the train, (my anger speedily evaporated). It was my first time in a Pullman and I felt uncomfortable. Many speculations arose before me. Would I be able to acquit myself with credit before the student body? Would I have myself adequately in hand? Would I be successful in this, my first appearance before a white student body, especially, inasmuch as it happened to be one of the most outstanding colleges of the country? At first, I yielded myself up as a willing prey to these rampaging thoughts. Then, after their surgings had passed, I relapsed once more into my confident self.

I asked a porter to bring me a table and immediately transformed my section of the car into a study. Passengers going to and fro looked at me in amazement. Could not fathom what a Negro could have to write that was so important. And I enjoyed their astonishment as I worked feverishly on.

But I had to pause. Nature in her alluring loveliness compelled me. Beautiful afternoon—slanting, warming rays of the dying sun, the lordly Susquehanna—must pause to gaze upon it. It flows down from Pennsylvania —my Passion Flower—she is there. My thoughts fly to her. Who knows but that these crystal, gleaming waters might not have nourished her, made her to bloom in all her radiant splendor. The river passes even as I muse upon it. Like all lovely things in life, like happiness, these are evanescent, momentary, ever in flux.

Lo! The river again. I love the water, so calm, placid, serene, almost inviting one to drown his sorrow, disappointment, pain in its healing, lulling midst. Water and romance—sunbeams sparkling on glassy surfaces, undulating waves, a little boat, twilight or eventide, stars, moon, and you.

Wilmington with its ugliness and barrenness of memories jars my brain, interrupts my lovely thoughts. Then dirty, vice-ridden Chester. Ah, yes, Anne Valentine, who nourished a well-developed superiority complex, only to have it destroyed by us. Then Ada—Ada, charming, roguish. Sarah Pride, well.

Ah, West Philadelphia—North Frazier Street, a black dress, turquoise collar, black hair, flashing eyes, eyes that dared not meet mine, myself ill, inspired, enraptured, Sundays, parties. Riverton—Lola Garth, New York, Newark, Riverton. Happiness, bliss, fire-flashing eyes, honeyed, maddening lips, kisses, rapturous embraces, clinging arms. Delightful rides—you and I—Camden, Dowingtown, Trenton. Rain, laughter. Desire. Kisses, woods, lips. Kisses, then heavenly days, bliss, incomparable brown body, towering passion. Life in its fullest and sweetest. Life, surging abundant, undeniable, pulsating madness, ecstasy, majestic mountains of belonging consuming soul-fire, soul conflagrations. Spirits blending. Life fluids intermingling, interflowing. Eden. Separation, memories, letters.

But such musings so engrossed me I quite forgot the task before me. Worked upon notes until I reached New Haven. Decided to retire. Had berth changed to the men's end of car. Cost me 75 cents more. Didn't mind it for I was a stranger, wholly uninitiated into the ways of Pullman travel. Didn't know where to disrobe. Only the Porter saved me. Must reward him. Couldn't sleep. My thoughts dwelt on the morrow.

Arrived at White River Junction, Vermont, at 3:27 a.m. 'Tis just a hamlet. Trains for Canada and Maine diverge here. Taxi met me. These hills are beautiful still. Even at this early hour their attractiveness impressed itself upon me. Snow there remained from last week's blizzard. Plenty of it. Piled four feet high in some places. The driver told me of Dartmouth. Hanover constituted the college only.

[No entry was found for March 19.]

Friday March 20, 1931

New York City

Mar[guerite] [Skeeter] came over today at 11:30. We cooked breakfast—bacon and eggs, cereal, toast, fruit, and milk. What a sweet girl. Tells me although she is engaged to marry, she looks upon it with little enthusiasm. I don't feel that she loves G____ as much as he believes. In fact, she confided to me that he was nice—too nice, almost. And whenever I hear a girl or woman state that a man is too nice, it ultimately means that his hold has waned or fast is waning. She would like a studio fitted up in Bohemian fashion and live her life as she desired. I doubt whether she would marry for a while. In fact, she has told me she would not do so. Fine girl. Seemed glad to know I was not married. May go to Howard University with her husband, if he is appointed next year. That means I shall miss her being in New York. Remained with me until 3:15. Cut classes.

Called upon G____ (Gladys MacDonald). Didn't know whether to fuss with me or embrace me. Told her not to do either on the street. Went upstairs a moment. Fought it out there. G____ (Gladys) is the same as ever. Likes me. Even in an amorous way. Too tall for me. Taking books for library.

Called on my former landlady Mrs. B[urbridge]. Not living up to her former moral plane. Has sunk. Manufacturing and selling whiskey. [Harry] Hipp won't go there.

Called on Mrs. Collier. Disappointed by her after sister's description. Small, of muddy, brown complexion. Lacking in personality. Cannot see why Collier married her, especially after he had gone with Mildred Payton. But, then, who can account for *l'affaire du coeur*?

Called upon Harry. Was eating his dinner. True to form, he rapidly bolted it and rushed away, much to the disguised discomfiture of his wife and mother-in-law. I know full well that I am an abomination to them, and also to Vickie (Ernest's [Bacote] wife). How these wives would like to see me married off. Harry walked along with me, telling of the boner that Helen [Notis] pulled. Just as she was leaving about a month ago, she turned to Muriel and said: "When you come to Newark don't be like Harry—never call on me." Then, turning to Harry, she asked, "Why didn't you tell me Florence [Bacote] was at Ernest's that Sunday I stopped there and he wasn't home?" Muriel, wifelike, smelled a mouse. She turned on Harry right before Helen. Told him she had felt such was going on. Reminded him that one Sunday last year she had gone to the station to meet Harry after a trip to Washington to see me and, lo, Florence got off the train with him. Harry waxed indignant over Helen's actions and looseness of tongue. But the poor thing did not know, was utterly in the dark about Harry's relationship with Florence. So was and is Bacote. By God, I fear this thing, have always feared it. What if something happens? They cannot keep it secret forever. If Muriel finds out it will wreck their marital life—although I don't believe Harry would mind. And Florence, it would kill her mother. What would my folks think of Harry? But most important of all, what will be R____'s [Bacote's] attitude toward Harry, especially since F____ [Florence] is his cousin? True, he might take the stand that F_____ knew what she wanted, but then could he ever forget that H_____ [Harry] stood in the position of father, brother, adviser, etc., to her, even as I did? Can he forget that after all, blood is thicker than water, that H_____ [Harry] has deceived him into thinking that the relationship is platonic? Will this explosion ultimately wreck the gang—if it occurs? I have counseled H_____ [Harry] to break off. He has promised he would. Yet, I know that F_____ [Florence] has such a hold on him that to break off now is well nigh impossible. His adherence to her is fanned by M_____'s [Muriel's] coldness. If she had the emotional make-up of E_____, H_____, or others that I know, she could so absorb his energy that he could not find time to carouse as freely as he does now—granting that it is the nature of the male to do so. He has told M_____ [Muriel] the same thing. Did so the night he returned from my home after Christmas.

As to F_____ [Florence], she thrills over the liaison. Told me that only one man in the world can thrill her. That is H_____ [Harry]. Too bad. He started her. No one else now can get a foothold. And poor B_____. He is just the fool—just the foil for her and H_____ [Harry]. I even doubt whether she cares for him, although H_____ [Harry] tries to make me believe she does. But he to whom a woman freely yields her body is the man she loves. Experience has only corroborated what history has shown. I wish the entire thing might have been avoided. I may be pessimistic, but optimism always fails me when I contemplate the direful consequences of this triangle. What will it mean? Ruptured romance for Muriel, but that I presume has already happened. Divorce? Scandal? Florence—talked about, scarlet woman and all that? People in Ansonia saying, "I told you so." Mrs. Bacote crushed, her soul wrenched by the utter crumbling of her faith in Harry? Theodore . . . seeking vengeance? Brown, the dutiful, patient lover, perhaps driven to frenzy by the double dealing of both the one he loved and him in whom he had imposed the utmost faith. Who can foretell what he might do? Then Muriel, the neglected, cheated wife, turned perhaps into a destroying angel—I shutter to think of it. And Bacote—his greatest agony the betrayal of confidence in his best friend. Upon me alone, then, would devolve the task of salvaging something from the wreckage. I alone knowing, foreseeing the storm, shout warnings in vain. Yet, when unheeded, utterly impotent to prevent the cataclysm. Oh, I pray God no such pass will ever come! But I fear it, I dread it; I, horrible to relate, even expect it.

Called H_____ (Helen) after a deal of thought. Invited her to go to the basketball game. She will meet me at Jim's at 10:00 p.m. Went to store. Met Carry[?]. Accompanied her home. Didn't know she was going to the basketball game alone. Would have taken her. Marguerite came in just before I left. Promised to see me at game.

Returned to Jim's. Helen came in at 10:00. Looked as pretty as ever. Was able to steal a kiss by dint of hard work. We did not mention the Washington Birthday weekend about which she rapped me two weeks ago. By tacit agreement we kept silent over it. What shall I do about her? Harry and Bacote counsel quit. Can I? I like her; but marriage? I am not ready for it. Harry told me she had shown an engagement ring to some girls in a department store and told them upon being questioned that it was from me. I don't believe it. Told Harry so.

Game was sickening. Marguerite came in dressed in red. Looked beautiful. Introduced her to Helen. One buoyant, blushing, full of life, talkative; the other (Helen) reserved, quiet, veiled. I had told both girls about the other. Green there. Never let (Marguerite) out of his sight. I danced with her. Told me the first time I heard a slow dance to come over and bump with her. Didn't. Left. Went to Newark. Love in emotional fires with E_____ [Helen]. But a black velvet dress saved us. First time I can ever remember such. Reached Ernest's about 5:00 a.m. I was utterly fatigued. Am doing myself incalculable injury by such late hours. But how could I do otherwise?

Saturday March 21, 1931

Ate a little breakfast about noon. Returned to bed. Remained there until 5:00 p.m. Could not sleep. Played checkers with R_____ (Bacote). We discussed E_____ (Helen). He feels that I should give her up. Suggests I tell her frankly. How can I? I like her. She may have hopes. If so, she has never broached them to me. Hate to hurt her, although the pain may be but incidental to the healing. Could do it at one time. Was heartless, then. Perhaps I ought to be that way now.

She called about 2:00 p.m. Told me she couldn't sleep. I knew why. But 'twas her fault. Asked that I take her to a dance tonight. Told her I had to go to New York to get my bag. Then, too, I was tired. Would go, however, because of the disappointment I had caused her on Washington's Birthday. She told me that it would rush me too much to go to the dance, but to come to see her. When I wavered, she reminded me that I at least owed her that much. I couldn't refute it. I promised.

Rushed to New York about 6:00. Arrived at Jim's. He was closeted with a Jewish mistress, wife of a druggist. Nice looking, about 40. We talked about a number of things. I mentioned the fact that R_____ [Bacote] and I had bought two genuine Panamas for $5.00 this morning. He then brought forth three of an even superior grade, which he had brought from St. Petersburg, Florida. He refused to state what he paid for them.

Knowing that I was a "third party," I contrived to leave after spending about a half hour.

Reached Ernest's about 9:45. Didn't even take time to shave. He took me to E____'s [Helen's]. She had just bathed and wore nothing but a slip and a dress. I understood. She was ardent tonight, filled with pent-up longing and yearning. Her kisses burned me, fell hot and almost supplicatingly upon me. She desired me to eat something with her. But I couldn't. Finally told her I'd take some cocoa. Couldn't find any. Took two cups of hot Ovaltine instead. And it worked to her woe. For with my utter helplessness resulting from physical exhaustion, I could have done nothing better calculated to induce sleep. And that is just what I did. . . . Left at 3:30. I stumbled into R____'s [Bacote's] and took two tablets to make me sleep. I felt as if any moment would be my last.

Sunday March 22, 1931

Awoke this morning about 10:20. When I rose I felt so weak and dizzy I returned to bed for fear of collapsing. My heart beat at a terrific pace. R____ [Bacote] advised me to eat and to drink some coffee. Said the latter would act as a stimulant. Suggested that perhaps one of the tablets would have been sufficient for me. After eating I felt a little steadier, but I returned to bed. Remained there until 12:00 noon, then called [the] station. Could get a train at 1:20 p.m. Called T____ [Edna]. How surprised she was to hear my voice. Asked when my train would arrive. Would meet me. Couldn't tell her. Asked her to find out at station, using the train's departure from New York, 1:00 p.m., as the index.

Arrived at the 30th and Arch Street Station at 2:50. Had telegraphed T____ [Edna], telling her I would get there at 3:13. Train did not stop as per the timetable. I was at the wrong station. Therefore, I walked through a subway passage to the 32nd Street and Market Station. T____ [Edna] was the first person I saw. Her face beamed as she caught sight of me. I was glad to see her. Would not let me kiss her in the station. Told me we were going to Bert's [Alberta S. Norwood's]. [John Wesley] Poe was at the window. Both he and Bert brightened up when I entered. T____ [Edna] gave vent to her joy at my arrival, after returning from the Y.W.C.A. on an errand. Remarked she was unspeakably happy. Also remarked that she would not tell what time she arrived at the station to meet me. Bert invited us to dinner at Mrs. Warwick's. Had lots of fun. Went therefrom to Almira's, while Poe and Bert went elsewhere. Almira could not believe it really was I. They were all well and my coming took on the aspect of that of a prodigal son. Waited long for Poe and Bert. Finally arrived with Poe overloaded with schnapps. He was boisterous. Hated to see him that way.

Went out to Edna's. Poe kept up a bantering conversation directed against poor Bert. Is tired of her now. And she, poor thing, having tasted that which she wanted so badly, is loathe to let him go. And he lacks the courage to tell her outright, but takes refuge in either real or assumed drunkenness to tell her he cares nothing for her. He kept talking to T____ [Edna]. She admonished him to turn around, she wanted to kiss me. Then, again, that she was so happy to have me with her again that she did not even know he existed.

Got Poe to (take) her (Bert) home. I feared her mother would detect his condition. She (Edna) suggested coffee. Made it. Got him in the kitchen. . . .

Poe and B[ert] left at 12:00. I had planned to leave at 8:45. Finally left at 12:30. . . .

Arrived in D.C. 5:00 a.m. Utterly fatigued.

22

Washington

Surveying Negro Employment

MONDAY MARCH 23, 1931

Rose a trifle rested at 9:30. 'Twas raining. Called L____ (Lillian) [Mickey] to inquire whether she had gone. Evidently she had. Would have taken her downtown. Stomach upset. Ate no breakfast; two oranges.

Called upon Mr. Neal at the Washington Railroad and Electric Company to get the questionnaires he promised to fill out for me. Was not at his office. From there, went down to the Capital Traction Company. Saw Mr. Hibberly, assistant vice president. Gave me fine information. Employs 100 Negroes as a base force in a group of over 1,000. Numbers vary after warm weather sets in due to extreme track repairing. Negroes mostly unskilled laborers in track repairs. Have linemen's gang, however. Headed by a Negro. Paving done by them. Employees have been in service years and years. Asked him why no Negro motormen or mechanics were hired. Could not do so. Whites would refuse to work with them. Would not do to mix races. No welfare program. No chance of their getting higher jobs. Wages range from $20 to $40 a week. Turnover compares favorably with that of whites. Depression has not affected them. Trench-digging apparatus has, however. Labor efficient. Best for such work under white supervision.

In the afternoon, went out to the Chapin-Sacks Ice Cream Company. Hires about twenty Negroes. Most laborers. No chance for advancement here. No ice cream makers. Managers says he has never seen any. One Negro helps pasteurize milk, another is garage man, but most of them are doing janitor or porter work. Pays about $22 a week. No comparison between whites; [they] are doing different work. Went by B's. She wanted me to go to show with her. Refused in the interest of sleep. Came home and retired about 8:30, only to be awakened by Kirlen, who came in about 9:00. Made short shrift of him, however. Oh yes, dropped by office today but could not get in. Woodson will think that I have forsaken the survey.

Tuesday March 24, 1931

After breakfast this morning, stopped at the office. Woodson asked me where I had been. Told him right in town for the past day. Reminded him of my failure to get in yesterday. Told me I must get a key. Feared survey was languishing. Assured him that it was not. Gave me letters. Inquired how I had fared at Dartmouth. Was pleased when I reported.

Went immediately therefrom to the Washington Railroad and Electric Company, where I called upon Mr. Neal, its vice president. The information I received was certainly heartening. They employ over 400 Negroes in a total of over 1,300. Janitors, porters, truck drivers, firemen, and track men predominating. Machinery has displaced some as in the case of the Capital Traction Company. The depression has not. I ought to state that this total includes the employees of the Potomac Electric Company. Employees are reliable. Turnover no greater than for whites. Negroes best workers on tracks, where heavy work is required. Wages ranged from $4 to $5 a day. Little turnover. Depression has not affected them. Employers here seem to take paternalistic attitude to Negro workers. Many tell me organization is like one family. Mr. Hibberly of the Capital Traction stated such; so did Mr. Neal, who rejoiced that they took care of their aged or incapacitated Negro employees.

I find that few or no Negroes work in the iron or steel business here. That is a white man's job. Interviewed four such places today. No Negroes were hired, either because the owner knew of no skilled Negro help; because white machinists would not work with them; because the employer did not feel that Negroes could perform such labor; or because trade union machinists barred Negroes from working at the craft in union shops. In addition, I found no Negro helpers. These are white boys who are advanced from helper to apprentice to machinist. Of course, Negroes are excluded from the machine shop as mechanics either by the machinist union or, if it is an open shop, by the refusal of whites to work with them. One man told me he had seen a few Negro machinists.

Went to Rosslyn. B[ertha] was not there; neither was anyone at home.

In the afternoon, I obtained a deal of interesting information from several laundries. Among them, they employed almost 1,100 Negroes who represented nearly 85 percent of the total employees. The laundries, next to the government service and hotel and house work, form the leading outlet for Negro labor and the principal source of Negro female industrial labor. In some of them, like the Bergman Laundry, they perform nearly all sorts of work with the exception of truck driving and clerical work. The management feels that since the drivers must come in contact with white women, it is better to have white drivers. Their work here, as in others, is highly satisfactory. No different from the white. Information as interesting was gleaned from Page's Laundry and Toberman's.

The prize, however, insofar as Negro employment is concerned, must be awarded the Palace Laundry. This is the largest laundry in Washington and virtually all the work is done by Negroes. Of the more than 500 employees more than 450 are Negroes. They do all sorts of work. In fact, the manager—a refined and cultured official, whose curled and pointed mustache and debonair airs reminded me of a Frenchman—told me that their colored help was the best in town and that they run the laundry. They are the markers, sorters, shakers, shirt ironers, starchers, washers, and even do all the dry cleaning. He told me that no one makes less than $10, and that on piece work, the earnings of a girl might go as high as $23. Negroes have the incentive to work, for through the manifestation of skill and ability, they are able to rise into better-paying jobs. This is unique in the laundries, for in nearly every other branch of endeavor, save in contracting and paving, the Negro begins as an unskilled worker and ends as such. Here a Negro man has charge of the washroom, and another Negro is in charge of the cleaning department. All drivers are Negroes.

This company not only has the most modern plant—a thing of beauty for a laundry—but what is unique is its extensive welfare work. It maintains sick benefits for its help. They pay about 25 cents a week and receive a certain amount of money a week when incapacitated by illness. This also entitles them to free medical and dental attention throughout the year. A medical clinic and a dental clinic for both races are located here. There is also a cafeteria where lunch is served at cost. White uniforms are furnished the girls daily. The drivers—all colored—wear corduroy uniforms and caps. Shirts and ties even are furnished, and there is absolutely no excuse for untidiness or uncleanliness, for they may put on a clean shirt every day if they desire. (One of the drivers, himself, is authority for this statement.) The working atmosphere in the laundry is all that could be desired. The entire building is light, clean, airy, and well ventilated. Music, furnished by radio, is furnished to every department of the laundry. The management finds it keeps the help in better humor and relieves the monotony of the work, besides making for a certain rhythm in untiring motions.

I asked the manager how his colored employees reacted to his welfare campaign. He told me at first it was extremely difficult to get them to join the sick benefit club which gave them so many benefits in respect to dental, medical care, and so forth. Moreover, he found it hard to persuade them to come to the cafeteria. Asked my opinion. I ventured to say that the Negro was new to industry, knows little about cooperative efforts, and was timid and diffident about eating in the company of whites, since he had been barred so long from the opportunities of becoming accustomed to [eating] in white restaurants and hotels. He remarked that after a deal of effort, they were finally coming to see the virtues inherent in the company's efforts in their behalf. After much fulsome praise of his Negro employees by the manager, I set off in company of a Negro driver, whom he designated, to view the plant. The manager himself would have escorted me but a business call detained him.

I marveled at the sanitary conditions under which these Negro girls worked. So different from the laundries in Virginia, South Carolina, Georgia, and Florida, as reported by the Women's Bureau of the Department of Labor. Plenty of light, no overcrowding. Girls dressed in white uniforms. At some tables white and colored working together. A Negro man beside a white woman, both doing similar work. In the washroom, where a Negro was in charge, the floor was dry, dryer than in the Manhattan Laundry. I looked into the toilets—that is for men. They were clean, no odor. There are shower baths and lockers of steel. These also were clean, although a few clothes, socks, etc., were lying on the floor, but this may be attributed to the fact that the men were dressing. Of course this is a Southern city, and there were different sets of toilets, two for the white and colored. A waste of time and money that is one of the results of prejudice. The cafeteria, too, was divided in twain: one side for white, one for colored, with a barrier in the center. Both races work together, both eat the same food, but must do so under the edict of physical separation in all things social, although that barrier be no more substantial than a serving table. Segregated conveniences usually redound to the disadvantage of the Negroes. That was evident not only in the dental clinics, where fewer conveniences and apparatus were noted—although they might be transferred—but also in the cafeteria. Here, the floor on the Negro side was uncovered. On the white side, the floor was overlaid with heavy linoleum, which gave it the appearance of white and black blocks of marble. On the whole, however, this laundry offered the most wholesome environment for workers both black and white, and especially for the latter, that I have ever seen.

Before my tour was finished, I had gone into every department of the laundry, into the shipping department. Cautioned the driver who had escorted me through the plant not only to take care of his job, but to admonish all his fellow workers to do the same. I reminded him of the scarcity of jobs, of the fact that there no longer remain jobs which the Negro could look upon as wholly his own, that they were on trial, and their job tenure would endure only so long as they rendered efficient service—that is, satisfaction. He assured me all the boys realized the value of a chance for steady employment and that it was almost unthinkable for a fellow to stay out [or] either otherwise demean himself on the job.

Returning to the office, I thanked the manager for my inspection trip through his plant and assured him that he had shown me something novel in a laundering establishment. I referred to the welfare service, wholesome working environment, and the monopoly of positions by Negroes. He asked whether I had seen the dry cleaning department, which is run altogether by Negroes. To my negative response, he added that I should inspect it. Called the head of that department and asked him to show me through it. The latter is a white man, Mr. _____. He told me that he had the finest dry cleaning crew in Washington. It is work calling for skill and intelligence. The head spotter is a Negro, Mr. Sutton. He was attired in an immaculate white uniform and was just then going over a piece that had been dry cleaned to see whether all spots had been (removed). If not, by a special chemical process, adopted to different kinds of spots, he would remove them. The dry cleaner is a Negro. Upon him rests the responsibility of thousands of dollars, for the slightest mistake would ruin a garment that could cost the company dearly. All the pressers, likewise, are Negro. Delicate silks, crepes, suits, and other garments are cleaned and pressed here and the head of the department remarked that he has the most efficient crew in town.

All of this made me feel good. It corroborated my cherished idea that efficiency will win recognition; that it is not so much what a man says he can do, but what he is actually able to produce. The workers seem satisfied, and well they might be, for they have hope. They know that through a manifestation of greater skill, they will be rewarded with better paying jobs. Then, too, a higher class of colored girls goes into this work. This is because their industrial opportunities are limited. White girls with less education work in stores where their prestige is higher but remuneration smaller. Then, anything that smacked of laundry, until recently, has been looked upon with aversion by white girls. Stopped at the office. Woodson was busy. After dinner wrote letters. Took clothes to B[ertha]. Made arrangements to sell M_____ a set of books on Thursday.

WEDNESDAY MARCH 25, 1931

Met B[ertha] downtown at 10:00 and took her to Rosslyn. Left her while I went over to interview employers of Negro labor in Foggy Bottom—a part of Georgetown down on the riverfront. The first man I struck was a contractor who lays composition floors. Tells me all his actual work is done by Negroes. They mix the composition and so forth. Best labor he has ever had, he told me. Virtually no turnover. Men have been with him for years. Plenty of chances for advancement. In the cement and paving companies, Negroes do nearly all the labor, although one firm told me that their trucks were driven by white men because the drivers have to come into contact with foremen of construction gangs, and they get along better and transact business better than Negroes. Wages 45 cents to 62½ cents an hour.

At the Rogers-Wilkens Flour Milling Company, where almost 20 Negroes out of 60 employees work, the treasurer seemed very reluctant at first about giving out any information. Finally told me, however, that they hired Negroes as laborers in warehouse, as janitors, etc. One held a responsible position in the warehouse. No turnover. Asked if they employed Negroes on trucks. Did so once. Changed because Negroes were unreliable and dishonest. Returned to Rosslyn. After lunch I left again for Georgetown.

Before going, however, B[ertha] told us that the Bishop ([Charles Emmanuel] Grace, who founded the House of Prayer as a means of mulcting thousands of Negroes out of their pitiful savings) has returned to America without his bride. That astounded me, for she had told me just two weeks ago that he had gone to marry a very beautiful Cuban girl, daughter of a rich planter. Now it appears that the senorita has jilted him. She is nineteen, he about forty-five. Their disparity in ages might have exerted such influence. I had already remarked to B[ertha] that he would possess her legally, [but] someone younger actually.

It seems, too, that the bishop has suddenly become persona non grata at Cousin Winnie's and Susie's who, for the past six or seven years, have been boarding and lodging him gratis. They even moved without telling him. It seemed that, at first, the furnace broke down in the middle of winter and all subsequent efforts to induce the bishop to have it repaired proved futile. Then on top of that, it has reached the ears of my good cousins that another woman had bought a bedroom suite and had fixed up her home preparatory to entertaining the bishop upon his arrival here with his bride from the Antilles. Had prepared a sort of bridal suite or something. Now such knowledge made Cousins Winnie and Susie exceedingly perturbed—nay, I say wrathful, if they would dare display anger toward a "celestial being." They did, however, get up courage enough to question his spiritual highness as to the truth of these rumors that he would soon take up his abode elsewhere and bereft their home of his sanctimonious, devil-chasing, and healing presence when in town. What was to become of the bed, hallowed by his having touched it with his body, and of the dining room suite, upon which his "holiness" alone had eaten. So exalted was his presence that no humble creature save Cousins Winnie, Susie, or B[ertha] could enter, and then only in the category as servant to the "most high."

To these queries, the "Holy Person" returned an answer befitting to one of such celestial parts and attainments. He flatly told my cousin he would go when he desired and where he desired, and in effect, reminded them that they had been honored above mere mortals by having been blessed with his presence in their home. "I think I have done well by you to stay here," was his retort. Yes, in effect, he had, because God knows I never could have stood them. It was humorous, yet pathetic.

I asked B[ertha] what attitude the people had taken toward his impending marriage. She told me many of them had become disillusioned, disgusted. They thought he was divine, even God, and he had no need of a wife. I ventured to say: Fools! So long as he enjoyed a multiplicity of women, he was their God, for, unlike mere mortals, he owed allegiance to none. But, as soon as he decided to make one woman his own and to conform as ordinary persons to social customs and demands, presto, he is dragged down from his pedestal of divinity, and the man whom they had robed in the luster of a God, whom they had worshiped as the Christ himself, they now disrobed, stripped him of all immortality, and he now stood revealed unto them as just a common man, with all the weaknesses of earthly flesh.

Both Cousin Grace, Rose, and B[ertha] agreed with me. They were vindictive, said he would suffer for misleading these poor people. I feel that his end is almost near. The people are opening their eyes. B[ertha] says attendance has fallen off. Even Cousins Winnie and Susie are staying home at night, as if they had sense, rather than flocking to church. No punishment could be too severe for that man. He ought to swing for exploiting these poor people, while he rides about in all the majesty and luxury of a king in Cadillacs, Pierce Arrows, and Packards, with liveried chauffeurs, etc.

Went back to Foggy Bottom. Interviewed linoleum dealers, cement and gravel plant owners, and the paving contractors. The most interesting information came from Crawford's Contracting Company. Most of their skilled work, besides engineers (and) machine operators, is done by Negroes. About 200 Negro laborers are employed, the number increasing in the summer months. All the cement finishers, asphalt layers, and concrete mixers are Negroes. They also drive the trucks. Wages range from 40 cents to 62½ cents an hour, and sometimes go as high as 70 cents an hour, the bookkeeper told me. The men are very reliable. No difference between them and whites; if any, it is in their favor. Some have worked for Crawford so long that they are just being carried. Others have known Crawford so long that if they are laying streets, they believe they are still working for him. Their skilled labor gives fine satisfaction. No complaint. Do cement finishing better than whites. Machinery has displaced some. The depression, too, has hurt them, but not so much as it has other companies. The reason that Negroes do not operate the machines is because most of the men are mechanics who have learned to run them in the factory and are capable of making all repairs on them.

A storm coming up, I returned to Rosslyn just in time to get some ice cream before taking my cousins to work. Took B[ertha] home. Stopped by office. Woodson asked me to come in tomorrow to straighten out list of people to whom books had been sent in Philadelphia and who had not received or not accepted them. Left note for Miss Dunlap to that effect. Received from Dartmouth check, also. Had been received at the office before my arrival from Dartmouth. Glad to get it, for I had begun to wonder.

While eating dinner, I recounted to Woodson some of my findings. Elated. Asked whether I wrote them down. Assured him I did. Remarked that it was as necessary to get the information from places where Negroes were not employed as it was those establishments that freely hired them. Told him I was doing that, also. Took packages to station. En route back to B[ertha]'s to school.

Thursday March 26, 1931

Returned to Foggy Bottom this morning. No Negroes in three iron-working establishments. In one, no Negroes had applied. In another, a Negro blacksmith had worked. Employer had tried others but none could learn trade. Said few skilled Negroes. Train whites as machinists from helpers up. In other instances, Negroes do not apply for jobs. Most of labor unskilled. Careless, too.

Went to Rosslyn at 12:10 to take Cousin Rose to market. Gained information about oystermen. Saw Negroes shucking oysters in stalls, 35 cents a gallon. Get 50 cents when shucking for individuals. Work highly seasonal. Busiest time around Christmas and holidays. Then, can make $6 to $7 a day.

Man told me that 15 or 16 men are kept so busy, (they) hardly have time to eat. Work [is] hard on hands. Sometimes pain so at night can hardly sleep. Nowadays the oyster season is dead. Some days men don't make a penny.

All of these men are floaters. Pick up a few pennies here and a few there. Clam openers get 5 cents a dozen. Many Negroes work on the oyster boats. One of them told me that he acted as oysterman, pilot, and salesman for the white man for whom he works. The latter, who owned the boat, was a drunken sot, he told me, and that if he (the Negro) did not take charge and sell his wares, he (the white man) would not make a penny. His words carried veracity, for not only did he wait upon my cousin, but a few minutes later, I beheld the swaying figure of a bearded, booted, and overcoated man ambling toward us. He approached us and began praising his oysters. His breath, meanwhile, smiting our nostrils, reeking with the foulness of stale, bad whiskey. I interviewed a number of these fishermen and oystermen. In most cases, there are two men to the boat, the white owner, and the Negro who is a man of all work. They eat, sleep, drink, and work together. No Negroes own any boats at the wharf here. Some did a few years ago.

The oystermen, I should relate, operate in government-built stalls. They pay no rental. Government even furnishes coal. Stalls were the outgrowth of the protestations of women for greater sanitation in the oyster business. The men used to open oysters squatting about on the ground. Now they have a shed with a little stove and separate stall for each man. It is interesting to see them work, the ease with which they open the oysters. They wear a leather finger over their finger of the right hand, which holds a sharp, thin knife. The left hand holds the oyster. With great deftness they open the shell, pick up the oyster proper with the knife and forefinger and drop it in a container, then wash their right hand in a can of warm water. The process is then repeated ad infinitum. 'Twas interesting to watch.

En route back to Rosslyn we nearly met with a serious accident. Driving up 26th Street, I had almost reached K Street when I beheld a Chevrolet sedan coming in the opposite direction. As it reached the intersection of 26th and K, a Ford roadster bearing a group of high school cadets reached there about the same time and attempted to turn south into 26th Street. There was imminent danger of a triple smash-up with the Chevrolet sandwiched in between. I pulled over to the curb and stopped. I saw the Chevrolet driver making frantic efforts to swerve his car to prevent his being struck amidships by the Ford. The boys in the Ford, apparently oblivious to what might have happened, realized only too late how fast they were traveling. They could not stop. The Chevrolet could not clear the path of the Ford in time. The result was a zig-zagging, a frantic yell, a blood-chilling crash, and the noise of shattered glass, as the Ford struck the heavier Chevrolet off balance and turned it completely upside down. The wheels still revolved in air. My blood froze for a second. Cousin Rose threw down her pocket book. Then, I jumped out, hurried to the wrecked car just as the occupants were emerging. Thank God, except for a cut arm, no one was hurt! I got back in the car all atremble because of what might have happened. Cousin Rose was visibly perturbed. I myself was far from being composed.

Did nothing further all afternoon, for I had eaten too many oysters. Returned to the office to check up on books returned from Philadelphia. Had Miss Dunlap write [John Wesley] Poe, Miss ——, and Sarah Pride, telling them their books had been returned. Think the latter will take them. Poe is to get in touch with the other.

Woodson unfolded some interesting schemes today. Told me he intended having some pictures, 19" × 24", made of eminent Negroes. Felt they would sell well. I shared his opinion. He suggested pictures of Lincoln, Douglass, Booker T., and Paul Laurence Dunbar. I felt Phillis Wheatley and Toussaint L'Ouverture ought to be added. He agreed. Computed lists in order to set selling price. Told me he could get them made for $40 a thousand or 4 cents apiece. Mailing tubes would cost 10 cents. Postage 10 cents at the highest. Total cost 24 cents. The picture would sell for $1.00. I suggested 50 cents for the agent, giving the Association 25 cents or 100 percent on investment. Would not suit Woodson. Held out for 35 cents. Couldn't arrive at understanding. Wisely postponed it.

He evidently felt exuberant today. Informed me of a calendar he had [James Lesesne] Wells working on. Would be ready by October. That also would sell for $1.00. I didn't warm up to this proposition as ardently as to the picture project. Calendars can be secured too easily gratis.

I then told him of my plan to publish the "Negro Hero Tales," dealing with the lives and achievements of African military heroes, empire builders, historians, etc. Informed him also of Edna Jefferson Gaines, who had promised to help me write them. In fact, she was going to put them in language for children. Since Mrs. Gaines teaches retarded children, in my opinion, I told him, she was eminently qualified for the work. He seemed impressed. Told me he would write her. I interrupted to say that she might come down here over the weekend. He wrote the name down, however, and asked that I bring her in to see him when she comes to town.

About the pictures, now. It was found that there existed no large pictures of Toussaint L'Ouverture or Phillis Wheatley from which we might secure copies. Therefore, Woodson stated that some would have to be painted. I asked why smaller pictures 5" × 8" could not be enlarged. He responded that the effect would be similar to that of a person afflicted with smallpox. The face would be full of holes. I suggested Lois Jones to do the work. Woodson did not know her. Asked about her. I told in glowing terms of her accomplishments, how she had led her class at the Boston School of Art, of her service with Charlotte Hawkins Brown at Sedalia, and, of her beautiful artwork. Told him that she was the best among her group. He asked whether she was better than Wells. I felt she was and told him so. He countered that Wells did fine work, which I admitted. But I held steadfastly to the point that Lois was his superior. He yielded to my exuberant laudations of Lois, and told me to give her the pictures in miniature for her to enlarge. It was understood that the work would be purely a trial and that the compensation would not exceed $10.00 apiece. I accepted it for Lois, knowing that it would ultimately mean additional work for her. Went to dinner quite elated. Woodson seems pleased over the prospects of the survey.

Took B[ertha] to the movies. Saw Otis Skinner, a truly great actor, in one of the finest screen productions I have ever seen. 'Twas a classical drama of the Orient with the scene laid in Arabia. Otis Skinner as Hajj, the Beggar of Bagdad, played a difficult and inspiring role. He was in turn beggar, charlatan, murderer, lover, suffering father, and beggar again. The language was picturesque, ornate, elegant. I thrilled to it. So did B[ertha]. But the majority of Negroes could see no virtue in it. They enjoy jazz-maddened pictures.

SATURDAY MARCH 28, 1931

A miserable day. Bought pair of shoes. Went to B[ertha]'s. Wrote. Returned to office. Took books to station.

Called upon Lois. She was tickled to know I had thought of them sufficiently to put work in their hands. Gave her pictures of Toussaint and Phillis Wheatley, about 5" × 8". She is to reproduce and enlarge them to 17" × 22". Told her I had praised her to Woodson as being a better artist than Wells. The latter does our illustrating now. Is a Harmon medalist. But Lois [was] the best in her art school at Boston. And she does beautiful work. She can do it. Would give them to me in two weeks.

SUNDAY MARCH 29, 1931

Spent virtually the entire day with the M[ickey]s. Breakfast, ride, blowout, dinner. Went to movies alone at night. I must find someone here whom I can see on Sunday. Was dreadfully lonesome tonight.

MONDAY MARCH 30, 1931

Hoped to interview at least ten persons today. But, alas, for the schemes of men! First, the battery refused to work. Could not start the car. 'Twas beastly cold. Left it. Went to breakfast. Returned disgusted. Read *Seed* by

Charles G. Norris.[1] The story is a plea for birth control, setting forth the opposing and protagonistic forces. Takes a family as the example. Depicts the misery and death of women from too rapid breeding and the strain that finally kills them in an endeavor to provide for them. Contends that rich should have more children. Poor in proportion to means to care for them. Singles out Catholic Church as main obstacle to birth control. Forceful book. Sees society dying off at top. Best brains going that way. I feel, like many others, that it is compensation, else the poor man's son would never get a chance to rise.

Went out about 3:45. Interviewed the managers of two laundries. One hires Negroes in almost every position—the Arcady. The sole exception are the drivers. Done by whites. Feel they can contact people better. Most of the employees are Negroes. They do everything.

The Ambassador Laundry, which is much smaller, has also the smallest percentage of Negroes, only 25, or one-fourth of the entire working force. Nearly all the skilled work is done by whites. No Negroes do marking or sorting. They are chiefly shakers and washers. The manager could only account for it by the fact that they were thus employed when he took charge and that he had never seen fit to change them. Whites drive trucks. Could or would offer no satisfactory explanation there.

Stopped at the office. Told Woodson of battery and tire trouble. Advised me to get tires tomorrow.

TUESDAY MARCH 31, 1931

Went down to southwest Washington this morning. Got some interesting information down there. Interviewed wholesale grocers, beverage manufacturers, cap makers, bakers, etc. The most interesting returns came from a cap maker. Showed the unwillingness or inability of Negroes to take advantage of opportunities to learn trades. A Jewish cap maker told me that he had tried more than thirty-five Negro boys in an endeavor to teach them the cap-making trade, starting them as apprentices at $10 a week and increasing their pay until their earnings reached $40 to $45 a week for the same period. None, however, wanted to start at such a small salary. Desired $20 to $25 a week. Then would work only a certain number of days a week. This astonished the proprietor, who hails from Trenton, New Jersey, where labor, both black and white, with whom he had been accustomed to dealing, proved much more efficient. Told me both races made poor laborers here. Hired a colored girl as a seam sewer. Very reliable. Likes colored people;

1. Charles Gilman Norris, *Seed.*

90 percent of trade gained from Negroes. Therefore, would prefer to hire them. Then, too, although he failed to admit it, Negroes will work cheaper.

A beverage concern could not use Negroes on its trucks because the drivers were also salesmen, who had to deal with white entrepreneurs. Negroes could not function smoothly in that capacity because of the attitude of whites here. And Negro business is so inconsequential that, in response to my query, [I was told that] it would not pay to have a Negro salesman to solicit Negro business.

At a wholesale grocery establishment—Horton and Company—where a Negro is in charge of the shipping room, I received another interesting observation. Everything that comes in, everything that goes out of the building is checked by him. He has about twenty to twenty-five fellows working under him. Yet, it was some time before the men would give him the respect and subordination due him as a foreman. They would come in late, argue with him, stroll out to chat during work hours, and do every conceivable thing to embarrass him, expecting him to overlook it because they were Negroes under a Negro foreman. But with honor to him, he asserted his authority, and, with the backing and confidence of his employer, was able to maintain discipline by rewarding diligence and efficiency and weeding out the insubordinates and troublemakers. He gets $40 a week.

Went to see B[ertha] at night. Found a telegram from E_____ (Edna) on my return. Arriving here tomorrow evening at 7:55 p.m. Asked that I meet her if convenient. Felt no elation. Didn't even care whether she came or not because I wanted to rush this survey along, and I know only too well that she would be a retarding influence. Then, too, I was getting a cold. Strange, though, I never warm up to the prospects of a liaison. My joy comes later.

23

Washington

Continuing the Survey

WEDNESDAY APRIL 1, 1931

Rained terribly hard today. Took I____ [Lillian Mickey] to work. Started to return to office. Didn't.

Worked quite diligently today. Secured returns from a number of wholesale houses that were more or less interesting. One man told me Negroes did all his work. Were excellent. Another that the only Negroes employed in more than 200 employees were about twenty-five Negroes who were janitors, maids, porters, and the like. This was the Auth Provision Company. No Negroes as sausage makers or butchers, etc. Disappointing. Manager just told me he could not use them in any other capacity.

A department store manager (Kann and Company) informed me that out of approximately 800 employees, but eighty-five were Negroes, working as truck drivers, maids, stock girls, porters, janitors, etc. Asked him could he hire colored sales girls. Told me it would be impossible because of the attitude of Southern whites here. Would not stand seeing a Negro behind the counter. Told me they could do the work just as well. Waste of Negro brain power. Prejudice among white customers forces these proprietors to pay out larger items for salaries to these white employees, when a better grade of Negro labor could be hired cheaper.

Saks and Company employs Negroes only as janitors [and] elevator operators. According to the manager, there are no more jobs upon which they might be hired.

Went to Hill and Tibbetts to get tires. Took almost two hours. Arrived late for dinner, reaching the Y at 7:15. Woodson there. He told me of the impending struggle to remove [Mordecai] Johnson from the presidency of Howard University, backed by a triumvirate of scoundrels—Perry Howard, Judge [James A.] Cobb, and Emmett Scott.[1] The latter, "Dr." Scott, is the smoothest, petty politician in the race, a low-down, grafting, crafty, underhanded, suave, scheming, self-inflated egotist. I have not one shred of respect for Scott, nor did I ever possess such. He is the mainspring, the brains, the source of the conspiracy to oust Johnson. (Not that I hold any brief for the latter.) Judge Cobb is not familiar to me. I have met him but once, and he did not impress me on that occasion—the banquet we gave for the Negro congressmen.

Perry Howard is execrated, where thinking Negroes are concerned, as the man who accepted a $4,000 bribe from the Pullman Company to kill the Pullman Porters' Union. A rascal, a former Republican dictator of Mississippi, but who was turned out of office with the advent of Hoover to the White House. These three, then, are the self-appointed committee of three to undo Johnson. Scott gives all the information he can. Cobb assembles the data, and Perry Howard is the attorney for the malcontents.

Scott—like [Theodore] Roosevelt with [William Howard] Taft—has soured on Johnson because he cannot rule him. Was instrumental in having Johnson appointed. Expected to rule him. Finding that Johnson was too independent to be his creature, he now seeks his academic head. What the outcome will be cannot be ascertained until April 14th, when the Board of Trustees meets. Woodson styled Scott one of the smoothest Negro politicians in the country, a past master in the art of petty political intrigue. I agreed.

Felt Johnson was doing a good piece of work for the school. Miss King, the keeper of the cafeteria, asked my opinion of Dr. Johnson. I responded that he easily ranked as one of the two foremost Negro ministers in the country and as one of the gifted orators of the day.

1. Mordecai Johnson's tenure as president of Howard University was marked by controversy during what Rayford W. Logan, in *Howard University: The First Hundred Years, 1867–1967,* 184–292, called his "embryonic years," 1926–1935. Logan's discussion of Johnson's conflict with James A. Cobb and Emmett J. Scott, however, is based solely on minutes of the Board of Trustees and of the Executive Committee. Perry Howard is not mentioned in this account. Lisio, *Hoover, Blacks, and Lily-Whites,* 98–105, treats Scott's, Cobb's, and Howard's political roles during the Hoover administration. Examples of newspaper accounts can be found in the *Norfolk Journal and Guide,* April 4, 1931, 1; April 18, 1931, 1 and 14. Examples of Carter G. Woodson's public adverse comments on Scott, Cobb, and Howard can be found in "Historian Sees Danger in Political Activity of Howard Univ. Official," *Baltimore Afro-American,* July 4, 1931, 2; and "Mu-So-Lit Prexy Ignores Letter of Woodson," *Baltimore Afro-American,* May 2, 1931, 2.

Had to terminate the discussion in order to meet T_____ (Edna), who was to come in on the 7:55 train. Did not even have time to dress before meeting her. Just arrived at the station in time to reach the waiting room when I spied her coming toward me, a porter carrying her bag and fur coat.

She was dressed entirely in black, or rather only black showed, with the exception of a bandeau of flowers on her chic hat—a new style that resembled the steel helmets worn by the poilus of France during the World War. A black, almost form-fitting coat draped her, falling almost to her ankles. Her face lighted up as she saw me. I shook her hand. Perhaps something in my touch made her feel that I intended to kiss her. Such action never dawned upon me. I cannot say I felt the least emotion at seeing her, unless it was a realization that I was sorry she had come. In the middle of the week, with much work to do, and I knew myself. How could I work about her? Then there was B[ertha] who had wanted me so badly. B[ertha] who loves me as no other woman ever has or ever will love me. Then, too, there was no place to take her.

That was exactly the question she asked me when I returned to her from the post office, where I had left her sitting in the car. Where in Washington? I asked whether she had a plan in mind. Her answer was in the negative. The Hotel Whitelaw? Dangerous, people know me. 'Twould ruin me here in D.C. She asked about the "Y." All right, but then. Well, she would try the Whitelaw. Told her the price was prohibitive. She called. Wanted $3.00 a night. She agreed that was out of the question. Asked whether anyone had a room at Howard Manor. Came up to ascertain. Neither manager nor Gertrude at home. Came out. She seemed to feel I was a little disgruntled. Told me she would go to the "Y." Drove her there. She secured a room. I promised to return within an hour to take her to dinner.

Raining tonight. Had rained all day. I had got wet, too. Felt an incipient cold. When I returned for T_____ [Edna], she told me she liked rain because it symbolized the day with me.

Went to dinner at Harrison's. Stayed an hour and a half. She would not eat because I didn't. But I had already eaten at 7:15.

Leaving Harrison's, we drove around the reservoir. She told me that I had never acted so devitalized, that it was as if I did not desire her to come here. Told me my letter with its matter of fact tone had prompted her to come. I responded that I merely stated the facts. Told me that with all the honors that were falling my way—Dartmouth, President's Negro Housing Conference, and all—yet, she was only a school teacher. Talked about the "Hero Tales." That is what ostensibly brought her here. Wanted to know whether she could put in tomorrow browsing over them. Told her she could see Woodson, also that I would take her to the Congressional Library. Then, just like her, she told me she wanted to be kissed lots of kisses. I did kiss her, not those rhapsodic embraces we had indulged in on other occasions, but more rational kisses. I scolded her for wearing a spring coat on a damp and chilly night like this. Told me she did not feel cold. I was not satisfied, however. Took her back to the "Y." Returned home at 12:30. Not at all pleased with T____ [Edna]'s presence here. Could not warm up to her, and I know she felt keenly my indifference.

THURSDAY APRIL 2, 1931

Surprised to find T____ (Edna) at the breakfast table this morning as I entered. Wore a dark blue dress with pink bow on the shoulder. Liked the bow, but not the dress. She asked me about the dress. Told me that she had bought it especially for me, as she had two others which she had with her. I responded that I liked the bow. I thought it was extremely becoming to her complexion. She only exclaimed, "damn," and laughed the laugh of disappointment. Frankly, I did not like the dress and was too candid to lie about it merely to please her. She ate virtually nothing.

'Twas a fine day, and I had hoped that she would ride with me to the Congressional Library, where I would leave her to look over various hero tales by other authors, so that she might get the hang of the thing. But when she mentioned shopping, I gave up the intention of asking her. Left promising to see her at dinner, 5:30.

Spent a most profitable day. Secured returns from the Palais Royal. Has almost 100 Negroes there in warehouses, on trucks, one or two in stock rooms, clerks, [and] in the cafeteria as sandwich makers. Mrs. Tingley, the employment manager, told me that in many cases they were more reliable than whites. Saw no reason why they could not be used as clerks, and it was only the prejudice against them here that prevented their being used in that capacity. Said she was free from it. Asked her whether she was a Washingtonian. Replied affirmatively.

The firm of Woodward and Lothrop (has) 2,100 employees, about 300 Negroes—warehousemen, tea room doormen, elevator operators, porters, janitors, etc. No responsible positions. Little turnover. Same as whites. According to Mr. Grey, they can do all sorts of things any whites can.

Unsuspectingly he let me know the great waste of Negro brain power here. Told me that he has Negro college men and women running elevators and working in the tea rooms. Said so with pride. I rejoined that no white boy or girl with such education would have to do such. He asked me why such a condition existed. I told him that limited opportunities in white business houses and the inability of meager Negro business enterprises to absorb these prepared workers accounted for it largely. Told me that many of the colored girls make more than the whites. Whole fountain force is white; tea room colored. Asked him whether it was done purposely so. Told me he didn't think so. Asked whether white patrons would object to being served by Negroes at the soda counter any more than they would in the restaurant. He had never thought of that. No, he could not use them as clerks. For Chicago (I had purposely alluded to the use of Negroes as salesmen in the department stores of Chicago) it was all well and good, but this was Washington and the policy of the store was in a measure directed by the attitude of the white patronage, which would never brook seeing Negroes in such positions as clerks.

In N. B. Moses, the conditions were almost identical. Negroes were truck drivers, porters, janitors; very reliable; stayed in their place; and all such tommyrot. In essence, in these large department stores, the Negroes are either janitors, porters, elevator operators, maids, or truck drivers. And in the Woodward and Lothrop, they are not even that. Whites are doing such work.

At the office of the *Washington Star,* I had the pleasure of meeting one of the most interesting men I have yet interviewed. He is Captain Ruth, a man about forty years of age, friendly, cordial, well met, a man seemingly deeply interested in the Negro. He is superintendent of the plant. Told me he had a fine group of Negro workers, some sixty-six of them. He was interested in the Negro, so was the company—in fact, interested in all its employees. Realizing the small earning power of the Negro, Mr. Ruth told me that every effort is put forth to help deserving employees. The company has an extended welfare program for its employees. Buys homes for them, and they pay it back on easy installments; will save their homes for them if they are unable to keep up payments. Gets them out of trouble; keeps them out of the clutches of sharpsters; gives them group insurance, $1,000 for 50 cents a week; free medical and dental treatment; and runs a cafeteria where meals may be had at a nominal cost!

What astounded me more than anything else was the frank statement by Mr. Ruth that more brain power was wasted by the Negro than by any other group in this country, and simply because the Negro is discriminated against in the matter of securing work, thus forcing both men and women, many of them equipped with college education, to accept work as porters, janitors, elevator operators, and the like in order to live. Domestic and personal service, and the menial jobs in business places is the asylum for all the blasted hopes of Negroes who have aspired to something higher, but finding the door of opportunity shut fast against them, have found at least sufficient return to keep body and soul together. With their superior education, they are usually bossed by some white whose intelligence is far below theirs. Yet the white knows no limits to his own possibilities. The Negro, on the other hand, will begin as a porter and 40 years later will still function in that lowly capacity. His reward will be "Sam is a good janitor, faithful and reliable, stays in his place. Just like one of the family." I think of my dad sometimes. After 42 years of faithful service as a teamster for a large brass and copper manufacturing company, he was finally rewarded with a janitor's job, while white men who came into the company later had become superintendents and managers. Talked for a long while with Capt. Ruth. His interest led me to promise him a copy of the *Negro Wage Earner.*

Dropped by office. Woodson busy. Told me that books were waiting to go to the post office. Put them in the car and went to dinner. Ate with T____ (Edna). Fussed because she had lost a whole day. Told her she ought to have come to the library with me. My retort was her going shopping. Had expected to see Woodson today. Told her she could see him tomorrow. Plainly, she was not at all pleased with my attitude. By the way, she had moved, too. Was now living at a Dr. Whipper's in 511 Florida Avenue. Room at the "Y" had been reserved.

Took her to Howard Manor to meet Mrs. [Mayme] White. Taylor, manager of the Federal Life Insurance Company, was here. So was Violet (Hemsley). Forgot Taylor's name. They made T____ [Edna] feel right at home. I dressed. Later we went out to Falls Church. Called on Cousin Mag (Margaret). She insisted on calling me Ernest. Showed folks some beautiful rugs, comforters, and fancy jars, all of which she had made or painted. Lives all alone in a large house sitting about 1,000 feet from the main road. T____ (Edna) wanted to buy some of her rugs.

Returned home. Told fortunes. Violet struck the nail on the head in two instances. Told me someone here loved me to distraction, but that I had very little interest in her. Also, that I was going to a meeting shortly. Took T____ (Edna) home. Returning. Mrs. White and Violet told me they liked her. She liked them. Wanted her to stay overnight, but I vetoed it. Felt they would talk about her. She wanted to stay but declined because of me. . . . Promised to take her to meet Dr. Woodson tomorrow. She looked forward to discussing with him her plan to write some African hero tales for children.

FRIDAY APRIL 3, 1931

After breakfast, Took T____ (Edna) to meet Woodson. Arrived there at 10:30. Left her downstairs while I went up to ascertain whether Woodson was busy. Upon my informing him that T____ (Mrs. Gaines) was downstairs, he asked me, "Mrs. Gaines?" "Yes." "Married?" "Divorced." "Are you aspiring?" "Allah forbid!" With a chuckle I went downstairs and returned with the lady. They greeted each other. Woodson had already met her at Cheyney.

What an interview! Woodson clearly had met his match. Nothing he could say daunted the impetuosity of Edna. How she talked. She exuded confidence, optimism. Every query Woodson fired at her she answered with finality, which caused him to look at me in admiration. She would write the tales. I told her (for it was my idea) that the Negro was not to be played up, that we were interested only in putting them in an entertaining manner before the children.

We had to overcome some peculiar notions of Woodson. First, he wanted to include about 200 stories. Would have been self-defeating, for such a bulky volume would tend to repel rather than attract the child; secondly, it would cut off future revenue, because, by putting out these stories in different volumes a greater income will be realized; thirdly, it doesn't pay to incur too much expense with a novel undertaking. Give the public these tales in small doses. Have several volumes. We (that is I) made Woodson see my point and Edna supported it. Decided to have no more than twenty tales in a book, about the size of *African Myths,* ten pages to a story. These tales would deal wholly with African heroes.

To Woodson's contention that anthropologists and Negro history detractors would hold that although these characters were black, they were not Negroes but Mohammedans, I replied that the title would take care of that. It suggested nothing Negroid. It would be African heroes. We decided then to make this first book deal with Negroes who have achieved in Africa. It would be the first in a set of four. The other three to delineate the accomplishments of Negroes in (2) Europe, in (3) Latin America, and in (4) continental United States.

A capital idea! Then as regards illustrations, Woodson asked whether we intended there should be any. Both of us agreed that such were almost indispensable. Woodson acquiesced, but felt they would have to be in black and white, for colored illustrations were too expensive.

Who now was to do the art work? Woodson suggested [James Lesesne] Wells, who usually illustrates our books. Edna named Alan Freeland, a Philadelphia artist, who is supervisor of art in the Philadelphia school system. I returned the name of Lois Jones. Praised her as one who understood child psychology, something which is indispensable in such work. Woodson agreed. Edna, also. She made up her mind to see and talk with Lois. I promised to take her there.

An interesting point now came up. Edna asked about a course of study for club purposes. Woodson said he had no such thing already drawn up. Edna suggested a syllabus or outline. Her plan was too comprehensive, however.

Would necessitate four years' work on each topic, that is, the Negro in Africa, in the New World, in the United States, etc. I felt that it would be far better to give the members of the club a general idea of Negro History, which course could take a year. Then if the club decided to study any special phase of the Negro over the period of a year, it could do that, having already provided the basis for such. Both saw my idea. Woodson promised to get out such an outline.

Then another important subject, how best to get over Negro History in children's groups. Edna suggested the project method. This was "Greek" to both Woodson and me. Woodson inquired what she meant. Edna explained that the dramatization of some aspects of Negro History or some character would be the vehicle by which the setting and exploits of the character could be suggested to and worked out by the children. She contended that by lantern slides, moving pictures, and the like, a great deal of history might be told, and in a way highly interesting to children. In other words, the project method is going from the known to the unknown. Woodson replied that the teachers in the South would know nothing about such methods.

I took issue here, for I knew full well that at Tuskegee, Hampton, and other Southern schools the teachers were instructed along such lines in the summer. I saw such projects worked out in Tuskegee last summer on corn, wheat, etc. It took Woodson a long time to see Edna's point, but at last, more silenced than convinced, he told her to work out such a project and send it to him. She returned that she could not do so until after August.

About the time for the stories to be published, Woodson wanted them by July 1. Edna felt that this date would be too early, for she had hoped to write some of them while at Columbia University during the summer. It was finally agreed to set the date as August 1. The reason given by Woodson was that printing costs were lower in the summer.

Edna is naturally dramatic. Many were the times as she talked to Woodson that her eyes closed or flashed, or her arms stretched forth in magnificent gestures to emphasize her remarks. I was secretly amazed to see Woodson shooting covert glances at me, the while, with a smile playing about his lips. Clearly he was impressed with Edna. Several times, however, I feared that her interest in me would betray itself to Woodson, for despite the fact that she was talking to him, often she was gazing directly into my eyes.

We left there at a quarter of two after having spent more than three hours there. It ended the longest interview I have ever known Woodson to give anyone since I came there.

I took Edna to the Howard Manor where she had an engagement with Mrs. White. En route she told me that Woodson held quite a deal of respect for my opinions. I laughed.

Had taken citrate of magnesia the night before. Had not acted. Now my stomach actually felt as if it would bust. Edna suggested I drink a lot of water. Did so. Went therefrom to B[ertha]'s. Beautiful day. After lunch went to Hecht's. Could do nothing there. Took B[ertha] for a ride in beautiful Potomac Park. Day beautiful at the Potomac—clear, serene, reflecting the golden glory of the sun, miles and miles of green sward; men and women horseback riding, canoes skimming over the smooth, rippling surface of the water. Love-making near the water, spring, flowers, water, love. We looked and I thought of springs of several years ago when we two walked in this same park with our eyes and hearts for each other only. The spell was getting her. She wanted to go out to do—what she did not know. I understood. She wanted me. That is why she asked what I intended to do tonight. But such was impossible. T____ [Edna] was here.

Ate dinner late. She told me that I have been most indifferent, that it was because of the tone of my letter alone that she came here. Complained that I assumed such a haughty attitude toward her that it made her feel that I seemed to be fearfully expecting her to do something wrong, to explode, or whatnot. I laughed and blamed such an attitude, if one existed, upon the fact that we were in D.C., where one's business is everyone's business.

She called on Lois. I took her there. Went downstairs to dress. Took up the poem Lois is to copy for me. Returned to 306. Were to go out. Fellows for V[iolet] and M[ayme] did not appear. Played bridge, told jokes. Have become better acquainted with my landlady. She considered me snobbish. Allah forbid! Again asked T____ [Edna] to stay overnight. Again I vetoed it. Afraid they'll talk. Don't want to be compromised. Don't know what they might say about T____ [Edna]. Women are so "catty." Left. Went around reservoir. . . . I took her home, both of us agitated and flushed by searing crimson flames of love that we could not down. Retired, not to sleep, but to dream.

SATURDAY APRIL 4, 1931

We took our last breakfast at the Y this morning. T____ [Edna] came in a trifle behind me. Looked tired. I marvel at her amazing vitality! And yet, is it vitality? She gets little sleep, and if she feels drowsy at midnight, is usually wide awake in the early morning hours. Her boast is that when others are preparing to go to bed she is then just in the mood to go out and "clown." I fear, however, that in the long run she shall pay the penalty by some sudden breaking down of her nervous system. One cannot successively and interminably crowd 730 days into 365. Yet, withal, she is not merely a butterfly, but ranks as one of the best teachers in the city of Philadelphia.

I have much respect for her intellectual powers. She is well read, likes the arts, even as I do. In short, she is well-rounded, which all will contribute not a little to her untimely disability, or demise, unless she slackens her pace. One would be a fool to seek to follow her example.

After breakfast took her out Rhode Island Avenue N.E., with me, while I interviewed the manager of the Bedell Bed Company and the National Radiator Company. The Negroes employed in the former are largely truck drivers and helpers. Only one is employed by the National Radiator Company. The manager recognized me. Used to live in the Partner (Apartments on 15th and U streets N.W.), where I ran an elevator during my school days. Kindly disposed toward Negroes. So, too, was the bookkeeper, a native of Louisiana.

Told T_____ [Edna] I would try to find some place where we might go and lose ourselves from the world. But she told me her word had been given to Mayme and Violet to go to Baltimore or to some roadhouse on the Baltimore Pike. . . .

Took her home. I went to the office. She had a dinner engagement with Miss Weatherless. Was surprised to find them at the Y.M.C.A. where I take my dinner. Sat at another table in order to give them chance to chat, although I would have preferred sitting with T_____ [Edna].

Promised I would come back to Miss Weatherless's for T_____ [Edna]. Did so after an hour and a half. Took books to post office. . . .

Brought her to Mayme's, then took her up to see Lois while I dressed. Mayme told me we would leave as soon as their fellows came. By the time I had dressed it was 10:30. No one had come yet. Went up after T_____ [Edna]. Told Mayme and Violet we were going to the Mickeys' and could be reached there in case their escorts arrived for the Baltimore trip.

Went to the Mickeys'. What a lot of fun we had here. There were only Mr. and Mrs. M_____, her sister, and a Dr. Greene. They had already imbibed and all were feeling quite jovial. Formality was dispensed with. Edna, new dress and all, sat on the floor at my feet. Mrs. M_____, at first a little dazed from the effects of highball, talked very little, but later she opened up. And Edith—she is always talkative. Bushrod, however, carried off all talking honors. These highballs, daring stories, ribald jokes, hot biscuits, bacon and eggs, coffee. Greene told the darnedest toast I've heard yet, beginning "Rock of Ages cleft for me." Bushrod, determined to break my cold, induced me to drink highballs—good gin and fruit juice. I felt quite light in the head. They tell me 'tis good for me. Lillian marveled at my drinking.

At 1:00 think of Mayme and V. Call them. No one has come. About 1:30, T_____ [Edna] goes down. Stays so long I am sent for her, since the collation is being held up for her. . . .

About 2:30 we left Mickey and returned to our apartment. . . .

SUNDAY APRIL 5, 1931

Had breakfast. I lay out the food. Mayme cooked it. . . .

Went to Baltimore in the afternoon where a singular and vulgar incident happened. Just as we entered the city, M[ayme] desired to visit the ladies' room of a filling station. It was all right until the operator saw me in the car. Then he refused her by telling her someone was in there. Another told her someone else had the key. She, knowing they were lying, spoke to a policeman, who referred her to a sergeant, who in turn did nothing. Unable to secure admission to the toilet, she threatened to do something drastic unless he show her the consideration and courtesy that one would ordinarily show a dog.

He still refused, so she relieved herself in a field, then smeared the filth in such a conspicuous place that he was forced to clean it after her. The filling station man called a policeman to have her arrested. But what could he do? To think that one could be so inhuman as to refuse a person the privilege of discharging so vital a bodily function. 'Tis every bit as heartless as refusing a dying person a drink of water. We were shocked when Mayme told us what she had done. T_____ [Edna] remarked it was the Jew in her. She came near wrecking the car in her anger when she resumed driving.

Went to Mrs. Means. Party stupid. Hostess an alcoholic, addicted. Drunk when we arrived, became so helpless that the party became a failure. She even tried to jump out of a second story window. T_____ [Edna] tried to catch her but was rewarded with a kick. I led her away from the window. Husband a druggist. Fine man. She has the money. Beautiful home.

Left Baltimore at 10:30. Returned to Mayme's. . . .

MONDAY APRIL 6, 1931

Remained in all day while it rained and snowed outside. My cold was worse; fever, headache, cough. Ought to have attended to it before, but then there was T_____ [Edna]. How long, I thought, shall this thing, this madness continue? What will be the effect on me, on her? Where is it leading us? Just how much is she beginning to think of me? I am sure I do not love her. She interests me, would intrigue any man. But love? No, even though she felt and expressed the fact last night that I did love her but refused to admit it. I have never loved anyone. Came closest to loving N_____. Must pray over this matter.

Went to Mickeys'. Took them to wedding. Returned. They told me of Negroes' lack of propriety, how an usher had yelled across the room for Mrs. Mickey to move. Bushrod was incensed, disgusted, and rightly so.

Keene, a friend of Mayme, prescribed for my cold. I took quinine. Violet prepared hot lemonade for me. Retired.

Tuesday April 7, 1931

Spent the entire day reading a novel or lying in bed. Citrate of magnesia taken the day before failed to act. Mayme started it by giving me coffee. Mrs. Mickey gave me salts. Then it acted and—. Terrible day. Rained and snowed. Wouldn't go out. Called Woodson, told him I would be in tomorrow. Asked me whether I had taken castor oil as he suggested Saturday. Responded negatively. Told me had I done so, I would have been okay.

Wednesday April 8, 1931

Anniversary of T_____ [Edna]'s coming. Woodson called me at 7:00. Asked me to come to the office within forty-five minutes. Did so. He was going to Baltimore to speak on Negro Business. Wanted me to be there when the girls arrived.

Spent a most interesting day collecting material. Contacted about eighteen employers. Received interesting information. First was the Pioneer Laundry on Rhode Island Avenue. All the mechanical work is done by Negroes, two are doing clerical work, and six mechanics. Would rather have watched them while they wait on customers in the office and do all the work in the washroom. But there is not a single Negro girl. Strange when they constitute from 60 to 90 percent of the force in some laundries. The manager told me he has tried them. Can't get stable, reliable force. Blames it on the out-of-the-way location of laundry. Feels that Negroes cannot afford car fare. Would rather work nearer home. True, to great extent. Likes colored, he says. Even though Negro stole $300 from him, still employed them. Can't employ Negroes as drivers, for they must be salesmen also and disputes can be more satisfactorily handled by whites. Feels only way he could use colored drivers would be to have a white route man in charge.

In contrast to the few positions held by Negroes here, the Pullman Laundry, a few doors down the street, employed forty-seven Negroes out of seventy-two in every capacity except supervisory, mechanical, and repairing.

Some of these establishments that I visited today hired no Negroes at all. One, the Fleischmann's Yeast Company, with 190 employees, had not a single Negro on its roster. The manager, Mr. Meers, explained it by saying that the shop was strictly union, dominated by the Cereal and Soft Drink Workers Union. It supplied all the help. The only time when Negroes could have been employed was during rush times when a lot of coal has come in and had to be stored away. The union would even send the men to do that. And occasionally when white men were not available, they would send a few Negroes, giving them cards enabling them to work. The union's [exclusion] of Negroes tightened when the whites rose against the Negroes' scabbing.

At the Price-Wilhoit Specialty Company, maker of candy specialties and peanut butter sandwiches, the manager and stockholder, Mrs. Nelson, told me no Negroes were employed because she found it difficult for Negroes and whites to work together harmoniously. Has thirty-five employees. Says she would have to have all white or all colored. Used to have colored shipping clerk, but people could not get along with him. Most of the time such a person must be an "Uncle Tom" in order to hold his job. The infamy of it!

Good Humor Ice Cream Company employs none, also.

The other bits of interesting information came from two chain groceries—the American Stores and the A & P (Atlantic and Pacific). Together, these companies employ about 1,050 men and women. The A & P, much the larger, employs 800; the American Stores 250. Yet, each hire only two Negroes apiece and as janitors only. And despite this, Negroes constitute, I'll wager, a greater comparative percentage of their patronage than the white group because their low earning power compels them to trade where their money will go farthest. I asked the managers this question—prefacing it by saying that in Chicago, New York, Philadelphia, and several other cities, where their companies had stores in Negro settlements or where Negroes constituted a large percentage of their clientele, Negro clerks, men and women, were employed. I also stated that such an act not only showed the Negroes that the companies appreciated their patronage, but by giving employment of that character to Negroes, it automatically increased the Negro trade of such stores. The latter would respond to show their gratitude. I also told them how well this arrangement worked out in Woolworth's 5 and 10 cent stores, Walgreen Drug Stores, and Sears and Roebuck.

Both managers were interested. The American store employment manager seemed kindly disposed. Said he: "There is no feeling about Negroes waiting on white customers. A Negro used to wait on customers at one of the Old Dutch Markets. I have seen them acting in such capacities in privately owned stores. I feel that D.C. people would accept it quicker than the people of the North. But Negroes have never applied as clerks. We shall take it into consideration, for in business one must take advantage of every opportunity." This was the most encouraging answer I had yet received.

The A & P employment manager, Mr. Wilson, went even further. He told me that such an idea had already occurred to him. Felt it capital. Had such brought to them once before, he remembered. Opened new store in Deanwood Heights. A Negro minister irked by a prejudiced clerk demanded Negro clerks for this store in an all-colored neighborhood. Fired the clerk or changed him and the same situation continued to obtain. Yet, he thought so much of putting colored clerks in stores that he wrote a letter to Mr. S. W. Zink, the General Superintendent. Felt that at least they could be put in stores, the whites to wait upon whites and Negroes upon Negroes.

I felt more or less elated, for if I could open up opportunities for Negroes as clerks in these stores, it not only would give me great satisfaction, but would likewise provide an opening for the many high school and college boys and girls here, who, because they can secure nothing better, are cleaning cuspidors, running elevators, and acting as porters.

Thursday April 9, 1931

Went to Sears and Roebuck. Employs eight Negroes out of 140. Porters, janitors, one a stove fixer. Employment manager, a New England woman, finds that they cannot employ Negroes as clerks, etc., because of Southern prejudice here. Did so after I mentioned the fact that Negroes were so employed at Sears and Roebuck in Chicago, one department being entirely manned by them.

At Hackingers, a lumber company, I also found some interesting information. They employ a number of Negroes as drivers, cement mixers, asphalt layers, etc., both skilled and unskilled. Lofflers, [a] meat-packing plant, has a few colored as butchers, smoked meat men, janitors, (and) porters, while at the Phillips Sausage Plant, they make sausage, butcher, etc. Found a white laundry that employs no colored. Is a small concern, however. A stone cutter, Durity, told me he employed no Negroes. Had seen no stone cutters among Negroes here. Only ones he recalled were in Charleston, South Carolina. Were skilled, too.

After dinner came down to B[ertha]'s. She was expecting me. . . .

Friday April 10, 1931

Today was unprofitable. Went down to see Ellen Adams at night about making domestic service survey. Could not do so. Sister is ill. She must run the business. Bought a half-dozen shirts this morning.

Saturday April 11, 1931

Hectic day. T_____ [Edna]'s party. Came home at 1:45. Mayme and V[iolet] not ready. Got her car in readiness. Polished my bag. Had hoped to leave at 3:00, but these women! At 4:30, just as I finished dressing, I was informed by V[iolet] [that] M[ayme] had gone down to Hecht's for shoes and that we would meet her there. I was furious, but withheld my comments. Left the apartment about 4:40, first wiring T_____ [Edna] that we would stop at her home for her.

Made the trip in four and one-half hours. Mayme drove to Baltimore, thirty-three miles, I, the rest of the way.

T_____ [Edna] and about ten people awaited us at her home—Betty, Mark, Tristy, and others. Washed, took some refreshments, and left for the inn. Everyone felt hilarious. T_____ [Edna] was dressed in white. Looked tired. Had been drinking, too. Don't know why, but I acted cold and indifferent on the way out to the inn. Perhaps it was my revulsion against such unrestrained hilarity. Perhaps it was— Oh, well—

The Porhessing[?] Inn sets about 1,000 feet back from the main highway to Trenton, about eighteen miles from Philadelphia. [John Wesley] Poe was there with Bert [Alberta S. Norwood].

[No entry was found for Sunday, April 12.]

Monday April 13, 1931

Rose at 9:15. A little rested but actually unfit for work. Took breakfast at Thurston's. Met Peter Richardson, lawyer and Howard alumnus. He told me that the law school alumni are hot after [Mordecai] Johnson, president of Howard. Intend to get rid of him. Held meeting Friday night. Voted for his resignation. Felt that his policy in running the law school, as well as the entire university, is calculated to weaken, rather than strengthen, the university.

Fact is, they are opposing Johnson's appointments. Richardson feels that they will be successful in forcing Johnson out. To my query as to whom they would recommend for Johnson's place, he had nothing to say. Anyone can tear down. Requires a genius to build. Personally, I am against Johnson, but I resent his being sacrificed and ridiculed before the other group and our whole race put out on an exhibition of shame because of the scheming of a coterie of petty, grafting politicians (as Woodson describes them) of the meanest ilk—men like Perry Howard, Emmett J. Scott, and Judge Cobb.

Made several contacts today. Secured data from Lansburgh's Department Store, as well as Garfinkle's. Lady clerk at Lansburgh's asked why I desired information about whites. Had to placate her. Told her I merely desired it in order that we might have some basis of comparing the efficiency of the Negro worker. Otherwise the information gleaned concerning the Negroes would have little relative weight. She gladly complied to my soft soaping.

Went to bed early. Kirlen called. Refused to see him.

Tuesday April 14, 1931

Beautiful day. Went down to see Mr. [S. W.] Rutherford, head of the National Benefit Insurance Company, to give him some idea of my findings concerning the survey of Negro labor here. Told him of my ingenious method of extracting information from white employers and managers, informed him of the opportunities open to Negroes especially in laundries, the fact that Negroes generally refused to work under Negro bosses, and gave instances where such had been tried only to fail. He seemed delighted to know that there was the possibility of getting Negroes positions as clerks in chain stores like the A & P, American Stores, and others. Was elated so much so that he told me he would call the committee sponsoring the survey to a luncheon at the Whitelaw Hotel next Tuesday and have me talk to them.

Mr. Rutherford impressed me as a very plain man, impressionable, but having much common sense. He did not want this information played up, because it would impede my getting additional data on this problem from whites. He is a very busy man, attending to a thousand and one things. He was frequently interrupted by his secretary and other persons coming in to ask questions or whatnot. Moreover, he is active in community work. Even now he was soliciting among his employees donations for the NAACP. He had already aided largely the drive for Nannie Burroughs's school. Told me he would inform Woodson of my work.

After the interview, Mr. Rutherford had his secretary, one Miss (Mae) Wright, to show me through the plant. There are employed here almost 200 men and women. A fine organization, though lacking the spirit of the North Carolina Mutual.

This afternoon, Bertha and I went down to Potomac Park to view the cherry blossoms. What beauty! Great clusters of snow-white blossoms turned the park into a fairyland. With the sun on the Tidal Basin, which was surrounded by the cherry trees, and a soft, caressing breeze, which wafted the dropping blossoms about, the whole park took on the aspect of a miniature paradise. And thousands of persons drawn hither by the grandeur and beauty of this rare show, gazed, wondered, and exalted in this lovely spectacle of nature. It made B[ertha] quite lovesick.

24

Washington

Completing the Survey

WEDNESDAY–Sunday April 15–19, 1931

Several high points stood out in these days. One occurred the 15th when [Mordecai W.] Johnson, president of Howard, was unanimously endorsed by the Board of Trustees of the university. The students in their excessive joy built such a bonfire on the campus that it appeared as if the very school itself were burning down. I was glad he had been retained. Vindicated the race and spelled anathema to the schemes of the arch-plotters—[Emmett J.] Scott, [Perry] Howard, and [James A.] Cobb.

Another highlight dealt with the survey. It seems that certain new industries are barring Negroes from their plants. This is true of three new laundries opened within the past six months. Two of these—the Sterling in Georgetown employs no Negro girls, has fifty-odd whites, and but one Negro in the washroom; the other, Carrolls Laundry, employs none. The reason given by the first was that he brought his help from the soda factory here. Doesn't appear so, for he never hired more than five or six in the plant. The other maintained that they have been in operation only for six months and began with whites. Perhaps it is policy. But the chief reason for this departure, no doubt, is the fact that cheap white labor is plentiful due to the scarcity of jobs, and the employers are giving preference to their own race. We would do the same.

Another case illustrated the tendency of Negroes to lose what jobs they have. At the Chevy Chase Dairy, the second largest in the town, the employment manager told me the policy is to displace Negroes by whites. Therefore whenever a job becomes vacated by a Negro, a white will step in regardless of the type of job. In the best-paying work, such as drivers-salesmen, there are six Negroes. They are rapidly being displaced, I was told, not because of any prejudice against them, but because whites are able to bring in larger sales. They will be replaced by whites, I was told. Only one will be retained. His job will be preserved only because he has one of the best runs of any salesman. This man, I was told, had contacted the maids in the rich section of Chevy Chase and through their intercession was able to hold his own on his route. Most of the laborers, of course, are doing menial labor, such as stable or garage labor, washing bottles, etc.

A third important event was the drive for $1,000 by the first of May, for which a meeting was called on Thursday, April 16th. The immediate cause is to help to raise a total of $7,500 for the research fund for the Association for the Study of Negro Life and History. This will match $7,500 given each year for three years by the John D. Rockefeller Fund. Its gift is conditional upon a similar amount raised by us from other sources. We must raise $1,000 here. About $4,000 has already been subscribed. The rest is either promised to Woodson on his speaking tours through Kansas, Texas, and Oklahoma and from other parts of the country. If we do not raise the necessary $7,500, shame upon the Negro race. They do not deserve the benefactions of the white group. Several methods were proposed, such as teas, socials, etc., but my suggestion [was] that we secure a committee and apportion to each member an amount aggregating $1,000. This amount—$100 per each 10 persons, $50 per each 20 persons—was to be solicited by the several members. Next Tuesday evening was designated for the next meeting. The place would be the same, the Y.W.C.A.

I also received final instructions from Mr. [John M.] Gries, executive secretary of the President's Conference on Home Building and Home Ownership, that the Committee on Negro Housing would hold its sessions April 24 and 25. I wrote him signifying my willingness to serve on these dates. I am not expecting any radical changes in the Negro housing situation to follow. That is predicated upon the low earning power of the Negro. Economic, pure and simple. Then, too, his lower living standards.

Oh, yes, went to see H(elen) M(assey) about making a survey of domestic service among Negroes here. Wanted someone who showed little color. Felt they could secure information desired because they would be more readily admitted to a white home than a dark girl. Then, to a very fair person, the housewife might open up and tell frankly her attitude toward hiring Negroes as servants. Had tried to get Ellen Adams. Could not serve. Sister ill. Called on H(elen) after meeting (Thursday). Has apartment. Just got home as I knocked. So glad to see me. Had engagement, but canceled it. We talked, we rode. She bought ginger ale, made me take whiskey for my cold. It made me tipsy. We talked, caressed, discussed a thousand and one things. She has a fine disposition. Divorced, small, pretty, straight black hair, rather thin, however. Asked me whether I thought she was thin and raised her dress showing me her small but shapely brown thighs. Caresses, mad kisses, half nude, brown body, madness, burning desire. But no, it could not be. Left at 2:45.

Mickeys [Lillian and Bushrod] are very kind to me. Went to baseball game with them on Sunday after having had breakfast with them. Returned from game and had dinner. He has not been well; a tooth has bothered him. In fact, after having two extracted on Friday afternoon, he suffered hemorrhage, fainted, and had to send for his wife. She in desperation called me about 6:30. Violet [Hemsley] took the message. Told me when I came in. The worst was over then, however. . . .

Monday April 20, 1931

Interviewed real estate men today and secured some interesting information from them. It seems that the depression has meant little to the Negro working for these companies because they are performing, for the most part, indispensable labor, such as janitor, porter, elevator man, or charwoman. And buildings must always be kept clean and means of locomotion furnished, if the building is kept open at all. Negroes do most of this work. One firm, the Rust Company, has at least 200 in its 80 buildings. Shannon and Links has about 70. The Herbert Company, Capritz, Brenninger and Sons, and others have similar or dissimilar numbers. In some of the big buildings, white boys run the elevators. This is the case in the Investment Building at 15th and K and several others.

Turnover is large among these workers. There are many reasons, chief of which is poor pay—$60 to $65 a month for elevator operators, $30 to $40 for janitors. Of course, he gets his quarters, but he is superintendent, janitor, elevator operator, etc., for either he or his wife must work the relief shift when the regular operator is not there. Then, lack of hope, no advancement, the fact that many persons, students, go into this work as a means to an end, working during the winter months and returning home in summer or seeking more remunerative work (all act to inflate the large turnover). There is also the humiliation of such work, especially in white apartment houses. The difference in social position is less pronounced where Negroes work for Negroes.

Naturally, there would be complaints. Some employers can't keep them on the job. Others say they are too lazy and shiftless to work. Others are prone to go to sleep on the job. The rent manager of the Rust Company told me that they stay out so late at night they are not fit to work next day. He had to fire a Negro janitor last week because he caught him asleep three times during working hours. Another complaint—and this was the first time I had actually heard a concrete case—was the failure of Negroes to stay in their place. Only last Friday, he had to fire another Negro janitor for attempting to kiss a white charwoman, even though she may have desired to be fondled by a black man. He seemed to have a well developed sense of "separaphobia" anyway. Felt that Negroes should keep to themselves, not frequent white stores like Woodward and Lothrop where they are not wanted. I remarked that the whites would not let us long remain to ourselves, even if we desired it.

One of the most significant cases of the blighting effects of the depression showed itself in the virtual wiping out of the firm of Harry Wardman and Company. A few years ago, especially when I was at college here, Wardman was the outstanding contractor in the District [of Columbia]. He built everything. As such, he employed more Negroes than any other firm in the District. He was their friend, giving them economic as well as social aid. At one time, two years ago, he employed 700 Negroes. Among them were gangs of bricklayers, carpenters, engineers, plasterers, etc. The lull in business wiped out this company. And, today, the construction manager told me, they have but four men. Pathetic but they are fighting to start again. The public ought to be with him, especially the Negro public, but then we do so little building.

A day well spent. Took B[ertha] for a ride this afternoon while I gathered information. Went to the Charles Tompkins Company but can't get information until tomorrow morning. Mae Wright, secretary to [S. W.] Rutherford, who showed me about the building last week, called. Went to see her, but she was out.

Tuesday April 21, 1931

Put some notes together early this morning for my talk to the members of the committee sponsoring the survey of unemployment among Negroes that I am now making. There were about a dozen persons present, all prominent in their several walks of life—S. W. Rutherford, chairman, President of the National Benefit Insurance Company, largest Negro-owned business in the world; John R. Hawkins, financial secretary of the A.M.E. Church, Republican committeeman, etc.; Emmett J. Scott, notorious for his secretary-treasurership of Howard University and arch-conspirator against President Mordecai Johnson; Mrs. McAdoo, executive secretary of the Y.W.C.A.; Campbell Johnson, Executive Secretary of the Y.M.C.A.; and three prominent Negro ministers. (Dr. Woodson, of course, was present.)

With a few introductory remarks, Rutherford then introduced me, telling the committee that my findings had stirred him so that he felt the entire committee should have the benefit of them.

I began by telling first of my manner of contacting white men, making them respond by informing them that we are endeavoring to increase the working efficiency of the Negro worker. It really makes them talk. Failing, I resorted to subterfuge.

To date, I told them I had interviewed about 170 employers, employing 26,000 men, of whom 6,400 were Negroes. Ratio comparable to Negro element in District population, about one-fourth.

The best opportunities for Negro employment are found in government work, 11,000 are working here; then public utilities, like gas, electrical, and street railways, with several thousand. Next came building and paving operations; laundries; lumber yards; coal yards; real estate firms (as apartment house workers, chiefly); moving and storage companies; sand, gravel, and cement companies; bottling works; and auto laundries. The latter are new industries employing Negroes in entirety, and giving work even to Negro women, who do the polishing. It seems to me that the Negro who does most of the washing and polishing of cars should have had initiative enough to have started such himself. But he is ever the "follower after" instead of the leader.

In all these industries, the Negroes are freely employed. They constitute most of the workers in laundries, in some cases up to as high as 90 percent. They do all sorts of work. In some lumber yards, only the clerical force is white. In coal yards, the same often obtains. Because of their peculiar fitness for heavy unskilled labor, in the opinion of white businessmen, Negroes do most of the laboring work on the streets for electrical and street car companies and sand, gravel, and cement companies. They do, likewise, all the bottling, but whites are the salesmen, hence get the big money.

Lesser opportunities for Negroes are found in such industries requiring more skill as bakeries, automobile garages, sales agencies, gasoline filling stations, ice cream companies, printing establishments, paper manufacturing companies, millinery companies, milling concerns, film companies, and chain stores. In these industries, either the trade unions, the policy of the company, the fear of offending white workers by hiring Negroes, or incurring the dissatisfaction of patrons, or his failure to apply, or a medley of these factors bar large numbers of Negroes from these fields of labor.

Third, there are industries which are so highly skilled or unionized so that the Negro can't get in. These are iron and steel-working plants (which perforce are small here), machine shops, cooperage plants, coppersmiths, plumbing and tinning, ice cream plants, yeast companies, and smaller and new laundries.

As to the opinion of whites concerning their Negro workers, criticism ran all the way from favorable comments such as, "they are the best workers I have ever had," to the statement that, "they are too goddamned lazy to work." Some favorable comments follow: "They are the best class of laborers." "They are desirable because they stay in their places." "You can do more with colored labor than white labor." "If you cuss out a Negro, he will be better for it on the morrow, but if you cuss a white man, he will tell you to go to hell and ask for his time. Therefore, I like the Negro because I find him easier to manage." "They are not impertinent like white men." "They are the most efficient workers I ever had." "They are honest." "They are faithful." "I would trust them with anything I have." "They are no different from white workers."

Opposed to these favorable opinions were others not so complimentary to Negro workers. An almost general complaint is that the Negro is "lazy and shiftless." One man, the superintendent of a chain store company, told me Negroes were "too goddamned lazy to work." Then told me *I* had used strong language when he read his own words, which I had taken down verbatim. (I fear much of this is true.) Others say they are "eye servants." "Whites work harder when the boss is away. Negroes loaf or sleep." Another quite general complaint is that some Negroes won't work in warm weather. Much of this is true. "They can sit in the [shade] while their women work." "They get drunk," I have heard innumerable times. One man told me that "drink is the greatest curse of the Negro race." Other complaints were that "Many Negroes won't come to work after Sundays and holidays." Thirty-three were absent from work at a large chain store warehouse on a Monday morning, much to the chagrin of the superintendent.

Dishonesty, the tendency of the Negro to undermine his own group, the failure to work a full week if the pay is raised, impertinence, and failure to stay in their place completed the criticisms of black labor. It is only fair to state that all these faults are prevalent, too, among white workers. Some employers are fair enough to admit it. Others see it as a racial trait. But in reality, it is intensified and magnified because of the racial attitudes involved.

The main obstacles in the way of Negro advancement to better jobs fell into (several) categories I gleaned from my investigation. First are those external influences, such as the attitude of the employer who is wedded to the theory that Negroes cannot do certain work. This is coupled with "policy," the custom of hiring whites for these jobs, Negroes for less desirable ones; the objection of white workers to Negroes being employed with them—bakeries, machine shops, and as clerks in department stores; the objections of the patrons, potential or actual, such as occurred at Thompson Dairy here when whites visiting the plant demanded that a Negro working at one of the milk machines be discharged. He stood out so conspicuously in his white uniform that the owner had to remove him from the job. Was the only Negro so employed. Then, the trade union. It bars the Negroes from a yeast plant—where more than 150 persons are employed laborers—in bakeries (isolated case), in printing plants, machine shops, electrical shops, tile and terrazzo work, and others. In other instances, Negroes have lost some jobs on trucks, delivery wagons for laundries, in bottling works, sand and gravel companies, etc., because whites disliked to deal with Negroes in a business way. For this reason, too, they have been forced to yield their jobs in long-distance hauling, in some instances. The feeling, then, persists among white businessmen that whites are better fitted to contact white businessmen.

To a large measure, these attitudes are deplorable in their consequences, because not only do they prevent favorably inclined white employers from hiring Negroes, but it also acts as a boomerang to them, for they could hire colored men cheaper, increasing their profits. . . .

Wednesday April 22, 1931

The most important information today was gleaned from the plant and route managers of Fairfax Farms Dairy. The latter told me that they could not use Negroes as route men because they are too unreliable. They won't come to work early in the morning. Milk must be delivered about 1:00 a.m. Negroes either having a big time or asleep. Many a time at 1:00 a.m., the manager told me, he has walked up and down Seventh Street looking for men to work the bottle machines. Has even gone to the men's homes. Such undependable labor would ruin their business, especially in face of competition from other dairies. I went away knowing they spoke true and feeling almost helpless because of that knowledge. Woodson marveled at this information. Could not get questionnaire at Chestnut Farms Diary.

Took B[ertha] for a ride in the afternoon.

Thursday April 23, 1931

Interviewed several plumbers today. Negroes find almost no opportunity in this work, not even as helpers. The excuse is this trade is highly unionized. Negroes are used to dig the ditches, etc., before the plumber begins work. An awning company official also told me that he can't use Negroes. First, there are very few awning makers here. The chief reason, however, is that women do most of the work and the manager, a Southerner, feels that it is not wise to mix the races.

Saw Lelia Coleman tonight. Nice looking, brown-skin girl. As supple as a snake. Wild. Danced with and for me. Sent me into emotional tantrums by the way she twisted her body. Her mother is very liberal. Cautioned her daughter that she ought not do the "slaps" for me, then went out so that she could. A slow, rhythmic dance in which everything rises except the feet. She is as lithe as a serpent.

Friday April 24, 1931

Conference on Negro Housing met today at the Department of Commerce. Is Negro end of President Hoover's Conference on Home Building and Home Ownership. Miss Nannie Burroughs is chairman. Details are given in another booklet.[1] Charles Johnson, T. Arnold Hill, Zack Hubert, (and) President [Joseph S.] Clark of New Orleans University [Southern University, Baton Rouge, Louisiana] in attendance.

We were presented to President Hoover at the White House at 12:40. Received us in the Reception Room. Greeted us affably as we filed by and shook his hand. Told the man ahead of me, Mr. Leon Harris from Moline, Illinois, to do a good job on this survey. Hoover has not the features of a man of strength. Not impressive as chief executive. Does not manifest that indomitable will of Teddy Roosevelt, nor the academic lines of a [Woodrow] Wilson. A good-natured, smiling, middle-class man who might pass for a prosperous restauranteur, or even saloon keeper, was the impression I gleaned.

[No entry was found for Saturday, April 25.]

Sunday April 26, 1931

The Mickeys invited me to breakfast this morning. Spent several hours chatting afterwards. Mr. Mickey has been bothered with a bad tooth. We decided to go to the baseball game, or rather I did. Mickey could not go. Saw New York put up a stupid brand of baseball. In the first inning, [Lou] Gehrig hit a home run with [Lyn] Lary on first. The latter ran from third to the dugout without touching home plate. Consequently, the umpire called Gehrig out for theoretically passing Lary on the base lines. Yankees thus lost two runs. Then Dusty Cooke, playing right field for New York, slid on the wet grass and dislocated his collar bone. Bereft of outfielders, [Joe] McCarthy had to put [Charlie] Ruffing, a pitcher, in the outfield. Later in the game, with a chance to tie the score, Rice ran [Ben] Chapman off 3rd

1. Probably another of Greene's notebooks.

base. Such juvenile baseball. The Yankees lost 9 to 7, by the margin of the two runs they threw away in the first inning.

MONDAY APRIL 27, 1931

Finally succeeded in getting the information from Thompkins Construction Company. Told by an official that they hire a goodly number of Negroes, not as many as formerly. Do all kinds of work—cement finishers, bricklayers, engineers. Felt that Negro as union man abuses privilege, that unionization destroys, to some extent, the working efficiency of the black laborer. Asked why, the official told me that they begin to take advantage of the company. Told me he had a Negro union man who ran a compressor. Was listed as an engineer. One morning they wanted to get up steam early for a job. Compressor needed repairing. Union rules state that the engineer must be on the job at all hours that compressor is working. The Negro was asleep. Coming on the job about 7:00 and finding that the machine was running, he promptly put in a bill for $3.50 which, according to union rules, was due him for the time the air compressor had been in operation. This claim, just enough, however, inexpedient, so irked this official that the man was summarily discharged and every time this official sees his name on an employment slip, he "blackballs" him. Wonder what he would have done had it been a white man? Paid it, no doubt.

Leaving there, I went to Blue Plains, the school for incorrigible Negro boys, to see if I could induce Mr. Tucker and his teachers to contribute anything to the drive for the Association. Told me would do something. Did not know how much. Listed many reasons why he could not give much. His father had recently died. Mother looked to him for things, while not actually dependent upon him. Moreover, many of the twenty-nine teachers had been ill. Yet withal, he, as I knew, expressed an active interest in the Association and promised that he would do all in his power to help us. Asked me to bring some literature, which I promised to do tomorrow.

Returned to Washington. Went to the game. Nearly froze as New York and Washington played a twelve-inning game, which Washington finally won after the Yankees had twice sewn up the game.

TUESDAY APRIL 28, 1931

Kirlen called me this morning. Took him to breakfast, but first hurried off to the Griffith Consumers Company to secure information from one of the Griffith brothers. He has about eighty Negro truck drivers. In fact, all their trucks are manned by Negroes. Get drunk, shoot craps, etc. Most of these are the floaters who come in to make a little money to tide them over a few days. The regular hands are sober, industrious, honest, and home lovers. Asked whether he could employ Negroes as coal salesmen, Mr. Griffith responded that he had never thought [of] such a procedure, but he assured me that if I could furnish proof that they were being successfully used in that capacity elsewhere, he would gladly hire them. Told me that it would require different types of salesmen for different localities—for instance, a suave, intelligent, and cultured person for Le Droit Park and other fashionable sections and a man more nearly approximating the level of such Negroes as here in Southwest. Didn't actually believe this necessary. Then, too, Mr. Griffith felt that Negroes seemed to prefer dealing with whites. Have more confidence in them. I told him otherwise, although I knew I was falsifying.

Later went to the Elite Laundry. Here I received a very stinging criticism of the Negro. Before I had time even to ask the manager, Mr. Gardiner, about the possibilities of Negroes getting better jobs in his establishment, he exclaimed with considerable heat: "You know as well as I that your people will not work under one another. There is more prejudice among your own group than between the whites and blacks. I have a young fellow here who is capable of being a foreman, but every time I have sought to elevate him to that position the envy and jealousy of his own people have made it impossible. Then, I have another colored girl who is very bright. Sometimes she does clerical work for me. She ought to be a supervisor or the like. But the colored girls won't stand for it. I have never experienced such attitudes. Then, you ask, can they secure better positions? They stand in their own light. Those who won't accept responsibility refuse to allow others to do so. Can work under a white but not a Negro."

Pointed and acrid as were his words, justice and fairness prompted me to agree with him that it is true. I have seen and heard too much about it. Mr. Gardiner was also in bad humor over a dinner given by the Elite Laundry workers where Mrs. McAdoo, Secretary of the Y.M.C.A. where the banquet took place, compelled whites and blacks to sit together at the same table. Gardiner felt that it was a liberal step for the two to eat in the same dining room at different tables and that a common table might be worked up to gradually. You can't cram an idea into a person overnight. Customs of long standing cannot be eliminated in a moment. These attitudes are the result of centuries of thinking and implantation of ideas—puerile and inconvenient and obnoxious to us as they are. But public opinion must undergo a metamorphosis without force. We can assist but not coerce. He called Mrs. McAdoo "a white nigger." [Gardiner] said, "I realize that as long as the white man lives, the presence of the mulatto will always remain a living evidence of his sin."

Received some more interesting information from the American Ice Company. Tells me that the company will not hire Negroes on their ice routes because the driver must deliver ice when the family is out. He must, therefore, be honest, for he has the keys either to their homes or to their apartments. These absent housekeepers feel that a white man is more honest and reliable, thus the exclusion of the Negro. The official hastened to assure me, however, he did not mean Negroes were not honest. On the contrary, he declared, he would prefer Negro drivers. They show less initiative than the white ones and won't quit your service to go into business for themselves, taking your customers with them. Thirteen to fourteen white drivers did that last year. It hurt us. Sam Blick, another ice man, won't employe white drivers for this reason.

Wednesday April 29, 1931

Got returns, finally, from the Chestnut Farms Dairy Company. Have Negroes, about seventy-eight of them, in many capacities. Most of them, however, are laborers either about the plant or garage. Some are drivers-salesmen, others special delivery truck drivers. Had a task getting this data. Went there until I was ashamed to bother the girl at the information desk.

My friend Roy Plummer, M.D., gave me $5.00 toward the campaign this morning. He was about to send in $1.00.

Received data from the Bailey Sign Company and the Wall Paper Company. Both of these have laid off men recently.

Saw I____ this afternoon. Told me that she often thinks of December 15, 1929. Assured me that I gave her the greatest sexual stimulation she had ever experienced. She even feared lest she cry out my name in the arms of her husband.

Saw Mrs. Mickey. Informs me she will have her tonsils removed Saturday. Is quite depressed. I assured her she has naught to fear. Don't believe she has TB. Both she and her husband are very kind to me.

Thursday April 30, 1931

Received some surprising information today concerning the tile and mosaic business here. Italians control about 75 percent of the work. They have virtually driven out the (other) whites. No Negroes work at the trade. Can't join the unions. Simply frozen out. Work calls for great skill, therefore, few Negro mosaic workers. Electrical and plumbing contractors, too, have no Negroes for the same reason. Union blocks them. Some of these plumbers, however, will employ them as plasterers.

Another interesting bit of information came from the Harris Jewelry Company, largest jewelers south of Philadelphia. Here a Negro shipping clerk is employed with about thirty Negroes under him. Was glad to learn he had no trouble with them. Desiring to find out why Negro jewelers were not hired, I asked the shipping clerk to take me to the workshop. He did. The foreman received me affably as I interviewed him and the workman at the bench. Was told Negro jewelers are few. Union does not exclude them here, for there is no union. Disbanded several years ago because they could not have apprentices and guarantee them a certain scale of wages and, at the same time, be responsible for any articles they might ruin. An old German jeweler told me he once worked beside a Negro in New York. Was a German from one of the African colonies. Had learned trade in Germany. Was exceedingly efficient.

From a window washing company, the American, I learned they have thirty-five men. Fired whites. Now have all Negroes. Can make as high as $9.00 a day.

Called on Mae Wright, Rutherford's secretary, tonight. Small, slim, exceedingly so. Has beautiful hair, worn in a long bob parted in the center. Very engaging and charming personality. Only thing mars her are pock marks on her face. Passion, yea God! She responded to my kisses like a leaf caught in a typhoon. She shook, her eyes half closed, her breathing became labored, she pushed me from her only to draw me to her time and again. She shuddered as I kissed her lips, her eyes, her neck. She finally told me as I was leaving that she had best see me next December when the weather is cold. Mutual passion. But what is life without it?

Friday May 1, 1931

Interviewed construction companies and window washers. One employed no Negroes. Said they wouldn't work. Another employed three-fourths Negroes in total force. Construction managers tell conflicting stories. All hit by depression. Largest loser, Hyman, had 200 Negroes last year. Has none now. Not even bidding on jobs. Out-of-town firms are underbid[ding] local contractors. Employ rebate system of wages. Pay men union wages, ostensibly. Day after payday, men return certain amount. In reality, are scabs. Hyman would not have nerve to do it. One construction company, Breninger, employs Negro bricklayers at union wages. Union Paving Company, on other hand, pays them 62½ cents an hour for cement finishing, while the Pittman Company pays Negroes union wages of $1.25 an hour for the same work. All of which shows the exploitation of the Negro worker. Take advantage of their labor's helplessness.

Saw I____ tonight. How alluring! Nearly took away my breath. . . .

Saw Mrs. M[ickey]. Told me she was going to the hospital tomorrow. Fears she has TB. I believe she is more nervous than anything else. Asked me to take her.

25
In Retrospect

[AUGUST 1931]

Since May, [the] notations in my diary have been very haphazard. This was due to several causes: 1) the writing up of the survey, which left precious little opportunity for other epistolary efforts; 2) mental fatigue induced by working nights as well as days on the above mentioned study in an effort to leave Washington by July 1; 3) social engagements, which have demanded my attention and to which I have inclined more regularly than hitherto; 4) one particular object of my attention who has been paramount in the absorption of my time.

Despite the absence of such jottings, several interesting and personal happenings have occurred since my last communings. I list them and comment as follows:

On the seventeenth of June, (1931), the Negro newspapers appeared with glaring headlines, stating that R. S. Rutherford and S. W. Rutherford, president and secretary-treasurer, respectively, of the National Benefit Life Insurance Company, the largest business owned and operated by Negroes, had been ousted by the board of directors.[1] This was indeed shocking information, for had not the old man, "S. W.," founded, fathered, and built up the company to its present greatness? It was the only Negro organization that gave regular employment to hundreds of the race. I felt that something must be wrong. Woodson expressed the same fear upon his return from Atlantic City at the end of the week. Said it had upset him greatly.

It later developed that the Rutherfords—father and son—had been charged with misappropriation of certain benefit monies; that they had

1. For an example of coverage by the African American press, see *Norfolk Journal and Guide,* July 18, 1931, 7.

formed a syndicate, consisting of themselves and Mortimer Smith, the comptroller of the company; and had sold the same, ostensibly as National Benefit stock, but the returns accrued to Rutherford, Smith, and Rutherford. More scandal! Too bad.

Terrible blow to Negroes' confidence in race business. Never thought such of Rutherford. Then, upon the announcement of the resignation of the Rutherfords, the white actuary of the company, [Alfred] Dawson of New York, committed suicide. John T. Risher, a racketeering lawyer and real estate man, was elected president. He promised an investigation, threatened to prosecute the Rutherfords, but soon backed down when confronted with the accusation that he had actually condoned, while a member of the board of directors, the actions of the Rutherfords. Although the Rutherfords are out, Risher either had to back down, or relinquish his office as president and even stand trial. Evidently, he chose the former, for in some mysterious manner all indictments against the Rutherfords are suddenly quashed.

Still, the upheaval has hurt the company, for Georgia, Texas, and one or more Southern states have called upon the company to show cause why it should continue business in these states. In Georgia and another state, a receivership was appointed. A sad mess, with the new president so involved that he could not prosecute the culprits without injuring himself, credit impaired, and confidence in a once great institution shattered.

A little before this debacle, John R. Hawkins, president of the Association for the Study of Negro Life and History, resigned. I certainly had anticipated it, for only an insensate human could have endured the thrusts of Woodson's pen. The latter had stigmatized Hawkins as a cheap, venal politician in league with (Emmett J.) Scott, (Judge) Cobb, and others to oust (Mordecai) Johnson and, thus, discredit not only the head of a great race institution, but the race itself. So caustic had become Woodson's written comments about these men, and Hawkins included, even to the calling of their names, that I felt it would only be a question of time before Hawkins, out of a sense of self-respect, would have to resign.[2]

2. John R. Hawkins was president of the National Negro Republican League, and Woodson's criticism of the involvement of members of the league in efforts to remove Mordecai Johnson as president of Howard University angered Hawkins. In his letter of resignation, Hawkins said: "As president of the National Negro Republican League, I know that it has in no way by word or act attempted to exploit any institution, and your charge is without foundation." He continued: "As president of the Association for the Study of Negro Life and History, I feel that your conduct in this matter is wrong, unjust and injurious, and the way you are prostituting the office of the director of the Association for the Study of Negro Life and History leads me to feel that I can, as president, no longer approve of such

I don't know what has come over Woodson. His diatribes against influential persons certainly do not redound to the advantage of the Association, however calculated to do so. Yet, every week, in every Negro newspaper, there appear these releases, which, instead of imparting historical information, have degenerated into the veriest of muckraking. The Association is losing friends, when it stands in direst need of funds. Yet, it seems that Woodson is intently bent upon wrecking the very edifice which by his own sacrifices and the philanthropy of others he has erected. This has led some people to the conclusion that Woodson is crazy. And he does do many things which the obviously sane man would eschew.

Anyway, Hawkins resigned on June 13. Woodson received the letter in Atlantic City. I waited until Tuesday to get his reaction. It was that Hawkins's resignation was a blessing, this coming fast upon an expression of regret. Then, a tirade against Hawkins. He was a trickster, a philanderer. He was woman-crazy, and actually kept a woman in an apartment in D.C., which was common knowledge to everyone. In self-righteous indignation, he added "I could not be as Hawkins, Scott, and others who sell their race and their souls for a mess of pottage." And with this, he turned up his nose in the characteristic Woodson fashion.

Just before going to West Virginia, I was taking him to the station. During the course of our conversation, he promised me a salary for July, told me that my fellowship from last year had been renewed, and informed me that John Hope, President of Atlanta University, had been elected president of the Association. Oh, yes, just what difference Rutherford's tenure of secretary-treasurership of the Association will make in light of his present misfortunes it is difficult to say. Frankly, however, I am glad to see a churchman's name erased from the presidency of the Association, even though it is but an office of show.

Sunday August 16, 1931

Spent the day prosaically enough. T_____ [Edna] was invited to breakfast by the M[ickey]s. Later played golf. Elated at my driving, although I suffered a corresponding reversion in mashie and putter play. Lolled about the park for couple of hours. Home. Read over chapters of survey in conjunction with M_____ and T_____. Latter works along faithfully with me. Love? After dinner a friend of B_____'s came in. Took them for drive. Later returned

---

conduct, and that it is my duty to resign from the office as president of said association." *Baltimore Afro-American,* June 20, 1931, 1.

home. Danced quite familiarly with L_____. She resented it, but B_____ had asked her to be nice to his friend. Starts many a woman on the wrong path. . . .

We leave for Hampton tomorrow.

26

Third Summer Selling Trek

Monday August 17, 1931

Today resumes my third summer selling trek in five years. Got books, etc., ready, directed girls at office where to send mail, and instructed Miss De Mond (Dr. Woodson's secretary) to send me the copy of the concluding chapter of the survey as soon as it is ready. Woodson wants to know where I am. Told girl to tell him I had gone to Hampton. I don't even feel that I should inform him personally, since his attitude before leaving for Atlantic City was hardly calculated to induce me to do so. In fact, I felt rather like telling him to go to hell.

Returned home preparatory to leaving at 12:20. Both T____ (Edna) [Gaines] and M____ (Mayme)[White] out. T____'s (Edna's) daughter (Barbara) had come down this morning. Seven years old. Looked decidedly better than when I saw her in the winter. Informed [James] B[rowning] we could not leave until about 2:00. T____ (Edna) returned at that time. Had to dress. I was impatient.

At 4:30, Mayme had not come. Finally called, saying car was being overhauled. We decided to leave at midnight. B____ (Browning) and I played golf. B[rowning] is excellent driver. Mine was good in spots. Decided to take our clubs with us.

Returned. Saw L____ (Lillian) and B____ (Bushrod Mickey). Hated to leave them. Both seemed loath to have me go. Caught a few hours' sleep from 9:30 to 12:55.

M____ (Mayme) continually whined she was not going. Got both T____ (Edna) and me out of patience. Had to make up her mind for her. Left.

TUESDAY AUGUST 18, 1931

Left Washington at 1:00 a.m. Taking T____ (Edna) with me, filled me with apprehension as to my ability to see Marguerite (Skeeter) in Suffolk. But, perhaps it can be arranged.

My car held books, B____ (Barbara), T____ (Edna), and I. M____ (Mayme) took the luggage in her car.

Arrived at Hampton 8:15, without incident. Then the fun started between T____ (Edna) and M____ (Mayme). The latter wanted to eat before finding lodgings. T____ (Edna) desired to find accommodations first, in order that she might wash and change clothes. M____ (Mayme) sulked. Then they went to the Bayside Hotel at Buckroe Beach. Here they inquired of a room. It was $21.50 for the week. They would put in a cot for B____ (Barbara). E____ (Edna) felt it was too much. Told M____ (Mayme). She flew off. Told T____ (Edna) she had made a fool of her.

I counseled staying with a private family in the interest of their purses. T____ (Edna) took my suggestion. Back to the campus. I saw the commandant, Captain [Walter R.] Brown, who referred me to private homes in Phoebus and Hampton.

M____ (Mayme) then complained of her car. Water was leaking. Still wanted to eat first and then wanted the car repaired before finding lodgings. Directed her to campus garage. Then T____ (Edna), who had B____ (Barbara) on her hands and who had become exasperated with M____'s (Mayme's) childlike antics, asked me to take her to one of the homes that she might get located. And she did not want to be with M____ [Mayme].

There I was now between two fires. Told M____ (Mayme) I would locate places for them and they could meet us (Browning and me) in Phoebus. Where Captain Brown had directed us, no one was home. A neighbor, however, directed us to a Mrs. [J. I.] Fountain. T____ (Edna) got a room there. Accommodations tentatively were made around the corner for M____ (Mayme).

When she drove up, however, she became incensed because T____ (Edna) had not waited to take a room together. Pouted, said she was going home. In reality, I didn't give a damn so exasperated was I. Yet, I urbanely informed her that I had made arrangements for her and regretted her decision to return to D.C. However, I removed all our luggage from her car. B____ (Barbara) was tired. I, tired, dirty, and unwell and my patience was fast approaching the breaking point.

Took B____ (Browning) to a restaurant in Hampton. It was dark, dismal, dirty, a typical (Southern Negro) place, the best offered. Oh, it's uncomfortable and inconvenient to be a Negro at times. I couldn't eat.

Returned to T____'s (Edna's) home. There sat M____ (Mayme) in the car after an hour and a half. Asked if she had come in to see T____ (Edna). Replied she had. Expected T____ (Edna) to come to her. Informed her T____ (Edna) did not even know she was there. Left her. Went home. Lay across bed and slept. B____ (Browning) woke me about 1:30 to tell me she (Mayme) decided to stay. Had a room next door to us. We stayed in Hampton at Dr. [William E.] Atkins's. Jesse, the daughter, was a classmate of mine.

Both of us (Browning and I) were disgusted. B____ [Browning] was a rank stranger (a history teacher at Miner Teachers' College,[1] who, lured by my experiences at Hampton last summer, wanted to earn a few dollars selling books). I determined from this time on never again to bother with women on business trips.

After a nap, tried to find the golf course. Went to the wrong one. A Negro boy advised us not to go in because attorney ____ was practicing. It was a whites golf course. Thought it extremely well kept for a Negro course.

Returned, took T____ (Edna) and B____ (Barbara) in an effort to find dinner. I had drunk citrate of magnesia. It had not acted, therefore, I did not want dinner. Got hot tea. What a place to drink it in. Old boards that showed unpainted on the in- as well as the outside. An oil lamp burning. Water three cents a glass. Must be scarce here or rather these places do not have city water and are not progressive enough to have an artisan well.

Sat and watched the waves for a while. They were beautiful as they rolled shoreward. They displayed opalescent colors of blue, green, and white. It was a gorgeous sight against the blackness of the water and the heavens. Went to bed about 11:00.

Wednesday August 19, 1931

Called upon Mr. [Albert O.] Goodale, director of the summer school, after breakfast. Gave me permission not only to set up an exhibit, but also wanted me to address the summer school. Had no time to prepare, for five minutes after leaving his office, it was time for assembly.

Told the students the purpose of Negro History, the reasons for and some achievements of Negroes, and the means of disseminating this knowledge. They listened very attentively. Received many congratulations afterward from both white and black. An African especially congratulated me because I dwelt to some extent on African contributions.

1. In 1930, James Browning was listed as a member of the history faculty at Howard University.

Will put up an exhibit tomorrow. Did nothing, particularly in the afternoon. It rained. Bought fish, had them cooked. Then M_____ [Mayme] and B_____ [Browning] ordered something else.

Went to bridge party and dance at Parker's Auditorium in the evening. Met a few folks, particularly a Miss Wyche.

Thursday August 20, 1931

Set up an exhibit in Ogden Hall this morning. Teachers swamped the stand after chapel. Interested, but few of them have any money. Was forced to cut the deposits from $4.00 to $2.00 on the large set. Most of the teachers, although they could take a smaller set at a correspondingly smaller down payment, yet preferred the larger combination. Experienced the same efforts of teachers to purchase books as last year. Many are from rural districts where salaries are small, yet have spent ten weeks in summer school. Consequently, they are unable, offhand, to make arrangements for books. Yet wanting them, they ask for various considerations. Some desire the books forwarded $9.98 C.O.D. Others wanted the deposit reduced. Still others would like to get them after school starts. Others, more ambitious, see an opportunity of getting these books in Negro county schools. In fact, several county supervisors spoke to me concerning such. They want me to address their county institutes. One told me she had 71 teachers, all of whom would no doubt buy. Another suggested that I come to North Carolina in the winter to speak to them, at which time they would pay expenses.

Met Mrs. Espey, sister-in-law of Naomi Espey, an old Howard University sweetheart. Looks like an Indian; in fact, she is part Indian. Quite friendly. Wants to see me. I made arrangements to take her out tonight. Do so, but it rains. Great God! How it rained! Descended in such sheets that the streets ran deep with water. I could not drive. Did not get beyond the gate. Revels in the fact that she is married and is true to her husband.

Car went bad. Water got in the distributor. Could not get it started and ruined the battery trying to do so. Had to be towed more than three miles. In vain, however. It only started after a mechanic had worked upon it for an hour. All the while, Mrs. Espey was highly perturbed, fearful that she would not get back to the dormitory on time. She was due back at five minutes of ten. Cost me $2.00, but I got her to her dormitory on time.

Went back to Mrs. Fountain's to see E_____ (Edna). M_____ (Mayme) and B_____ (Browning) were parked in front of the house. E_____ (Edna) sat in the back seat. The former (Mayme and Browning) seem to get along famously. Rode around a while and went home about 12:00. Sold four sets of books.

Friday August 21, 1931

Rainy and cold again today. I shall certainly appreciate the sunshine, if it ever comes out again. Teachers again! How pitiful some of them look! So suppressed, so downtrodden, with fear and timidity written upon their features. Not all of them, however, present this aspect, for some have aggressiveness, assurance, capability, and even sophistication stamped upon them. These are mainly city teachers and are easily distinguishable from the more underprivileged rural school workers.

Sold four sets of books today. Collected eleven dollars. E____ (Edna) was more or less elated with the day, while I could not share her reaction. To me it was a dull day.

Went to call upon the Reverend Mr. [B. H.] Johnson, pastor of the Queen Street Baptist Church. Is a big, sleek, well-fed, dark-complexioned man. Laughed, wisecracked, pleaded lack of money, took no books. Gave me an interesting sidelight on industrial conditions in Hampton. Most of the men work either in the Newport News shipyard, at the government stations, such as Fortress Monroe, Langley Field, or at Soldiers Home in Pheobus. Others fish and crab or work as common laborers. Now, however, work in the shipyards has lagged. The fishing, crabbing, clamming, and oystering industries are becoming smaller each year due to the exhaustion of the beds. This minimizes chances of employment for Negro men. As a result, according to Reverend Johnson, Negro women virtually support their households in Hampton. They work in domestic service as maids, cooks, and the like. Others find employment in the crab factories as pickers, preparatory to the canning of the same; still others open clams or shuck oysters. According to Reverend Johnson, some of these women earn from $4.00 to $5.00 a day, being paid 5 cents a pound for all crab meat picked.

Went to the wharf with Reverend Johnson to get some fresh crab meat. For the first time I had an opportunity to see how crab meat was canned. The building itself was only a shack with a concrete floor. The live crabs are first packed in a giant steel basket which holds about a half-ton. This is then raised by means of a crane and lowered into an enormous cylindrical iron vat through which steam circulates. The vat is then tightly closed, the steam turned on. After a certain space of time, the basket is lifted out of the steam bath and the crabs are strewn along a long table. Women, sitting on wide benches, pick out the crab meat. Negro women and girls furnish the labor. They make fairly good wages at crab picking. They are paid, the foreman told me, 5 cents a pound for the meat, and added that a good picker can pick 100 to 150 pounds a day, thus earning from $5.00 to $7.50 daily. The foreman then conducted me into another room where the actual canning takes place. This work is done by whites (two white men). It is cleaner.

Much oystering also is done here, and Negroes play an important part in the industry. It is chiefly a winter industry. Shucking is usually done by Negroes. They get 35 cents a gallon and can make between $3.00 to $4.00 a day. The company that I was visiting cans crabs in summer and oysters in winter. Not as much money can be made shucking oysters now, I was told, because not only are the oyster beds becoming fewer, but oysters are smaller. Clam opening also furnishes occupations for many Negroes. According to the foreman, they are paid 30 cents a gallon for them. A clam opener makes more than an oyster shucker, first, because the clams are larger and second, because they are more plentiful. A good opener can amass from 20 to 25 gallons at the end of a day's work, which means from $6.00 to $7.50 earned.

Promised to take Edna to a dance at Parker's. Given for tennis players. Took her home, then I went to the library to abstract Gordon Hancock's article on the changing status of Negro labor for *Social Science Abstracts* of Columbia University. Nothing new in it. Abstracted it in one sentence. Home, dressed, returned for E_____ (Edna). Did not enjoy myself. E_____ (Edna) did not dance. I danced once with Miss Wyche. But just as I entered, Mrs. Espey from Florida left to get back on the campus at 11:00 and the other Miss Wyche was engaged.

Told E_____ (Edna) she would be paid $3.00 a day for her services. Refused, but I was adamant. Told her she could not assist me under other circumstances. After many remonstrances, she finally became silent, as she usually does when she does not wish to anger me. I do not want to feel obligated to her. Neither do I wish her to remind me of her gratuitous services at some future date.

SATURDAY AUGUST 22, 1931

Cold and rainy again today. Business was almost nil. We collected but $1.00 for a copy of *African Myths.*

Took Mrs. Espey to the Community Center in the afternoon. Failed to see Mr. Bowman, the director. Also failed to find Mr. [William S.] Parker, the druggist. [R. Nathaniel] Dett advises me to stay for music convention.

Had trouble with the car after taking E_____ (Edna) and B_____ (Barbara) to movies at Ogden Hall. Came out, starter would not work. Had to crank it. Late getting back for E_____ (Edna). Was standing in the rain. Patient as ever, never fusses because of my tardiness. By the time she had put B_____ (Barbara) to bed, dressed and gone for Miss _____, a soror, it was eleven o'clock when we arrived at the dance. I got one dance only. Certainly did not enjoy myself.

Returned, sat out in the car until about 3:00 a.m., then could not start the car. Would have remained there indefinitely had not a car bringing someone home where Edna lives given me a shove. I am thoroughly exasperated with the car.

SUNDAY AUGUST 23, 1931

Rose at 12:00. Went to dinner. Ate heartily. Met several musicians, among them Mr. Hill of Indianapolis; Miss Smith of Terre Haute, and Miss ____ of Indianapolis. Also caught a glimpse of a pretty black girl whom I took at first glance to be Miss [Lillian?] Carter, a young lady of Phoebus who promised to take a set of books from me.

Browning and Mayme left after dinner for D.C. Foolish of Browning, I thought, since possibilities were bright for his doing business here. Will see him in D.C. next week. Rode around for a while. 'Twas cold, rainy. Felt more like going to bed and told E____ (Edna) so. Met Captain [Earl] Wilson, Hill, and others. E____ (Edna) suggested a party. Wilson named Parker's place, but could not go there until 9:30. He had engagement with Mrs. E____. I had to speak. Hill had to sing. We arranged, therefore, to get together at Parker's at 9:30.

Talk at [J. W.] Patterson's church seemed to grip people. The Reverend wants to arrange a special meeting for me some time later in the fall. His wife told me I made her feel that the Negro had done everything. Woodson would be pleased to hear it.

Met at Parker's. He has a nice party room over his drug store. Played cards, danced. Folks wanted fire water. W____ [Wilson?] took them to Buckroe Beach where they got it. Edna drank, then had to go out and sit on a railing. Water was beautiful, but black. Waves, starting out like tiny, white lights, rolled inland unceasingly. I picked up shells and dispensed them to the group. Returned to Parker's. E____ (Edna) and I leave about 3:00 a.m. Terrible hours. All this makes me feel I must break loose from E____ (Edna) or ruin my health.

MONDAY AUGUST 24, 1931

Opening morning of the convention. Our exhibit in Ogden Hall proves an attraction to the delegates. We are frequently mistaken for musicians. By the way, when we arrived this morning, the janitor had removed our tables. Thought we had gone. Had to replace them.

Met many interesting people today: Mr. and Mrs. Carl Diton, famous musicians; Miss [Lillian] Le Mon, the President of the Convention; Mr. B. K. Thomas of New York City; Mr. Kemper Herrold, famous violinist; and others. The most outstanding one in my estimation, however, was a Miss Lenora Pritchett, a beautiful, black girl from New York City. She is a social worker, the executive secretary at the Utopia (Children's) House on W. 130 Street. She is beautiful, with large expressive eyes and a charming personality. Her voice is like music. She inquired where to purchase tickets for the convention activities and, through this informal channel of introduction, we became acquainted. Was drawn to her immediately. Is about my height, a little plump, well formed, but her personality captivated me. Asked her whether she had seen much of this section. She answered negatively. I, thereupon, offered my services to show her some of the beauty of Hampton and its environs. She graciously accepted. Promised to see her at 6:00 p.m.

The delegates are intensely interested in the books. Not only do they subscribe, but some have even suggested that I tell the convention about them. Spoke to Miss Le Mon. She told me she would try to make a place for me on the program tomorrow. Edna is also trying to arrange such through Mrs. Diton.

We had an unpleasant occurrence at chapel time while a program was being rendered. E_____ (Edna) has become interested in the work. Wants to have her mother come for B_____ (Barbara), which will enable her to travel with me through the county selling books. I flatly told her I would not take a woman with me in this work. Asked why, I told her that the presence of a woman handicapped a man who had to depend to a great extent for success on social contacts. Women buy more books than men, and women do so largely upon sentiment. If a man is unencumbered by a woman, local ladies will assist him in putting over his proposition. But they must have attention; and he cannot give it to them, if he brings a woman with him who likewise is expecting the same. Then, too, there is the question of morality, public opinion, Woodson, the Association. To this E_____ (Edna) said she didn't care, but I am concerned with what construction the public would put upon my traveling with a woman. She cited motor trips to Philadelphia by fellows and girls, as instances, but I overrode those as irrelevant. They do not go before the public.

Then she made it personal. Told me I would not take her, but I would take Mayme [White] and Violet [Hemsley]. I laughed, it was so ridiculous. Added, I would take no woman with me. Then she did just what I hoped she would not have done. Asked me why had I accepted her services here? Told her she forced them upon me and I was paying her for her assistance. Asked why I did not remunerate her for reading the manuscript upon which she worked harder than selling books? Told her that was a favor any one of the girls I know would have been happy to do for me. To have offered them pay would have been tantamount to an insult. Reminded her, too, that she read a chapter whenever she felt so-minded. But regardless of what she said or felt, under no consideration would I take her or any other woman on a bookselling trip with me. She restrained her tears as best she could in my presence, then got up and bounded outside. I was so angry, I felt like refusing to even permit her to sit behind the table. But she does not long remain angry at me. In fact, she coddles me so, I forget my anger.

Tuesday August 25, 1931

Books selling well. I am to speak in the morning. The dance. We fuss again.

E_____ (Edna) won't go. Tells me she is in my way. I don't admit she is not. Felt I wanted to take Miss P_____ [Lenora Pritchett], which is true. E_____ (Edna) says she will wait for me to give her a ride after the dance.

Arrived at dance. Take and meet Miss P_____ [Pritchett]. Dance. We go to Old Point. Unforgettable beauty. Remain until 12:45.

Returned. Took E_____ (Edna) for ride to Buckroe Beach. Love. Home at 3:30.

Wednesday August 26, 1931

Sit from 9:00–12:00 in the convention hall awaiting an opportunity to speak. Delegates reporting so long-winded don't get chance. Go over to Ogden Hall. E_____ (Edna) has had no breakfast. Dett induces me to return. Mrs. Le Mon introduced me. Time short. I speak about eight minutes. Met Mrs. [Carrie Booker] Person from Tulsa. Result, several musicians bought books.

See Lenora. Overslept at 10:00. Sorry she could not hear me. I play golf for a little while. Edna arranges it for me.

Concert at night splendid. Miss Harmon fine artist. Boat ride. Delightful. Lenora and I separated, yet yearned for one another. We slip off. Have poem to her. Can't read it. Tell her of it. She is excited and pleased. I promise to read it to her tomorrow. Water is beautiful. E_____ (Edna) and I fuss again. Tells me I only want people who will do something for me. Want her for sex only. [She] said I told her that in park in D.C. Infuriates me. She weeps and begs my pardon. Said I would not like Lenora if she could not assist me.

Thursday August 27, 1931

Lenora and I steal a march. Go to Soldiers Home. I read poetry to her. She is supposed to leave at noon. Yet, I see her in the afternoon. She lives with a Miss Chaplain, a splendid woman. Meet Miss Freeman.

Removed exhibit. (The Hampton City) librarian tells me she will put in order. Also will hire a Negro assistant. Mr. Turner takes *Wage Earner* book.

Is to be billed for $2.00 in October. Mr. Goodale is given *Wage Earner.* Feels Negro History best means of uplifting race. Take boat ride. Later go for ride. E____ (Edna) gives me up to L____ [Lenora]. We are happy.

Friday August 28, 1931

We leave for Norfolk. Arrived about 12:00. Am given list of names. Taken to Mary Cook's out in (a beautiful suburb of the city). Met Mr. Brooks, a real estate man here. Gives me important information on housing. Return. Meet Evelyn Lightener. Taken for ride by Cook.

Saturday August 29, 1931

Mrs. Lightener took me to meet Mrs. Fuller, Miss Brown, Mrs. Palters, and Reverend [Richard H.] Bowling. They take books. I go to Berkeley. Meet Dr. [G. Hamilton] Francis, who takes combination. Meet Reverend [J. C.] Diamond. Will speak at union meeting tomorrow night. Will go to Berkeley tomorrow morning to see a Mr. Reid. Meet Dr. Francis, former member of child welfare commission. West Indian, fine man. Impressed me. Takes set. Doctor refers me to Reverend Diamond and [J. A.] Valentine. Former of the old school. Has nice home. Plenty of children. He, himself, is large, tall, spare. Sort of "Uncle Tomish." Wants me to speak at the union meeting of churches tomorrow night in South Norfolk. Sends me to Reverend Valentine who is presiding officer, spare, thin, excellent talker. More intelligent than Diamond. About [Charles H.] Wesley's age. Glad to have me tomorrow. Can't give honorarium. Choir will get receipts. I'll go anyway. Will at least be opportunity to spread Negro History gospel.

Meet a Mr. Reid, postal service man. Has fine home. Well read. Will see me tomorrow afternoon. Will have more time to look over books. Things cheap here. Watermelons five and ten cents. People can't give them away. Cantaloupes and potatoes [are] drags on hands of farmers.

Back to town. Take dinner. Have suit pressed. See E____ (Edna). Take her for a ride. First time, she reminds me, I have kissed her in forty-eight hours. Lovely road; drunken white drivers.

Sunday August 30, 1931

Go to Berkeley in the afternoon. Try to take Miss Brown with me, but she had gone to Durham. E____ (Edna) went to Richmond with Mary Cook. First Sunday without her in seven weeks. A break for both of us. Guess we'd been getting on each other's nerves. The old saying of intimacy breeding, etc.

Spoke at service in evening at St. James Methodist Church in Berkeley. People elated. Long, drawn-out program. Woman in trio surprised me and elicited laughter and applause by singing bass. Reverend [Davis F.] Gladney, formerly of Suffolk, accuses me of collecting money, $1.25, and neglecting to send book. Started to raise Cain. Quieted him by showing how ridiculous was his assertion when I have personally given books to schools. Told him that, like many others, he refused to accept the books when sent him. Of course our own office may have been in fault. Apologized. I gave him a book *(African Myths)* for a dollar more. So appeased that he offered to help me sell books Wednesday by taking me to the homes of prospective buyers.

Monday August 31, 1931

Rose early this morning to do a full day's work. Had just eaten breakfast when E____ (Edna) called. Wanted me to come up at 10:00. Promised, stopped at Mrs. [Mildred] Peters's first. Latter and Mrs. Montero will buy tomorrow.

Went to Mary's, where E____ [Edna] was stopping. Had enjoyed a fine trip to Richmond. Mary wearies me by her gossiping and also by her reference to so-called "blue-bloods" among Negroes. Then, too, she has a superiority complex, based on nothing more than her light skin color. So many Negroes feel the same. She revels in the acquaintanceship of people, social climbers, who are doing things and also doctors and their wives, who are doing the people.

Horrors, they are going downtown. E____ (Edna) goes to a bridge party tonight, therefore, must buy shoes. Before she can broach it to me, I tell her I am going to Suffolk. That ruined her disposition for the day. Informs me she hoped I would have gone yesterday. [She] did not want to be in Norfolk and know that I was in Suffolk. I had previously told her Marguerite had invited me down for two weeks and this recollection hurt her. Took dinner with me, asserting the while that she did not want to detain me. I became a trifle impatient and told her frankly that I would not have invited her to dinner if I had not intended to give her the time.

Thereafter, I took her back to Mary's. Inquired when I would return. Told her tomorrow morning. I left feeling that I was being restricted and confined by E____'s [Edna's] presence. Were it not for her, I should have spent the week in Suffolk.

The road to Suffolk was extremely narrow. Likewise it has many curves. Arrived safely at 8:30, however. Marguerite was tickled to see me. Had not been out all day.

Mr. [H. P.] Reid (the county farm demonstration agent) and his wife were there. They tell me conditions in Virginia are terrible. Fine crops, but people can't get anything for them. Potatoes can't be given away, and watermelons, cantaloupes, and other fruits are almost worthless.

Took Marguerite and Carrie for a ride. Marguerite is disappointed because I can't stay longer. Feels I am either married or that I have someone with me in Norfolk. Latter is the case. I shall take her to Belleville tomorrow. Stayed at the Peeles' [James and Odella].

TUESDAY SEPTEMBER 1, 1931

Called on Dr. Hoffler, a young fellow, this morning and, after a little persuasion, sold him two sets of books and collected $6.00. Went from there to a Dr. De Loatch. Sold him a set and collected $1.00. Had to use a lot of salesmanship upon him.

Gave Mrs. [Lillian] Huskerson some books and damaged pictures for her school (Nansemond High, which her husband's indefatigable labor has built up). She was extremely grateful.

Called for Marguerite at 12:15, more than an hour late. She was ready. Took Carrie also.

Horns! Lost an order that might have given me about $50 commission. The Church of God and Saints of Christ Colony had already sent a representative to our office to pick out the books he felt were needed for school. The son of the bishop, Howard Plummer, who transacts the business, was very sorry. I was sorrier. Wouldn't bother with pictures.

They are not planting this year. The ground, in accordance with their faith, is resting and does so every seventh year.

These people are restless. They impress me as desiring to get away from here, but know not whither to go. The women appear so indifferent and woebegone.

Rushed back to Suffolk. Disappointed because of failure to land the order. Marguerite wants me to come down and bring her back to New York. Would like to. Told her I'd let her know. Asked about a picture. Would let her know about that, too.

Rushed pell-mell back to Norfolk to keep an engagement with Mr. P. B. Young, the owner and editor of the *Norfolk Journal and Guide,* one of the leading Negro weeklies. My errand was to interrogate him on the housing situation in Norfolk. Spent almost an hour with him and secured interesting sidelights on these conditions among Negroes here. His comments are contained in another section under the caption of "Impressions of Norfolk." [This section of the diary was not located. The following is a summary found in a transcription made by Greene.]

(According to Young, the economic status of Norfolk Negroes is bleak, indeed. Most men work at unskilled jobs, loading and unloading ships, working on streets, and as porters and janitors. A few have skilled jobs at the Navy yard. There are of course a small group of professionals—teachers, doctors, lawyers, and a few social workers. The *Journal and Guide* is the leading Negro-owned business. Small groceries, barber shops, hairdressing parlors, and mortuaries are also found. Employment, Mr. Young said, is irregular with many Negroes, as well as whites, out of work. Wages range from 35 to 50 cents an hour for unskilled labor.

Housing conditions, except for the upper class, are poor. In older sections of the town, ramshackle houses may have water in the house but toilets in the backyard. Even in sections near the river, where indoor toilets are found, most houses do not have hot water. Yet rent is fairly cheap. Mr. Young cited an apartment house, of six flats each, where a four-room apartment with bath rented for $15 a month. Yet rent-gouging was common. Now he says the situation is reversed. The housing supply exceeds the demand. One can now get a six-room house for $15 a month. Was grateful for his observations.)

Returning to Mrs. Poole's, I found that Mrs. Carter desired to see me. E____ (Edna), too, had called asking me to come immediately to Mrs. Cook's. Before responding to the latter summon, however, I called upon Mrs. Carter. She wanted to see me in respect to discounts on certain books bought in combination for children. Told her I'd send her such information after an interview with Woodson.

Got my laundry. Took a nap of about a half hour. Ate dinner, took a shower, and went out to Mrs. Cook's. There I played cards and was bored by the gossiping of Mrs. Cook and the other ladies. I read alone in the living room awhile as they panned and pinioned this and the other lady.

Recited a few poems in response to Mrs. Cook's request. She read some of hers. Thinks mine are good. I don't. Her's are too prosaic in some cases, but one or two show that she possesses poetic feeling. In one she attains imaging that I have as yet been unable to achieve.

She makes me feel that she is unhappy. And this despite her outward appearances to the contrary.

Wednesday September 2, 1931

This is supposed to be my last full day in Norfolk. E____ (Edna) and Mrs. Cook are supposed to go to Portsmouth. They asked me to bring books for them at 10:00. I do. They finally decide not to go.

I went to Berkeley, however. My "good friend" Reverend Gladney, who was to accompany me to the homes of prospective buyers, failed to do so. I, nevertheless, sold two sets of books to friends of Miss Catherine Browne. Received only $2.00 deposit, however.

Some of these homes in Berkeley are wretched hovels, and side by side with fine dwellings. The streets are largely unpaved, no gutters, and puddles of water stand in the streets.

Went to Portsmouth. Fine contrast to Norfolk. Streets cleaner, better paved. Negroes' dwellings are better constructed and maintained.

Sold Mr. and Mrs. Riddick a set of books. Collected only $2.00, however. Sent me to a Mrs. Chapman and Mrs. [M. D.] Bullock. The latter bought and gave a $2.00 deposit. The former wants me to send them later.

Returned to Norfolk. Saw Mrs. Peters. She cannot take books now. I shall have to send them. Mrs. Poole's brother-in-law, Mr. Collins, will take some books from me tomorrow morning. At the same time, he will show me an insurance policy. He is the chief deputy for the St. Luke Insurance and Fraternity of Richmond, Virginia, of which Mrs. Maggie Walker is president.

Back to the Cooks'. E_____ (Edna) is already high. There are highballs. There are punch, milk shakes, salads, and other refreshments. E_____ (Edna) asks that I take some, but oh, no. I take a milk shake. Put about two teaspoons of whiskey in it. Enough for me. The highball I gave E_____ (Edna) makes her sleepy. She reclines while Mary (Mrs. Cook), dreamy-eyed, converses with me. Her soul hungers for its mate. She is like the canary in the cage—desiring to be free but not knowing how to release herself. Ernest gives her home, ease, comfort, social prestige, but not happiness, that solace and contentment that comes from a communion of souls, from an understandability of temperaments.

Her poem, "The Flight of the Soul," the best thing she has done, depicts the restiveness of her inner self. She wears the mask. She is by nature aesthetic; her husband is pragmatic. She loves art, literature, music; he woos the dollar. She fears a defection on her part would result in his utter degeneration. Yet, she desires it. Married at eighteen. Just twenty-seven now. He was her first fellow. Unfortunate! 'Tis always better to love often before marriage than afterwards. One can pick and choose then and have some basis of comparison for the choice. Mary didn't have it. Yet, one can't have perfect bliss here. Many women would be elated to have such a husband as Ernest, even if his greatest aim in life is a million dollars. God knows our race needs money. We need, therefore, a few more Ernests.

For all her fear, M_____ (Mary) has met one man who fits in with her temperament. He is Robert Bagnall, field secretary of the NAACP, a friend of her father and old enough for her father. But he is cultured, refined, and has contact and was attracted by Mary. Stayed at her home once for a weekend. Ernest can't bear him. Arranged to show her New York, but she wisely refused the invitation.

She asked my advice. What was she to do? I could not answer. I could only submit to her one of three alternatives, either to separate from Ernest and find her soul happiness elsewhere, thus, working the ruin of her husband; continue to crush her aesthetic yearnings in order to conform to his utilitarianism; or stay on and seek some inspiration clandestinely as many others do, always mindful, however, of the consequences attendant upon detection.

She remained seated for some time enjoying my answers or remarks, interrupting frequently to congratulate me, until suddenly we realized that we had robbed E____ (Edna) of an entire evening. Mary, therefore, retired, and left the house to us.

And after a brief but ardent love-making, we parted, I to go to my lodging; she to her room. She was happy.

Thursday September 3, 1931

What an unusual number of happenings were crowded into today.[2]

Thursday September 3, 1931

Early this morning made preparations for leaving Norfolk. Had breakfast with Edna and Barbara. Bade farewell to Ernest and Mary. She promised to remember our conversation. Said it had helped her. I went to Hampton. Spent more than three hours conversing with people whom I had met during my three visits here. Many persons inquired about Dr. Woodson, Dr. Wesley, Dr. Mordecai Johnson, and others. Those who met me in 1927 were happy that I was associated with Dr. Woodson.

Hated to leave beautiful Hampton. So did Edna.

Trip to Washington was enjoyable. Stopped in Williamsburg. Took dinner in Richmond. Barbara slept much of the way.

2. The entries for 1931 end abruptly with this statement. The next diary entries found among Greene's papers were made in 1933. In a transcription made years later, probably in the 1970s, Greene added to the September 3, 1931, entry and made an entry for September 4. He also added a retrospective summary of activities and some conclusions to sum up the results of the bookselling campaign. The events recounted in these entries were probably modified at the time he made the transcript. The editor found that the transcript departed from the original in important respects. Changes were made to improve the literary quality of the writing, to add interpretation that was not made originally, and for personal reasons. The editor has included these entries as a means of bringing closure to this set of events and to let Greene speak to the meaning and significance of events chronicled in these diary entries. Moreover, the editor largely agrees with Greene's interpretation of the contributions and significance of the bookselling campaign.

Reached Washington about seven-thirty p.m. Edna and Barbara went to Mayme's, who greeted them affably. I went to the Mickeys'. Later, they called Edna. She came up after putting Barbara to bed. Spent an enjoyable time over refreshments, chatting, and recounting our experiences. Lillian tried to get Edna to spend a few more days in Washington, but the latter said she had to go back to Philadelphia to prepare for the opening of school. She expects to leave about noon.

FRIDAY SEPTEMBER 4, 1931

Drove Edna and her daughter to the Union Station at eleven this morning. She and Mayme embraced before leaving. Guess that they had forgotten their verbal altercation at Hampton. Edna was in good spirits. Asked whether I would stop in Philadelphia en route to Columbia University. Told her my plan was to spend a few days with my parents in Connecticut before returning to New York.

After seeing them safely aboard the train I went to the office. Dr. Woodson was glad to see me. Told me, however, that although books were being ordered, many persons did not accept them C.O.D. Same as last year. I responded that it reflected the seriousness of the Negro's economic condition. Also told him of bringing the work of the Association to the attention of people from various parts of the country by speaking to the Music Convention, by the book exhibit at Ogden Hall, and also by speaking to the summer school teachers attending Hampton and to the Union Meeting in Norfolk.

The campaign is over. Back in Washington after ten months on the road. We had covered a great part of the South, the Midwest, and the eastern states of Pennsylvania, Delaware, and eastern Maryland. We even set foot for a few hours in old Mexico.

The trip was enlightening. I saw firsthand the desperate economic situation of Negroes, especially in the South. Hundreds of thousands of idle sharecroppers and farm laborers wandered about looking for jobs. Hundreds of owners were losing their farms, joining other farmworkers in a rush to the towns and cities seeking employment. Victims of drought, boll weevil, falling prices, white competition, and cheaper Mexican labor, for the first time since Reconstruction, the plight of Negro farmworkers is indeed desperate. In urban areas, similar conditions prevailed. Negroes have been forced to divide menial labor with unemployed whites, leaving many black porters, waiters, janitors, [and] sanitary workers without jobs. White women now compete with black maids, waitresses, nurses, cooks, washerwomen, and scrubwomen for what traditionally were considered "nigger" jobs, increasing the ranks of unemployed blacks. Worse, it has wrought havoc upon the Negro family where, in too many instances, women were the main support of the home. Hard hit, manufacturing and other industrial concerns—automobile, steel, meat packing, railroads, and mining—have dropped thousands of workers. Negroes, traditionally the last hired and first fired, have suffered most. Skilled workers—carpenters, bricklayers, plumbers, electricians, and others—already limited by exclusion from unions, added to the growing numbers of unemployed Negroes. In short, the very economic foundations of Negro existence in America are crumbling. The same is true, to a lesser degree, of all Americans.

With the deterioration of the Negro work force, black business and professional classes face a bleak future. Many Negro businesses, never lusty, and mainly groceries, restaurants, hairdressing parlors, barber shops, mortuaries, pool rooms, and dance halls, have been forced to close. Even the few banks, newspapers, and insurance companies, while tenaciously striving to survive, have seen some of their competitors close their doors. Professionals—lawyers, doctors, and others—have also seen their clientele melt away, or if treated, pay either in kind or not at all. As a result, many doctors and lawyers (except in Oklahoma and Houston) unexpectedly pleaded inability to buy books. Teachers, on reduced salaries or jobless, although interested and desiring the books, often were unable to take them. Even in the Philadelphia area such instances were not uncommon. One physician, however, became so enamored with the work of the Association that he begged me to remain in Philadelphia. He promised to give me an office, guarantee me a salary of $10,000 a year if I would revise Dr. Woodson's books so that they would be understandable to the man on the street. The books would be published in paperback and sell for no more than one dollar.

To me, the campaign was extremely broadening and intellectually revealing. I met all sorts of people—farmers, farm laborers, unskilled laborers, male and female domestic workers, mechanics, [and] businessmen: small shopkeepers, bankers, insurance magnates, newspaper owners, ministers, doctors, lawyers, dentists, teachers, school principals, [and] college presidents and administrators. Dr. Woodson's name and my association with him proved an "open sesame." College presidents, school teachers, ministers, and businessmen welcomed and extended me and my coworkers every courtesy, which often kept us from being hungry and lacking accommodations. I made many friends among these people, which afforded me associations that I never could have enjoyed at my age. Lastly, we met many young college women who invited us to their homes, entertained us at parties and picnics, and used their influence to aid us in selling books. From the experiences gained on this trip, I deeply regretted not having traveled about the country before making a study of the *Negro Wage Earner.* For me the trip was unforgettable. By the way, one by one the fellows dropped off: one because of proximity to his home in Oklahoma, a second because of disillusionment with selling, and another returned with me to Washington. Only one, [John Wesley] Poe, who became my close friend, carried on in Philadelphia after Woodson called me back in March to survey Negro Employment in the District of Columbia.

Finally, what benefits, if any, accrued to the Association from the campaign? Several.

First, we carried the message of Negro History to the people, many of whom had never heard of Dr. Woodson or the Association for the Study of Negro Life and History. Second, we contacted schoolchildren, teachers, ministers and their congregations, [and] business and professional people, all of whom manifested an interest in Negro History and the Association. Third, we also took the message to white persons in Virginia, North and South Carolina, Mississippi, [and] the Southwest and Midwest, not to omit Pennsylvania and other parts of the Eastern Shore. Fourth, we also made the Association and Dr. Woodson's efforts known to Women's Clubs, social welfare institutions, and fraternal and Greek-letter organizations. Books were sold, whenever and wherever possible. Failing, we left reminders of the Association and Woodson's work in the guise of leaflets. These were blanks for purchasing books. Left with people, presently unable to purchase books, they were reminders where such could be purchased at a future date.

Neither the Association, nor the salesmen, reaped a golden harvest from our ten-months' bookselling campaign. It must have increased the sale of publications, however, for Dr. Woodson, himself, wrote me in Philadelphia informing me that the Association was selling more books now than before the depression. Whatever the result, it was a great advertising campaign.

27

Back in New York City

FRIDAY SEPTEMBER 30, 1932

What I have feared for more than a month has been verified. Lenora [Pritchett] is engaged. The news came from Violet, a friend of ours. Although I had been expecting the same, since Lenora had declined to see me following her return from Oak Bluffs, the disclosure dealt me a staggering blow. I realized then more than I have realized during the past four weeks that I love Lenora—love her as I have never before loved a woman. Never had I met a girl whose personality, charm, and beauty cast such a subtle spell over me as Lenora. We were soulmates from the moment we looked upon one another.

It was a little more than a year ago when we first met at Hampton, one of nature's garden spots. Can I ever forget those events: our causal meeting in Ogden Hall, the invitation to show her the surrounding country, the gorgeous beauty of Soldiers Home, the beach at Old Point? Lenora and I under the moonlight—just we two—all alone in the world. Then New York. Both of us learning to care, learning to love. Dr. Thompson—his proposal—Lenora's reaction—her preference for me—my failure to propose—her determination not to see me again—her struggle—my struggle—now her engagement.

And it need not have been thus. She gave me every opportunity to win her, did everything except actually propose to me, because she loved me. But I had reasons for remaining silent. Lack of funds, my work, poor health.

But I love her and I daresay she loves me. Violet has talked to her and she has reasons to believe as much. And I feel like a person without goal, rudder, or anchor. It seems as if everything worth striving for is gone. Everything—now since she is gone—will be nothing more than dead sea fruit.

I had to jot down this notation. It is the biggest upset in life since 1926. Still, I alone am at fault. A word from me would have won me eternal bliss. Unspoken, it dashed the cup of happiness from my lips.

Broken though I am, however, I cannot fall. I must go on. She would desire that I do so. I must not break faith with her. I dare not falter, lest I destroy her confidence in me and rejoice that she chose otherwise.

We might have been so happy. That we are not in position to be so, I alone am culpable. And though I write it with my heart's blood, I wish her every happiness, every contentment, every joy, and that supreme contentment, connubial bliss, that only comes to those whose hearts and souls blend in transcendent oneness.

Farewell Lenora. We met—we loved—we parted. Yet, our souls are one. Across the vast reaches of space illimitable, our souls shall still commune. Thus, unseen to mortal eyes, our souls shall meet, shall still laugh and love as before. You are still mine; I am yours alone.

Thursday October 6, 1932

I saw Marguerite [Skeeter] this morning. She is such a dear girl. Poured out her heart in sympathy with me, and in response to my statement that Lenora was engaged, embraced me and whispered: "I am still here, Rennie." She is one of God's sweetest creatures. Yet, even her words could not fill the void left by Lenora's loss.

Friday October 7, 1932

I spoke at Hunter College today to a group of girls called the International Club. My topic was background of Negro History. Both whites and blacks congratulated me on my fine presentation. Yet there was no elation for me. Indeed a depressing fit of futility seized me. Honors meant nothing. I was thinking of my inestimable loss—Lenora. And en route back uptown I determined to see her. I stopped at Florence [Bacote]'s office and had her call Lenora to find out whether she was at her office. I knew I could never go to her home. She was in. I immediately went thither.

She rose to greet me in her same intimate manner when I entered her office. Her "hell-o Rennie" carried with it the same soft intonation that I knew so well. Violet was there, but she left immediately. I hardly knew how to begin. We could scarcely look at each other. I told her of my suffering since I last saw her, of my love for her, and my regret that I could not during the summer say something definite. I could not refrain from chastising myself for foolishly scorning such a precious possession, I reminded her. She retorted that she had given me every opportunity. I agreed that it was my fault. She recalled our first meeting, our evenings spent together, our walks, our readings. Then her eyes welled with tears; mine, too.

I left after spending more than two hours with her. She assured me we could still be friendly, even though she were married. It was like rending my heart to take leave of her.

At night I saw her at a benefit given for the Scottsboro boys.[1] My heart was so heavy at seeing her with her fiancé that, when passing her accompanied by Thelma Holland, I could not speak for fear of crying.

Saturday October 8, 1932

This was a most miserable day. I could not work and could not get Lenora out of my mind. My spirits are at their lowest ebb. It is noticeable to everyone.

Sunday October 9, 1932

I called Lenora about two o'clock. In a burst of emotion, I told her I loved her, could neither forget her nor do without her, and asked her to marry me. Poor girl! Words failed her for a while. Then she said: "Rennie, I must think it over. Give me time." I told her I would. It embarrassed her, I know, but it certainly made me feel better. I have made a mess of the whole affair.

Harry [Hipp] called me. Later he came up. He told me that Lenora had asked him to come over tomorrow night. She wanted to talk to him. I told him what I had done. He replied that she would be a fool to give up Thompson now for me. Muriel [Hipp] believed so too, but added, in case Lenora did, I should have to marry immediately.

1. On March 25, 1931, nine African American youths were among the hoboes aboard a freight train traveling between Chattanooga and Memphis by a winding route that went through sections of Alabama and Mississippi. The black youths were arrested in Scottsboro, Alabama, and charged with raping two white women who were aboard the train. By April 9, 1931, all of the youths had been found guilty; eight received death sentences and one was sentenced to life in prison. The case became a cause célèbre. The International Labor Defense, a Communist Party organization, took over the defense. By holding benefits and through other means, the Communist Party raised an estimated $1 million. In spite of new trials and evidence that cast doubt on the youths' guilt, the International Labor Defense was unable to either free the men or get the death sentences changed. The NAACP took over the major burden of the defense after 1935, and, finally, a deal was made that resulted in long prison terms for five of the youths. The last of the Scottsboro boys was not freed until 1950. See Dan T. Carter, *Scottsboro: A Tragedy of the American South.*

Monday October 10, 1932

Harry, after a deal of coaxing, came up tonight. He had just left Lenora. He appeared deeply moved. He told me there was no hope, related how Lenora had bared her heart to him. She loved me, gave me every opportunity to propose, but I remained silent even though Thompson was hounding her for an answer. She held that it was too late to change now, that the invitations were being printed, their engagement has been announced, the doctor has ordered furniture, and some presents have already been received. Now I asked her to break her engagement. She felt that I had had many affairs. My poetry showed that. "Yesterday," she added, "he told me he was writing poetry to me, and he will forget me like the others. It was just another affair to him." Thus, Harry said, she hit the crucial spot.

Yet, Lenora told him that I ought to marry, that it would help my work. In essence, the affair had reached a point where to break the engagement was impossible. This news crushed me, but I did not despair. I sent her five or six poems tonight.

Called Lenora. Refused to see me. Told me she would call me by Thursday.

Tuesday October 11, 1932

Mrs. Holley felt deeply grieved when I reported to her the unfavorable outcome of the interview. However, she encouraged me by telling me it would come out all right. I am not so optimistic. If I could only see her personally, I feel she could not refuse me. Therefore, I went to Violet, her friend, to enlist her aid in arranging a meeting with Lenora. Violet agreed and promised to call me after six.

Saw Helen Tynes. When I told her of my predicament, she laughed. Told me it served me right. Then she suggested that I kidnap Lenora, take her to the city hall, and marry her. She would like the romantic flavor of it, Helen thought. I was not so sanguine.

Harcourt [Tynes] became very thoughtful over the matter. He held I should not marry now. It would interfere with my work. Yet, he ventured if I loved Lenora, well—.

Tonight I wrote Lenora. It was my supreme effort in love-letter writing. It was only my second. I told her that she and Thompson were not mated and, therefore, marriage to him could be productive of unhappiness only. I recounted our soul union, told her to refrain from entering into such a union, rather than endeavor to get out after once getting in. I set forth all her possible objections, then demolished them. I reminded her that marriage is a gamble at best and should be entered into only under the most favorable auspices. I suggested diverse ways in which the engagement might be broken. I told her that Thompson could not appreciate what she had to offer and brought up the many fine things we could do together, even to collaborating in the writing of books. I then asked her forgiveness for some of the things I said, ending by telling her it was only my soul calling to its mate.

Violet didn't call.

Wednesday October 12, 1932

Lenora crushed me today. She called while I was at Harry's. Harcourt, Helen, Murial, and Woody Robinson were there when she called. I could not hear on account of the noise made by the children. She told me it was too late. I begged to see her. She gently refused me. I told her I would come to her office. She replied it would be no use. I asked her to wait until I called her from the street.

Instead, I hailed a taxi and went to her office. There I was told she had gone out. I called her home. She was not there. I then called the Utopia House and gave a fictitious name. Lenore[2] answered. She told me she had received my letter, thanked me for it, but regretted it was too late now. Nothing could be done. According to her, they were secretly married in September. I don't believe it, but from the pathos in her voice and by the halting way in which she spoke I gathered that she was making her supreme effort to go through with a bad bargain. The ceremony in November, she said, will merely satisfy the public.

I feel she is not married, but is both afraid to see me or to have me persuade her further, lest she weaken. Long intervals obtained between our words for upon several occasions I felt like breaking into tears. I feel guilty of wrecking four lives: mine, Lenora's, Thompson's, and Pansy's. I asked her to forgive many things I said in my letter. She replied that she accepted it on its face value. She no longer believes I am trifling with her.

I left the phone booth forlorn and dejected. I managed to straighten up a little before reaching Harry's, where all of them began to josh me. I was invited to dinner by Harry, but it was not food I wanted. I desired to be alone with my loss.

Thus the last chapter is written in the most beautiful episode of my life. An ideal romance, with princess, poetry, flowers, everything to make it complete. Yet, my own procrastination shattered it, destroyed forever the only sublime thing in my life, a noble love for a good, beautiful, and lovely woman. I loved her. It grew until it overpowered my resistance. It forced me to capitulate. But too late.

2. The name is spelled both *Lenora* and *Lenore* in the diary and in correspondence.

[Tuesday] November 22, 1932

This day shall never fade from my memory. I sat in church and witnessed the loss of my dearest treasure. So overcome was I with grief and pathos because of my bereavement that I could not pen what was in my heart.

28

First Days at Lincoln University

Friday [September 1,] 1933

E[dna] [Gaines] helped with final preparations for leaving. Called on Ethel Harris. Returned books. Felt like weeping when I left. From there went to Marguerite [Skeeter]'s. Kissed me. Told me she had seen Lenora last night. Latter asked about me. Leaving for Atlanta tomorrow. I returned home. Got Mrs. Holley's amount[?] of $148. She gave me $12.

From there went to station. Had trunk and books shipped express C.O.D. Shall ask [President Charles W.] Florence to advance money for them.

Stopped at Ernest [Bacote]'s. Turned car over in his name. E[dna] moody. Ate dinner at Ernest's. Hated to leave him.

Drove to Philly, arriving about 7:00 p.m. Rained, in keeping with my being there with E[dna]. She drove to station with me. Hired boy to take car back. From her talk, she intends for me to marry her. Asked whether I was engaged to Helen, or whether I intended to marry her in the future. Told her the truth, no. Would not come to Chicago Christmas if I did. Left her, feeling I should give her up, or at least I should not allow her to come to Chicago at Christmas. What about Lenora?

Too worried about E[dna]'s remarks to read. Just thought about her. Sleepy too. Filipino porter on Pullman. Displaced Negroes. Travel very light. Retired 11:40 p.m.

Saturday [September 2, 1933]

Read poetry on train. Spent $1.20 on breakfast. Could ill afford. Going 1,200 miles from home with $30. Read civics. Arrived St. Louis at 7:30. All white porters at Union Station. Not as obliging as Negroes. Expect more.

Passengers from Pullman carried own luggage with that as reason perhaps. One porter exclaimed, "What kind of car is this?"

Arrived on campus in 15¢ taxi. Cheapest yet. Went to Florence's home. Had not arrived. A Mr. [Norval P.] Barksdale there. French teacher. Referred me to men's dormitory. Took me there and introduced me to dean of men, Mr. [James C.] McMorries. Fine fellow, little older than I. Former Y.M.C.A. student secretary. We chatted. He told me of difficulties under which Florence worked: political, etc. Gave me a nice room, private bath, etc. Place beautiful but lonesome, seems like 1,000 miles from nowhere. Hungry; McMorries referred me to Negro lunchroom at foot of campus. Too many flies and bugs. Nowhere for Negro to eat. Went to drug store. Would not serve me. Bought pint of ice cream. Got two wooden spoons. Returned to campus, ate, cried. Determined to go back East.

SUNDAY [SEPTEMBER 3, 1933]

Rose at 10:20. Read civics. Went to breakfast with Mr. McMorries at little inn run by former professor's wife. Husband dropped because of woman-chasing proclivities. Told me of attraction here. Came here because of Florence. Stocky, brown fellow, about 38. Have not seen any prof[essors] yet. Went through administration building. Built 1930. Cost $250,000. Splendidly furnished. I am down for government and history. Don't know anything about former. Saw baseball game.

Campus is beautiful, rolling hillside with lovely shade trees. Has tennis courts, golf course, etc.

State Legionnaires meeting here today.

Received special from Edna this morning. Wanted to be first to greet me and asked that I write her first. She deserves it. Yes, she does, yet I love Lenora.

Dropped in to see Florence. Not in. Ate and talked with the Barksdales until he came in. Talked, told jokes, laughed. He walked along the beautiful campus with me. Told me future here for me. Retorted I would give my best.

This is a gorgeous night. The moon, pale and silvery white, shines down from a sky flecked with soft, fleecy vapor. Her brilliance has put to flight the stars, and she has cast an aura of silvery loveliness on the campus that transforms the world into a terrestrial paradise.

Appendix

Three Poems by Lorenzo J. Greene

A June Night

Soft and sweet the night—
Fragrant night—
Perfume from fairest flowers,
Incense of mortal love,
Rising to heaven above
Nectar celestial.

Soft and clear the night—
Wond'rous night—
Bright moonbeams from above,
Silvering the verdant nook,
Drowned in the shimmering brook,
Gliding before us.

Soft and still the night—
Amorous night—
Scattered about the glen,
Others in whispers spoke,
Gently the stillness woke,
Breathing love's story.

Soft and warm the night—
Charming night—
Only the sailing moon
Beamed from her placid way,

While in my arms you lay,
Smiling upon me.

Soft and calm the night—
Blissful night—
Dark eyes looked into mine,
Shy arms about me twined,
Warm, lingering lips met mine,
In found caresses.

Soft and sad the night—
Parting night—
Tears like two lustrous pearls,
Gleamed on her lovely face,
As with a last embrace,
Gently we parted.

June 11, 1925

Out of the Mist

It was evening when night's mantle
Wrapped the sylvan glades in silence,
And a hush stole over the landscape,
Beckoning to rest the weary;
Noiselessly, the heavenly beacons
Rushed to their celestial stations,
Gleaming like uncounted jewels,
Jewels in the moonless heavens.

There beside the lapping water
Of the wood-bound lake before me,
Lake where memories of childhood
Clustered in fond recollection,
Gazing, I sat, into spaces,
Heedless of the stars above me,
Of the lapping of the water,
Or the mist from it ascending.

Chin in hand, and elbows resting
Firm upon my knees—immobile—
Long with straining eyes, I searched
The naked emptiness about me;
For my thoughts, to youth returning,
Brought the bitter past before me,
And the tears by vision blinded,
As I dwelt on her who loved me.

Suddenly, I heard a whisper,
Whisper like a note celestial,
Softly sounding from the water,
From the peaceful, lapping water,
And it woke me from my musings,
From those mournful meditations,
And I bent my startled glances
Fast upon the lake before me.

But I could not see the water,
Though I heard it faintly lapping,
As it gently washed the pebbles
That close at my feet were lying;
For a misty cloud hung over it,
Shrouding it in ghostly whiteness,
Like a vaporous thing ascending,
Mounting to the moonless heavens.

All at once a lovely maiden,
Wreathed in mist, appeared before me,
Up I leaped, amazed, astounded,
"Maybelee" I wildly shouted,
For the sweet face there before me,
Wreathed about in mist ascending,
Was the playmate of my childhood,
And the lost love of my youth.

Mid the vaporous veil ascending,
Like a river-nymph majestic,
Rising in transcendent beauty,
With her raven tresses loosely

Over her mist-clad bosom falling,
Awed, bewildered, I beheld her,
As her arms toward me extending,
Soft she called me to the water.

Eagerly my heart responded
And, aloud her sweet name sounding,
Laughing-weeping-arms extended,
Jubilant, I rushed to greet her,
Rushed into the lapping water,
In the vapor to enfold her,
From her misty shroud to win her,
Hold her, keep her mine forever.

Mad with ecstasy I reached her,
And with ardent arms embraced her,
Kissed her face, lips, mist-draped bosom,
But, O Christ! 'Twas but a phantom!
For my arms held empty vapor,
And my lips pressed damp, cold moisture;
For she with the mist ascended,
Mounted to the moonless heavens.

Disappointed, crushed, I stood there
Knee-deep in the mocking water,
Calling to her; vainly clutching
At her aerial robe ascending,
But in vain; my only answer
Was the lap-lap of the water,
And the taunting of the hillsides
Flinging back their scoffing echoes.

So I fled the misty mirage,
Rushed down to the dormant village,
And, despairing, sought my chamber,
Hoping slumber might dispel her;
But throughout the night I heard the
Jeering lap-lap of the water,
Saw her, robed in mist, ascending,
Mounting to the moonless heavens.

To a Lady

To Mae
I looked into your
eyes
And all the world
dissolved
Into a nothingness
And only you in all your
loveliness
Remained.
I looked into your
eyes
And their soft magic
like
The Orient
Charmed and entranced me
Drew me irresistibly
to you
I looked into your
eyes
And lo my very soul
Stirred and awoke
I looked into your eyes
And straight there came
To me
A yearning for all time
To hold you and to always
call
You mine.

Editor's Bibliography

GOVERNMENT PUBLICATIONS

The President's Conference on Home Building and Home Ownership. *Negro Housing: Report of the Committee on Negro Housing.* Prepared by Charles S. Johnson. Washington, D.C.: National Capital Press, 1932.

U.S. Department of the Interior. Bureau of Education. *Survey of Negro Colleges and Universities.* Bulletin, 1928, no. 7. By Arthur J. Klein. Washington, D.C.: U.S. Government Printing Office, 1929.

White House Conference on Child Health and Protection. *Preliminary Committee Reports.* New York: Century, 1930.

NEWSPAPERS

Baltimore Afro-American, 1930–1931.

Cleveland Gazette, 1930.

New York Times, 1930–1932, 1985.

Norfolk Journal and Guide, 1930–1932.

Pittsburgh Courier, 1930–1932.

BOOKS AND PERIODICALS

Atlanta University Bulletin, 1928 and 1935–1936.

Beeth, Howard, and Cary D. Wintz, eds. *Black Dixie: Afro-Texan History and Culture in Houston.* College Station: Texas A & M University Press, 1992.

Bowers, Claude G. *The Tragic Era: The Revolution after Lincoln.* Cambridge, Mass.: Riverside, 1929.

Branch, Taylor. *Parting the Waters: America in the King Years, 1954–1963.* New York: Simon and Schuster, 1988.

Brawley, Benjamin. *A Short History of the American Negro.* Rev. ed. New York: Macmillan, 1922.

Brawley, James P. *Two Centuries of Methodist Concern: Bondage, Freedom and Education of Black People.* New York: Vantage, 1974.

Carter, Dan T. *Scottsboro: A Tragedy of the American South.* New York: Oxford University Press, 1969.

Catton, Bruce. *Never Call Retreat.* Vol. 3, *The Centennial History of the Civil War.* Garden City, N.Y.: Doubleday, 1965.

Cellini, Benvenuto. *Autobiography of Benvenuto Cellini.* Trans. John Addington Symonds. New York: Modern Library, 1927.

Colonial Williamsburg, Inc. *Official Guidebook.* 5th ed. Williamsburg, Va.: Colonial Williamsburg, 1965.

Desantis, Vincent P. *Republicans Face the Southern Question: The New Departure Years, 1877–1897.* Baltimore: John Hopkins Press, 1959.

Dowd, Jerome. *The Negro in American Life.* New York: Century, 1926.

Ellsworth, Scott. *Death in a Promised Land: The Tulsa Race Riot of 1921.* Baton Rouge: Louisiana State University Press, 1982.

Franklin, Jimmie Lewis. *Journey toward Hope: A History of Blacks in Oklahoma.* Norman: University of Oklahoma Press, 1982.

Goggin, Jacqueline. *Carter G. Woodson: A Life in Black History.* Baton Rouge: Louisiana State University Press, 1993.

Gosnell, Harold F. *Negro Politicians: The Rise of Negro Politics in Chicago.* Chicago: University of Chicago Press, 1935, 1966.

Greene, Lorenzo J. *Working with Carter G. Woodson, the Father of Black History: A Diary, 1928–1930.* Ed. Arvarh E. Strickland. Baton Rouge: Louisiana State University Press, 1989.

Greene, Lorenzo J., and Carter G. Woodson. *The Negro Wage Earner.* Washington, D.C.: Association for the Study of Negro Life and History, 1930.

Heintze, Michael R. *Private Black Colleges in Texas, 1865–1954.* College Station: Texas A & M University Press, 1985.

Hine, Darlene Clark, ed. *Black Women in America: An Historical Encyclopedia.* Vol. 1. Brooklyn, N.Y.: Carlson, 1993.

Howard University Magazine (October 1964).

Hutchinson, Arthur Stuart-Menteth. *If Winter Comes.* Boston: Little, Brown, 1921.

Journal of Negro History 15–19 (1930–1934).

Kerlin, R[obert] T[homas]. *Negro Poets and Their Poems.* Washington, D.C.: Associated Publishers, 1923.

LaGrone, Clarence Oliver. *Dawnfire and Other Poems.* Detroit: Lotus, 1989.

Lamon, Lester C. *Black Tennesseans, 1900–1930.* Knoxville: University of Tennessee Press, 1977.

Lisio, Donald J. *Hoover, Blacks, and Lily-Whites: A Study of Southern Strategies.* Chapel Hill: University of North Carolina Press, 1985.

Logan, Rayford W. *Howard University: The First Hundred Years, 1867–1967.* New York: New York University Press, 1968.

Lynch, John Roy. *Reminiscences of an Active Life: The Autobiography of John Roy Lynch.* Ed. John Hope Franklin. Chicago: University of Chicago Press, 1970.

Malval, Fritz J., comp. *A Guide to the Archives of Hampton Institute.* Westport, Conn.: Greenwood, 1985.

Meier, August. *Negro Thought in America, 1880–1915: Racial Ideologies in the Age of Booker T. Washington.* Ann Arbor: University of Michigan Press, 1963.

Morehouse College. *Annual Catalogue, 1929–1930* and *1930–1931.*

National Association for the Advancement of Colored People. *One Year's Work in Race Relations: 1930, 21st Annual Report.* New York: National Association for the Advancement of Colored People, 1930.

Norris, Charles Gilman. *Seed.* New York: Doubleday, Doran, 1930.

Papini, Giovanni. *Life of Christ.* Trans. Dorothy Canfield Fisher. New York: Harcourt, Brace, 1923.

"The Restoration of Colonial Williamsburg in Virginia." *The Architectural Record* 78 (December 1935): 355–458.

Robinson, Wilhelmena S. *International Library of Negro Life and History: Historical Negro Biographies.* New York: Publishers Company, under the auspices of The Association for the Study of Negro Life and History, 1970.

Rout, Leslie B., Jr. *The African Experience in Spanish America: 1502 to the Present Day.* Cambridge: Cambridge University Press, 1976.

Sand, George [Mme. Dudevant]. *The Intimate Journal of George Sand.* Ed. and trans. Marie Jenney Howe. New York: John Day, 1929.

Scally, Sister Anthony, comp. *Carter G. Woodson: A Bio-Bibliography.* Westport, Conn.: Greenwood, 1985.

Schor, Joel. *Agriculture in the Black Land-Grant System to 1930.* Tallahassee: Florida A & M University, 1982.

Southern Workman 59 (1930).

Spear, Allan H. *Black Chicago: The Making of a Negro Ghetto, 1890–1920.* Chicago: University of Chicago Press, 1967.

Spero, Sterling D., and Abram L. Harris. *The Black Worker: The Negro and the Labor Movement.* New York: Atheneum, 1931, 1959.

Strickland, Arvarh E. *History of the Chicago Urban League.* Urbana: University of Illinois Press, 1966.

Thornton, Mary Lindsay, comp. *A Bibliography of North Carolina, 1589–1956.* Chapel Hill: University of North Carolina Press, 1958.

Toppin, Edgar A. *A Biographical History of Blacks in America since 1528.* New York: David McKay, 1971.

Vandercook, John W. *Black Majesty: The Life of Christophe, King of Haiti.* New York: Harper and Brothers, 1928.

Weare, Walter B. *Black Business in the New South: A Social History of the North Carolina Mutual Life Insurance Company.* Urbana, Chicago, London: University of Illinois Press, 1973.

Wesley, Charles H. *Henry Arthur Callis: Life and Legacy.* Chicago: Foundation Publishers, 1977.

Who's Who in Colored America: A Biographical Dictionary of Notable Living Persons of African Descent in America. 5th ed. Brooklyn: Who's Who in Colored America Corp., 1940.

———. 6th ed. Brooklyn: Who's Who in Colored America Corp., 1944.

Who's Who in Colored America: A Biographical Dictionary of Notable Living Persons of Negro Descent in America. New York: Who's Who in Colored America Corp., 1927.

Wilkinson, Frederick D., ed. *Directory of Graduates: Howard University, 1870–1963.* Washington, D.C.: Howard University, 1965.

Wilstach, Paul. *Tidewater Virginia.* New York: Blue Ribbon Books, 1929.

Woodson, Carter G. "Proceedings of the Annual Meeting of the Association for the Study of Negro Life and History, Held in New York City, November 8–12, 1931." *Journal of Negro History* 17 (January 1932): 1–7.

Work, Monroe N., ed. *Negro Year Book: An Annual Encyclopedia of the Negro, 1937–1938.* Tuskegee, Ala.: Negro Year Book Publishing, 1937.

Writers' Program of the Work Projects Administration in the State of Virginia. *Virginia: A Guide to the Old Dominion.* American Guide Series. New York: Oxford University Press, 1941, seventh printing, 1964.

Wynia, Elly M. *The Church of God and Saints of Christ: The Rise of Black Jews.* New York: Garland, 1994.

Index

Page numbers in italics refer to photographs.